New Approaches to Ezra Pound

New Approaches to
EZRA POUND

*A Co-ordinated Investigation of
Pound's Poetry and Ideas*

EDITED WITH AN INTRODUCTION BY
EVA HESSE

UNIVERSITY OF CALIFORNIA PRESS
Berkeley and Los Angeles: 1969

Acknowledgments

MY THANKS are due to Professor Richard Ellmann for permission to include his essay 'Ez and Old Billyum', which first appeared in German in my symposium *Ezra Pound: 22 Versuche über einen Dichter*, Athenäum Verlag, Frankfurt 1967, and is now also included in his *Eminent Domain: Yeats Among Wilde, Joyce, Pound, Eliot and Auden*, Oxford University Press, Inc., New York, 1968, and Oxford University Press, London, 1969, as well as to Professor N. Christoph de Nagy, who allowed me to abridge slightly the fifth chapter of his monograph *The Poetry of Ezra Pound: The Pre-Imagist Stage*, Francke Verlag, Berne 1960. Professor Boris de Rachewiltz's essay is a substantially condensed but at the same time somewhat amplified version of his *L'Elemento Magico in Ezra Pound*, published by Del Pesce d'Oro, Milan 1965. Donald Davie's essay adapted from his *Ezra Pound: Poet as Sculptor*, copyright © 1964 by Donald Davie, is reprinted by permission of the Oxford University Press, Inc., New York, and Routledge & Kegan Paul, London. Acknowledgment is made to the *Times Literary Supplement*, London, for permission to use that part of the essay by Christine Brooke-Rose which appeared in their issue of 10th June 1960. Professor George Dekker's essay, which originally appeared as Chapter IV of his *Sailing After Knowledge*, 1963, is included by permission of Routledge & Kegan Paul, London, and of Barnes and Noble, Inc., New York. Professor Leslie Fiedler's essay which originally appeared in his *Waiting for the End*, 1964, is included by permission of Stein and Day, New York, and Jonathan Cape Ltd., London. The extract from Professor R. J. C.

ACKNOWLEDGMENTS

Atkinson's *Stonehenge*, 1956, is reprinted by permission of Hamish Hamilton, Ltd., London. Ezra Pound material covered by U.K. copyright is reprinted by permission of Faber and Faber Ltd., London. Thanks are due to the New Directions Publishing Corporation for permission to use extracts from the following works by Ezra Pound: *Personae* © 1926 by Ezra Pound; *The Cantos*, copyright 1934, 1937, 1940, 1948, © 1956 by Ezra Pound; *A Lume Spento and Other Early Poems* © 1965 by Ezra Pound; *Literary Essays* © 1918, 1920, 1935 by Ezra Pound; *Guide to Kulchur*, All Rights Reserved; *Pavannes and Divagations* © 1958 by Ezra Pound. Acknowledgment is further made to Harvard College Library for permission to quote from a letter by Ezra Pound in their possession. All other extracts from material by Ezra Pound are reprinted by permission of Mrs Dorothy Pound, Committee for Ezra Pound, All Rights Reserved.

Contents

CONTENTS

Introduction

by EVA HESSE

————————>>>>>>>§<<<<<<<————————

Ezra Pound's *Cantos* are not a poem but a conspiracy. This shrewd comment by George Dekker[1] is one which few readers who are more than casually acquainted with the poet's forty-years' epic would wish to contest. For in reading the *Cantos* the subconscious mind is induced to perceive inter-relationships in matters of literature and life which had not hitherto been apparent.

Although these links may sometimes exist solely in the mind of the poet, or perhaps of the reader, the process involved is essentially one of poetic osmosis. As the curiosity of the reader quickens, the fragments of the poem begin to organize themselves into meaningful patterns.

It is doubtless this peculiar spell worked by Pound's poetry which excites some of the more irrational reactions of critics. On the one hand we have found, in the past, an irritatingly devout endorsement of practically all that the poet has ever written or said. Such indiscriminate acceptance wrongs Pound's intelligence by disregarding the gradations between his ideas and opinions, and attaching excessive importance to plus or minus marks that he has handed out in prose on various occasions in response to specific and transient situations. At the other extreme we occasionally encounter the philistine reaction of the isolated critic who experiences personal pique at the realization that, but for the higher poetic standards which Pound and Eliot have done so much to set, his own verses might have earned greater recognition.

[1] *Sailing After Knowledge*, London 1963, p. 107.

13

Between the two extremes there are a number of serious critics who, having been caught in the Poundian net during a relatively early phase of their literary development, are now going through the motions of extricating themselves by a somewhat forced display of objectivity that bears many strange fruits. As a result, Pound, who is certainly open to legitimate attack on a variety of fronts, is as likely as not to be censured for the wrong reasons.

Oddly enough, the inductive process of the *Cantos* is set in operation in the reader's mind irrespective of whether he broadly accepts or rejects the inferences that the poet wishes to be drawn from his juxtaposition of facts and fiction, sense impressions, snatches of conversation, literary quotations, multiple allusions and recorded events. In other words, they continue to 'make Cosmos'[1] in the reader's head. Considering the didactic ambitions of the *Cantos*, this in itself is no mean achievement.

Since Pound realizes that 'civilization is individual',[2] the ideal city towards which he is working must necessarily be built in the reader's mind, so that each individual reader becomes the 'Prince' for whom this Machiavellian poet is writing. In Canto LXXIV he even confesses to the conspiracy:

> and that certain images be formed in the mind
>> to remain there
>>> *formato locho*

> . . .

> to remain there, resurgent *ΕΙΚΟΝΕΣ*

Quoted from Guido Cavalcanti's *Canzone d'amore*, the term 'formato locho', meaning literally 'formed space', is rendered freely by Pound in Canto XXXVI as a 'formed trace' in a man's mind.[3] The seminal images, εἰκόνες, are not intended to impart specific knowledge as much as a certain almost sensual quality of knowledge, and to implant this at a depth at which it

[1] Canto CXVI. [2] *Literary Essays*, London 1954, p. 355.
[3] Pound's rendering is here based on the Laurentian Cavalcanti manuscript in which he read 'un formato locho', whereas in more reliable

will influence the assimilation of all subsequently acquired information. Pound considers poetry rather than prose to be the more effective means of bringing this about, and it is in this light that we should understand his observation that 'prose is NOT education but the outer courts of the same'.[1]

All art depends in the final analysis on communication that is to a greater or lesser extent incomplete. Norman Mailer, a man of many illuminations, has said that a work which is altogether explicit is not art. It is not art because it does not allow the audience to respond with their own creative act of imagination—'that small leap of the faculties which leaves one an increment more exceptional than when one began.'

The leap in communication demanded by Pound's device of the *forma* (cf. Donald Davie, pp. 210–4) is considerable, for it confronts the reader not with an idea but with an early phase of ideation in which the image has not yet developed beyond 'a radiant node or cluster . . . from which, and through which, and into which, ideas are constantly rushing'.[2] Otherwise expressed, it is that vortex of ideas which draws the reader personally into the creative process, providing him with a strange sense of enjoyment which, as Miss Brooke-Rose notes (cf. p. 243), is not to be found elsewhere in literature. Genius has here, for once, become democratic, but as in any real democracy a conscious effort is required on the part of those concerned if the principle is to function. True democracy is, as Juan Bosch has had reason to point out, a product of capacity and vigilance.

If poetry at the level of the *forma* does not follow a thought

manuscripts we read 'non formato locho'. In his earlier versions of the Canzone dated 1912 and revised in 1920 and 1931, he nevertheless gives the correct translation, i.e. 'unformed space' (cf. *Translations*, London 1953, p. 139). It must therefore be concluded that he did not always translate the Canzone from the Laurentian text that he chose to have printed *vis-à-vis* his translation. His personal objection to the reading 'non formato locho' is recorded in 'The Canzone: Further Notes' appended to the essay on Cavalcanti (1934) in *Literary Essays*, p. 187.

[1] *Guide to Kulchur*, first ed. 1938, p. 144.

[2] Pound, *Gaudier-Brzeska: A Memoir*, London 1916, p. 106.

through to the end but stops at the penultimate phase of ideation, the reader is necessarily forced to complete the thought process. This is what the Japanese poet Katue Kitasono, whom Pound quotes, has termed 'idioplasty' (cf. J. P. Sullivan, p. 236), a process that takes place in the reader's mind where the poem's language gives rise to imagery that in turn creates for him an overall texture of meaning.

'Idioplasty' (from ἰδιόπλαστος, self-formed) thus naturally depends greatly on the reader's mental capacity. All exegesis of poetry might be regarded as being, to a significant extent, idioplasty, and as such, forming an extension of the poem read. In generating a kind of corona or chromosphere around the poem, idioplasty is liable to lead the reader to subjects that may sometimes lie far outside the specifics that the poet originally had in mind. One of Hokusai's 'Thirty-six Ways of Looking at Mt Fuji' depicts the mountain as a distant speck on the horizon while a huge wave is on the point of breaking in the foreground. This is still a valid way of looking at Fuji, and even though there are as many different ways of looking at the *Cantos* the idioplastic process in the individual reader's mind will never be entirely fortuitous but will follow, at whatever distance, the outline presented by the poem itself.

Mr Kitasono goes on to discuss the danger of reversing this process, i.e. of proceeding from idioplasty to language, a practice which he rightly diagnoses as the rhetorical method that is likely to be indulged by 'religionists, politicians, and satirists'. Yet this is the very procedure that many critics assume Pound to have followed. It is an assumption that may account for a great many wrong-headed exceptions taken to his poetry that are not based on ideas derived directly from the poetry itself but from the poet's prose dicta. In other words, there is an uncircumspect tendency to take the evidence of Pound's prose much more seriously than that of his poetry.

Yet, as regards the poetry, the inescapable inference to be drawn from the concept of the *forma* so brilliantly treated by Professor Davie is surely that the *Cantos* constitute an 'open form' despite the fact that the poet himself may not have realized this from the outset. At their best they represent a lifelong attempt to formulate truth from experience rather than to impose a set of premeditated truths upon reality, or, as Pound has put it, to 'shave off the nose and ears of a verity'[1] in order to make it fit more snugly into the coffin of a system.

Thus the probability that the *Cantos* will remain unfinished, not leading to an ultimate formula but ending with the poet's end as a poet or a man, does not imply a formal failure as has so often been assumed, but on the contrary is entirely consistent with a form of poetry that is shaped and sustained by life itself.

Pound's resolute eclecticism, which has always rendered him incapable of accepting any ready-made system in toto, appears for some reason to have disqualified him as a thinker. At least there seems to be some general consensus among critics that his views on any matter of philosophical moment are of negligible value. It will be noted that similar criticism is not levelled against poets whose ideas fit more conveniently into some prefabricated system—such as Eliot and, to a certain extent, also Yeats. 'We think because we do not know', Pound has said, and it would seem reasonable that the thoughts of a man in the actual process of thinking aloud in his poetry should have some claim to our interest, especially when they so frequently touch upon some of the more advanced conceptions of the age.

The suggestion that the *Cantos* are an open form is supported by the fact that the voyage on which Odysseus-Pound embarks can only be regarded as an adventure or an experiment if the hero, steering by periplus rather than by an Aquinas map, does not actually know which course to set in order to reach his Ithaca. Unlike Dante, who embarks upon a conducted tour of first hell, then purgatory, and finally paradise, and has only to follow the schema, Odysseus-Pound strikes out into the unknown in the mere hope of reaching Ithaca and paradise, but with the possibility of shipwreck and ultimate failure remaining with him all the time as an essential element of the whole venture.

---

[1] *Guide to Kulchur*, p. 127.

Odysseus himself, we may recall, gave way to landlubberly despair whenever he was to 'set forth on the godly sea' (Canto I).

Pound's *Cantos* should therefore be seen as that form of poetry which Robinson Jeffers has called 'a means of discovery, as well as a means of expression'. But poetry as a means of discovery—for poet and reader alike—is diametrically opposed to that rhetoric ('persuasion' according to Aristotle) which, in literature, requires the finite and closed form. 'We make out of the quarrel with others, rhetoric,' Yeats was to confess in *Anima Hominis*, 'but of the quarrel with ourselves, poetry. Unlike the rhetoricians who get a confident voice from remembering the crowd they have won or may win, we sing amid our uncertainty.'

While both Yeats and Pound, let it be said, were so well aware of the nature of rhetoric, to which they themselves occasionally succumbed, particularly in their political prose, their poetry is a different proposition altogether. There, as Richard Ellmann shows (cf. p. 85), Pound instinctively rejects all 'premature synthesis'.

For Pound there was never any prefabricated system of orthodox thought to fall back upon as there was for Eliot, whom he taunted on one occasion with being 'too weak to live with an uncertainty'. The scale of values on which future civilizations might be built consequently had to be established by empirical means, and any values which he might wish to borrow eclectically from systems of the past or present had first to be made new and tested against his own experience.

In this sense the *Cantos* would appear to belong squarely within the framework of the 'poetry of experience' that has been analysed so well by Robert Langbaum, although he did not in fact apply his analysis to the epic poem under discussion which would corroborate his argument no less convincingly than his own examples. In creating new values the poet, according to Langbaum, who calls him 'the romanticist' but establishes an unbroken line of descent from romanticism to modern classicism, 'employs two modes of apprehension, sympathy and judgment . . . sympathy being always ahead of judgment, and certain whereas judgment is problematical'.[1]

This describes Pound's procedure in the *Cantos* to perfection while at the same time indicating the directions in which the poem's successes and failures are to be sought. The urge to mend the breach between object and value that Langbaum notes in post-Enlightenment poetry comes close to defining the *raison d'être* of the *Cantos*, viz. the poet's deep-rooted conviction that there is, as Goethe has it, 'an uncharted pattern in objective things that corresponds to the uncharted pattern within the subjective being.'

It is not generally realized that, underlying all of Pound's actions, critical assessments and poetic techniques, there is one fundamental pattern of thought which might be described as the pattern of congruity: the fact and the value ascribed to it must tally, neither part must exceed the other lest, as with *usura* in Canto XLV, 'the line grow thick.' It is this equilibrium of mind that Pound perceives in 'mediterranean sanity', and it is essentially as much an aesthetic as a moral or economic perception.

We should not lose sight of the fact that, in its wider metaphorical sense, the history of monetary systems and coinage that forms a recurrent theme in the *Cantos* revolves around the question of the 'just price' that man should be required to pay for the gifts of nature and civilization: an attitude of mind reflecting a sense of responsibility for the whole of life. In its positive aspect, the theme of money in the *Cantos* is seen to be a token of that *sinceritas*, or common honesty, on which all human commerce, and hence all human society, is founded. In its negative aspect, it stands for *usura*, the cancerous growth of the cells gone mad and proliferating at the expense of the organism as a whole. Rhetoric is an inflation of value based on a scarcity of fact, and is the tool of the mountebanks of information, public relations and propaganda, while excess of fact and lack of evaluation lead to blinkered academic specialization which,

[1] *The Poetry of Experience*, New York 1957, p. 27.

19

unmindful of the vital interrelationships between the disciplines, produces mere bureaucrats of knowledge.

Either way, by inflation or deflation, the currency of human knowledge is debased. Pound appears to have been sharply aware of both evils. When he first entered upon the literary scene at the turn of the century, values had become divorced from facts to the point where they could be used as abstract counters, to be juggled with at will to form various systems of speculative thought, whereas facts and concrete entities were treated as mere phenomena. His early critical strictures were for this reason directed almost exclusively against the abstract tendencies of western thought—the usurious interest levied upon the 'manifest universe' vouchsafed to man.

In opposition to this trend he recorded his conviction that 'Any general statement is like a check drawn on a bank. Its value depends on what there is to meet it.'[1] Generals, he points out later in the *Pisan Cantos*, should have an army of particulars to back them up.

This compulsive urge to establish a balanced relationship between ideas and concrete reality was to have far-reaching consequences for Pound's poetic technique. But its implications extend even to ontology: evil, according to his lights, is quite simply a lapse from the 'green world' as the true measure and ultimate criterion of all human effort:

> . . . it is not man
> Made courage, or made order, or made grace,
> Pull down thy vanity, I say pull down,
> Learn of the green world what can be thy place
> [Canto LXXXI]

Sin, to Pound's way of thinking, is whatever does not square with reality; it is a deficiency of being, exactly as it was, less recently, for the Neoplatonists. His allergy to all manifestations of such disparity in economics, politics, literature, religion or philosophy, which always indicated to his mind the presence of

---

[1] *ABC of Reading*, London 1951, first ed. 1934, p. 25.

INTRODUCTION

some insincerity, acted as the constant irritant that kept his
poetic faculties alive for so long, even though it was to lead him
in economics and politics far out of his depth. At any rate the
striving for congruity may be said to account for practically all
of his aesthetic insights and technical innovations, which are
consequently fraught with ethical and philosophical implications.
That this fact is still widely disregarded may be due to certain
curious current notions about his alleged 'nominalism'.

The earliest indication of this mental disposition was of
course his discovery in Provençal poetry of the absolute
consonance of words and music, *motz el son*, which he took to be
a manifestation of the *forma* found in Melic poetry and later,
as far as European languages are concerned, in Elizabethan
lyrics. The double relationship here involved is a validation of
the intellect by emotion, for, as Pound insists, 'Poetry is a
centaur. The thinking word-arranging, clarifying faculty must
move and leap with the energizing, sentient, musical faculties.
It is precisely the difficulty of this amphibious existence that
keeps down the census record of good poets.'[1]

The qualities of rhythm and melos accordingly became for
him the test of a poet's sincerity, the proof of 'the whole man'
being behind the poem written. At the same time these qualities
represent the instinctual, animal component, for if melopoeia is
'poetry on the borders of music', music itself is 'perhaps the
bridge between consciousness and the unthinking sentient or
even insentient universe'.[2] Properly attuned, the poet's voice
becomes the voice of inarticulate creation.

Pound's demand for an absolute rhythm—'that this correspondence be exact, i.e., that it be the emotion which surrounds
the thought expressed'[3]—is closely related to his belief that in
poetry it is really the subjective, emotional, subconscious
strata that validate whatever ideas are advanced. In other words,
his conception of rhythm and metre points to just those dimensions of his writings that have been so consistently overlooked

[1] *Literary Essays*, p. 52.   [2] op. cit., p. 26.
[3] *Translations*, p. 24.

by critics who have persuaded themselves that Pound is a man of many wrongly reasoned arguments and no innards.

This demonstrates the danger of literary criticism that assumes idioplasty to have been the poet's point of departure. But, as he himself has said, the strength of the arts is precisely that 'their statement is a statement of motor forces. Argument begets but argument. . . . The artistic statement of a man is not his statement of the detached and theoretic part of himself, but of his will and his emotions.'[1]

Translated into Langbaum's terms, the 'sympathy' is more far-reaching and momentous than the 'judgment'. The pattern of congruity evidenced in these demands for exact correspondence between emotion and thought is reinforced by the demand for the *mot juste*, for 'the application of word to thing',[2] only this time with the emphasis reversed towards articulation, leading finally to the Confucian principle of *chêng*[4] *ming*[2], which is for Pound characteristically not so much a stylistic as an ethical principle, viz. 'finding the precise word for the inarticulate heart's tone means not lying to oneself'.[3]

Allied as it was to the Imagiste movement, the *mot juste* brings us to the image which, in Pound's definition, is yet another connecting device—'an intellectual *and* emotional complex in an instant of time'. With Pound, moreover, the image turns into a stratagem for reducing the symbol, which in the hands of the Symbolists had become an arbitrary counter, to its concrete core, for 'the natural object is always the adequate symbol'.

That this is a realization his predecessors had lost sight of completely or, at most, glimpsed only in isolated instances and at considerable personal cost, may be concluded from Oscar Wilde's observation in *De Profundis* : 'The great things of life are what they seem to be, and for that reason, strange as it may sound to you, are often difficult to interpret. But the little things of life are symbols.'[4]

---

[1] *Patria Mia*, Chicago 1950, first publ. 1912, pp. 77–8.
[2] *Literary Essays*, p. 21. [3] *Confucius*, p. 47.
[4] *The Letters of Oscar Wilde*, Ed. Rupert Hart-Davis, London 1962, pp. 454–5.

INTRODUCTION

The belief in the message inherent in the factual was to lead Pound to his most important device of allowing juxtaposed realities in the form of facts, events, quotations from documents and snatches of conversation to create their own meaning. This does not in any way imply a total repudiation of the subjective or mystical approach: the poet is merely letting the *vox mundi* of outer reality blend with the *vox humana* of his own inner reality, the one reinforcing the other.

The use of what Eliot, thinking along parallel lines, was to term the 'objective correlative' is a much older stratagem than is generally supposed. Eliot himself picked it up, albeit unconsciously and indirectly, from Sanskrit philosophy, and it was apparently also known to the eleventh century T'ang poet Wei T'ai, who wrote: 'Poetry presents the thing in order to convey the feeling. It should be precise about the thing and reticent about the feeling, for as soon as the mind [of the reader] responds to and connects with the thing, the feeling shows in the words: this is how poetry enters deeply into us. If the poet presents directly feelings which overwhelm him, and keeps nothing back . . . he cannot . . . strengthen morality and refine culture, set heaven and earth in motion and call up the spirits.'[1]

Leaving aside the spirits for a while, we find that in using the objective realities of other human, vegetable or mineral existences (cf. Albert Cook, p. 362), the poet has developed the three main technical devices of the *Cantos*: persona, ideogram, metamorphosis. In turn, these represent the othernesses of persons or of natural and supernatural things in order to stake out the boundaries of the poet's own being within the 'manifest universe'. As a natural corollary of this two-term relationship, he sees himself throughout as discovering, rather than inventing, his meaning. Any meaning with which reality may be invested by the individual must perforce seem counterfeit to a mind as attuned as Pound's to the notion of congruity. In fact his deep-rooted distrust of alleged artistic creation 'ex nihil', which he places on a par with moneys created 'out of nothing' by the

---

[1] Translated by A. C. Graham in *Poems of the Late T'ang*, London 1965.

bank, may be traced throughout his writing, where it assumes increasing proportions with the years. True originality for Pound, as for Eliot in his Introduction to Pound's *Selected Poems*,[1] is simply development as seen against the backdrop and reality of tradition. 'The so-called major poets', Pound observes, 'have most of them given their *own* gift but the peculiar term "major" is rather a gift to them from Chronos . . . it has been given them to heap together and arrange and harmonize the results of many men's labour. This very faculty for amalgamation is a part of their genius and it is, in a way, a sort of modesty, a sort of unselfishness. They have not wished for property.'[2]

We note that genius here consists in actualizing structures already latent in reality. The magnetic lines of force—to use the poet's own metaphor—already exist, but their presence does not become visible to the eye until physical iron particles are introduced within the magnetic field. Hence the emphasis placed in the *Cantos* on the re-erection of statue, altar and temple, for art 'is, religiously, an emphasis, a segregation of some component of that intelligence [the *intellectus agens*, cf. J. P. Sullivan, p. 241] for the sake of making it more perceptible.'[3]

The *forma*, or component of the divine intelligence, which although latent is so palpably present to the artist's mind, is of course, philosophically speaking, a factor in Aristotle's *entelechia*, the universal muscle flexed between the potential and the actual which even in antiquity seemed best illustrated by the sculptor's simultaneous perception of things in three dimensions :

'as the sculptor sees the form in the air
before he sets hand to mallet,
'and as he sees the in, and the through,
the four sides
'not the one face to the painter
[Canto XXV]

This is also the manner in which the main motifs of the *Cantos* take shape and materialize, and the reason why they

[1] London 1928. [2] *Literary Essays*, pp. 48–9.
[3] *Guide to Kulchur*, pp. 189–90.

can never be exhaustively treated in two-dimensional prose, critical or otherwise.

Pound's peculiar 'sculptural' awareness of his themes (cf. Donald Davie, pp. 198–214) is of paramount importance in that it provides him with an astounding immediacy of access to some of the profoundest intuitions of prehistory. Thus he seems to sense instinctively that the earliest canons of architecture (and here we would include Woodhenge and Stonehenge) were arrived at by representing the convolutions and figures of the dance as retraced pathways between the two worlds. The pattern of the dance reproduces the primitive Stone Age concept of the 'spiral of entry' that leads to the point where the divine life-force is thought to enter the temporal (cf. Boris de Rache-wiltz, p. 189 ff). This yields a clue to the original significance of the myth of Amphion, who built the walls of Thebes with the music of his lyre, and of the defences of Troy, which rose to the sound of Apollo's music in a dance :

> Templum aedificans, not yet marble,
> 'Amphion!'
>> [Canto XC]

The dynamic arts of music and dance here merge directly with the static arts of architecture and sculpture. The 'spiral of entry', an atavistic memory of the labyrinthine passageways of the caves in which paleolithic man lived and out of which the cult of the Great Mother arose (cf. G. R. Levy, *The Gate of Horn*[1]) appears in the *Cantos* in the shape of the Cretan maze. The centre of this maze was, significantly, the dwelling place of the Great Goddess, here called Ariadne, 'the Most Holy One', whom Pound invokes in a fragment of Canto CXVI, his very last Canto to date, just as in a slightly earlier fragment we find the lines :

> To reign, to dance in a maze.
> To live a thousand years in a wink.
>> [Canto CXIV]

[1] London 1948.

as the consummate expression of archetypal authority, which rests on the alignment of heaven and earth, or on following the divine pathways which, as Miss Levy says, are 'themselves currents of energy: "I am the Way and the Life."'

If the *Cantos*, in so far as they criticize temporal values that fail to square with perennial values, are the poet's dialogue with history past and present, it stands to reason that the subjective reality of their author cannot be quite as absent as the reader might conclude from the long poem's pragmatic phalanx of particulars. Moreover, if the pattern we have traced is valid, the *Cantos* must, as Forrest Read remarks (cf. p. 140), have an 'overplot' and an 'underplot'.

The private and quasi-mystical underplot is interleaved with the objective overplot through the poet's technique of presenting 'factual atoms'. Again it is the poem which provides the clue, for when Odysseus-Pound calls himself 'no-man' or 'Οὖτις' (in Cantos LXXIV, LXXX and LXXXIX), and elaborates this with the line 'Odysseus the name of my family', he is calling our attention to a time-honoured mystical issue.

The question of identity, widely discussed in mediaeval mysticism, rests on the recognition that the soul can have no direct knowledge of itself and becomes aware of its existence only through its contents. Basilius (329?–379) formulated this idea metaphorically in the words: 'As our eyes, which see external things, do not come to see their own image unless they glance into a mirror, whence their gaze is thrown back at them as a wave is thrown back from the shore, thus our mind, which perceives externals, cannot come to know itself unless it glance into the Scriptures.' That is to say, the soul cannot be its own object; it cannot 'delight in itself' (Canto XC), but only in its functions or its objects.

Such is also the argument of Richard St Victor, contrasted by Pound with modern psychoanalysis, which might be defined as a *l'âme-pour-l'âme* movement. The self can read itself in its empirical objects—which include books—but it cannot lay hold of its unalloyed essence.

At the centre of Pound's creative vortex (cf. the early poem

'Plotinus', Richard Ellmann, p. 58) we invariably discover this psychic vacuum from which, as the mystics agree, all images and all empirical content are absent. But it is precisely this void which constitutes the threshold or, as Pound repeatedly calls it, the gate of higher being or of inspiration (cf. Canto XLVII; also 'And that all gates are holy', Cantos XC, XCIV, C).

The Middle Ages had many similes for this paradox of identity, one of which, the *scintilla rationis*, or divine spark, standing for the focal point within the individual at which all time is conflagrated, seems to appear in the very last line of the *Cantos* to date :

> A little light like a rush light,
>   to lead back to splendour.
>   [Canto CXVI]

It is the void in man's nature which constitutes his mind's quintessence, for man is a biologically adaptable, non-specialized animal. We have come to see by now that Odysseus-Noman is, by necessity, a protean Everyman, and thus the ideal persona for Pound's sea voyage; and we may note how the periplus of the *Cantos* encompasses both Homer's and Dante's *nostos* in the external and the internal range of experience.

The search for identity employs the devices of persona, ideogram, and, above all, metamorphosis, which Pound has called the 'bust thru from the quotidien into "divine or permanent world" '.[1] In all this the poet approaches very close to Nietzsche's conception of the Dionysian element in poetry, outlined in *The Birth of Tragedy From the Spirit of Music*, which reverses Aristotelian poetics in a way which Pound, having formulated a similar idea in the concluding lines of his early programmatic poem 'The Flame', would probably endorse.

Nietzsche advances the theory that 'the ego of the lyric poet

[1] Letter to Homer L. Pound, April 11, 1927, *Letters of Ezra Pound*, London 1951, p. 285.

reverberates from the abyss of being: his "subjectivity" in the sense of our modern aesthetes, is an illusion . . . the lyric poet's images are nothing but himself and, as it were, only different projections of himself by virtue of which he, as the moving centre of that world, is entitled to say "I". Only of course this self is not the same as that of the conscious, empirically real man, but is the one and only truly existing and eternal self which resides at the root of things and by means of whose images the lyric genius sees right through to the root of things.' He goes on to show how man, as long as he is imbued with purely subjective volition and desire, can never at any time be a poet: 'Only in so far as the poetic genius, in the act of artistic procreation, merges with the original artist of the universe, does he acquire any knowledge of the permanent nature of art, for in that state he miraculously resembles the uncanny figure in the fairy-tale which can turn its eyes inward and look at itself: at that stage he is both subject and object, he is poet, actor and spectator all in one.'

In the case of Pound, this unfolding of the ego into 'poet, actor and spectator' becomes particularly evident in the *Pisan Cantos*, where the author appears to strike a more personal note, which persists through *Rock-Drill*, *Thrones* and the final fragmentary Cantos CX to CXVI. Yet this personal touch is, as Nietzsche points out, itself only a mask of the poet's enormous underlying impersonality, and so the terms subjective and objective, as applied to Pound, should always be taken in their full paradoxical import. Thus in emphasizing the 'private', 'emotional' and 'irrational' elements in the *Cantos* I am only trying to correct an imbalance that has long prevailed in earlier critical studies notwithstanding the numerous clues that point in this direction.

I refer here to the complete neglect of a pervasive nocturnal side to the poet's venture in the *Cantos*, an aspect to which he himself would seem to be explicitly alluding in what might well be taken as his final summing up of the *Cantos* as a poem:

And Laforgue more than they thought in him,
. . .

And I have learned more from Jules
                    (Jules Laforgue)
                              since then,
Deeps in him . . .

                              [Canto CXVI]

That Pound should place this acknowledgment of a Symbolist poet at the end of his long epic is only surprising as a contrast to the massive evidence of his prose repudiations of Symbolism, particularly in the essay entitled 'Vorticism'. Laforgue had derived from German Romanticism more elements than the irony (or *logopoeia*) that he found in E.T.A. Hoffmann and, perhaps more indirectly, Novalis. (Pound is, however, probably unaware of Laforgue's German antecedents.[1]) During his appointment as Reader to the Empress Augusta, Laforgue discovered in the Berlin aquarium those 'deeps' that were to become for him 'the symbol of promised Nirvana', and subsequently a leitmotif in his poetry: the motif of nature in reverse, an immutable anti-world that he once described as the 'immobile unique bliss of inorganic aggregates', and as 'the silent deeps which know only eternity, for which Spring, Summer, Autumn and Winter do not exist.'[2]

This calls to mind the numerous submarine sequences in the *Cantos*, such as the reference to the nymph Eleutheria transformed into coral in Canto II, the cave of Nerea-Thetis glistening with salt crystals in Canto XVII, the nocturnal voyage of the sun passing under the ocean in Canto XXIII ('With the sun in a golden cup / and going toward the low fords of ocean'), and many other kindred images throughout the poem, all of them characterized by a strange unearthly beauty.

It would surely not be far off the mark to see in these subaquatic motifs, which eventually become an essential element

[1] Cf. *Novalis und die französischen Symbolisten* by Werner Vordtriede, Stuttgart 1963, pp. 43–97.
[2] Jules Laforgue, *Moralité légendaire Salomé*, 1888.

in the 'great healing' and transfiguration of Canto XCI, a variation on the theme of Persephone's mineral vegetation of jewel-fruit and golden boughs (cf. Guy Davenport, pp. 160–173), the mirror-world that is inimical to the surface reality of things.

We have already frequently encountered this world in the early *Cantos*, in the 'valley under day's edge' of Cantos IV and XXI, in the 'gemmed field' and the artificial landscape at the end of Canto XX, in the nymph Phaetusa 'by meadows of Phlegethon' in Cantos XXI and XXV, and in some significant lines in Canto XXVII referring to the two-way vegetation of Persephone: 'The air burst into leaf. / "Hung there flowered acanthus, / Can you tell the down from the up?"'. Later, in Canto XCIX, we find the line 'a mirrour to flowers, as water is to the moon', likewise strongly suggestive of the underworld.

The idea of this antipodal vegetation of metal and precious stones is not of course a mythopoeic invention of the nineteenth century, even though the Symbolists did base their aesthetic and philosophy of a supernatural and almost evil purity and refinement upon it. The theme has actually come down to us from Sanskrit legend by way of the Arabian tales of Aladdin's cave and other subterranean themes; it is further evident in the trees buried upside down at Abydos and Deir el Bahri, as also in the Sumerian and Assyrian motif of the kishkanu tree of the underworld with its fruit of lapislazuli; in the Greek world we come across it in the myth of the golden apples that Heracles was required to secure from the garden of the Hesperides, and in Roman times it appears in the golden bough which was to give Aeneas access to Persephone-Proserpina's other kingdom. As early as in the last line of Canto I we find the theme of Aphrodite, goddess of the sea, sometimes also called Nerea or Thetis, 'Bearing the golden bough of Argicida' as she prepares to embark on a voyage which is a mirror image of that of Odysseus and his ill-starred companions.

Argicida, meaning 'slayer of the monster Argos', is an appelation of Hermes, the god who summoned the souls of the dying into the underworld. Aphrodite is here therefore not

only the goddess of beauty but also the goddess of death.
Aeneas, who defended Troy and, after its destruction, set
out to rebuild the archetypal city, is thus seen from the beginning to be a double of Odysseus who helped to destroy it,
the voyages of both Aeneas and Odysseus being a return to
origins and an effort to regain lost kingship; creation and
destruction, like beauty and death, are here compounded.

Aphrodite and Persephone could well be regarded as identical
in that the preparations for the Greater Mysteries at Eleusis,
which were concerned with the ἄνοδος, or Rising of Persephone
from the dark and wintry world of Dis, were also referred to by
the ancients as the Birth of Aphrodite from the sea. Laforgue's
static subaquatic world is most frequently associated by Pound
with the goddess of beauty, manifestly so in Canto XVII, where
he describes the cave of Nerea with its light 'not of the sun',
but also elsewhere:

> And she said : 'Otreus of Phrygia,
>   'That king is my father . . .'
>   and saw then, as of waves taking form
> As the sea, hard, a glitter of crystal,
> And the waves rising but formed, holding their form.
> No light reaching through them.
>
>   [Canto XXIII]

and, with its strong suggestion of the reversal of the processes
of surface reality:

> and saw the waves taking form as crystal,
> notes as facets of air,
> and the mind there, before them, moving,
> so that notes needed not move.
>
>   [Canto XXV]

The establishment of a connection between Aphrodite and
Persephone seems to come quite naturally to artists. Botticelli
in his 'Primavera' as well as in his 'Birth of Venus' links the
arrival of Aphrodite with that of Flora (or Persephone-Kore)
and vice versa. There is a continuity of existence among the

gods who live in the 'light *compenetrans* of the spirits' (Cantos
XCI and C).

But we may also observe that Pound, while employing a
leitmotif of nineteenth-century Symbolism, transmutes its
significance partly by going back through history to its original
meaning and partly by re-living it for himself. This is well
illustrated by his jewel-cum-colour imagery, and especially the
sensual topaz-to-amber regions of the spectrum and the metaphysical triad of blues, each having, as John Espey was early to
show in his *Ezra Pound's Mauberley* (1955), a specific mystical
significance :

> Will not our cult be founded on the waves,
> Clear sapphire, cobalt, cyanine,
> On triune azures, the impalpable
> Mirrors unstill of the eternal change?
> ['Blandula, Tenella, Vagula',
>   *Personae*]

But above all we have, as the unifying image of the whole
Cantos, the crystal, the 'white light' in which all colours are
contained. This suggests that the poem, as it progresses,
undergoes a change from the liquid melt of the poet's experience
into a hard and finely structured mineral substance, a sort of
'organic' stone. The symbolist use of precious stones to signify
an artificial static purity has here undergone a characteristically
Poundian development: 'Crystal waves weaving together
toward the gt/ healing' (Canto XCI).

The new understanding conveyed to readers of the *Cantos* by
Boris de Rachewiltz's observations (pp. 195–197) on Pound's
vicarious palingenesis may be augmented by a closer inspection
of the poet's revaluation of aestheticism in his pre-Imagist
stage.[1] Here again we do not find any outright rejection of
aesthetic values, but rather the 'logical development of his
predecessors' noted by T. S. Eliot.

The truth is that Pound accepts the late nineteenth century's

[1] Cf. N. Christoph de Nagy, *The Poetry of Ezra Pound: The Pre-
Imagist Stage*, Berne 1960.

almost religious estimation of artistic sensibility as well as its cult of Beauty, but with the qualification that this does not exonerate the poet from all social responsibility as it did the aesthetes and the decadents, who derived from Poe by way of Baudelaire the idea of Bohemian licence.

Poe defined the poetry of words as 'The Rhythmical Creation of Beauty. Its sole arbiter is Taste. With the Intellect or with the Conscience, it has only collateral relations. Unless incidentally, it has no concern whatever either with Duty or with Truth.'[1] Pound takes exactly the opposite stand: the very fact that artistic perceptivity is so far above the average human capability causes him to see artists as the 'antennae of the race', so that the artistic gifts of the individual properly belong to humanity as a whole. It is because the gods send their messages to Odysseus and the goddesses bed with him, because he alone has heard the sirens singing, that he is responsible for his companions. Such is the situation of the poet as summarized in Canto XX, where Pound refers to the lotus-eaters of pure aestheticism:

> What gain with Odysseus,
> They that died in the whirlpool
> And after many vain labours,
> Living by stolen meat, chained to the rowingbench
> That he should have a great fame
> And lie by night with the goddess?

The chorus of the nameless dead of past and recent history, of those who have never known the good life, all the lost lives which never attained articulation, keeps dinning in the poet's ears, driving him onward, both in the *Cantos* and in his personal and political engagement. His choice, for his early personae, of poets who had 'lived their poetry', indicates, as de Nagy points out, the direction his life was to take. At the same time it reveals a profoundly non-intellectual tendency, a desire to invest his energies not in the writing of books and poems alone, but also in life itself, in personal and collective endeavour.

[1] Poe, *Works*, Vol. VI, p. 12.

Viewed from this aspect, the vicarious occult processes to which he chooses to expose himself in the *Cantos*, leading him if not to madness at least to the outermost borders of rational thinking, are strangely consistent with what he so prophetically defined in *Patria Mia* as 'our American keynote'. Discovering this 'national chemical' in Whitman, he describes it as a 'desire for largeness, a willingness to stand exposed :

> Camerado, this is no book;
> Who touches this touches a man.

The artist is ready to endure personally a strain which his craftsmanship could scarcely endure.' And Pound adds that the strength of the American genius is that it 'will undertake nothing in its art for which it will not be in person responsible'.[1]

Thirty years later we find him repeating the same conviction upon his arrest by the U.S. Army in Genoa in 1945 : 'If a man isn't willing to take some risk for his opinions, either his opinions are no good, or he's no good.'[2] Since active adherence to this belief rather than to any other led to the Pisan cage, followed by twelve years in a hospital for the criminally insane, we see that it was more than mere theory.

This deeply felt responsibility for and to the whole of humanity ultimately causes the poet to assume the classic role of the poet as *vates*, of the seer and soothsayer, with all its attendant dangers to life and sanity.

In his somewhat paradoxical acceptance of this role in consequence of his belief in the aesthetic sensibility, Pound carries on the literary tradition by referring back to its very beginnings. Yet another of his patterns of thought here emerges, for in turning back to beginnings he quite often arrives— perhaps even stumbles upon—some of the more advanced concepts of our era. Expressed in three-dimensional terms, the development of his mind might be likened to the growth of a tree, where each year the trunk acquires a new ring—a historical process which does not imply 'simple recurrences or cycles,

---

[1] *Patria Mia*, p. 63.
[2] Charles Norman, *Ezra Pound*, New York 1960.

but continuous creative renovation' (cf. Forrest Read, p. 142).

The method has been demonstrated with telling effect in Miss Brooke-Rose's analysis of a key passage in Canto XCI, where she shows how Pound, by using various layers of language as indicators of historical time, penetrates the subsoil of recorded and authenticated history to reach down to the underlying magma of myth and the archetype.

Once the eye is focussed on the *forma* as the constant factor behind the variable forms of history, Elizabeth I of England, of the Welsh House of Tudor and—the Welsh having been the original Britons—the first 'British' queen to reign over England since the defeat of the Britons by the Saxons, is revealed as being in the same 'profession' as Helen of Troy, of whom it will be remembered that she was no mortal woman but Nemesis' daughter 'Helle' or 'Persephone', a goddess of death and rebirth. The motif of Stonehenge, which is here brought into the context of the oldest British tradition that tells of the direct descent of the Britons from the archetypal city of Troy, completes the cultural cycle.

By using a Mediterranean frame of reference in his themes as well as in his polyglot quotations, we therefore see that Pound has been true all along to the oldest and most enduring tradition of the English language, that strong Mediterranean strain which has stimulated English letters throughout the centuries from Laȝamon and Chaucer to Shakespeare, Byron, Shelley and Rossetti.

Seen in this light, the *tour de force* by which the poet presents the Homeric 'hinter-time' Nekuia passage in Canto I in an approximation of the metrics of the *Seafarer* appears as a thematic rhyme of great subtlety and depth. In the megalithic temple-and-tomb of Stonehenge, monumentalizing the lost cause of the sun-and-moon kings of prehistory, we find moreover yet another instance of that pattern of thought which links the prehistoric past with the present and the future, since it arises out of those timeless archetypal concepts of which the Irish poet Æ (George Russell) has said: 'There are no nations to whom the entire and loyal allegiance of man's spirit could be given. It can only go out to the ideal empires and nationalities in the womb of time, for whose coming we pray.'

With this in mind it is very difficult to accept the view advanced by Marius Bewley that history does not become for Pound, as it did for Eliot, 'a perspective capable ... of leading towards a final transcendence'. Mr Bewley bases his argument largely on the long-standing misconception of Pound being a 'nominalist' (a point that J. P. Sullivan disposes of on p. 237 f).

But, and perhaps more importantly, a critical consensus on Pound's treatment of history appears to be establishing itself which is clandestinely grounded on theological prejudgments. Even such a discriminating mind as Donald Davie's is apparently not entirely unaffected by this current trend, for in his book on Pound we read :

'Pound has made it impossible for any one any longer to exalt the poet into a seer. This is what Pound has done to the concept of the poetic vocation. . . Charles Olson in the fifth of his *Mayan Letters* declares that Pound's egotism, the fact that Pound recognizes only Confucius and Dante as his betters, "creates the methodology of the Cantos" wherein, "though the material is all time material, he has driven through it so sharply by the beak of his ego, that he has turned time into what we must now have, space and its live air." And so, because Pound's egotism in the *Cantos* "destroys historical time," Olson decides that it is "beautiful". . . . Whatever more long-term effect Pound's disastrous career may have on American and British poetry, it seems inevitable that it will rule out (has ruled out already, for serious writers) any idea that poetry can or should operate in the dimension of history, trying to make sense of the recorded past by redressing our historical perspectives. The poet may one day be honored again as a seer. Within the time-span of the individual life, his insights may be considered as not just beautiful but also true; and so they may, when they operate in the eschatological time-span of religion. . . . But the poet's vision of the centuries of recorded time has been invalidated by the *Cantos* in a way that invalidates also much writing by Pound's contemporaries.'[1]

Add to this line of reasoning Bewley's following remarks, in which he quotes from Noel Stock's *Poet in Exile*,[2] and we arrive at the crux of the argument : 'The failure of the religious aspect of the *Cantos*, if it may be said to exist, is intimately associated with the failure of Pound's historical sense in the poem as Mr Stock shows : "Pound has consistently failed to see or admit that Christianity . . . coincides with a great change in human sensibility. Something was already happening in Virgil's time which that sensitive soul perceived; with the establishment of Christianity some three centuries later that something was manifest. It was no less than the death of the old gods of the hearth and the city and the tribe—Eleusis it should be remembered was only a local religion—and their replacement by the conception of one God for all men. . . . But that above all else which casts serious doubts about Pound's treatment of religion is his silence about Christ and the central Christian dogmas in a poem that purports to deal with history over a great span of time." '[3]

The operative word in this argumentation is of course Davie's term 'eschatological', for it is Christian eschatology that views historical time as an objective linear progression from the creation of the world to the Last Judgment—a view that can scarcely be reconciled with the conception of historical progression by rings of growth, where each new ring encompasses all previous rings instead of leaving them behind once and for all. It is precisely this heretical non-linear view of history that accounts for Pound's very early perception that 'all ages are contemporaneous'.

It is this too that compelled him to write out the text of the *Cantos* as a palimpsest on which the writings of many hands are superimposed one upon the other, thus giving each meaning its depth in time. Yet the simultaneity of all time does not in any

[1] *Ezra Pound: Poet as Sculptor*, New York 1964, pp. 243–4.
[2] Manchester University Press, Manchester 1964.
[3] *The Southern Review*, Autumn 1965, pp. 923–4.

way eliminate from the *Cantos* the time factor as is being currently claimed. Nor does Pound reject time *per se* when he says 'Time is the evil. Evil' (Canto XXX), where he is simply referring to the mummified corpse of Inez de Castro enthroned next to her husband, the king 'still young there beside her'. This may be taken as Pound's comment on the asynchronism between time levels which allows dead, dogmatized and superannuated form to hang over the present and hold sway over the living. Time is evil only in so far as it acts as a barrier to living contact.

For Pound it is not the past that has been moving towards us in linear progression, but he himself and his poem that move into the past. In line with modern scientific concepts, history for Pound is a space-time continuum, or a field of force. Thus time in the *Cantos* is not the objective, abstract and graduated time of calendar and clock that academic historical studies take for granted, but the subjective time of individual experience: 'Time is not, Time is the evil, beloved / Beloved the hours' (Canto LXXIV).

This dissociation between objective and subjective time at once removes the objection that Davie bases on Olson's remark about Pound turning time (by egotism, of all things!) into 'space and its live air', namely that 'poetry is an art that works sequentially by its very nature; therefore it inhabits the dimension of time quite literally'.[1] Since it is the mind of the poet that moves through history, no contradiction in terms can be held to exist between the *Cantos'* microstructure (their metric measured by the poet's subjective time, his breath or 'psyche', cf. Hugh Kenner, p. 334) and their macrostructure, the accumulated records of history. As far as Olson's rejection of time in favour of space is concerned, one is reminded of Mrs Margaret Fuller's remark that she was prepared to 'accept the Universe'. To which Carlyle replied: 'Gad, you'd better.'

Pound has himself made it amply clear that he is aware of this dissociation and, by introducing the idea of the periplus in a definition derived from Victor Bérard's *Les Navigations*

---

[1] *Ezra Pound: Poet as Sculptor*, p. 246.

d'Ulysse ('not as land looks on a map / but as sea bord seen by men sailing', Canto LIX), has shown that he is not even attempting to arrive at an eschatological pigeon's-eye view of history: 'we do NOT know the past in chronological sequence . . . what we know we know by the ripples and spirals eddying out from us and from our time.'

Here then, history is not so much an object of scholarly study as a world to be experienced. Far from ever having been an academic scholar—despite one unfortunate claim that he once made to that effect to Louis Untermeyer in 1932— Pound has always been a dilettante in the original sense of the word. Dilettantism is even an essential aspect of his cultural criticism in that it deliberately flouts the current restrictive specialization of all knowledge, whereby the individual disciplines are generally sealed off in a vacuum and reserved for experts to whom they are considered to 'belong'.

This is a development which, despite or even because of the advances of modern science in its various fields, is likely to throw us back into another dark age of ignorance; it must be seen as a negative by-product of the encyclopaedist classification of knowledge on a purely mechanistic principle—'only the alphabet for a filing system', as Pound has observed.

Pound's practice of trying to establish links between the various branches of knowledge is, moreover, in accordance with the poetry of experience in that it seeks to deal with what Langbaum defines as 'the central question posed by the Enlightenment—the question of tradition, of how, after the collapse of the traditional authority of values, to find and justify new values.'

The attempt to answer this question should, again according to Langbaum, be seen as 'in large measure literature's answer to science, . . . we can understand it as essentially a doctrine of experience, an attempt to salvage on science's own empiric grounds the validity of the individual perception against scientific abstractions.' It is the effort of modern man to 'reintegrate fact and value after having himself rejected, in the experience of the Enlightenment, the old values.'

Yet the purpose of this movement is 'not in the end to reject intellect and discipline but to renew them by empirical means.' In this sense, then, Post-Enlightenment poetry is really 'not so much a reaction against eighteenth-century empiricism as a reaction within it, a corrected empiricism. It is, as Mill suggested, the necessary corrective for the skeptical analytic intellect.'[1]

Unless these considerations are ignored it would seem to reflect a singular lack of critical sensibility to subject Pound's dialogue with history—so entirely different from the scientific historical method in which the historian effaces himself—once again to the 'skeptical analytic intellect', or even to pretend that Pound's 'sense of history' is inferior to that of Eliot who, after all, simply reverts to Pre-Enlightenment tradition and disregards all that has occurred in the intervening period.

As to the alleged failure of the religious aspect of the *Cantos*, this charge is tenable only if one arbitrarily restricts the meaning of the word 'religion' to apply to Christianity alone and, even within these narrow limits, turns a blind eye to the results of anthropological research which have, one would think, established clearly enough important dissociations between the highly syncretic teachings of the faith—if one ignores or belittles the Greek mystery cults—and the philosophy on which Christian dogma and sacrament are in so large a measure based (cf. Werner Jaeger's *Early Christianity and Greek Paideia*, 1962).

One of Pound's pet unappreciated savants, Tadeusz Zieliński, made a fine distinction between theocratic religions 'in which an impassible abyss separates the divine from the human', and theanthropic religions 'which allow a connection between the two natures in the shape of a god-man or even a man-god.'[2]

Since all theanthropic elements in Christianity, embodying as they do the pith and marrow of the teaching, derive, as Zieliński shows, from the Mediterranean mystery cults (which, far from being confined to Eleusis alone, also flourished in Egypt, Minoan Crete, Samothrace, Thrace and Phrygia), whereas the

[1] *The Poetry of Experience*, pp. 21, 22, 27.   [2] *La Sybille*, 1925.

theocratic elements all go back to the monotheism of the Old Testament, there is a certain justification for Pound's claim that the real 'Old Testament' of Christian teaching is to be found in Hesiod and Ovid, and that 'Christ follows Dionysus' ('Hugh Selwyn Mauberley', III). His purely theanthropic religious beliefs are, in addition, kin and kindred to the conception of his *magnum opus* as an open form and to his penchant for regarding the creative process not as invention *ex nihilo* but as a process of continuous discovery by which things are actualized in the temporal sphere.

Creation would accordingly appear to be more of a continuous process taking place within the world, something in which man may participate, than is allowed for by the monotheistic conception, which sees the world as having been created in a single operation from without, thereby confronting man with the *fait accompli* of a ready-made universe and precluding or severely limiting all human creativity. It may indeed be asked which of the two cosmogonies is the more religious. If transcendence means going beyond the self to enter and participate in another level of existence, there is surely much to be said for not drawing as rigid a dividing line between creature and creator as monotheism requires. Pound sees the universe as being sustained by an Ovidian continuity which is manifest in the principle of metamorphosis, where graduated transitions are possible from inorganic rock to organic vegetation, from vegetation to animal, from animal to man, and from man to gods (plural) or 'divine states of mind', and from gods back to inorganic or organic hypostases. And it is this universal cyclical movement that he would record in the *perpetuum carmen* or 'permanent metaphor' of his *Cantos*.

The mask or persona is intimately connected with the metamorphotic principle in that it is the device by which the experience of transcendence, of passing 'beyond your bonds and borders' ('The Flame') is made manifest. Individual existence is resolved in the mystical experience in which a present exists outside of time and all being reveals itself as one continuous bloodstream coursing through the arteries of reality. This is the supreme realization of the dying Heracles that 'It all coheres';[1] it is the great synthesis and 'healing', where the voice of the universe, of external fact, becomes one with the poet's individual voice, reverberating, as Nietzsche has said, from the abyss of being. Thus the light imagery of the *Cantos*, the 'light tensile' (Canto LXXIV), stands for the umbilical cord that links the individual with the universe.

Participation in an existence other than one's own is, moreover, at the root of all religious experience, a fact well attested by the masked animal dancers depicted on the walls of paleolithic caves, whose sympathetic magic bespeaks a profound intuition of the indivisibility of life. We might further recall the Dionysian cults of Eleusis in which the masked ritual of Attic comedy (animal masks) and tragedy (heroic masks) arose from the dance in honour of the demigod Dionysos (Zagreus, Iacchus, Bacchus), who was given the epithets *dithyrambos* and *digonos* (Twice Born), having been born once on earth and once in heaven.

Plato and Euripides both interpreted the epithet *dithyrambos* as 'He of the Double Door', thus identifying Dionysos as the semi-divine mediator between the natures of man and god. We may surmise this to be the reason why Dionysos is so frequently associated in Pound's mind with Christ.

The mutuality of all being—on which the feeling of social responsibility that we have mentioned earlier is also grounded—finds a psychological basis in the Neoplatonic teaching that 'omniformis omnis Intellectus est', that the mind can assume the shape of all things (cf. Cantos V and XXIII). The human mind is, by definition, *polytropos* (*Odyssey*, I, 1) and *polymetis* (*Odyssey*, XXI, 274), like that of Odysseus; it is not fixed in systems and dogmas. Precisely this quality causes the gods to take an interest in Odysseus, so that Pound can have Zeus say: 'A chap with a mind like THAT! The fellow is one of us. One of US.'[2] The quality of being *omniformis*, of being able to encompass within the mind the living, interpenetrating intelligences of the world, must, of course, also apply to the divine creative mind.

[1] Pound, *Women of Trachis*, 1954. [2] *Guide to Kulchur*, p. 146.

Plotinus translated these conceptions into the terms of his cosmic dynamism : God (or rather the One that, for Neoplatonists, is beyond personification) is *thinking* the universe, and this divine motor of self-realization itself forms the universal process : 'The primary cause of all things is also their ultimate end', says Dionysos Areopagita. In Neoplatonic thinking the urge of all living things to return to their primary cause thus constitutes a mystical vortex which informs both Eros and Intellect :

> drunk with the 'ΙΧΩΡ of ΧΘΟΝΙΟΣ
> fluid ΧΘΟΝΟΣ strong as the undertow
> of the wave receding
>
> [Canto LXXXII]

The retrograde movement of Pound's mind, which makes him try to lay hold of ideas at the early stage of the *forma* and is discernible in all of his moral, social and literary opinions, appears in this sense to be of the true nature of religion in so far as religion is a link binding man, both metaphysically and historically, to his origins. In this light it is hardly an exaggeration to say that the *Cantos* are more deeply imbued with religion than any other poem of our time. It is also worthy of note that the cyclical pattern of thought here manifested makes Pound in one way literally the most anachronistic of thinkers, while at the same time enabling him to include within his range various territories that have not hitherto been touched on in literature and which science is only just beginning to consider.

The mental feedback control which continuously compels Pound to refer back to origins as a corrective aid in evaluating contemporary phenomena is also the underlying cause of his profound intuitive sympathy with ancient Chinese thought. China's age-old orientation towards beginnings, and especially such where recorded history merges with archetypal legend, is deeply congenial to his way of thinking. Marcel Granet has pointed out in *La pensée Chinoise* that the concept of exemplary existences, such as those of the Chinese sage kings Yao, Shun and Yü, has relieved the Chinese of the necessity of having to invent a world of abstractions outside of the human world, and so enabled them to retain a flexible idea of order. For over twenty centuries this constant testing of phenomena against origins has acted on Chinese mental life as an agent of *hsin*[1] *min*[2], the renewal of the people, a process which, as Professor Needham has observed, has been many times repeated, more often attempted, though never so deeply achieved as now.

It might be counted among Pound's achievements that he recognized the affinity between the Confucian idea of the *tao*[4], the process of reality as a circular movement around the axis or centre of things, and the Neoplatonic vision of the universal process—which Hegel was to call 'history'—as a cycle which is set off by the 'Unmoving Mover' to which it eventually returns. Pound's mystical Neoplatonic interpretation of Chinese philosophical concepts is perhaps the most interesting development in Neoconfucian thinking since the teachings of the Ming-dynasty philosopher Wang Yang-ming (1472–1528), who incidentally puts in a fleeting appearance in Canto LXXXVII along with Nakae Tōju (1608–1648), who carried the lamp of Wang's new idealistic Confucianism with its doctrine of the unity of knowledge and action to Japan.

There is no reason to believe that fundamental Chinese thinking will ever be surpassed or outmoded by occidental ratiocination any more than the thought of Plato, Aristotle and Plotinus has ever become a negligible quantity in successive European cultures. Future students of Pound's works may find an examination of his equation of certain concepts of the Neoconfucian syncretic philosophy of the Sung-dynasty scholar Chu Hsi (1130–1200) with those of the mediaeval European Philosophers of Light far more rewarding than any discussion of his so-called 'translations' of the Confucian books, which in point of fact are not translations at all but highly imaginative variations and 'commentaries' on the texts of the kind that have been indulged in by Confucians of all ages. They are the outcome of one of the most serious, albeit certainly the oddest, positive responses to Chinese thought by an occidental mind— and so belong to the history of ideas.

INTRODUCTION

If Pound has done much to make his readers aware of the civilizing influence of Chinese culture, it was the historian of Japanese art, Ernest Fenollosa (1853–1908), who first guided his interest in this direction. 'The duty that faces us', Fenollosa had written with regard to the Chinese, 'is not to batter down their forts or to exploit their markets, but to study and to come to sympathize with their humanity.... The Chinese have been idealists and experimenters in the making of great principles; their history opens a world of ... achievement, parallel to that of the ancient Mediterranean peoples. We need their best ideals to supplement our own.'[1] He went on to prophesy that, once translated into the terminology of human experience, the Chinese tradition will show itself, as far as the European mind is concerned, to be an extension of the *Iliad*, an idea that Pound obviously has attempted to realize with his versions of the Songs (*shih*).

Fenollosa's ideas here ran parallel with some of those of his more widely known contemporary, the Scottish anthropologist James George Frazer, who posited the fundamental comparability of all religious, mythical and ritual concepts. It is, incidentally, because of the Christian claim to a monopoly on truth that Dionysus serves Pound's purpose in the *Cantos* better than Christ.

Such insights inevitably lead away from the still prevalent ethnocentrism of European thinking and towards that cultural relativism that Johann Gottfried Herder (1744–1803) anticipated almost two centuries earlier.

The achievement of seeing all human cultures, no matter how far separated in time and space, as parts of a single living organism, and thus of perceiving a fundamental unity beyond the plurality of cultures, must be credited to Leo Frobenius, a spiritual descendant of Herder and the von Humboldts, who wrote: 'We no longer live under a single horizon. The frontiers, the geographical divisions, the critical attention paid to racial factors—all these requirements of the specialized sciences have

---

[1] *The Chinese Written Character as a Medium for Poetry*, New York 1920,

been set aside. We see the earth in its entirety: we hold all [phases of culture] in equal esteem. Nothing is of greater or of lesser interest to us. The vast process of becoming unfolds before our eyes as a single unity, from the first stone flints of diluvial cultures to the flower of Greek civilization or of the Gothic spirit. The whole of it one huge tree, the tree of heaven, Ygdrasill.'[1]

This pluralistic and relativistic mode of thinking, although still anathema in many disciplines, is nevertheless emerging into the foreground in certain fields of modern science. In physics it has found expression in the probability calculus and in Heisenberg's Uncertainty Factor. Elsewhere attention is being focussed upon non-Aristotelian logic, non-Euclidian geometry, 'non-grammatical' linguistics. The *a priori* categories of knowledge, such as space, time, and causality, have all but been abandoned. Einstein was the first to question what had hitherto been considered unshakable axioms of thought. 'Concepts that have proved useful in imposing order on things,' he warned, 'tend to assume such an authority over us that we forget their lowly origin and accept them as immutable law. Thus they come to be marked off as "logical imperatives". And it is precisely these which have so often blocked and impeded the path of scientific progress for long stretches of time.'

Taken seriously, Einstein's admonishment could lead to the development of a kind of virtue—the tolerance of other people's otherness that has for so long been lost to occidental civilization, and the strength to live with uncertainties, which would be a mark of intellectual honesty. That fine old physicist Max Born even goes as far as to say: 'Conceptions like Absolute Rightness or Ultimate Truth are figments of the mind that should be excluded from any field of scientific inquiry. This loosening up of thought is in my view the greatest boon that modern science has bestowed on humanity. For it is precisely the belief in a single truth which one supposes to be in one's

[1] *Vom Kulturreich des Festlandes*, 1923; cf. 'Ygdrasill' in Cantos LXXXV and XC.

possession that lies at the root of all the iniquities in the wide world.'[1]

When Fenollosa contended, at a very early date for such ideas, that poetry agrees with science rather than with logic, coming events were casting their shadows before them. He had indeed put his finger on the essential link between science and poetry—the structure of the sentence seen as a mirror of natural and mental processes. We may observe in this context that physical science has for some time now discarded the naive conception of matter, manifest in the subject-predicate division, for that of the 'field of force'. Thus it has come to be recognized that things are really their functions, a plurality of functions. or as Fenollosa would have said, verbs : 'All processes in nature are interrelated; and thus there could be no complete sentence (according to this definition) save one which it would take all time to pronounce.' So much for the closed form.

The belief that in language we are not dealing with static mental counters but may be 'watching things work out their own fate' (Fenollosa) caused Pound to advance from the image to his ideogram (conceived as a cluster of pictograms or word-pictures and not to be confused with the Chinese ideogram) and to polyvalent logic. The imagistic poem still follows the Aristotelian dialectical process of thesis, antithesis and synthesis—as is quite apparent from Pound's early quasi-haikus and other short Imagist poems, in which we invariably find two concrete images juxtaposed in such a way as to fuse into a sudden meaning. It is a process which takes place entirely within the reader's mind, recording 'the precise instant when a thing outward and objective transforms itself, or darts into a thing inward and subjective.'[2]

The method of the Poundian ideogram, on the other hand, breaks away from the thin-blooded progressions of occidental syllogization by blending the metaphoric overtones of words and their multiple correspondences into an intricate fabric of

[1] 'Symbol und Wirklichkeit', *Universitas*, Stuttgart 1958, XIX p. 817 f.
[2] Pound, *Gaudier-Brzeska*, p. 103.

meanings, thereby recovering for poetry the full echo area of each word. Syntax yields to parataxis.

Stylistically speaking, parataxis begins where the ancient dispute over sentence structure broke off. This had been concerned with the relative merits of the *connexio verbalis*, as the external linkage provided by grammar, and the *connexio realis*, as the internal linkage provided by inner necessity, the first culminating in the balanced rhetorical period of Baroque language and the latter in the erratic manner of much modern verse. Carried to extremes, the *connexio realis* may strike the reader as sheer incoherence, but it is nonetheless, by its very definition, entirely different from automatic or aleatory writing. Pound has extended this technique by juxtaposing concrete particulars that he considers meaningful in the conviction that they will speak for themselves. The grammatical link becomes irrelevant, contrived and artificial once we regard things as 'bundles of functions' (Fenollosa, cf. also J. P. Sullivan, p. 240), where the resultant amalgam of meanings provides a plural relationship instead of the dialectical one deemed by convention to be essential.

While Pound's method necessarily contains logical incompatibilities as well as paradoxes, it might be argued that syllogistic contradiction cannot arise at the level of the *forma* because ideas have not there attained the degree of abstraction which would make it possible to use them separately and play one off against the other. The *forma* is the concrete stage of the incipient idea.

The sequence of themes recorded on the two-dimensional printed pages of the *Cantos* is the nearest the poet can approach to the three-dimensional cluster that every motif forms in his mind. This process—often dealing in metaphysical concepts—which relies on external objective reality to a degree hitherto unprecedented in occidental literature, is peculiarly close to the mystical mode of contemplation that we find exalted in the late cantos. For contemplation involves, as Richard of St Victor (one of Pound's favourite ecclesiastics) points out, the *liber volutas* (free flight) of the mind and the *mira agilitate circumferri* (the wondering encirclement) of its object, thus abandoning, like Pound in his ideogram, the central perspective of a single onlooker.

In the foregoing we have sought to point up some aspects of the almost incredible internal coherence achieved in the *Cantos* by a poet who has in recent years repeatedly dismissed his long poem as a failure. It may well be so in his eyes, for it is quite conceivable that, while he did not set out with a fixed formula, he has been adding canto after canto throughout the years in the firm belief that such a formula, a finite form, would eventually emerge, so that the poem would lead to that paradise in which the poet's intensely subjective, emotional impulse—his 'sympathy' in Langbaum's sense of the word—would prove to be commensurate with the expansive, objective, reasoned effort of his 'judgment'. No one would claim that this has been realized in the *Cantos*. 'Nothing living can be calculated,' Kafka has said, and in this sense the *Cantos* would certainly seem to be a living poem.

While it is true that Pound is known to have expressed, in unpublished private letters and broadcasts, some of the most purblind and even vicious notions of his generation, it is no less true that his fundamental instincts and sympathies have generally been sound. In a well-reasoned analysis of the political implications of the ideas of Pound and other right-wing writers of the first half of the present century, John R. Harrison arrives at the final conclusion that 'As Pound was the only one of the writers under discussion to work for a fascist country during the war, it may seem paradoxical to say that he was the most democratically-minded of them; but I believe this to be the case. He had a genuine concern for the underdog, whether individually or in the mass.'[1]

As to the periodic aberrations to which we have referred, literary history tells us that these are, regrettably, more the rule than the exception among poets and writers. We may recall, for instance, that Elizabeth Barrett, in a letter to her friend Mary Russell Mitford, recorded how Wordsworth had stamped his foot with rage on learning that the death sentence

[1] *The Reactionaries*, London 1966.

on a Chartist leader had been mitigated to transportation,[1] and that Professor Ernest Samuels has described the parochial anti-Semitism of Henry Adams, which was so akin to that for which Pound blamed himself to Allen Ginsberg[2] in Venice two days before his 82nd birthday in 1967. More serious still, it is a matter of historical fact that Tennyson publicly condoned the bloody 1885 massacre, with trimmings, in Jamaica,[3] and that Yeats counted as an intimate friend—and even celebrated in verse—Kevin O'Higgins, who had been in large measure responsible for the seventy-seven judicial murders carried out in the Irish Free State from 17 November 1922 to 2 May 1923.[4] And in recent years we ourselves have witnessed the spectacle of a small coterie of 'advertised litterati' (Canto XCV) unequivocally defending in public what by any standard must be condemned as an unjust war. Aristotle of course made a distinction between intellectual and moral virtù. And if certain writers may be considered to possess intellectual virtù, it does not go without saying that they must unfailingly exhibit moral virtù on all occasions as well.

In Pound's case our prime attention is claimed not by the element of paranoia but by certain visions and illuminations which can assume for us a value of which the poet himself may be unconscious. Nor is there, as Lucien Goldmann has observed, anything at all absurd in the notion of a writer or poet not apprehending the objective significance of his own works. In fact this is an essential factor in the new empirical—as opposed to Aristotelian—poetics.

Heere's fine Reuolution, if wee had the tricke to see't. And there is indeed much in Pound's *Cantos* and in his less apodictic prose statements which can hold significance for a consciously post-Poundian generation in much the same way as, in another

[1] *Henry Adams: The Major Phase*, London 1965.

[2] Michael Reck, A Conversation between Ezra Pound and Allen Ginsberg, *Evergreen Review*, New York, June 1968.

[3] Geoffrey Dutton, *The Hero as Murderer: The Life of Edward John Eyre*, London 1968.

[4] Dorothy Macardle, *The Irish Republic*, Dublin 1937.

discipline, earlier generations derived from Hegel a workable dialectic and the concept of 'claims of conscience' which are manifest in the moral imperatives that are beginning to inform the social and political thinking and responses of a new generation.

'Litterae nihil sanantes' writes Pound (quoting John Adams) in his very last canto, but goes on to ask :

> And as to why they go wrong,
>   thinking of rightness
> To confess wrong without losing rightness.
> [Canto CXVI]

Pound's great quixotic venture based on the belief that individual existence, when fully explored, will yield up a meaning independent of any preconceived answers of religion, philosophy or political doctrine, seems to have failed. Yet the enormous naiveté on which such faith was founded does not necessarily nullify the achievement. As it proceeds, the poem develops its own logic and, in the process, becomes an inexhaustible record of the *condition humaine*. One has in fact to be thankful that the poet insists on his failure, for it spares us from seeing the *Cantos* as just another success story—that most vulgar of all the fetishes of the Western world. Let us therefore accept Pound's self-disparagement with the one reservation that, if the *Cantos* are a failure, they are at all events a failure worth most of the successes of the age.

Scholarly studies of Pound's work began with Lawrence Richardson's essay 'Ezra Pound's Homage to Propertius' in the *Yale Poetry Review* in 1947, Hugh Kenner's two essays in the *Hudson Review* in 1949 and 1950, and an essay by Hugh Gordon Porteus in Peter Russell's symposium of the same year. Hugh Kenner followed up in 1951 with the first comprehensive study of Pound's works—*The Poetry of Ezra Pound*, and Warren Ramsay's seminal essay 'Pound, Laforgue and Dramatic

Structure' appeared in *Comparative Literature*. Porteus' 'Ezra Pound and His Chinese Character: A Radical Examination' contained some of the acutest observations ever made on Pound's Leibnitzian misapprehensions with regard to Chinese characters; to complete the picture it remained only for Achilles Fang, in his subtle introduction to *The Classic Anthology Defined by Confucius* (Pound's versions of the Songs, 1954) to make it implicitly clear that Pound should primarily be seen as a Confucian poet rather than as a translator of Confucian texts. The following years saw a number of remarkable breakthroughs in Pound criticism—John Espey's analysis *Ezra Pound's Mauberley* in 1955, Donald Davie's first essay on the *forma* in 1956 (later expanded in his *Ezra Pound: Poet as Sculptor* 1964), Angela Chih-ying Jung's unpublished thesis *Ezra Pound and China* in 1955, Barbara Charlesworth's unpublished thesis *The Tensile Light: A Study of Ezra Pound's Religion* in 1957, Earl Miner's chapter on Pound's poetry in *The Japanese Tradition in British and American Literature* 1958, N. Christoph de Nagy's *The Poetry of Ezra Pound: The Pre-Imagist Stage* 1960, J. P. Sullivan's analysis *Ezra Pound and Sextus Propertius* 1964, and N. Christoph de Nagy's second penetrating monograph *Ezra Pound's Poetry and Literary Tradition: The Critical Decade* 1966.

Parallel with these special studies there have been a number of more general works, the more important being *The Annotated Index to the Cantos* edited by J. H. Edwards and W. W. Vasse in 1957; Clark Emery's *Ideas Into Action* in 1958; M. L. Rosenthal's *A Primer for Ezra Pound* and G. S. Fraser's *Ezra Pound* in 1960; George Dekker's *Sailing After Knowledge* and Donald Gallup's *A Bibliography of Ezra Pound* in 1963.

Finally, no general survey, however condensed, should neglect to acknowledge that, at least from January 1950 to 1965, some of the most perceptive Pound criticism on record has appeared *hors concours* in anonymous reviews in the *Times Literary Supplement*.

The present collection of essays pays its respect to this impressive record of scholarship by avoiding wherever possible any re-examination of fields which have already been competently explored elsewhere. Rather than attempt to present another all-round evaluation, the book ventures for the most part into hitherto uncharted regions of Pound's work. Since many of the essays have been specially written, I should like to record my gratitude to contributors for their willingness to treat special themes and to pursue lines of investigation that often led beyond the limits of conventional literary criticism.

RICHARD ELLMANN

Ez and Old Billyum

———————— ❦ ————————

Ezra Pound, after attending the service for T. S. Eliot in
Westminster Abbey in January 1965, memorialized an
even older association with W. B. Yeats by visiting the
poet's widow in Dublin. His friendship with Yeats began in
1908, six years before he met Eliot. In a shrunken literary
scene, it is tempting to try to piece together the substance of
this once drastic connection, now diminished to history.

At the time of their first meeting in London, Pound was
twenty-three to Yeats's forty-three. He did not, like James
Joyce six years earlier, find Yeats too old to be helped. Instead
he declared, with humility and yet some arrogance of his own,
that Yeats was the only poet worthy of serious study,[1] and in
later years he recalled without chagrin having spent the years
from 1908 to 1914 in 'learning how Yeats did it'.[2] What he
learned was the 'inner form of the lyric or the short poem
containing an image,'[3] as in 'The Fish',

> Although you hide in the ebb and flow
> Of the pale tide when the moon is set,[4]

and 'the inner form of the line,'[5] probably its rhythmical merger
of 'dull, numb words'[6] with unexpected ones. Yeats offered

[1] Ezra Pound, 'Status rerum,' *Poetry* I. 4 (January 1913), p. 123.
[2] Letter to Michael Roberts, July 1937. *The Letters of Ezra Pound
1907–1941*, ed. D. D. Paige (New York, 1950), p. 296.
[3] Pound, 'Harold Monro,' in *Polite Essays* (London 1937), p. 9.
[4] Pound, 'The Later Yeats,' *Poetry* IV, 2 (May 1914), pp. 65–66.
[5] Pound, 'On Music,' *New Age* X. 15 (8 February 1912), pp. 343–4.
[6] Yeats, *Dramatis Personae* (London, 1936), p. 53.

further an example of 'syntactical simplicity';[1] he had, for example, cut out inversions and written with what Pound as late as 1914 considered 'prose directness', in 'The Old Men Admiring Themselves in the Water',

> I heard the old, old men say,
> 'Everything alters.'[2]

That Pound had already studied Yeats intently before coming to London is disclosed by the volume *A Lume Spento*, which he published in Venice on his roundabout way to England from Wabash College, and has republished in 1965 with a new preface describing the poems as 'stale cream-puffs'. They are so, but show something none the less about the baker. The second poem, 'La Fraisne' (Old Provençal for ash tree), has a long 'note precedent' in Latin and Old Ezraic. Before explaining that the speaker in the poem is Miraut de Gazelas when driven mad by his love for Riels of Calidorn, Pound indicates that he wrote the poem in a mood like that of Yeats's *The Celtic Twilight*, a title which was intended to suggest a vague borderline between the physical and metaphysical worlds. He felt himself 'divided between myself corporal and a self aetherial', or as he defines it further, 'trans-sentient as a wood pool'. Such states in which time is contained and transcended possess Pound again, most notably in the descriptions of paradisal moods in the *Cantos*, but 'La Fraisne' itself does not come up to this degree of sentience. In the course of his self-exegesis, Miraut identifies himself with the ash tree; at one time he was a wise councillor but has now left 'the old ways of men' to lose himself in sylvan metamorphosis. He seems to follow the lead of two characters in Yeats's early poetry, Fergus who abdicated to drive his brazen cars in the forest,[3] and another royal abdicator, Goll, who belongs to the same dynasty as Arnold's 'Mycerinus'. Pound's line, 'Naught but the wind that flutters in the leaves,' echoes 'The Madness of King Goll,' where the refrain is:

[1] Pound, 'This Hulme Business,' *Townsman* II. 5 (January 1939), p. 15.
[2] Pound, 'The Later Yeats,' *Poetry* IV, 2 (May 1914), p. 66.
[3] Yeats, 'Who Goes with Fergus?'.

'They will not hush, the leaves that round me flutter—the beech leaves old.'[1] Miraut's thought that he is merging into the boles of ash wood owes something, like Pound's other early poem, 'The Tree', to Yeats's poem, 'He thinks of His Past Greatness when a Part of the Constellations of Heaven' :

> I have been a hazel-tree and they hung
> The Pilot Star and the Crooked Plough
> Among my leaves in times out of mind. . . .

Other lines in 'La Fraisne', where Miraut has 'put aside this folly and the cold / That old age weareth for a cloak,' and where he announces, 'For I know that the wailing and bitterness are a folly,' echo words like 'wail' and 'folly' of which Yeats was fond, and derive more particularly from his poem, 'In the Seven Woods,' where the speaker has 'put away the unavailing outcries and the old bitterness / That empty the heart'. Blistered in Provençe, Miraut has been patched and peeled in Yeats's first, third, and fourth volumes of verse,[2] as well as in *The Celtic Twilight*.

Yet the proximity to Yeats does not prevent 'La Fraisne' from being identifiably Pound's configuration. Yeats portrays the madness of King Goll as a heroic state of mind superior to sanity, while Councillor Miraut's mental condition is more equivocal, even pathetic. Pound diverges also, after three stanzas, from the formal regularity on which Yeats always insisted, so that he can attempt to capture his hero's fragmented consciousness. In a passage, bold in 1908, he makes use of a series of broken sentences :

> Once when I was among the young men . . .
> And they said I was quite strong, among the young men,
> Once there was a woman . . .
> . . . but I forget . . . she was . . .
> . . . I hope she will not come again.

[1] The wording of this line was changed somewhat later.

[2] 'The Madness of King Goll' is from *The Wanderings of Oisin and Other Poems* (1889); 'He thinks of His Past Greatness . . .' from *The Wind among the Reeds* (1899); and 'In the Seven Woods' from the volume of the same name (1904).

. . . I do not remember. . . .

I think she hurt me once, but . . .
That was very long ago.

These are perhaps the most important dots in English poetry.
They show Pound already essaying what in *Mauberley* he calls
a 'consciousness disjunct'. In the later poem the pauses represent hesitations instead of panicky repressions:

Drifted . . . drifted precipitate,
Asking time to be rid of . . .
Of his bewilderment; to designate
His new found orchid. . . .

In the *Cantos*, like Eliot in *The Waste Land*, he usually leaves
out the dots, as if no one expected any longer the kind of
constraint that prevailed in earlier poetry. But this mode begins
in 'La Fraisne'.

If Pound translated Yeats, then, like one of his troubadours,
sometimes literally and sometimes freely, Yeats responded to
the change in atmosphere with which Pound surrounded his
borrowings, and he did not dismiss him as an imitator. When
he read *A Lume Spento*, with which Pound must have introduced
himself, he called it 'charming', an adjective Pound knew to
be reserved.[1] Still Yeats could hardly have read the poem
entitled 'Plotinus' without being tempted to rewrite it, syn-
tactically and otherwise:

As one that would draw thru [sic] the node of things,
Back-sweeping to the vortex of the cone. . . .

And then for utter loneliness, made I
New thoughts as crescent images of *me*.

The vortexes are premonitory of Pound's later vorticist movement, but they also, with cones and crescents, anticipate
metaphors of *A Vision*. Pound cannot be said to have put them

[1] Pound, letter to Williams Carlos Williams, 21 October 1908, in
Letters, p. 4.

into Yeats's head, for Yeats knew Plotinus well already, but he must have given them a new spin.

He liked better Pound's next important book, *Personae*, which appeared in April of the following year, 1909. The title proudly drew attention to the very point that had vexed William Carlos Williams in the first book, the assumption of a series of exotic roles.[1] For Pound it was an attempt, by encompassing more situations and moods, to follow Walter Pater's advice and extend the self horizontally. Yeats's purpose in the seemingly similar doctrine of the mask, which he was then cultivating in early drafts of *The Player Queen*, and must have discussed with Pound, was a vertical deepening of the self by fusion with its opposite. For Yeats, Pound's theory, like Arthur Symons's version of Pater's impressionism, was too volatile and rootless, and suspiciously international. But beyond the theory he detected the young man's extraordinary talent; and Pound wrote elatedly to Williams, just after *Personae* was published, 'I have been praised by the greatest living poet.'[2] This snub almost silenced Williams.

Yeats was in fact as pleased with his new friendship as Pound was. In December 1909, he wrote Lady Gregory that 'this queer creature Ezra Pound . . . has become really a great authority on the troubadors'.[3] So much erudition of course amused him a little too, and now or later he humourously accused Pound of trying to provide a portable substitute for the British Museum.[4] He liked the way Pound devised to recite verse so that it sounded like music, with strongly marked time, yet remained intelligible, and he credited it with being a better method than that of Florence Farr which a decade earlier he had so highly praised. But he noted also that Pound's voice was bad, sounding 'like something on a bad phonograph'.[5]

[1] *Ibid.*, pp. 3–4.

[2] Pound, letter to Williams, 21 May 1909, *Letters*, pp. 7–8.

[3] Yeats, letter to Lady Gregory, 10 December 1909, in *The Letters of W. B. Yeats*, ed. Allan Wade (London, 1954), p. 543.

[4] Pound, letter to Sarah Perkins Cope, 22 April 1934, *Letters*, p. 257.

[5] Yeats, letter to Lady Gregory, 10 December 1909, *Letters of Yeats*, p. 543.

It may have been just the American accent emigrating into an Irish ear. Pound, for his part, thought Yeats's method of 'keening and chaunting with a *u*' absurd, and while he could effect no improvement, he obliged Yeats to admit, after half an hour's struggle, that poems such as those of Burns could not be wailed to the tune of *The Wind among the Reeds*.[1] Both poets enjoyed condescending to the other.

Pound, as he began to flabbergast London with his passionate selections and rejections, found that his allegiance to Yeats was not shared by other writers whom he respected. The movement away from nineteenth-century poetry had begun. As John Butler Yeats wrote his son, 'The poets loved of Ezra Pound are tired of Beauty, since they have met it so often. . . . I am tired of Beauty my wife, says the poet, but here is that enchanting mistress Ugliness. With her I will live, and what a riot we shall have. Not a day shall pass without a fresh horror. Prometheus leaves his rock to cohabit with the Furies.'[2] T. E. Hulme was already in 1908, when he and Pound met, denouncing the romantic bog and leading the way to the classical uplands; by his rule Yeats was wet and dim when he should have been dry and clear.[3] T. S. Eliot, who battled Yeats for Pound's soul a few years later, declared Yeats an irrelevance in the modern world.[4] By 1912 D. H. Lawrence, originally an admirer of Yeats, could say, 'He seems awfully queer stuff to me now—as if he wouldn't bear touching,'[5] and he objected to Yeats's method of dealing with old symbols as 'sickly'.[6] Another friend

---

[1] Pound, letter to Felix E. Schelling, 8 July 1922, *Letters*, p. 180.

[2] Letter from J. B. Yeats to W. B. Yeats, 12 March 1918, J. B. Yeats, *Letters to His Son W. B. Yeats and Others*, ed. Joseph Hone (New York, 1946), pp. 244–5. (Pound made a selection of J. B. Yeats's letters for publication.)

[3] A. R. Jones, *The Life and Opinions of Thomas Ernest Hulme* (London, 1960), pp. 29–31.

[4] T. S. Eliot, 'A Foreign Mind' (review of Yeats's *The Cutting of an Agate*, *Athenaeum* 4653 (4 July 1919)), pp. 552–3.

[5] Lawrence, letter to A. W. McLeod, 17 December 1912, *The Collected Letters of D. H. Lawrence*, ed. Harry T. Moore (New York, 1962), I, p. 168.

[6] Lawrence, letter to Gordon Campbell (19 December 1914), *ibid.*, I, p. 302.

of Pound's, Ford Madox Ford, though not unreceptive to monstrosity, informed Pound that Yeats was a 'gargoyle, a great poet but a gargoyle'.[1]

Pound's determination to make it new combined with this voluble pressure to stint a little his admiration of Yeats as a model. Writing in *Poetry*, the then new Chicago review, in January 1913, he explained that Ford and Yeats were diametrically opposed because one was objective, the other subjective. While he grandly pronounced Yeats to be 'the only poet worthy of serious study', he felt compelled to warn that the method of Yeats 'is, to my way of thinking, very dangerous'. The magistrate was severe: 'His art has not broadened much during the past decade. His gifts to English art are mostly negative, i.e., he has stripped English poetry of many of its faults.'[2] Yeats continued to fall short. In 1913 Pound wrote Harriet Monroe that Ford and Yeats were the two men in London, 'And Yeats is already a sort of great dim figure with its associations set in the past.'[3] In the *Pisan Cantos* (LXXXII) the two men are weighed again,

> and for all that old Ford's conversation was better,
> consisting in *res* non *verba*,
>> despite William's anecdotes, in that Fordie
> never dented an idea for a phrase's sake
> and had more humanitas

Such reservations did not prevent Pound from regarding Yeats as a splendid bridge from Mallarmé and the Symbolists,[4] which he could afford to traverse on his way to founding imagism and then vorticism. These movements, full of don'ts, extolled light, clearness, and in general a Polaroid view of the verse line.[5]

---

[1] Pound, 'This Hulme Business,' *Townsman* II. 5 (January 1939) 15.

[2] Pound, 'Status rerum,' *Poetry* I. 4 (January 1913) pp. 123–7.

[3] Pound, letter to Harriet Monroe (13 August 1913), *Letters*, p. 21.

[4] Pound, letter to René Taupin (May 1928), *Letters*, p. 218.

[5] 'And now one has got with the camera an *enormous* correlation of particulars. That capacity for making contact is a tremendous challenge to literature.' Pound quoted in *Writers at Work* (Second Series) (New York, 1963), p. 41.

Pound knew, however, as Hulme, Lawrence, and Ford did not know, that Yeats was still adaptable, and as eager to leave the nineties behind as they were. The books of verse he published in 1904 and 1910 reacted against his early manner, but he was still dissatisfied, and kept looking about for incitements for further change. Pound was a perpetual incitement, mixing admiration with remonstrance.

Another spur, now improbable, was Rabindranath Tagore, whom Yeats met in June 1912. Tagore's poetry brought together, Yeats felt, the metaphors and emotions of unlearned people with those of the learned, coupling the fastidious with the popular.[1] Yeats remarked to Pound, unhinged by the same enthusiasm, that Tagore was 'someone greater than any of us— I read these things and wonder why one should go on trying to write.'[2] Pointing to a description in Tagore's poem, 'The Banyan Tree,' 'Two ducks swam by the weedy margin above their shadows, and the child . . . longed . . . to float like those ducks among the weeds and shadows,' Yeats proclaimed, 'Those ducks are the ducks of real life and not out of literature.'[3] His friend Sturge Moore was helping Tagore with the translation, and Yeats joined in the task, arguing with Moore about words.[4] (He allowed Tagore to use the word 'maiden,' though in a later stage of dictional disinfection when he was translating the *Upanishads* with another Indian, he insisted upon the word 'girl'.)[5] Soon he recognized that Tagore was 'unequal' and sometimes dull, but he saw mainly 'great beauty',[6] and wrote a fulsome introduction to *Gitanjali*.

[1] Yeats, 'Introduction' to Rabindranath Tagore, *Gitanjali* (New York, 1916), pp. xiii–xv.
[2] Pound, letter to Harriet Monroe (October 1912), in Harriet Monroe, *A Poet's Life* (New York, 1938), p. 262. Cf. Pound, 'Rabindranath Tagore,' *Fortnightly Review* XCIII (N.S.), 555 (1 March 1913) pp. 571–9.
[3] Pound, 'French Poets,' in *Make it New* (New Haven, 1935), p. 245.
[4] W. B. Yeats and T. Sturge Moore, *Their Correspondence 1901–1937* (London, 1953), pp. 22, 190.
[5] Yeats, letter to Dorothy Wellesley (21 December 1935), in *Letters of Yeats*, p. 846.
[6] Yeats, letter to Edmund Gosse (25 November 1912), *ibid.*, pp. 572–3.

Pound's own role in the modernization of Yeats began at first, like that of most mentors, uninvited. In October 1912 he persuaded Yeats to give *Poetry* (Chicago) a start with some new poems. Yeats sent them to Pound for transmittal, appending a note to ask that the punctuation be checked. The note was bound, as Pound said ruefully later, to 'create a certain atmosphere of drama'.[1] He could not resist exceeding mere compliance by making three changes in Yeats's wording. In 'Fallen Majesty', he impudently if reasonably deleted 'as it were' from the final line :

Once walked a thing that seemed as it were a burning cloud.

In 'The Mountain Tomb', he worried over the lines,

Let there be no foot silent in the room,
Nor mouth with kissing or the wine unwet,

and altered 'or the' to 'nor with'. Then with 'To a Child Dancing upon the Shore',

Being young you have not known
The fool's triumph, nor yet
Love lost as soon as won,
Nor he, the best labourer, dead,
And all the sheaves to bind,

Pound thought long and deep and then changed 'he' to 'him'.

At peace, he sent the poems to Harriet Monroe with the comment : 'I don't think this is precisely W. B. Y. at his best . . ., but it shows a little of the new Yeats—as in the "Child Dancing". "Fallen Majesty" is just where he was two years ago. "The Realists" is also tending toward the new phase.'[2] Pound, though he had liked the hardness of 'No Second Troy',[3]

[1] Pound, unpublished letter to Harriet Monroe (4 November 1912), in University of Chicago Library.

[2] Pound, letter to Harriet Monroe (26 October 1912), in University of Chicago Library. It is slightly misquoted in Monroe, *A Poet's Life*, p. 264.

[3] Pound, 'The Later Yeats,' *Poetry* IV, 2 (May 1914), 66.

was weary of prolonging the celebrations of Maud Gonne as she had been twenty years before. On the other hand, he welcomed the increasing directness that Yeats now usually aimed at. He conveyed something of these opinions to Yeats, and at the same time duly informed him of the small changes he had made. To his surprise, Yeats was indignant at this American brashness, and Pound had to carry out mollification proceedings as recorded in his letters to Miss Monroe. For rhythm's sake Yeats insisted upon restoring the spiritless 'as it were' to 'Fallen Majesty', though a year later he rewrote the line to get rid of it. But Pound's other two revisions shook him. At first he modified the second passage to read, 'Nor mouth with kissing nor *the* wine unwet,' but by the proof stage he recognized that unwet wine would not do, and Pound's version, 'nor with wine unwet,' appears in *Poetry*. In the third instance, the battle of the pronouns, he insisted upon 'he' rather than 'him', but, made aware of the grammatical sin, put a period after the third line to replace the comma. On November 2 Pound transmitted these partial restorations to Miss Monroe with the remark, 'Oh *la la*, ce que le roi desire!'[1] Later the same day he reported a last change, eliminating 'Nor' before 'he':

Final clinic in the groves of philosophy.

Love lost as soon as won. (full stop)
And he, the best labourer, dead

peace reigns on parnassus.[2]

Still spellbound by Tagore's verse, and still stung by Pound's criticism, Yeats felt the challenge to his powers. It was probably now that he confided to Pound, 'I have spent the whole of my life trying to get rid of rhetoric. I have got rid of one kind of rhetoric and have merely set up another.'[3] For the first time in

[1] Pound, letter to Harriet Monroe (2 November 1912), in University of Chicago Library.

[2] Pound, letter to Harriet Monroe (same date as above, but sent separately), University of Chicago Library.

[3] Pound, 'French Poets,' *Make it New*, p. 245.

years he asked for help, as his letters to Lady Gregory of 1 and
3 January make clear. In the former he writes: 'I have had a
fortnight of gloom over my work—I felt something wrong
with it. However on Monday night I got Sturge Moore in and
last night Ezra Pound and we went at it line by line and now I
know what is wrong and am in good spirits again. I am starting
the poem about the King of Tara and his wife ["The Two Kings"]
again, to get rid of Miltonic generalizations.'[1] (Pound had
made 'Miltonic' a derogatory epithet.) He was later to re-
define what he and Pound had crossed out as 'conventional
metaphors,'[2] presumably those turned abstract by overuse. In
his second letter to Lady Gregory he indicates that the whole
experience has given him diarrhœa:

'My digestion has got rather queer again—a result I think of
sitting up late with Ezra and Sturge Moore and some light
wine while the talk ran. However the criticism I have got from
them has given me new life and I have made that Tara poem a
new thing and am writing with a new confidence having got
Milton off my back. Ezra is the best critic of the two. He is full
of the middle ages and helps me to get back to the definite and
the concrete away from modern abstractions.'[3]

A letter which Pound sent Harriet Monroe summarizes the
sound principles if not the questionable taste he must have
communicated to Yeats. In terms ostentatiously graceless he
called for 'Objectivity and again objectivity, and expression;
no hind-side-beforeness, no straddled adjectives (as "addled
mosses dank"), no Tennysonianness of speech; *nothing* that
you couldn't in some circumstance, in the stress of some
emotion, *actually say*. Every *literaryism*, every book word,
fritters away a scrap of the reader's patience, a scrap of his

[1] Yeats, letter to Lady Gregory (1 January 1913), in 'Some New
Letters from W. B. Yeats to Lady Gregory,' ed. Donald T. Torchiana
and Glenn O'Malley, *Review of English Literature* IV. 3 (July 1963) 14.

[2] Yeats, 'A General Introduction for My Work,' in *Essays and Introductions* (London, 1961), p. 525.

[3] Yeats, letter to Lady Gregory (3 January 1913), quoted in A. N.
Jeffares, *W. B. Yeats: Man and Poet* (New Haven, 1949), p. 167.

sense of your sincerity.'[1] Though Yeats had been able to re-construct much of his diction, he needed a jolt to complete the process. This Pound, by virtue of his downrightness, his good will, his unintimidatable character, his sense of himself as shocker, was peculiarly fitted to administer. For him, as for Auden later,[2] poems were contraptions, and most of them were inefficient and needed overhaul. He had trained himself, like no one else, for the very task Yeats demanded of him. That Pound was able to give advice, and Yeats, notwithstanding age and fame, to take it and to admit having taken it, made their friendship, unlike many relations of literary men, felicitous.

The experience was, like most medicine, more than a little painful for Yeats; having requested Pound's help once, he had to submit to occasional further reproofs. He showed Pound 'The Two Kings' when it was finished, and Pound informed him, and said later in a review of *Responsibilities*,[3] that it was like those *Idylls* written by a poet more monstrous even than Milton. Yeats wrote his father of this harsh verdict, and his father re-assured him by saying that the poem had supremely what Tennyson never achieved, namely, concentration. Yeats took heart and believed that Pound this time was wrong. But he was none the less gratified when Pound, on reading the untitled last poem in *Responsibilities*, and especially the last lines,

> till all my priceless things
> Are but a post the passing dogs defile,

remarked that Yeats had at last become a modern poet.[4] An image of urination had finally brought Pound to his knees.

Yeats, while acknowledging Pound's critical penetration and quite liking him as a person, was perplexed about his poetry. He quarrelled with the rhythms of its free verse as 'devil's metres'.[5] Many of the poems did not seem to Yeats fully achieved. When in 1913 Harriet Monroe offered him a prize

---

[1] Pound, letter to Harriet Monroe, in *Letters*, p. 49.
[2] W. H. Auden, *The Dyer's Hand* (New York, 1962), p. 50.
[3] Pound, 'The Later Yeats,' p. 67.   [4] Interview with Mrs W. B. Yeats.
[5] Pound, 'The Later Yeats,' p. 65.

for 'The Grey Rock', Yeats urged her to give it to Pound instead; he said candidly, 'I suggest him to you because, although
I do not really like with my whole soul the metrical experiments
he has made for you, I think those experiments show a vigorous
creative mind. He is certainly a creative personality of some sort,
though it is too soon yet to say of what sort. His experiments
are perhaps errors, I am not certain; but I would always sooner
give the laurel to vigorous errors than to any orthodoxy not
inspired.'[1] The following year he spoke at a *Poetry* dinner in
Chicago, and said again of Pound, 'Much of his work is experimental; his work will come slowly; he will make many an
experiment before he comes into his own.' But he read two
poems which he judged of 'permanent value', 'The Ballad of the
Goodly Fere' and 'The Return'. The latter he complimented,
in that slightly histrionic rhythm for which Joyce mocked him
in *Ulysses*, as 'the most beautiful poem that has been written
in the free form, one of the few in which I find real organic
rhythm.'[2] He quoted it again later in *A Vision*,[3] where it jibed
with his theory of cyclical repetition. He was consciously,
doggedly, allowing virtue in Pound's work, though he had no
wish to enroll in the new school which his former pupil had
opened. On many matters they continued to dispute, and Pound
summarized almost with satisfaction the quarrelsomeness of a
meeting the next year: 'The antipodes of our two characters
and beliefs being in more vigorous saliency.'[4]

During the winter of 1913–14, and the two following winters,
Yeats wished to be away from London with a secretary who
could do some typing and also read Doughty's poems and
Icelandic sagas to him. He had formed the plan with Pound as
companion in mind,[5] and Pound with misgivings agreed to

[1] Yeats, letter to Harriet Monroe (? December 1913), in Monroe,
A Poet's Life, pp. 330–1.

[2] Yeats, speech given in March 1914, *ibid.*, p. 338.

[3] Yeats, *A Vision* (New York, 1938), pp. 29–30.

[4] Pound, unpublished letter to Harriet Monroe (24 December 1915,
at Stone Cottage), in University of Chicago Library.

[5] Yeats, letter to J. B. Yeats (5 August 1913), *Letters of Yeats*, p. 584.

put himself out for the sake of English letters. He expected that Yeats would sometimes amuse him but often, because the occult was so irresistible a subject, bore him.[1] To his partial surprise, life with Yeats in a four-room Sussex cottage proved contented and placid. He wrote Williams that Yeats was 'much finer *intime* than seen spasmodically in the midst of the whirl.'[2] With more polish he described life at Stone Cottage nostalgically in Canto LXXXIII:

> There is fatigue deep as the grave.
> The Kakemono grows in flat land out of mist
>> sun rises lop-sided over the mountain
>>> so that I recalled the noise in the chimney
> as it were the wind in the chimney
>> but was in reality Uncle William
> downstairs composing
> that had made a great Peeeeacock
>> in the proide ov his oiye
>> had made a great peeeeeeecock in the . . .
> made a great peacock
>> in the proide of his oyyee
>
> proide ov his oy-ee
> as indeed he had, and perdurable
>
> a great peacock aere perennius
>> or as in the advice to the young man to
> breed and get married (or not)
>> as you choose to regard it
>
> at Stone Cottage in Sussex by the waste moor
> (or whatever) and the holly bush
>> who would not eat ham for dinner
> because peasants eat ham for dinner
>> despite the excellent quality
> and the pleasure of having it hot

---

[1] Pound, letter to Isabel Pound (November 1913), *Letters*, p. 25.
[2] Pound, letter to Williams (19 December 1913), *Letters*, p. 27.

    well those days are gone forever
        and the travelling rug with the coon-skin tabs
    and his hearing nearly all Wordsworth
        for the sake of his conscience but
    preferring Ennemoser on Witches

    did we ever get to the end of Doughty :
        The Dawn in Britain ?
            perhaps not

While Yeats's aristocratic fasts and his reaching over Wordsworth for witches amused Pound still, he recognized that these
two foibles received a kind of immortal warranty by their
reflection in 'The Peacock' and 'The Witch'.

At Stone Cottage Pound taught Yeats after a fashion to fence,
while Yeats offered reciprocal lessons, as dreaded, in spiritualism
and related subjects. These proved, however, more apposite
to his own interests than Pound had anticipated. For while
Yeats was writing essays for Lady Gregory's *Visions and
Beliefs in the West of Ireland*, setting them in the context of the
tradition à rebours, Pound was devoting himself to editing
Ernest Fenollosa's translations of the Noh plays of Japan.
These were just as crowded with ghosts and other extraterres-
trial creatures. East and West met in the astral envelope as
well as in Connemara. In the edition he now made of the
Noh plays Pound refers frequently to parallels furnished him
by Yeats,[1] and speaks with unwonted respect of such matters
as 'the "new" doctrine of the suggestibility or hypnotizeability
of ghosts',[2] though he preserves his dignity by an alibi: only
the merit of the Japanese poetry has brought him to this pass.[3]
Pound's versions of Noh convene a kind of grand international

[1] Ernest Fenollosa and Ezra Pound, *'Noh' or Accomplishment* (London,
1916), pp. 27, 44, 91, 106.
[2] *Ibid.*, p. 31. Pound was himself prompted to read in occult literature,
notably in John Heydon, first mentioned in the discarded Canto III and
later in *Guide to Kulchur*, p. 225. While in St. Elizabeth's Hospital,
Pound borrowed John Heydon's *The Holy Guide* again from Mrs Yeats and
quotes directly from it in Cantos LXXXVII and XCI.
[3] Fenollosa and Pound, *'Noh' or Accomplishment*, p. 44.

festival with entries from India, Japan, England, the United States, and Ireland. The Samurai are particularly at home in Kiltartan or Aran :[1]

'I've a sad heart to see you looking up to Buddha, you who left me alone, I diving in the black rivers of hell. Will soft prayers be a comfort to you in your quiet heaven, you who knew that I'm alone in that wild, desolate place ?[2]

'Times out of mind am I here setting up this bright branch, this silky wood with the charms painted on it as fine as the web you'd get in the grass-cloth of Shinobu, that they'd be still selling you in this mountain.[3]

'I had my own rain of tears; that was the dark night, surely.'[4]

The Noh plays were more to Yeats's taste than to Pound's; by 1918 Pound was prematurely dismissing them as a failure.[5] He linked them in this disgrace with Yeats's long essay, *Per Amica Silentia Lunae*,[6] which with its hypothesis of antiselves and daimons must still have seemed too occult for the mint assayer's son. Whether he also dismissed the prefatory poem to this work, 'Ego Dominus Tuus', is not clear, though his allusion to it as a dialogue of 'Hic' and 'Willie' (for 'Ille')[7] perhaps implies some dissatisfaction, beyond his unwillingness to resist polylingual jokes. He was prepared to believe again, as he said in 1920, that Yeats was 'faded'.[8]

Yeats had entered a period of much greater assurance. The Noh plays, so fortuitously put in his hands, had won without his being aware of it the battle with naturalistic drama which he had himself been fighting in beleaguered fashion. Here was the authorization he needed for leaving probability in the lurch by abolishing scenery so the imagination would be untrammeled, by covering faces with masks, by portraying character in broad strokes—emptied of Ibsen's convincing details—through iso-

[1] A point noted by T. S. Eliot in his review, 'The Noh and the Image,' *Egoist* IV. 7 (August 1917), 102–103.

[2] Fenollosa and Pound, p. 30.

[3] *Ibid.*, p. 132. [4] *Ibid.*, p. 33.

[5] Pound, letter to John Quinn (4 June 1918), *Letters*, p. 137.

[6] *Idem.* [7] Interview with Mrs W. B. Yeats.

[8] Pound, letter to Williams (11 September 1920), *Letters*, p. 158.

lating the moment in which some irrevocable deed separates a man from his fellows. He was also prompted to new and more reckless devices, the symbolic dance as a climax to suggest the impingement of the timeless upon the actual, the preternatural shudder from the sudden lighting-up of a ruined place, the assumption of someone else's human form by a spirit or god. Yeats saw how he might focus an entire play, as he had entire poems, on a single metaphor.[1] That the Noh plays were often blurred in effect did not ruffle him; the form, he saw, could be improved. He kept the strangeness and increased the dramatic tension, splicing natural with preternatural in order, unpredictably, to heighten the human dilemma. The Yeatsian paradox was to disintegrate verisimilitude by miracle for the purposes of a more ultimate realism.

The result was the first of his plays for dancers, *At the Hawk's Well*, and to some degree almost all his subsequent plays. Ezra Pound proved to have an aptitude for the criticism of drama as well. He offered many suggestions about scenery and timing,[2] he found the indispensable Japanese dancer, Michio Itō, and he helped Yeats to clarify the play. For a time it seemed that his dramatic ability might receive professional sanction. He wrote a skit which Yeats encouraged him to enlarge, thinking it might be suitable for presentation at the Abbey Theatre, but it was adjudged, by the then manager, too full of indecencies.[3] Then Yeats recommended to Lady Gregory that Pound fill in as manager of the Abbey for a four-month period, but this plan also was vetoed.[4] Surviving these rebuffs, Pound remained indispensable; he observed Yeats locked in struggle with a long unfinished tragedy, and suddenly proposed it made a comedy instead. The firecracker went off, Yeats was exhilarated, and *The Player Queen* reached completion.

[1] Yeats, 'Certain Noble Plays of Japan,' in *Essays and Introductions*, p. 234.

[2] Two letters from Pound to Yeats, in Mrs Yeats's possession, deal with the problems of staging the play. One has several sketches included.

[3] Pound, letter to Iris Barry (September 1916), *Letters*, p. 96.

[4] Yeats, unpublished letter to Lady Gregory (21 June 1916), in Mrs Yeats's possession. Pound had made clear he would not come as permanent manager.

In the midst of vorticism and daimonism both poets were distracted towards marriage. Yeats in 1916 felt duty bound to offer marriage to Maud Gonne, whom the Easter Rebellion had widowed, though he hesitated about bedding an obsessive conviction. He was not sorry when she refused. Pound saw her in the same way; when he wished to characterize Yeats's occult interests, just as when Yeats wished to characterize Pound's political ideas, each compared the other to Maud Gonne.[1] Yeats refused to renounce his memory of her as a symbol of eternal beauty, however, and about this time he wrote 'His Phoenix' (which Pound called 'a little bad Yeats'),[2] in which he contrasts her more gaily than usual with the current lot of women :

There's Margaret and Marjorie and Dorothy and Nan,
A Daphne and a Mary who live in privacy . . .

and concludes :

I knew a Phoenix in my youth, so let them have their day.

He was indulging here a private joke by making a list of Pound's girl friends. Among them Dorothy was preeminent. This was Dorothy Shakespear, with whose mother, Olivia, Yeats had been in love during the nineties. Pound married Dorothy in April 1916. The following year Yeats married Georgie Hyde-Lees, a cousin and close friend of Pound's wife, and Pound served as best man. The two poets met often after their marriages, and after Pound went to the continent in 1920, they met in Paris in 1922, in Sicily in 1925, in Rapallo in 1928, 1929–30, 1934, and in London in 1938. Yet, as so often, separate households made for a subtle disconnection of friendship.

Pound's work had become more ambitious. After *Lustra*, he wrote *Propertius*, *Mauberley*, and the first cantos. Yeats disconcerted him in 1916 by saying that Pound's new work gave

[1] Pound, letter to John Quinn (15 November 1918), *Letters*, p. 140; Yeats, letter to Lady Gregory (1 April 1928), *Letters of Yeats*, p. 738.
[2] Pound, letter to Harriet Monroe (17 May 1915), *Letters*, p. 60.

him 'no asylum for his affections'. Pound wrote the criticism to Kate Buss but cautioned her about repeating it.[1] Perhaps in part because he recognized some justice in it, Pound moved away from purely satirical poems like many in *Lustra*, and in the *Pisan Cantos* (LXXXI) he subscribes fully to Yeats's principle :

> What thou lovest well remains,
> > the rest is dross
> What thou lov'st well shall not be reft from thee
> What thou lov'st well is thy true heritage

It is hard to discover Yeats's views of Pound's new works. He told Pound in 1920 that he liked *Mauberley*,[2] and he tried to suspend judgment about the *Cantos*.[3]

His attitude towards Pound between 1915 and 1925 can however be elicited from *A Vision*, the book he began in October 1917 just after his marriage. In the characterology which formed a large part of this book, Yeats classified contemporaries and men of the past in terms of phases of the moon. Pound was slowly becoming an abstraction, something analysed at a distance. The early drafts, written between 1918 and 1922, placed Pound with Nietzsche as denizens of the twelfth lunar phase, called the phase of the Forerunner. He is Forerunner to men of fuller consciousness including, with chronological indifference, Yeats himself. But when the book was published in 1926, Pound's name was omitted; Yeats probably feared to give pain. While Phase 12 was not a bad perch, Pound occupied it in a disharmonious way. The phase-12 man who is 'in phase' follows Zarathustra's exhortation by heroically overcoming himself. (Yeats speaks elsewhere of Pound's effort at total

---

[1] Pound, letter to Kate Buss (9 March 1916), *Letters*, p. 72. Yeats was quoting a sentence of Tulka which he used as an epigraph to *Early Poems and Stories* (1925) : 'Give me the world if thou wilt, but grant me an asylum for my affections.'

[2] Pound, unpublished letter to Homer Pound (1 September 1920), quoted by Thomas Parkinson, 'Yeats and Pound : The Illusion of Influence,' *Comparative Literature* VI (Summer 1954), pp. 256–64.

[3] Yeats, 'Introduction' to *Oxford Book of Modern Verse*, p. xxv.

self-possession,[1] but does not seem to have regarded it as successful.) He is thereby enabled to assume his true mask, which is lonely, cold and proud, and to formulate a subjective philosophy that exalts the self in the presence of its object of desire.[2] While Yeats may have thought of imagism as offering an aesthetic philosophy of this kind, he had primarily in mind Nietzsche's projection of a superior world. In phase, the 12-mind is a jetting fountain of personal life, of noble extravagance. It loathes abstraction as much as Pound did, and everything it considers comes clothed in sound and metaphor.[3]

But if the man of this phase is 'out of phase', the result is much less satisfactory. Unable to discover his true mask, he assumes almost in frenzy a series of self-conscious poses.[4] Here Yeats must have thought of Pound's *Personae*, and perhaps of Pound's own Bergsonian statement in *Gaudier-Brzeska*: 'One says "I am" this, that, or the other, and with the words scarcely uttered one ceases to be that thing. I began this search for the real in a book called *Personae*, casting off, as it were, complete masks of the self in each poem. I continued in long series of translations, which were but more elaborate masks.'[5] Always in reaction, yet according to Yeats always hesitant, the out-of-phase man becomes a prey to facts, which drug or intoxicate him. More by chance than choice, he turns to a false mask, which offers instead of splendid loneliness the isolation of some small protesting sect; and he defends this role by 'some kind of superficial intellectual action, the pamphlet, the violent speech, the sword of the swashbuckler'.[6] He oscillates between asserting some pose or, if preoccupied with outward things, asserting a dogmatism about events which depends too much upon the circumstances that produced it to have lasting value.[7] Yeats is thinking here of Pound's adherence to Major Douglas's theories of social credit.

While Yeats pencilled Pound into Phase 12, he could not fail

---

[1] Yeats, Journal kept in January 1929, quoted by Richard Ellmann, *The Identity of Yeats* (New York, 1964), p. 239.

[2] Yeats, *A Vision* (1938), p. 128. [3] *Ibid.*, p. 127. [4] *Idem.*

[5] Pound, *Gaudier-Brzeska* (London, 1916), p. 98. [6] *A Vision*, p. 128.

[7] *Idem.*

to think of him also for Phase 23, which is the phase of our age and of its dominant art. Ultimately he decided to transfer Pound completely to this later and less desirable phase; he saw him as neither arch-individualist nor forerunner but as a dissolving mind, subject to losses of self-control. What immediately impelled this unhappy change of niche was the sight of Pound feeding all the stray cats in Rapallo in 1928. This undifferentiated pity, pity 'like that of a drunken man', was quickly connected by Yeats to the hysterical pity for general humanity left over from the romantic movement.[1] He had observed and blamed it in other writers, notably Sean O'Casey and Wilfred Owen.[2] All three now seemed to belong to Phase 23, the theme of which is Creation through Pity.

The man of Phase 23 studies the external world for its own sake, and denies every thought that would make order of it. Instead of allowing the fountain of the mind to overflow, as in Phase 12, he lets the cauldron of the world boil over.[3] Not only is causation denied, as Pound once remarked to Yeats, only sequence being knowable,[4] but even sequence [too] is destroyed. Yeats returned to this idea of *A Vision* in other essays, where he complained of the *Cantos* specifically: 'There is no transmission through time, we pass without comment from ancient Greece to modern England, from modern England to medieval China; the symphony, the pattern, is timeless, flux eternal and without movement.'[5] In subsequent art, violations like Pound's have ceased to appear violative, but Yeats was not yet accustomed to them. He found an Eastern parallel for such work not in Pound's favourite Easterner, Confucius (who to Yeats seemed an 18th-century moralist, pulpited and bewigged),[6] but in Sankara, the ninth-century founder of a school of Vedantism which conceives of mental and physical objects as 'alike material, a deluge of experience breaking over us and within us, melting

[1] *A Vision*, p. 6.
[2] Yeats quarrelled with O'Casey over *The Silver Tassie* on this account; his comments on Owen are in *Letters of Yeats*, pp. 874–5.
[3] *A Vision*, pp. 128, 166.   [4] Ellmann, *Identity of Yeats*, p. 239.
[5] Yeats, 'Introduction' to *Oxford Book of Modern Verse*, p. xxiv.
[6] Yeats, letter to Lady Gregory (7 April 1930), *Letters of Yeats*, p. 774.

limits whether of line or tint; man no hard bright mirror dawdling by the dry sticks of a hedge, but a swimmer, or rather the waves themselves'.[1] The new literature of the *Cantos*, of Virginia Woolf's novels, melted limits of plot, of logic, of character, of nationality, of authorship.[2] In a letter Yeats complained that Pound and his school prided themselves on what their poems did *not* contain,[3] all that might stop the flood, the conscious mind's capacity for intelligibleness and form.

Remembering his old view that Pound was too preoccupied with experiment, Yeats in *A Vision* asserts that in Phase 23 everything is seen from the point of view of technique and is investigated technically rather than imaginatively. Technical mastery offers the man of this phase his only refuge from masterless anarchy. Denying its subjective life, the mind delights only in the varied scene outside the window, and seeks to construct a whole which is all event, all picture. Because of this submission to outwardness, the man of Phase 23 wishes to live in his exact moment of time as a matter of conscience, and, says Yeats, defends that moment like a theologian.[4] He has in mind here Pound's imagist predilection, as well as his forever and dogmatically 'making it new'.

Yeats noticed also that men of this phase, not only Pound but Joyce and Eliot, were apt to contrast some present scene with a mythical one. The pendulum which they pushed so far towards fact was inexorably swinging back, but myth could assert itself for them only as a nightmare opposite. By holding apart what should be joined, the phase-23 mind heralds further loss and eventual extinction of personality, and a world in which rights are swallowed up in duties; force is adored, and society turns

---

[1] Yeats, 'Preface' to *Fighting the Waves*, in *Explorations* (London, 1962) p. 373. The mirror was of course an allusion to Stendhal's definition of the novel as a 'mirror passing down a road'.

[2] Yeats, *A Vision*, pp. 299–300, 165; 'Pages from A Diary Written in 1930,' in *Explorations*, p. 294.

[3] Yeats, unpublished letter to Harriet Monroe (8 February 1931), in University of Chicago Library.

[4] Yeats, *A Vision* (London, 1925 [1926]), pp. 210–11.

into a mechanical force.[1] At variance with some of his later prose, Yeats explicitly deplores here an inevitable alliance of this phase and its successor phases with a regimented state.

After the first edition of *A Vision* was published early in 1926, Yeats grew dissatisfied with some of it, including the pretence that it was translated from an Arabic manuscript. In 1928 he came to Rapallo intending to work on it some more. He showed Pound a poem he had translated 'From the *Antigone*', and was again convinced of his neighbour's critical acumen. After looking over what 'the Yeats' (as Pound jocularly called him) had written,

> Overcome, O bitter sweetness,
> The rich man and his affairs,
> The fat flocks and the fields' fatness,
> Mariners, wild harvesters;
> Overcome God upon Parnassus;
> Overcome the Empyrean; hurl
> Heaven and Earth out of their places—
> *Inhabitant of the soft cheek of a girl—*
> *And into* the same calamity,
> *That* brother and brother, friend and friend,
> Family and family,
> City and city may contend
> By that great glory driven wild—
> Pray I will and sing I must
> And yet I weep—Oedipus' child
> Descends into the loveless dust.[2]

Pound saw that the eighth line must become the second; he changed 'And into' to 'That in', and dropped 'That' before 'brother'. Yeats accepted the corrections. They may have given him an idea, which was half a jest, of complimenting Pound by prefacing *A Vision* with a series of papers under the common title, 'A Packet for Ezra Pound.' The irony of this tribute was that of all Yeats's books *A Vision*, with its detailed scheme of life and the afterlife, was most antipathetic to Pound's conception

[1] Yeats, *A Vision* (1925 [1926]), p. 213.
[2] In Mrs W. B. Yeats's possession. Ellmann, *Identity of Yeats*, pp. 131–2.

of art as liberated from deliberate rule or abstract theory. So *A Packet* would pit Yeats against his surest castigator.

Acting on this impulse, Yeats began the *Packet* with a description of Rapallo and then a discussion of the poet 'whose art is the opposite of mine'.[1] He summarized a conversation he had had with Pound about the *Cantos*, and explained the poem enough (as he wrote a friend) to keep Pound neighbourly.[2] He did his best, in fact, to present sympathetically Pound's mode of marshalling in spurts certain increasingly enforced themes, though he admitted being unable to overcome his feeling that the *Cantos* were fragmentary, that in them conventions of the intellect were abolished without suitable substitutions for them, and that discontinuity had become a shibboleth.[3]

Yeats also included in *A Packet* a letter to Pound warning the expatriate against accepting public office: 'Do not be elected to the Senate of your country. I think myself, after six years, well out of mine. Neither you nor I, nor any other of our excitable profession, can match those old lawyers, old bankers, old business men, who because all habit and memory, have begun to govern the world. They lean over the chair in front and talk as if to half a dozen of their kind at some board-meeting, and, whether they carry their point or not, retain moral ascendancy.'[4] Pound was not at all convinced. In Canto LXXX he responded,

> If a man don't occasionally sit in a senate
>   how can he pierce the darrk mind of a
>   senator?

As for the bankers, Pound's special detestation, he devoted his pasquinade, 'Alf's Eighth Bit', in the *New English Weekly* (1934) to reforming Yeats's view of them:

[1] Yeats, *A Vision* (1938), p. 3.
[2] Yeats, letter to Lady Gregory (1 April 1928), in *Letters of Yeats*, p. 739.
[3] Yeats, *A Vision* (1938), pp. 4–5; 'Preface' to *Oxford Book of Modern Verse*, p. xxiv.
[4] Yeats, *A Vision* (1938), p. 26. See also 'Preface' to *The Senate Speeches of W. B. Yeats*, ed. Donald R. Pearce (Bloomington, 1960), p. 25.

Vex not thou the banker's mind
  (His *what*?) with a show of sense,
Vex it not, Willie, his mind,
  Or pierce its pretence
On the supposition that it ever
Was other, or that this cheerful giver
Will give, save to the blind.[1]

The only other part of *A Vision* on which Pound commented directly was not from *A Packet*, but from the ending. Yeats wrote there: 'Day after day I have sat in my chair turning a symbol over in my mind, exploring all its details, defining and again defining its elements, testing my convictions and those of others by its unity, attempting to substitute particulars for an abstraction like that of algebra. . . . Then I draw myself up into the symbol and it seems as if I should know all if I could but banish such memories and find everything in the symbol.'[2] From Pound's point of view, symbols interfered with experience instead of letting experience coalesce into its natural pattern. In Canto LXXXIII he alluded to Yeats's perorative remarks, and connected them with 'Sailing to Byzantium' (a poem Pound had published in *The Exile* in 1928), where Yeats had asked to be gathered into 'the artifice of eternity'. Contrary to Yeats, Pound insisted,

> Le Paradis n'est pas artificiel
> and Uncle William dawdling around Notre Dame
> in search of whatever
>   paused to admire the symbol
> with Notre Dame standing inside it
> Whereas in St Etienne
>   or why not Dei Miracoli:
> mermaids, that carving,[3]

[1] Reprinted in *Personae* (New York, new edition, no date), p. 263.
[2] Yeats, *A Vision* (1938), p. 301.
[3] Cf. Hugh Kenner, *The Poetry of Ezra Pound* (London, 1951), p. 210, and Donald Davie, *Ezra Pound: Poet as Sculptor* (New York, 1964), pp. 180–1. As Davie points out, *Les Paradis artificiels* is the title of a book about drugs by Baudelaire. But the primary allusion is to Yeats's poem.

Pound differs with Yeats on architecture as on paradise; he ironically suggests that Mary's presence is diminished rather than enhanced by the symbolic portentousness of her cathedral. He subtly compares her to Yeats ingested into his own cathedral-like *Vision*. As churches Pound prefers lighter structures like St Etienne in Périgueux or Pietro Lombardo's Santa Maria dei Miracoli in Venice, and he repeats his earlier praise[1] of Tullio Lombardo's carvings of sirens or mermaids on the latter church. As literature Pound prefers to *A Vision* those poems of Yeats where the writer neglects 'monuments of unageing intellect' in favour of rapprochement with nature, as in 'Down by the Salley Gardens' from which Pound slightly misquotes a few lines later:

> as the grass grows by the weirs
> thought Uncle William   *consiros*

Yeats did not live to read the mixed blame and praise meted out to him in the *Pisan Cantos*, but he had another occasion to sample Pound's opinion of him. At the age of sixty-nine he wondered if he might not be too old for poetry. Fearing to outwrite his talent, he went to Rapallo in June 1934 primarily to show Pound a new play, *The King of the Great Clock Tower*. Pound was hard to divert from politics; he took the play, however, and next day rendered his verdict, 'Putrid!' In recounting this experience, Yeats allowed it to be thought that this was all Pound said, and that it was a sign, like his violent political *parti pris*, of a mind too exacerbated to be reliable.[2] But in an unpublished journal he does Pound more justice. What Pound told him was that the lyrics of the play were written in 'Nobody language' and would not do for drama. Far from defying this judgment, Yeats was humbled by Pound's criticism of his diction, willing as always to undergo any indignity for the work's sake. In his notebook he wrote, 'At first I took his condemnation as the confirmation of my fear that I am now too old. I have written little verse for three years. But "nobody

[1] Canto LXXIV, p. 8; Canto LXXVI, p. 38.
[2] Yeats, 'Preface' to *The King of the Great Clock Tower* (New York, 1934).

language" is something I can remedy. I must write in verse, but first in prose to get structure.'[1] He liked the new songs well enough to publish the play with a preface which, without mentioning Pound by name, wryly repeated his verdict. At the same time, as if to guard against any possibility that Pound's criticism might still apply even after revision, Yeats wrote another play on the same theme, *A Full Moon in March*, where the songs of the head (which is lopped in both plays) are more concrete. He also let Pound know, through Olivia Shakespear, that *The King of the Great Clock Tower* had been his most successful play at the Abbey.[2]

Pound was not won over; he had switched back to the pejorative view of Yeats's work as 'dim' or 'faded' that he had taken from time to time in the past, and he wrote Basil Bunting in 1936 that Yeats was 'dead', 'clinging to the habit of being a writer,' that the recent poetry was 'slop'. In another letter to Bunting he found 'increasing difficulty' in 'reading the buzzard'.[3] For Pound, Yeats, in spite of devoted ministrations, had come alive only for brief intervals. But at the last meeting of the two poets, which took place late in 1938 in London, Pound said he liked very much some of Yeats's recent poems,[4] and Yeats, accustomed to Pound's impertinent rebuff, was proportionately disarmed by his praise. Pound's most recent testimonial of quizzical admiration for Yeats was a parodic version of 'Under Ben Bulben' written in a Wabash version of Irish dialect, which he first published in 1958:

> Neath Ben Bulben's buttoks lies
> Bill Yeats, a poet twoice the soize
> Of William Shakespear, as they say
> Down Ballykillywuchlin way.

[1] Unpublished notebook of Yeats, begun Rapallo in June 1934.

[2] Yeats, letter to Olivia Shakespear (7 August 1934), *Letters of Yeats*, pp. 826–27.

[3] Quoted by Thomas Parkinson, 'Yeats and Pound: The Illusion of Influence,' *Comparative Literature* VI (Summer 1954), p. 263.

[4] Parkinson, *W. B. Yeats: The Later Poetry* (Berkeley and Los Angeles, 1964), p. 177.

Let saxon roiders break their bones
Huntin' the fox
          thru dese gravestones.

Yeats in his last years made a fresh effort to formulate his view of Pound without recourse, this time, to the symbology of *A Vision*. He was compiling his *Oxford Book of Modern Verse*, and the preface provided a good occasion to fence with his old fencing-master. As he thought about Pound and selected three of his poems ('The River-merchant's Wife : a Letter', a passage from *Propertius*, and Canto XVII), Yeats remarked to Dorothy Wellesley that Pound's work conveyed 'a single strained attitude', that Pound was 'the sexless American professor for all his violence'.[1] In the preface he said more discreetly : 'When I consider his work as a whole I find more style than form; at moments more style, more deliberate nobility and the means to convey it than in any contemporary poet known to me, but it is constantly interrupted, broken, twisted into nothing by its direct opposite, nervous obsession, nightmare, stammering confusion.'[2] The trait of nobility mentioned by Yeats was one that Pound had belauded in reviewing *Responsibilities* in 1916;[3] returning the compliment, Yeats prefixed the word 'deliberate' to explain how a temperament so commendably endowed could yield at moments to disorder. Not having achieved personal unity, Pound, in Yeats's view, had failed in his effort to get all the wine into the bowl.[4] Pound did not respond directly, though in the *Cantos* he remarks briefly, but twice, that Yeats, like Possum (Eliot) and Lewis, and unlike Orage, 'had no ground to stand on'.[5] Orage stood on the firm ground of Major Douglas's economics.

---

[1] Yeats, letter to Dorothy Wellesley (8 September 1935), in *Letters on Poetry from W. B. Yeats to Dorothy Wellesley* (New York, 1940), p. 25.

[2] Yeats, 'Preface' to *Oxford Book of Modern Verse*, p. xxv.

[3] Pound in 'The Later Yeats,' p. 67, speaks of 'a curious nobility, a nobility which is, to me at least, the very core of Mr Yeats' production, the constant element of his writing.'

[4] Yeats, 'Preface' to *Oxford Book of Modern Verse*, p. xxvi.

[5] Canto XCVIII, p. 37; Canto CII, p. 80.

Yeats was not so opposed to the agitation in the poetry of Pound as he often said. The Japanese professor Shōtarō Oshima went to see him in the summer of 1938, and expressed dissatisfaction with the poets collected in Pound's *Active Anthology*. Yeats replied, 'Even those pieces composed by ellipsis have a triumphant combination of the visual and the imaginative.'[1] He had come to identify Pound with ellipsis, and in some of his later poems he endeavours to incorporate a comparable effect within the stricter boundaries of his own verse. He attempts to produce disruption by a refrain which embodies all the hesitations, doubts, and unspoken thoughts which Pound conveyed by ellipsis or discontinuity. So in 'What Then?' the ghost of Plato is summoned to question in the refrain everything that has been affirmed in the body of the stanza:

> 'The work is done,' grown old he thought,
> According to my boyish plan;
> Let the fools rage, I swerved in naught,
> Something to perfection brought';
> *But louder sang that ghost, 'What then?'*

With such devices Yeats, who had generally conceived of reality under the figure of a sphere, acknowledges another force, which might be called the *anti-sphere*—a contemptuous, unassimilable force which mocks our enterprise. To represent the force by Plato's ghost is not the most anarchic symbol, yet it acknowledges incoherence as a domain. Perhaps Pound's liking for Yeats's last poems came from understanding that they were not unconcessive.

The relationship of the two men had long ceased to be that of master and disciple. Though Pound referred to Yeats as 'Uncle William' or 'Old Billyum', it was he who after 1912 often assumed the avuncular role. As a matter of fact, they be-uncled each other. The sense that Yeats could profit from his corrections must have reinforced Pound's sense of his own independent talent. To have kept Yeats up to the mark was a heady

---

[1] Shōtarō Oshima, *W. B. Yeats and Japan* (Tokyo, 1965), p. 104.

accomplishment. But Pound went his own way and notwithstanding his penchant for quoting Yeats in the *Cantos*, their later work is quite dissimilar. The principal and determining divergence between them is in their conceptions of form, which for Yeats is usually an hourglass, mined until it turns over, while for the later Pound, in so far as it can be characterized at all (and both he and his critics have had difficulty), it is an impromptu break-through, not to be rigged or enshrined. Yeats was eager to offset Pound's world, one of flow, with his own, which he considered to be one of arrest.

The two poets were equally engrossed in what Pound calls 'top flights of the mind',[1] moments often signalled in him by a pool of water, in Yeats by a sense of being blessed or birdlike or of shaking all over. Their metaphysics are not the same, however, for Pound at least on some occasions insists upon the power of the objective, external image to compel or lure the mind to recognize it, as if denying much of Yeats's subjectivism, while at other times he declares, 'UBI AMOR IBI OCULUS EST,'[2] or as he says elsewhere,

> nothing matters but the quality
> of the affection—
> in the end—that has carved the trace in the mind
> dove sta memoria[3]

The two positions are dovetailed by Pound's insistence that the writer needs above all 'continuous curiosity', to insure that enough life will be 'vouchsafed' for him to work with;[4] but curiosity and observation are, as he reiterates in the *Cantos*, only a start, the vital ingredient being love. While Yeats also asserted the importance of love, he meant by it something more passionate, sexual and individualized, less humanitarian, less cultural, than Pound meant. He thought, moreover, that too eclectic and international an orbit of affection could only diminish imaginative intensity.

[1] Pound quoted in *Writers at Work*, p. 56.   [2] Canto XC, p. 69.
[3] Canto LXXVI, p. 35; cf. Canto LXXVII, p. 44.
[4] Pound quoted in *Writers at Work*, pp. 41-2.

EZ AND OLD BILLYUM

Both writers agreed that they lived in an age of decline, 'beastly and cantankerous' for Pound,[1] 'half dead at the top' for Yeats.[2] ('My dear William B. Y. your 1/2 was too moderate,' the *Pisan Cantos* admonished.[3]) For Yeats the cure was to arrange experience stylistically[4]—Pound thought this procedure could only lead to premature synthesis, born from an insufficient 'phalanx of particulars'.[5] For Pound the cure was to probe, experiment, accumulate, until things shone with their intrinsic light—Yeats thought such experimentation might reach no end. Pound's view of experience is as 'improvisatory',[6] as informalist as Yeats's is formalist. The city of the imagination for Yeats is Byzantium, taken by assault; for Pound it is a kind of Ithaca, not arrived at but sporadically glimpsed, with lots of engrossing incidents en route. Pound's art in the *Cantos* is exploratory, Yeats's in his poems is exploitative. The poets face each other in an unended debate.

[1] Pound, 'Canto I' (Later completely revised), *Poetry* X. 3 (June 1917), p. 115.
[2] Yeats, 'Blood and the Moon'.   [3] Canto LXXIX, p. 65
[4] Yeats, *A Vision* (1938), p. 25.   [5] Canto LXXIV, p. 19.
[6] Yeats, 'Preface' to *Oxford Book of Modern Verse*, p. xxvi.

N. CHRISTOPH DE NAGY

Pound and Browning

———————❦———————

In the gallery of Ezra Pound's literary ancestors there stands, facing the line of 'last Romantics' from D. G. Rossetti to the young Yeats, the robust figure of Robert Browning, whom Pound succeeded as experimenter in the art of dramatic monologue.

The impact of Browning's poetry, or at least certain aspects of it, is felt in Pound's early poems along with certain tendencies which manifest the influence of 'aesthetic' poetry. Already the choice of individual words and expressions testifies clearly to the two lines of ancestry: poems which indulge in decorative mediaevalizing or the symbolical usage of esoteric words are found alongside others based, like 'Famam Librosque Cano', on Browning's conversational diction; and poems in which the sonority and cadences of Rossetti, Swinburne, Dowson and Yeats are recognizable contrast with unmelodious Browning-esque verses. But the most striking difference between the two currents is to be seen in the very principle which underlies the composition of the poems. Whereas the 'aesthetic' poems all tend to drift into a decorative or symbolic dream world and, through a gradual reduction in paraphrasable content, eventually into a *poésie à l'état pur*, most of those deriving from Browning, meaningful down to the minutest detail, appear as dramatic monologues and so provide the form for the Poundian 'persona'.

Yet despite the essential difference between the two currents, an important link may be shown to exist between them. Remembering that 'persona' means 'mask', and that Pound was greatly influenced by Yeats, who had already begun to use the technique of the mask in the 'nineties, we must first consider to what extent the 'personae' of the younger poet are related to the 'masks' of the older, always bearing in mind, of course, that the formulation of the Yeatsian theory of the mask, as distinct from its practice, took place much later than the publication of Pound's pre-*Ripostes* verse.[1] 'La Fraisne' (1908) seems to embody such a link; this persona is to all intents and purposes a dramatic monologue, but its envelopment in the Yeatsian mood and in particular a literal reference it contains to 'The Madness of King Goll' relate it to *The Wind among the Reeds*.

But despite the possibility of the 'personae' being, in their conception and function, not entirely uninfluenced by Yeats's masks, their form shows them, as well as certain other poems, to stand in direct line of succession from the poet whom Pound addresses in 'Mesmerism'.

The fact that Pound, who in 'Salve O Pontifex' worshipped Swinburne as the great master and whose poetics are based on those of the 'aesthetic' tradition, should also write a poem in homage to Browning is a further sign of the heterogeneity of the many, often conflicting, currents that converge in his early poetry. Browning's poetry, primarily a poetry of ideas, expounding and discussing religion, science and politics, represents largely all that against which the Pre-Raphaelites and the 'nineties, as also the Pound of 'Grace Before Song' and 'The Flame', set out to fight. Whereas Swinburne is apostrophized as the 'High Priest of Iacchus', the way Pound approaches Browning's person is light and jovial; the characteristic form of address is 'Master Bob Browning'—very likely an allusion to Browning's own 'Master Hugues of Saxe-Gotha', in which the 'poor organist' asks Hugues to explain his puzzling and obscure fugues.[2] Similarly Pound: 'Mesmerism', before being

---

[1] In the poems of *The Wind among the Reeds* Yeats speaks through mythological figures that are, however, supplanted in later editions by 'He'; this occurs for the first time in the edition of 1908.

[2]   Forth and be judged, Master Hugues!
Answer the question I've put you so oft:
    What do you mean by your mountainous fugues?
Robert Browning, *Poetical Works*, Vol. VI, p. 196.

Pound's tribute to Browning, is a witty and satirical criticism of some aspects of Browning's poetry, and in particular of the unnecessary and almost too consciously purposeful obscurity of his verse. The obscurity in Browning is due to the fact that he says both too much and too little. He says, or makes his characters say, too much, because, through his entirely synthetic style, he tries to capture various layers of a complex psychological state; and, from the point of view of an easy understandability, he says too little, because in his elliptic style he constantly omits important grammatical parts of the sentence.[1]

This elliptical style is to some extent responsible for the lack of euphony in Browning's verse. Pound, as the disciple and translator of the troubadours for whom poetry meant words set to music, was obviously repelled by tendencies in Browning's versification of which

> Irks care the crop-full bird? Frets doubt the maw-crammed
>   beast?[2]

represents an extreme example. And therefore it is not astonishing that Pound's weightiest, though still jovially expressed, reproach to Browning concerns the lack of musicality in his verse:

> You wheeze as a head-cold long-tonsilled Calliope,[3]

Yet the following verse already brings a change from blame to praise, and the rest of the poem embodies in crescendo Pound's homage, culminating in:

> Heart that was big as the bowels of Vesuvius,
> Words that were wing'd as her sparks in eruption,
> Eagled and thundered as Jupiter Pluvius,
> Sound in your wind past all signs o' corruption.[4]

---

[1] Paul de Reul, *L'art et la pensée de Robert Browning*, Bruxelles 1929.

[2] Robert Browning, 'Rabbi Ben Ezra' IV, *Poetical Works*, Vol. VII, p. 110.

[3] Pound, 'Mesmerism', *Personae*, 1926, p. 13.   [4] *Idem.*

POUND AND BROWNING

However, it will be noticed that Pound's praise of Browning in
'Mesmerism' is less particularized than his praise of Swinburne
in 'Salve O Pontifex'. What Pound admired in Browning—the
images of Vesuvius and Jupiter testify to this—was above all his
universality, his immense and insatiable interest in all human
problems. Pound also praises, after the line about the wheezing
Calliope, Browning's psychological insight:

> But God! what a sight you ha' got o' our in'ards,
> Mad as a hatter but surely no Myope,[1]

and finally Browning's integrity is stressed, his faithfulness to
Truth, his constant endeavour—best exemplified in 'The Ring
and the Book'—to seek, often by means of subjective points of
view, Truth itself:

> True to the Truth's sake and crafty dissector.[2]

However, nothing is said directly in the poem itself about
the dramatic monologue, although this is what one might
expect from a poet who in some of his 'personae' quite manifestly follows Browning and whose definition of his own
monologues is, moreover, basically a variation of the definition
most handbooks would give of the Browningesque monologue.
If in the content of 'Mesmerism' Pound does not say much
about his conceptions of the dramatic monologue in Browning,
the title of the poem and the opening words of the first line
make up for this to a great extent.

The Mesmerizer, i.e. Browning, is one who has power over
other souls and, by entering them, can command these souls
to come to life again as he chooses. Here one is induced to add
what Pound actually says about Browning in *The Spirit of
Romance* in connection with Ovid, the actual originator of the
dramatic monologue form: Browning is he who, in his monologues, raises the dead and makes them speak. And since
Browning is he who awakens the dead, one expects the young
Pound, who set out to bring back 'all the lost or temporarily
mislaid beauty, truth, valor, glory of Greece, Italy, England

---

[1] *Idem.*   [2] *Idem.*

and all the rest of it',[1] to learn more than one trick from the art of this 'Mesmerizer'.

Quite apart from the dramatic monologue, one meets in Pound's pre-Imagist poetry many signs of Browning's impact. One hears more or less distinct echoes of Browning's versification and in particular of his conversational rhythms in the poems of the cycle 'Und Drang', printed in *Canzoni* (1911), and especially in 'Famam Librosque Cano'. It is no exaggeration to say that some of the lines of this poem such as the following might have been written by Browning himself:

> Scrawny, be-spectacled, out at heels,
> Such an one as the world feels
> A sort of curse against its guzzling
> And its age-lasting wallow for red greed
> And yet; . . .[2]

Yet despite such 'shades of Browning' apparent here and there in Pound's pre-Imagist verse, the most important point of contact between the two poets is the genre of the dramatic monologue, which, brought to perfection by Browning,[3] was further developed by Pound as 'persona'. But what is the Poundian 'persona'? Does it designate a form of poetry or a function of poetry? Are only those poems to be considered as such in which the title or the poem itself informs us that the poet is speaking through some other person—Cino da Pistoia, Bertran de Born or Villon—as through a mask, and which, in accordance with Pound's own definition and the Browningesque device, present the nucleus of a drama in the form of a monologue? Pound himself tells us explicitly that his translations sometimes assume the function of a 'persona'. Can poems which are neither dramatic monologues nor translations be, from the viewpoint of their function, regarded as 'masks'? Answering this question one might be tempted to go so far as to say that a great number

---

[1] Herbert Bergman, 'Ezra Pound and Walt Whitman,' *American Literature*, XXVII, 1 March 1955, p. 60.

[2] Pound, *Personae*, p. 14.

[3] The dramatic monologue was by no means Browning's own invention.

of Pound's pre-*Ripostes* poems which are not monologues or translations can nevertheless be treated as 'personae' if—as in poems like 'An Anti-stave for Dowson' or 'The Tree'—Pound consciously and purposefully clothes the emotional content he wants to express in the form of one of his ancestors, thus using their form as a mask. Yet even if one is not willing to take such an extreme view, one is bound to notice the quantity of poems of a certain dramatic character which cannot be strictly considered as dramatic monologues although Pound is clearly speaking through another person. In Browning the situation is somewhat similar : practically all his poetry is dramatic, but he differentiates between *Dramatic Lyrics*, *Dramatic Romances*, *Dramatic Idylls* and finally *Men and Women*, a volume that contains most of the monologues proper. With Pound one must, moreover, be particularly careful in deciding what is a persona and what is not, for it is quite possible to encounter one where it is least expected. For instance, in his early poem 'Occidit' published in the 1909 edition of *Personae* (p. 36) but omitted from all subsequent editions, Pound starts off by painting a highly metaphorical picture of a sunset with an overtone of symbolism, and one has no reason to suspect that he is speaking through someone else. The second stanza, however, contains a comparison in which we are surprised to read :

> Hung on the rafters of the effulgent west,
> Their tufted splendour shields his decadence
> As in our southern lands brave tapestries
> Are hung king-greeting from the ponticells.

Since 'our southern lands' can hardly refer to Alabama or Tennessee, it is clear that the poet is speaking with the voice of an unidentified person, possibly a troubadour, for in 'Sestina: Altaforte', which is a 'persona' in every sense of the term, Bertran de Born begins his monologue with 'Damn it all! all this our South stinks peace'. But should 'Occidit' for this reason be classed among the 'personae'? Certainly not to the same extent as 'Cino' or 'A Villonaud'. 'Occidit,' however, shows that, even where there is no explicit indication of a poem being intended as a mask, one may sometimes hear a voice which is not Pound's own.

Surveying the totality of Pound's pre-Imagist poems in the light of his traditionalism, i.e. his endeavour to submit purposefully to a multiplicity of influences, one can distinguish as possible functional 'personae' four groups of poems : translations; poems whose form is so akin to that of other poets as to approach the condition of a mask; poems in which Pound is speaking through someone else but which are not monologues; and finally 'personae' proper, which are more or less consistent dramatic monologues and, even when they voice the words of a poet, go beyond mere translation. Only to the two latter groups is Pound's definition applicable :

'To me the short so-called dramatic lyric—at any rate the sort of thing I do—is the poetic part of a drama the rest of which (to me the prose part) is left to the reader's imagination or implied or set in a short note.'[1]

However, we are here considering only the seven poems that practically make up the last group, viz. 'La Fraisne', 'Cino', 'Marvoil', 'Piere Vidal Old', 'Sestina : Altaforte', 'A Villonaud : Ballad of the Gibbet' and 'Villonaud for this Yule'; only to these is the term 'persona' applied here.

Even if one had no knowledge of Pound's definition and his homage to Browning, one would look for a certain kind of affinity between a poet who, in 'Men and Women' alone, makes himself the mouthpiece of fifty different characters—many of them artists—and another poet who dons the mask of poets as different as Cino and Piere Vidal. The link between Pound and Browning is of particular interest because it concerns the most, if not the only, coherent group in the body of Pound's early poems. Though individually different, as will be shown, the 'personae' nevertheless show enough characteristics in common to constitute a group of their own : their group-like quality is, moreover, stressed by the fact that hardly any of them have been sacrificed by Pound in the course of various expurgations,

[1] Pound, *Letters*, p. 36.

so that, opening the *Personae* today, one would think of Pound primarily as the poet of the 'personae' even if the title were different. To demonstrate such a link one has to select from Browning's voluminous poetic works only the shorter monologues to the exclusion of those purely narrative. In fact the majority of the monologues that are likely to have helped Pound in forming his genre are to be found in the early collections, chiefly in *Men and Women* (1855).[1] And if we accept the definition Fuson gives of these Browning monologues we can apply it as a point of departure to most of Pound's 'personae':

'An objective monologue is an isolated poem intended to stimulate the utterance not of the poet but of another individualized speaker whose words reveal his involvement in a localized dramatic situation.'[2]

Not all of Browning's monologues fit equally well into this definition; Fuson selects 'The Bishop orders His Tomb' as a very characteristic specimen because it shows clearly the five 'touchstones' which, according to him, characterize the monologue. In Pound one meets a similar gradation; in 'Marvoil' one finds all five 'touchstones', in others only some. But poems such as these are allied to some of Browning's *Men and Women* through other aspects than those of technique. Their basic theme—the relationship of the poet to the 'others'—is developed by more than one artist through whom Browning speaks. Yet one notices as an important difference that whereas Browning presents various types of artists, the painters being the most numerous, all of Pound's major masks, with the exception of 'La Fraisne', are poets. Another—the most important—difference concerns, however, the style of the 'personae'. In Browning's best-known monologues we discern a high degree of what Fuson calls 'oral realism', which is indeed,

---

[1] Browning's first three collections containing short monologues are *Dramatic Lyrics, Dramatic Romances, Men and Women*; in later editions he distributed them differently but kept the original headings.

[2] Benjamin Willis Fuson, *Browning and His English Predecessors in the Dramatic Monologue*, Iowa 1948, p. 10.

on the level of language, the most decisive and predominant factor in this genre. The language serves exclusively as a vehicle for the dramatic conflict in which the speaker is involved. When we read, below the title 'The Glove', the words 'Pierre Ronsard Loquitur', we do not find, or even expect, a poem written in anything like Ronsard's manner. In Pound, on the other hand, or at least in those of his 'personae' in which the speaker is a poet, the situation is quite different. If we turn to the first 'Villonaud' we are struck immediately by the fact that the poem is permeated with allusions to, and quotations from, the poetry of Villon to such an extent that we ask ourselves whether what we are reading is not, despite a certain undeniable dramatic quality, primarily a free translation or at least a variation. One also finds in Pound sometimes, e.g. in 'Marvoil', a strict and literal reliance on the details of the biographical source, a great number of which are worked into the 'persona' and turn it into more than a dramatic monologue, in fact into a kind of biography in monological style. Of course one might say that Browning similarly used Vasari for his 'Andrea del Sarto', and that 'The Faultless Painter' constantly refers to questions of technique, whereby Browning is given the possibility of displaying his familiarity with even minor problems of the studio. However, in Browning all the details are subordinated to the presentation of the character and of the conflict in which he finds himself, whereas in Pound the basically dramatic references to biography and, in particular, to the verse of the lyrical poets who are speaking constitute partly the raison d'être of the poem; reading 'Villonaud for this Yule' or 'Sestina: Altaforte' one might wonder how far they fit into Pound's own definition of the 'dramatic lyric', and whether their function is ultimately not that of translation, even though in disguise. Against such an assumption one can point not only to 'Cino' and 'Marvoil', which are 'regular' monologues— 'Cino' contains hardly any reference to Cino da Pistoia's poetry and 'Marvoil' is written in irregular lines which would be unthinkable in a troubadour—but even to 'Sestina: Altaforte' itself: even into this poem, set in the most lyrical of all verse forms, Pound infuses elements which transform it into a monologue spoken in certain surroundings.

The two possible theses can obviously be reconciled. The Poundian 'persona' oscillates between two poles, the one being the Browningesque monologue and the other the more or less literal translation. There are 'personae' in which the poet's central preoccupation consists in revealing the dramatic involvement of a character; in others this aim is supplemented, though not superseded, by the endeavour to render in English—in the case of Villon Pound is quite explicit—what he considers to be the essence of the work of the poet through whom he speaks. Pound tries to bring the poets to life through their poetry, which is lyrical—nothing is more natural; but he also uses for this purpose the framework of the dramatic monologue, and this dualism of the underlying principles conditions the shaping of the 'personae'. Thus the definition Fuson provides of the Browningesque monologue, though basically applicable to the 'personae', must be extended if it is to include the characteristics of all of them:

'The Poundian "persona" is an isolated poem intended to stimulate the utterance not of the poet but of another individualized speaker—mostly of a poet—whose words, often borrowed partially from his own poetry, reveal his involvement in a localized dramatic situation.'

Beyond fitting this definition, the six or seven major 'personae' also share a common theme; the only other group to which this could be said to apply to almost the same extent is the one exhibiting the various facets of the conflict of the 'we' and the 'you'—the 'we', 'the bearers of the sacred flame', who are poor, lonely and frustrated by the 'you', the masters of the material world and therefore also of the products of Art. This fairly coherent group of 'personae' develops, with greater or less pertinence and intensity, this basic 'we' situation on various levels. With the exception of 'Sestina: Altaforte' all embody a movement of withdrawal from the world of the 'you': the sensitive old councillor of 'La Fraisne' escaping from the mockery of the healthy 'young men at the swordplay', Cino turning his back on the duplicity of eligible young girls, Marvoil banished from the presence of his lady by the holder of worldly power, or the speaker in the second 'Villonaud', sentenced to death together with Villon, deriding in his last hour all that on which 'you'-society is built. The 'personae' represent concrete instances of the 'we' attitude; it is the perennial 'Outsider' who speaks in them.

This basic 'we' attitude is clothed in various ways in the individual 'personae' as regards not only form but also content, very much as in Browning's own monologues, which are mostly divided into two main groups, the one consisting of 'static' monologues such as the well-known 'The Bishop orders his Tomb' or 'Pictor Ignotus', whose object is chiefly to give a synthetic view of the speaker's mind in all its complexity, and the other made up by monologues in which, through a more or less continuous narrative, a drama is evoked just before or after the climax. This latter group we associate with poems like 'Porphyria's Lover' or 'The Italian in England'. Variants of both can be found among Pound's 'personae': 'Cino' and 'Sestina : Altaforte' are glimpses of two states of mind with very little 'story' attached; in 'Piere Vidal Old' there is the unfolding of a drama; and 'Marvoil' seems to fall somewhere in between. In these, and in fact in all 'personae', one can observe that the dramatic quality diminishes and the lyrical increases as the Poundian 'persona' moves away from the Browningesque monologue towards pure translation: from 'Cino' and 'La Fraisne', which stands somewhat apart, through 'Marvoil' and 'Piere Vidal Old' to 'Sestina : Altaforte' and the two 'Villonauds'. This movement one notices even within some of the individual 'personae': the lyrical verve of the mask occasionally breaks through the framework of the dramatic monologue that has been imposed on it.

But what are the main characteristics of this Browningesque monologue, one of the two poles between which Pound's 'personae' oscillate? First and foremost the monologue is objective; the personalities evoked in Browning's monologues are unrelated to the poet's own; he takes no moral responsibility for the attitudes and reactions of his speaker;[1] one does not expect to find any existential connections between Browning and Fra Lippo Lippi, Abt Vogler or the Italian in England. He, as Pound puts it, brings the dead back to life, trying to present them as he thinks they were.

This degree of objectivity can obviously not be expected from Pound, who calls his monologues 'masks' and uses almost exclusively poets as such. Therefore one of the problems raised by the 'personae' consists in determining how far the different masks diverge from, or are similar to, the poet's own face.

Even if from the very beginning one does not expect to find in the general conception of Pound's monologues Browning's absolute objectivity, one nevertheless notices in the individual poems the endeavour to convey to the reader—through 'signals', as Fuson calls them—that it is not Ezra Pound but one of his literary ancestors speaking. The simplest of such signals is obviously the title.

Already in Browning the title is sometimes supplemented by a sub-title helping us to localize the dramatic incident out of which the monologist is speaking. Seeing under the title of 'The Bishop orders His Tomb' the sub-title 'Rome 15—' one knows that one is going to listen to a bishop who is ordering his tomb in a church of the Rome of the Cinquecento, and so the scene is set for the character's involvement in a localized conflict; after objectivity this is, according to Fuson, the second essential element of a dramatic monologue. The presentation of such an involvement necessitates first of all that the reader should be made aware of the place, and possibly also of the time, in which the action is staged. To convey such information as this through a sub-title is, for Browning, an exception; he usually does it the harder way and indicates the place, and occasionally the time, within the monologue itself. And Browning's unsurpassed skill in the handling of the monologue consists to a great extent in the manner in which through only a few hints, or only one hint, the 'stage' is set for the speaker within the poem, sometimes

[1] *Ibid.*, p. 13.

at the beginning or end, sometimes all through the speech. Browning's very first published monologue, the comparatively short 'My Last Duchess', already shows perfection in this point; apart from revealing in retrospect the drama itself, the monologue—with the help of only a few 'signals'—evokes in an extraordinarily suggestive manner the picture gallery and courtyard through which the monologist is walking while delivering his speech.

In Pound's 'personae', since to some extent they are meant to fulfil the functions of translation as well, the utterances of the speaker do not concentrate exclusively on the dramatic situation, some of them being contained in complex lyrical forms, and not enough space, as it were, is left within the poem for the localization. To remedy this deficiency Pound makes a rule out of what, for Browning, was the exception : the use of a sub-title— a 'short note' as he calls it—as an important secondary 'signal'. He goes much farther in the use of sub-titles than Browning, who only very occasionally indicated the place and century. In Pound the shortest sub-title, that of 'Cino', records not only the place, the year, and the persons present, but even describes the monologist himself in such detail as to suggest Shavian stage directions in miniature. In the stage directions to 'Sestina : Altaforte', which is a sestina embodying a monologue, the scene is indicated, the *dramatis personae* introduced, and even a sketch of the monologist's character drawn; in the note to 'Piere Vidal Old' Pound goes even further and, translating almost literally from the 'vida' of Piere Vidal, relates the foregoing history which, in an orthodox monologue, it would be the poet's task to 'bring in' step by step.[1] The sub-title sometimes also names the person or persons, as in 'Villonaud for this Yule', to whom the speech is addressed, i.e. the 'silent listener'.

This silent listener constitutes the third touchstone of a

---

[1] 'Et el si amava la Loba de Puegnautier, e madona Estofania de Son que era de Sardanha. . . . La Loba si era de Carcasses; eu Peire Vidals si se fazia apelar lops per ela, e portava armas de lop. Et en la montanha de Cabaret el se fetz cassar als pastors ab cas & ab mastis & ab lebriers, si com om fai lop; e vesti une pel de lop per donar a entendre als pastors &

perfect monologue, such as Browning's 'The Bishop orders his Tomb'. Fuson calls it the 'auditor focus'. The more dramatic and realistic and the less narrative a monologue, the more important the function of the silent listener becomes. Often the reader is kept aware of his or her existence throughout the poem not only by the monologist's remarks, but also by questions asked by the listener, then taken up and answered by the speaker. Sometimes, however, Browning proceeds differently and does not tell us until the very end of the speech to whom it has been delivered. Thus in 'The Italian in England' we first listen to the narrative about the devotion of an Italian woman to the speaker while he was hiding from the Austrians, and only in the last two lines do we learn about the background to the speech : we are at a meeting of some kind, perhaps of a revolutionary committee, where the Italian has been entreated to tell about his adventures.

In Pound's 'Piere Vidal Old', the poem itself is basically lyrical with stretches of narrative; only the last two lines turn it into a definite monologue; they express Vidal's anger and also his surprise at being seized by some men—men of the Countess of Penautier, as we know from the stage directions. The last two lines alone, beginning with 'Take your hands off me' and containing a 'normal' stage direction, create the dramatic situation. One imagines Vidal fleeing, occasionally stopping and shouting his impassioned words to the hills of Cabaret where, according to the Provençal biography given in Pound's note, he 'ran mad'; and also shouting at the men, yet in a manner which infers that they are something different from the traditional polite listeners of the monologue; then suddenly Vidal is taken by surprise. All this is brought home to the reader by adding to the stanzas a few disconnected words.

als cans qu'el fos lops. E li pastor ab lor cas lo cassero el baratero si malamen qu'el en fo portatz per mort a l'alberc de la Loba de Puegnautier.'
Ed. Camille Chabaneau, *Les biographies des Troubadours en langue provençale*, Toulouse 1885, p. 66.
In his stage directions Pound gives a literal translation of the last sentence.

In certain other 'personae', such as 'Sestina: Altaforte' or the second 'Villonaud', the auditor focus, and to some extent the localization, are linked up with, and conditioned directly by, the source—mostly the mask's own poetry—and develop more organically from the poem, yet their full significance can only be apprehended when the 'persona' is set against the poem or poems of which it is made. This applies even more to the language of the 'personae', corresponding to what Fuson calls 'oral realism', and in particular to their content (Fuson's 'psychological self-revelation'). In support of this it is necessary to consider the manner in which the individual 'personae' move between the two poles—the dramatic monologue and the various sources.

One of the major 'personae', 'Cino', is still strongly attracted to the former pole and distinguishes itself by its being almost completely unrelated to the monologist's own verse, free from any attempt to embody in English typical features of Cino da Pistoia's poetry. Nowhere outside 'Cino', mentioned in T. S. Eliot's earliest essay on Pound as one of the poems showing Browning's influence,[1] did the pre-Imagist Pound write anything that came so close to the orthodox monologue as does this. Cino Sinibuldi (da Pistoia), friend of Dante, poet of the 'dolce stil nuovo', produced a considerable bulk of poetry, written partly to a Bolognese Lady, partly to the renowned, and probably symbolical, Selvaggia. In his poetry he not only adhered strictly and monotonously to the Platonic pattern of Tuscan love poetry, but even within these limits he lay himself open to the charge of coventionality,[2] so that nothing will surprise the reader of Cino's verse, or of Pound's essay on him, more than to find him uttering cynicisms about women. But then Pound writes of his 'persona': ' "Cino"—the thing is banal. He might be anyone,'[3] which may be looked upon as

---

[1] T. S. Eliot, *Ezra Pound, His Metric and Poetry*, New York 1917, p. 10.

[2] *Storia letteraria d'Italia*, Il duecento; a cura di Giulio Bertone, Milan 1930, pp. 257–8.

[3] Pound, *Letters*, p. 39.

absolving us from having to establish any relationship between Cino and his poetry on the one hand and the dominant idea of Pound's monologue on the other. Yet Pound, by adding the sub-title 'Italian Campagna 1309, the open road', also supplies data that must induce us to recreate not from Cino's verse but from his biography the psychological state in which the monologue is spoken. In 1307, after the defeat of the 'Whites', Cino Sinibuldi went into exile from his native city, an exile to which there is more than one bitter reference in his poetry.[1,2] He possibly went to Lombardy or perhaps even to France and stayed for some time with Philippo Vergiolesi, whose daughter was long supposed to be the famous Selvaggia.[3] It is his exile that Cino blames in a well known sonnet he wrote in reply to Dante's rebuke for his inconstancy in love : having, far from all pure joy, become a wanderer, he confesses to find no comfort but in pleasure :

> Un piacer sempre mi lega, e dissolve,
> Nel qual convien, ch'a simil di biltate
> Con molte donne sparte mi diletti.[4]

If Pound's 'Cino' has any direct source, it is here, and it is with this sonnet in mind, together with Whitman's 'Song of the

---

[1] Sonetto LXXXI. Ad Agaton Drusi da Pisa :

> Druso, se nel partir in periglio
> Lassate 'l nido in preda de' tiranni,
> Son di gran lunga poi cresciuti i danni,
> E l'Arno al mar n'ando bianco, e vermiglio;
>
> Ond' io m'ho preso un volontario essiglio,
> Da che qui la virtu par si condanni,
> E per piu presto gir preparo i vanni,
> Perch'al vostro giudizio buon m'appiglio.

Ed. Sebastiano Ciampi, *Poesie di Messer Cino da Pistoia*, Pistoia 1826, p. 145.

[2] Cf. Sebastiano Ciampi, *Vita e memorie di Messer Cino da Pistoia*, Pistoia, 1826.

[3] *Ibid.*, Vol. I, p. 41.

[4] Ed. Sebastiano Ciampi, *Poesie di Messer Cino da Pistoia*, Sonetto LXXXVII, p. 151.

Open Road' to which the sub-title seems to refer, that we must listen to Cino as, after years of wandering from city to city, and apparently woman to woman, he bursts into his both sardonic and rhapsodic invective against the female sex. The whole poem illustrates the position to which the 'we'—here the poor singers —are reduced by the 'you', even in love; their praise is accepted, while they themselves are rejected. When Cino becomes intensely aware of this at a dramatically heightened moment on leaving a city after yet another disappointing experience, Pound cuts through his mind to uncover its various layers in their complexity—in a manner not unlike that of Browning's 'The Bishop orders his Tomb'. The whole poem gives voice to nothing but associations in the poet's mind—reminiscences, snatches of conversation and lyrical verses; there is no proper narration, nor is Cino involved in any particular drama other than, as it were, the drama of his whole existence, the 'we' existence. In this respect 'Cino' is related to 'Pictor Ignotus': there is little reference to the outside world, and there is no 'silent listener'. Yet Pound nevertheless conveys in an ingenious manner with the very first syllable that the poem is a spoken monologue and not merely a soliloquy. One pictures Cino stopping outside the city, shaking off its dust and exclaiming :

> Bah! I have sung women in three cities,
> But it is all the same;
> And I will sing of the sun.

However, he cannot stick to this good resolution because his thoughts keep returning to the women he loved, and this reminds him in turn of how they treated him; he then imagines what they think of him when they are alone and how differently they speak about him to their suitors. These associations Pound clothes in scraps of normal everyday language with which Browning's monologues, particularly 'Fra Lippo Lippi', abound. Finally, memory of the affronts suffered at the hands of those he has celebrated turns Cino's thoughts back to the sun he has set out to sing, and a kind of facetious 'Cantico del Sole' ends the monologue.

Thus 'Cino' is developed entirely along the lines of the dramatic monologue; a knowledge of Cino da Pistoia's poetry—except for one sonnet—does not help at all, and a knowledge of his life helps but little towards the understanding of Pound's 'persona'.

'Marvoil', the second 'persona' nearest to the Browning pole, on the other hand, cannot be fully apprehended without some familiarity with both the life and the poetry of the troubadour through whom Pound speaks. It still moves largely within the framework of the Browningesque monologue and is, moreover, the only one among the major 'personae' not to have any stage directions; yet nearly every line is packed with references to the life and poetry of Arnaut de Maruoil. Pound takes over many facts from the Provençal vida, but he also alludes to striking features of Arnaut de Maruoil's manner of writing, borrows from his recurrent themes and characteristic images, and even echoes the views of posterity. We are given many more facts than in 'Cino', chiefly because 'Marvoil' is quite a different kind of monologue. If 'Cino' was mainly a glimpse of a state of mind, 'Marvoil' unfolds a drama about the central event in Arnaut's life: his dismissal from the court of the Vicomte de Béziers. Pound draws his information on what has happened before from Provençal 'vidas': Arnaut de Maruoil had sung the praise of the Countess of Béziers, but when Alphonse II of Aragon appeared on the scene, the poor singer was banished and fled to Guillaume de Montpelier; from his exile he wrote several letters to his former Lady imploring her pardon.[1]

---

[1] 'Vos avetz auzit d'en Arnaut com s'enamoret de la comtessa de Bezers, filha del pros comte Raimon, maire del vescomte de Bezers, queil Frances auciron, quan l'agron pres a Carcassona; laquals comtessa era dicha de Burlatz, per so qu'ela fon noirida dins lo castel de Burlatz. Molt li vlia gran be Arnautz ad ela, e moltas bonas cansos en fetz de leis, e molt la preguet ab gran temensa; & ela vlia gran ben a lui. E lo reis n'Anfos, que entendia en la comtessa, s'aperceup que volia ela gran be ad Arnaut de Maruelh. El reis fo ne fort gilos e dolens, quan vit los semblans amoros qu'ela fazia ad Arnaut &, auzi las bonas cansos qu'el fazia d'ela. Si la occaizonet d'Arnaut, e dis tan e tan li fetz dire qu'ela donet comjat

It is at such a moment of letter-writing that he is caught in Pound's monologue; we see him in a cheap tavern, 'in this damned inn of Avignon'—a statement of locale—telling his story over a glass of wine to the other guests, whom he addresses as 'friends' in the first half, and talking to the hole in the wall in which he proposes to deposit his secret in the second. He has apparently been asked who he is and in answer he first introduces himself in a manner akin to that of Browning's Fra Lippo Lippi:

A poor clerk I, 'Arnaut the less' they call me,[1]

and then in a flash, as it were, he illuminates the drama of his love for the Countess of Béziers.[2] Here, in the first part, since we hear Arnaut de Maruoil speaking of the details of this drama, we immediately ask ourselves how far the facts he is referring to are drawn from his own canzoni. Does he now utter anything like a dramatic lyric synthesized from his own songs in the manner of some of the other masks? The contrary is the case. What comes forth in this retrospective monologue is that which had to be withheld and suppressed in Maruoil's own poetry: chiefly the hatred he feels for the King of Aragon and his naming of the Burlatz as the object of his love; the identity of the 'gent conquis', which Maruoil had been so careful to conceal, is disclosed. Unlike Pound's mask, Arnaut de Maruoil himself, since his songs mention the favours his 'gent conquis'

ad Arnaut, el vedet que mais nol fos denan ni mais cantes d'ela e dels sieus precs d'ela.

Arnautz de Maruelh quant auzi lo comjat, fo sobre totas dolors dolens; e si s'en parti com hom desesperatz de lieis e de sa cort. Et anet s'en au Guillem de Monpeslier qu'era sos amics e sos senher, & estet gran temps ab lui. E lai plays e ploret, e lai fetz aquesta canso que ditz: Molt eran dous miei cossir.'

Ed. Camille Chabaneau, *Les biographies des Troubadours en langue provençale*, pp. 12–13.

[1] Pound, *Personae*, p. 22.

[2] In his *Leben und Werke der Troubadours,* Friedrich Diez contests that Arnaut de Maruoil was less famous in his own lifetime than the other Arnaut—Arnaut Daniel. Pound's designation 'Arnaut the less' derives, in fact, not from a contemporary but from Petrarch or a still later source.

had granted him,[1] was particularly careful not to betray her identity. Nor does he reveal any trace of ill feeling towards Alphonse, King of Aragon, but actually addresses an envoi to him, a gesture in which one might see an attempt to placate a powerful rival.[2]

Thus the first part of Pound's 'Marvoil' tells us mainly about things that are absent from Maruoil's poetry, yet not all. In the second part Marvoil seems to turn away from his cronies and to set down what remains to be said in a letter. He ends the poem by addressing the hole in the wall in which he proposes to hide it, but there is no direct connection between this lyrical outburst and Maruoil's own songs.

Yet although the form of the monologue has nothing in common with Maruoil's poetry and the content of 'Marvoil' exhibits but few links with it even where one would most expect to find them, the elements that Pound does take over are particularly characteristic of the troubadour. All through his

---

[1] Cf. Canzone III, Cobla I, 1–10 :

> La franca captenensa
> qu'eu non puosc oblidar,
> e·il doutz ris e l'esgar
> e·il semblan qu'ie·us vi far,
> mi fant, dompna valens,
> miellir qu'ieu non sal dir,
> dinz del cor sospirar;
> e si per mi no·us vens
> Merces e Chauzimens,
> tem que·m n'er a morir.

Ed. R. C. Johnston, *Les poésies lyriques du Troubadour Arnaut de Marueil*, Paris 1935, p. 17.

This is the canzone to which Nostradamus attributes Arnaut's dismissal from the court of the count of Béziers; Nostradamus does not mention the business with King Alphonso. Jehan de Nostradamus: '*Les vies des plus célèbres et anciens poètes provençaux*, Nouvelle édition préparée par Camille Chabaneau et publiée avec introduction et commentaire par Joseph Anglade', Paris 1913, p. 43.

[2] Canzone XXI, Cobla VII, 2e Tornada, 39–41 :

> En Aragon al rei cui jois agensa,
> Tramet mon chan, cares cortes e pros,
> e lai o·is tanh humils et orgolhos

Ibid., p. 123.

songs and letters, Arnaut de Maruoil was haunted by the thought of his social inferiority in relation to his Lady, and while he usually dismisses this as something not pertinent to love, he is obsessed by it all the same.[1] He had been a clerk—as we know from the 'vida'—before he went to the Court of the Count of Béziers, and in a didactic letter of 400 lines, in which he assesses the virtues and vices of the various classes, clerks are accorded special attention.[2] All this comes to the surface when Pound's Marvoil begins his monologue with a reference to his former profession. But, more than this, the whole of the second half of the monologue is centred around a letter which Marvoil is writing as he speaks, and this is highly typical both of Maruoil's poetry and of his character. Of all the troubadours

[1] Canzone III, Cobla IV, 31–40 :

> Dompna, per gran tamensa,
> tant vos am e·us teing car,
> no·us aus estiers pregar.
> Mas plus fai ad honrar
> us paubres avinens
> que sap honor grazir
> e·ls bes d'amor celar,
> c'us rics desconoissens,
> cui par que totas gens
> lo deian obezir.

Ibid., p. 18.

[2] This Enseignamen, or didactic letter, begins : 'Razos es e mezura;' the lines about the clerks run as follows :

> Li clerc, per cui ancse
> Sab hom lo mal e·l be,
> Au pretz, si cum s'eschai,
> Aital cum ie us dirai ;
> L'un de bona clercia,
> L'autre de cortezia ;
> Li un de gen parlar,
> L'autre de rics faitz far ;
> Li un de gran bontat,
> L'autre de larguetat ;
> Et en aissi, senhors,
> Diversas son lauzors
> Donadas a chascun ;

Ed. C. A. F. Mahn, *Die Werke der Troubadours in provenzalischer Sprache*, Berlin 1846, Vol. I, p. 182.

Maruoil wrote the most perfect love letters, and whenever Provençal love letters are discussed, his are mentioned as excelling all others.[1] However, it was not so much physical separation as timidity that forced him to address his Lady in this manner; in fact, even before his exile, timidity caused him to express his feelings to the lady of his affections in the form of a letter:

> Amors m'a commandat escriure
> So que 'l boca non ausa dire.[2]

Maruoil seems to have vacillated between timidity and over-boldness, the latter inducing him to announce triumphantly—and incautiously—in a song, that his Lady had honoured him with a kiss. It is this first kiss which is to represent another link between the poetry of the real Maruoil and Pound's mask. Pound's Marvoil says:

> As for will and testament I leave none,
> Save this : 'Vers and canzone to the Countess of Béziers
> In return for the first kiss she gave me.'

This echoes a famous passage in Canzone XX, Cobla IV of the real Maruoil:

> Bem·aucizetz, quan mi detz un baizar,
> qu'anc pueys no fo mos cors meyns de dezir ;
> mas be suy folhs, quar m·en auzi vanar ;
> be·m deuria hom a cavalh atraire !³

However, the point where the connection becomes closest and Pound's 'persona' approaches the condition of translation

---

[1] a. Friedrich Diez writes : 'Der Liebesbriefe möge hier nur gedacht und bemerkt werden, daß sie mit Ausschluß der Form alle Züge des Minneliedes tragen. Arnaut von Marueil glänzt in diesem Fach.' Friedrich Diez, *Die Poesie der Troubadours*, Leipzig 1883, pp. 149–150.

b. Cf. also Karl Bartsch, *Provenzalisches Lesebuch*, Elbersfeld 1853, where Bartsch quotes under the heading 'XVIII. Brief' the only complete text of the letter of Arnaut de Maruelh 'Dona, genser que no sai dir'.

[2] Letter beginning 'Dona, genser qu'ieu no sai dir,' ed. C. A. F. Mahn, *Die Werke der Troubadours in Provenzalischer Sprache*, p. 151.

³ Canzone XX, Cobla IV, 25–28, ed. R. C. Johnston, *Les poésies lyriques du Troubadour Arnaut de Mareuil*, p. 115.

is in the last line of 'Marvoil'. Pound's poem ends with a simile that has been found by Maruoil's editor, R. C. Johnston, to be characteristic of the Provençal poet's manner of expression.[1] Pound's Marvoil keeps the image of his Beloved in his heart just like the troubadour, for whom 'el cor m'a miral ab que'us remir'.[2]

Maruoil's poetry, by no means considerable in bulk, is less outstanding for its particular originality than for a certain delicacy of expression. Apart from his fateful dismissal, the poet led a simple uneventful life, and sang the praises of only one woman. The far more versatile Piere Vidal, on the other hand, addressed songs of equal fervour to various ladies, wrote sirventes on diverse subjects, and spent the life of a wanderer not only in Provence and Italy but also in lands as distant as Cyprus and Hungary.

Why did Pound choose such different poets—Cino de Pistoia, Arnaut de Maruoil and Bertran de Born, who is different from either, for his three troubadour 'personae'? For Pound they obviously possess some quality that sets them apart as a group. This quality, however, lies as much in their lives or, more precisely, in the link between their lives and their poetry, as in their poetry alone. That is why Pound presents them as masks rather than confining himself to translating their poetry: it also explains why their lyrical poetry lends itself to use in a dramatic monologue. Since Pound links them with one another and, in his essay on Villon, also with Villon, who appears twice as a mask, we see that all four, so utterly different, nevertheless form a group. As Pound writes: 'Villon's verse is real, because

---

[1] 'Mais ce qui est plus particulier à Arnaut c'est cette image de sa Dame renfermée dans le coeur de l'amant par amour (qui joue un rôle si important dans la vie sentimentale de notre poète).'

Ibid., Introduction, p. xxv; Cf. Canzone V, Cobla IV, 25–29:

> Ves lo païs, pros dompna issernida,
> repans mos huoills on vostre cors estai,
> e car plus pres de vos no·m puosc aizir,
> tenc vos el cor ades e cossir sai
> vostre gen cors cortes, qui·m fai languir,

Ibid., pp. 45–46.

[2] *Ibid.*, Canzone IV, Cobla VII, 45, p. 24.

he lived it; as Bertran de Born, as Arnaut Marvoil, as that mad poseur Vidal, he lived it.'[1]

What Pound calls 'living one's verse' was exercised so consistently and carried to such extremes by Piere Vidal, author of highly polished but also most extravagant canzoni and sirventes, that he came to be what Pound calls him in the 'stage directions' —'The fool *par excellence* of all Provence', for in his life he actually practised the foolishness and excesses described in his verse. Overwhelmed with grief when one of his protectors, Count Raimond V of Toulouse, died in 1194, Vidal put on mourning, had his and his servants' hair and the ears and tails of his horses cut, but, together with his servants, let his nails and beard grow, and in this state he set out into the world. His behaviour with some of the women he sang was hardly less strange : Barral, another of his protectors, to whom he owed a great deal, was forced to turn him out of doors after he had stolen into the Countess' room one night, firmly convinced of his irresistibility. What made Vidal the 'fool *par excellence* of all Provence—'dels plus fols homes que mai fossen'[2]—was not merely his antics but also his naiveté : at one time he assumed the title of Emperor because the woman he married was the Byzantine Emperor's niece, and in particular the constant bragging in his poems about being the bravest fighter and the most successful seducer of women. And in order to demonstrate the truth of all this he did the craziest things.[3] Since his poetry abounds in long tributes to his own courage and charms, so

[1] Pound, *The Spirit of Romance*, p. 178.

[2] Ed. Camille Chabaneau, *Les biographies des Troubadours en langue provençale*, p. 64.

[3] Alfred Jeanroy, and he does not seem to be the only one, considers Vidal's bragging to be intended as a caricature of his fellow-poets and dismisses as incredible the anecdotes told in the 'vidas'. However, Pound does not share this view and accepts Vidal's songs and the anecdotes in the 'vidas' as facts.

Jeanroy writes : 'Non content de parodier le style de ses confrères, il s'amuse, semble-t-il, à faire de sa propre personne une caricature de la leur, outrant comiquement leurs prétentions au génie, aux dévorantes passions, aux énvirantes bonnes fortunes.'

Alfred Jeanroy, *La Poésie des Troubadours*, Paris 1934, Vol II, p. 152.

does Pound's monologue, which catches him at this maddest
moment of all when, in order to ingratiate himself with the
Countess of Penautier, Loba (i.e. She-Wolf), he clad himself
in a wolfskin and 'ran mad' in the hills of Cabaret.

The passionate words that flow from Vidal's lips in this
situation are not a monologue in the same sense as 'Marvoil' is,
nor are they variations on a particular theme as may be said of
'Sestina : Altaforte'. Ultimately the 'persona' presents a character by the narration of a number of incidents. However, the
emphasis is laid on the lyrical element, and, as has already been
shown, it is only the last lines that turn the poem into a proper
monologue. Pound's 'Piere Vidal Old' is in fact a single sustained outcry of the ageing singer who, though still bragging,
knows that his powers have left him. It is this bragging in the
past tense that gives the poem its peculiarly poignant quality
and also differentiates it from the many poems in which Vidal
vaunts his own courage, valour, generosity and success with
women. Examples of verse in this vein are available in plenty,[1]
and the first part of Pound's 'Piere Vidal Old' is little more than

---

[1] Cf. in particular the canzone beginning 'Baros de mon dan covit',
Cobla V :

> Ben es proat et auzit
> cum eu sui pros e cabals,
> e pos dens m'a enriquit,
> nos tanh qu'eu sia venals.
> cen domnas sai que cascunam volria
> tener ab se, si aver me podia :
> mas eu sui cel qu'anc nom gabei nim feis
> ni volgui trop parlar de mi mezeis,
> mas domnas bais e cavaliers desroc.

Ed. Karl Bartsch, *Peire Vidal's Lieder*, Berlin 1857, p. 84.
Cf. alsc the canzone beginning 'Ajostar e lassar', Cobla I :

> Ajostar   e lassar
> sai tan gen motz e so,
> que del car   ric trobar
> nom ven hom al talo,
> quan n'ai bona razo.

Ibid., pp. 61–62.

the further development of such themes with a few new ones
added : now that Vidal is a wolf, he perforce must sing of himself
as such, but all seen as part of a glorious past. The vigorous
over-confident bragging of :

> En totas res sembli bon cavalier,
> sim sui e sai d'amor tot son mestier
>
> . . .
>
> qu'anc en cambra no vist tan plazentier[1]

contrasts tragically in Pound's sestina with the old man's
meditation upon his past greatness :

> Swift as the king wolf was I and as strong
> When tall stags fled me through the alder brakes,
> And every jongleur knew me in his song,
> And the hounds fled and the deer fled
> And none fled over-long.

Then, in the second, more narrative part of the poem, Vidal
tells the fantastic tale about the night when the 'Loba' supposedly
yielded herself to him and he nearly killed her out of possessive-
ness. Although this incident is Pound's own invention, it is not
out of character with Vidal's songs, which occasionally display
intensely erotic streaks that are absent from those of most
troubadours.[2] However, 'Piere Vidal Old' is still far from being
a translation : its form does not follow that of any of Vidal's
songs, and in order to approach it one must be equipped with a
knowledge of Vidal's biography besides that of his poetry.

[1] Canzone beginning 'Drogoman senher, s'eu agues bon destrier',
Cobla VI, *ibid.*, p. 61.

[2] Cf. in particular the canzone beginning 'Plus quel paubres que jatz . . .',
Cobla VI :

> . . .
>
> car anc no vi tan bela ni gensor
> ni tan bona, don tenh qu'ai gran ricor,
> car sui amics de domna que tan val.
> e si ja vei qu'ensems ab mis despolh,
> melhs m'estara qu'al senhor d'Eissidolh.

Ed. Karl Bartsch, *Peire Vidal's Lieder*, p. 71.

This is far from being the case with Pound's 'Sestina: Altaforte', where a knowledge of the biographical details of the life of Bertran de Born will not greatly assist our understanding of the poem. Although more facts are known about the eventful life of the Seigneur of Altaforte, that prodigious 'stirrer up of strife', than about that of any other troubadour, Pound did not draw upon these or even upon his poetry with its many references to wars and treaties in order to create his 'persona'. Pound could have been expected to give us a glimpse of Bertran's character by interpersing the monologue with a host of references to the troubadour's activities recorded in the many 'vidas' and his poetry. Although he attempted something similar in his later 'Near Perigord', he did not in 'Sestina: Altaforte'. Had he done so, we might have had another, possibly more elaborate monologue in the manner of 'Marvoil'. But Maruoil's life was centred around a single event, which is evoked in Pound's poem, whereas Bertran's ceaseless activities, and their echoes in his poetry, are largely repetitive and all emanate from his love of strife. Dante likewise saw the Seigneur of Altaforte as a lover of strife and consequently put him into the 8th circle of Hell, where we meet him in Canto XXVIII of the 'Inferno', a meeting to which Bertran owes to a great extent our familiarity with his person. Pound refers to Dante in the 'stage directions', where he says of Bertran that he has 'dug him up again'. This disinterment was performed by relying mainly on a single poem, a sirventes which, since 'love of strife' was the driving force behind all of Bertran's activities, gives us the essence, as it were, of the man and his poetry. This sirventes— 'The Praise of War' as it is usually called—is not the only one in which Bertran gives way to his bellicose inclinations, but in the others, with one exception,[1] they are voiced in connection with some actual conflict or incitement to war, whereas here they make up the entire poem. Bertran's sirventes, like Pound's sestina, consists of vivid vignettes depicting various scenes of battle: the lining up of the warriors, the

[1] This other sirventes begins 'Mei sirventes volh far des reis amdos', but its structure bears no resemblance to Pound's poem.

fighting itself, the siege of a castle, the running wild of unmanned horses, each scene being introduced with a characteristic 'platz me', which is taken up in Pound's sestina, although translated in different ways, and dominates the structure of the poem just as it does in Bertran de Born. One of the rhyme-words repeated in every stanza is 'rejoicing', and various translations of 'platz me' are prefixed, as in Bertran de Born, to the vignettes that similarly make up Pound's sestina. Thus if Bertran sings

> E platz mi, quan li corredor
> fant las gens a l'aver fugir,
> e platz me, quan vei apres lor
> gran ren d'armatz ensems venir,
> e platz me en mon coratge,
> quan vei fortz chastels assetgatz[1]

Pound follows with :

> I have no life save when the swords clash.
> But ah! when I see the standards gold, vair, purple, opposing
> And the broad fields beneath them turn crimson,
> Then howl I my heart nigh mad with rejoicing

Pound here goes far beyond mere translation, first in that his vignettes are variations on the war theme and not literal renderings—the troubadour introduced his sirventes by praising the Spring, while to Pound 'In hot summer have I great rejoicing' seems more appropriate—but mainly in that his poem is a sestina and Bertran de Born's is not. Not only is Bertran's 'The Praise of War' no sestina, but not a single one of his other poems is either; furthermore, his songs and sirventes contain but one example[2] of the artful intricacy of the rhyme-structure in which the rhymes, instead of being simply repeated in all the stanzas in the same order as in most Provençal songs, reappear according to a special scheme from which the *cansos redondas*

---

[1] Ed. Albert Stimming, *Bertran de Born: Sein Leben und seine Werke*, Halle 1879, pp. 226–7.

[2] *Ibid.*, p. 102.

and the sestina form developed. The sestina, an invention of Arnaut Daniel, Pound's favourite troubadour, consists of six-line stanzas in which the same rhyme-words recur according to a fixed scheme. This makes it particularly unsuitable as a vehicle for any coherent thought. In the words of a specialist, the sestina is 'une rêverie où les mêmes idées, les mêmes objets se présentent à l'esprit sous des aspects successivement différents, mais qui conservent des uns aux autres une certaine ressemblance, ondoyant et se transformant, comme les nuages de l'air, comme les flots de la mer, comme les flammes d'un foyer.'[1] Yet since the six rhyme-words are, through their recurrence, constantly ringing in the listener's ear, if they are well chosen the sestina can express a lyrical content with rare intensity. Pound uses 'music, opposing, rejoicing, crimson clash, peace', which, together with the elements he took over from Bertran, create anew the bold, gay, provocative atmosphere of a time when the poet did have the power to 'stir up strife'. Yet, one may ask, can anything written in the complicated sestina form contain an element of drama; can it come anywhere near a dramatic monologue? In 'Sestina: Altaforte' it does, for Pound succeeded in turning the sestina, in spite of its repetitive and 'abstract' quality, into living speech, and in doing so he remained within the framework of the Provençal canzone and sirventes, and even within the framework of Bertran's 'The Praise of War' itself. The ingenious device he used consisted in shifting the envoi, which addresses the person or persons to whom the song or sirventes is dedicated, from the end of the poem, its usual place, to the beginning. The envoi contained in the *tornada* was largely a matter of convention, and often the person addressed had little to do with the actual poem. Sometimes, however, the envoi would reveal a point of importance in connection with the rest of the poem. Thus, at the end of his 'The Praise of War', Bertran orders, at least according to some manuscripts, his jongleur Papiols, who occurs in several of his envois, to go to Richard Cœur-de-Lion, whom he calls Oc-e-No, to tell him that

[1] Conte de-Grammont, *Sextines*, Paris 1872, p. 33; quoted from Alfred Jeanroy, *La Poésie lyrique des Troubadours*, Vol. III, p. 86.

there was too much peace.[1] Pound saw dramatic possibilities here and turned the Papiols of the conventional envoi into an organic constituent of the poem; Papiols is made the 'silent listener', so making an 'auditor focus' possible, and his presence is felt all through the poem. Whether or not the envoi appears at the end of Bertran's sirventes is of no real importance, and Stimming's authoritative edition reproduces a manuscript in which Papiols is not named at all. In Pound he is addressed as early as in the second line :

You whoreson dog, Papiols, come! Let's to music!

and through this an element of the dramatic monologue is infused into the sestina form. Largely through his device of addressing the jongleur, Pound succeeds in giving us a convincing character-sketch of the bellicose troubadour-baron of the twelfth century, who is bored to tears by peace, while at the same time reproducing in English some of the typical features of Bertran's most famous and most representative poem. Dramatic monologue and translation counterbalance each other, but we are considerably nearer the 'translation pole' than in 'Piere Vidal Old'. We approach even closer in one of the 'Villonauds' which, almost destitute of all elements of the dramatic monologue, borders on adaptation or variation.

'Villonaud for this Yule' is the only one of the 'personae' to be written in a verse form actually used by the original poet, and Pound himself tells us that the Villonauds are linked with Villon's poetry : 'The Villonauds are likewise what I conceive after a good deal of study to be an expression akin to, if not of, the spirit breathed in Villon's own poeting'.[2] Pound refers to 'the spirit breathed' in Villon's verse and not to any detail of technique; but he also tells us—in *The Spirit of Romance*—that

---

[1]   Papiols, d'agradatge
        Ad Oc-e-No t'en vai viatz
        E dijas li que trop estai en patz.

Ed. Antoine Thomas, *Poésies complètes de Bertran de Born*, Toulouse 1888, p. 135. This second tornada is not included in Stimming's edition.
[2] Pound, *Letters*, p. 36.

'Villon's art exists because of Villon' and 'It is not Villon's art, but his substance, that pertains',[1] and goes on, in a book devoted primarily to problems of form, to paint for us a portrait of Villon the man as seen in his poetry. Rarely in the whole of *The Spirit of Romance* does one feel Pound to be so personally involved in what he is writing about as in this chapter. Pound, like many others before him, admired in Villon above all the great sincerity with which he treats of his life in his poetry: 'Villon has the stubborn persistency of one whose gaze cannot be deflected from the actual fact before him: what he sees, he writes.'[2] Thus the poet and his poetry form a whole and the two are intimately linked. Yet Pound also remarks that: 'Much of both the "Lesser and Greater Testaments" is in no sense poetry,' and reading this one expects him to select for his 'personae' only a few elements from Villon's verse. This is precisely what Pound did; he ignored some of the most characteristic devices of both 'Testaments'. For one of his 'Villonauds' he adopted the form and mood of some of the interspersed ballads; for the other he did not rely on the 'Testaments' at all, at least not directly. That Pound, on the other hand, constructed two 'personae' out of Villon's work shows that he perceived in it a certain dualism which manifests itself all through the 'Testaments', among other things in the contrast between the sincerely pious beginning and the mockery of some of the 'legs'. This feature is much in evidence if one compares ballads such as 'les dames du temps jadis' and the brothel ballad about 'La Grosse Margot'. Villon, in Pound's words, 'has sunk to the gutter, knowing life a little above it, thus he is able to realize his condition, to see it objectively, instead of insensibly taking it for granted'.[3] Villon is therefore in a position to depict what is felt by one who has sunk to the level of the gutter and enjoys its pleasures; yet through awareness of the ephemeral character of these pleasures he has an enhanced consciousness of the ephemeral character of life altogether.

There is more than this in Villon, and since the time when

---

[1] Pound, *The Spirit of Romance*, pp. 168, 170.
[2] *Ibid.*, p. 168. [3] *Ibid.*, pp. 176–7.

Pound wrote *The Spirit of Romance* the celebrated sincerity of Villon has been seriously contested;[1] but these are certainly two basic—though perhaps not the only—attitudes reflected in the 'Testaments'.

Pound reserved, as it were, the form of the ballads in the 'Great Testament' for his evocation of the nostalgic Villon, of the Villon of the 'ubi sunt', and obviously had to find another form in which to bring back to life the Villon whom he himself calls 'thief, murderer, pander, bully to a whore', along with his associates. For in order to show Villon 'caught in filth and crime', it was essential to place him in a corresponding environment. Anyone who has read the 'Testaments' knows that nothing is easier than this, because in them Villon recreated the world—the Paris—in which he lived and the people he met. And if Pound intended to approach Villon at his farthest remove from 'les dames du temps jadis', the Villon of 'ce bourdel où tenons nostre estat', he might have adopted the characteristic device used by Villon himself in order to present his little world and its people. In his 'Testaments' Villon bequeathes various real or imaginary belongings to his friends, acquaintances and enemies, choosing such as are particularly suited—or, more often, eminently and facetiously unsuited—to the future heirs. Through the device of bequeathing and the invariably characteristic suitability or unsuitability of the 'legs', Villon draws, in the words of Gaston Paris 'des croquis, tracés avec la sureté de plume d'un caricaturiste de génie'.[2] That Pound wanted to follow Villon in this too is clear from the second 'Villonaud'. However, short of writing another 'Testament', he had to condense the method of characterization he found in Villon. He had to find a new form in which to bring Villon and his companions back to life and, coupling it with a selective principle with respect to the figures he would borrow for his poem, chose for his 'mask' only one section of the panorama of Villon's world. Strangely enough, the particular milieu that he chose was one which is but thinly represented in the 'Testaments': he

---

[1] Cf. in particular Fernand Desonay, *Villon*, Paris 1947.
[2] Gaston Paris, *François Villon*, Paris 1901, p. 137.

sets Villon among criminals of the rough sort. Although Villon actually always lived on the borderline between respectability, the demi-monde and straightforward crime, there are few allusions to the latter in his poetry written in French and only two figures in the 'Testaments' belong to the world of the Paris gangs. Yet between the composition of the 'Great Testament' and his disappearance from Paris Villon also wrote seven ballads in the slang of the 'Coquille', and Pound's 'A Villonaud : Ballad of the Gibbet' is more closely related to these than to the 'Testaments' themselves. Thus we see that Pound condenses, as it were, the method of characterization employed in the 'Testaments', but applies it to the world of the 'jargon' ballads.

Both 'Villonauds' are 'drinking-songs', although Villon never wrote songs of this kind, and in the second the method of indirect characterization adopted from the 'Testaments' consists in drinking to the health of Villon's various companions, present or absent, with toasts which give a short and facetious sketch of their 'careers'. Only a few of those companions occur in Villon's verse; in fact, the 'Testaments' mention hardly any criminals. The way in which one whom they do mention (together with Marianne Ydole of 'ce bourdel') is addressed in Pound's ballad illustrates particularly well the manner in which he condenses the method of the 'Testaments'. In both Villon leaves a facetious and characterizing legacy, a coat, to a rather suspect character so that he can hide under it the fowl he has stolen :

> Item, je donne a Jehan le Lou,
> Homme de bien et bon marchant,
> Pour ce qu'il est linget et flou,
> Et que Cholet est mal serchant,
> Ung beau petit chiennet couchant
> Qui ne laira poullaille en voye,
> Ung long tabart et bien cachant
> Pour les mussier, qu'on ne les voye.[1]

[1] Ed. August Longnon, *Oeuvres complètes de François Villon*, Paris 1892, p. 4.

While Pound, in the second 'Villonaud' manifestly confuses Culdou (who actually appears elsewhere in Villon) with Cholet, he follows Villon closely in the matter of the characterizing legacy of the coat:

> Culdou lacking a coat to bless
> One lean moiety of his nakedness.[1]

Then the function of the coat is indicated in the same oblique manner that is so often employed by Villon himself: the act of stealing the fowl is referred to as 'plundering' St Hubert, i.e. the patron saint of hunters. Pound similarly adopts Villon's basic method of characterizing his figures by linking them up with some object—a coat, a poignard or the gallows.

Most of the characters and the whole tone of the poem, however, connect Pound's second 'Villonaud' not with the 'Testaments', but rather with the slang ballads. These consist chiefly of advice and warnings to the robbers who made up 'la Coquille' as to the ways of performing their 'work' and avoiding capture. The ballads abound in references to the vocational hazards of the 'Coquillards'—prison, the wheel, and in particular the gallows—and Pound's very title, 'Ballad of the Gibbet' is an echo of these passages.[2] In some of his ballads Villon seeks to

[1] Pound, *Personae*, p. 12.

[2] Here is a characteristic passage from the first of Villon's jargon ballads about the gibbet, followed by the French translation:

> A Parouart, la grant mathe gaudie,
> Ou accollez sont duppes et noirciz,
> Et par angels, suyvans la paillardie,
>   Sont greffiz et prins cinq ou six;
> La sont bleffeurs au plus hault bout assis
> Pour le havage et bien hault mis au vent.

Translation:

> A l'échaufaud, la grand'place gaudie,
> Ou dupes près, accolés et noircis,
> Et par sergents, durs à la main hardie,
>   Sont mis en grappe cinq ou six;
> Là sont glaneurs au plus haut bout assis
> Pour le pain du bourreau livrés au vent.

Ed. Jules de Marthold, *Le Jargon de François Villon*, Paris 1895, pp. 94–5.

warn his companions of these dangers by sketching the ends of those who were not sufficiently cautious. These sketches may have been among the sources or at least the points of departure for those of Pound. Here is one of them in a French translation of Villon's jargon:

> Changez vos costumes souvent,
> Du rez de chaussé au front du temple;
> Et prenez garde, en vous sauvant,
> Que de la gorge on vous trouve ample;
> Montigny, pour ce, par exemple,
> Bien attaché devint caduc,
> Déraisonnant, pris de la tremble
> Dont l'enchauvreur lui rompt le suc.[1]

The monologue is not spoken by Villon himself but by the sixth of the companions who are to be hanged together with him. The elaborate stage directions inform us that we are in 'ce bourdel où tenons nostre estat'—a reference to the celebrated brothel ballad—at the moment that Villon is writing his moving 'Frères humains qui après nous vivez', to the sincere humility of which Pound's 'Villonaud' stands diametrically opposed. Pound, as already explained, saw a dualism in Villon, and he points up the 'low' aspects of his nature, the Villon 'caught in filth and crime' at the very moment when Villon is composing his song of contrition. Through this we are made intensely aware of the two poles between which Villon's life was swinging to and fro. Pound's second 'Villonaud' with its 'Drink ye a skoal for the gallows tree!' and

> Skoal!! to the gallows! and then pray we
> God damn his hell out speedily
> And bring their souls to his 'Haulte Citee'

reads like a cynical reply to 'Frères humains qui après nous vivez', and its ending is certainly a consciously inverted echo of Villon's:

[1] *Ibid.*, p. 99.

Prince Ihesus, qui sur tous a maistrie,
Garde qu'Enfer n'ait de nous seigneurie :
A luy n'ayons que faire ne que souldre.
Hommes, icy n'a point de mocquerie,
Mais priez Dieu que tous nous vueille absouldre.[1]

In Pound's first 'Villonaud' we are transplanted into the nostalgic world of the 'ubi sunt'. Whereas the three ballads Villon wrote on the illustrious dead in order to evoke a feeling of transitoriness are by no means particularly original, and two of them do not rise much above the level of their predecessors, this is quite different with 'La ballade des dames du temps jadis', where, in the words of Gaston Paris, Villon 'a su faire de ce lieu commun une des perles les plus rare de la poésie de tous les temps, d'abord en n'évoquant dans son rêve que des figures de femmes puis en les choisissant avec un art ou plutôt un instinct merveilleux, les unes à peine reconnaissables et passant vaguement devant les yeux, . . . d'autres éveillant les lointains souvenirs de la mythologie ou de l'antiquité.'[2] Although it is this ballad, together with 'Les regrets de la belle heaumière', that directly inspired Pound, he did not translate it, possibly because this had been done by Rossetti with a perfection that had also induced Swinburne, who otherwise translated all of Villon's ballads, to leave it untouched. Pound's own version, although it comes near to being a translation, is not a literal rendering but relies on several passages in Villon and, moreover, still discloses traces of the dramatic monologue. The ballad is not entirely lyrical and is spoken at a moment that is localized in time right at the beginning, where Pound borrows from the opening of the 'Lesser Testament' the familiar lines :

En ce temps que j'ay dit devant,
Sur la Noel, morte saison,
Que les loups se vivent de vent,
Et qu'on se tient en sa maison,
Pour le frimas, pres du tison.[3]

[1] Ed. August Longnon, *Oeuvres complètes de François Villon*, p. 121.
[2] Gaston Paris, *François Villon*, Paris 1901, p. 107.   [3] *Ibid.*, p. 4.

In Pound's 'Villonaud', whose form is, except for a change in the rhyme scheme,[1] identical with that of Villon's ballad, this is rendered:

> Towards the Noel that morte saison
> (*Christ make the shepherds' homage dear!*)
> Then when the grey wolves everychone
> Drink of the winds their chill small-beer
> And lap o' the snows food's gueredon.

Much of the indefinable charm of Villon's ballad lies in the evocativeness of the refrain 'Mais où sont les neiges d'antan?', which Rossetti translated 'But where are the snows of yester-year?' Pound adopts as his refrain a slight modification of Rossetti's line. In Rossetti the envoi reads:

> Nay, never ask this week, fair lord,
>   Where they are gone, nor yet this year,
> Save with thus much for an overword,—
>   But where are the snows of yester-vear?[2]

while Pound ends with:

> Prince: ask me not what I have done
> Nor what God hath that can me cheer
> But ye ask first where the winds are gone
> Wineing the ghosts of yester-year.

In general, Pound's 'Villonaud for this Yule' sounds much like Villon spoken by his two Pre-Raphaelite translators. It is not yet a literal translation, but the dramatic component is reduced to a minimum and the aim of the poet is almost entirely that of recreating a lyrical mood. Elements such as the drinking song may not derive from Villon in their details, but the structure of the poem, with the thrice-repeated 'Where are' and the refrain justify Pound's statement that his 'Villonauds' are 'an expression akin to, if not of, the spirit breathed in

---

[1] The rhyme in Villon is: a b a b b c b c
The rhyme in Pound is: a b a b a b a b
[2] D. G. Rossetti, *Collected Works*, Vol. II, p. 461.

Villon's own poeting'. If we go but one step beyond 'Villonaud for this Yule', we enter the domain of translation.

With the 'personae' Pound created a new literary genre which distinguishes itself from the Browningesque monologue not only by its form but in particular by its function. Browning, like a playwright, creates an objective character or a dramatic incident with which he has no personal involvement and sets it before the reader. Had Pound's intention been similar he would not have called his monologues 'personae', i.e. masks through which the actors spoke in the antique theatre, for his own masks are largely created to voice what he himself has to say in a personal manner. All have as a central theme the relationship of the poet to the world around him: even the old councillor of 'La Fraisne' represents the poet himself. In all but one of the 'personae' the poet is shown as the poète maudit, an outcast from a hostile world. In this one, the 'Sestina: Altaforte', however, he is shown not only as playing a part in this world, but as an active and even aggressive principle in it. Much of what Pound wrote and did in his later years seems to be foreshadowed in these dualistic attitudes.

Similar, though not identical, are the two attitudes in which Yeats, under the names of Michael Robartes, Owen Aherne and others, dramatized his own personality already before the turn of the century, although he did not elaborate his systematic theory of the self, anti-self and the mask until the essays of *Per Amica Silentia Lunae* (1918). Michael Robartes and Owen Aherne are crystallizations of the two poles of Yeats's personality: the dreamer of the Celtic dream and the member of occult brotherhoods (the private self) on the one hand and the fighter for Ireland (the public self) on the other,[1] and in the poems of *The Wind among the Reeds* he realized to a great extent what he said more explicitly in a later essay: 'If we cannot imagine ourselves as different from what we are, or try to assume that second self, we cannot impose a discipline upon ourselves though we may accept one from others. Active

[1] Cf. Richard Ellmann, *Yeats: The Man and the Masks*, London 1949.

virtue, as distinguished from the passive acceptance of a code, is therefore theatrical, consciously dramatic, the wearing of a mask.'[1]

Although the young Pound was so strongly under the spell of Yeats for it to appear unlikely that his idea of the function of the mask was conceived in complete independence of the older poet, the very first 'personae' bear so distinctly the stamp of Pound's own personality as it also manifests itself throughout all of his poetry and critical ideas that Yeats's impact should not be overestimated, if only because but a single persona, 'La Fraisne', is indebted to Yeats through its form. For Pound, the form of a 'persona' conditions to some extent its function. The 'personae' are an essential part of his traditionalism and in most of them he complements a personal attitude with real incidents drawn from the lives of certain poets of the past and with actual quotations from their verse. The 'personae' thus function as a loudspeaker that reinforces Pound's own voice. While on the one hand he is, as he says in 'Histrion', a medium through which certain dead poets can manifest themselves, on the other he turns them into masks. Yeats himself did not go beyond using symbolic personages: Aedh, Michael Robartes and Owen Aherne exist merely as masks of Yeats, whereas Maruoil in 'Marvoil' and Bertran de Born in 'Sestina : Altaforte' are reanimated beings in addition to fulfilling the function of masks. And if it has been said that the Poundian 'persona' oscillates between the Browningesque monologue and mere translation, it may be added now that, in its function, it stands halfway between an objective poem—monologue or translation—and a mask in Yeats's sense.

[1] W. B. Yeats, *Essays*, London 1924, p. 497.

FORREST READ

Pound, Joyce, and Flaubert :
The Odysseans

———————◦◦◦◦◦◦◦———————

In the first versions of *The Cantos*, probably begun in 1911 or
1912 and under intense composition in 1915, Ezra Pound
projected the speaker of his poem, himself, as a Dantean
visionary in the act of seeking what he defined in his first canto
(later discarded) as a 'rag-bag' for the modern world 'to stuff
all it's thought in'. His subject was the modern mind, his guide
was Robert Browning, his model was Browning's *Sordello*, and
the structure of his 'new form', a version of Browning's 'meditative, semi-dramatic, semi-epic story', would 'follow the
builder's whim'.[1] The choice of Browning reflected his belief in
1915 that *Sordello* was the last great poetic narrative, itself
Browning's version of the 'personal epic', the post-romantic
autobiographical poem which at the same time sought the
objective validity of actual history. But by 1922, having completed eight cantos, Pound had lost confidence in the form of his
'rag-bag'. He wrote to his father at the end of 1919 'done cantos
5, 6, 7, each more incomprehensible than the one preceding it;
don't know what's to be done about it' (letter at Yale). In
1920 and 1921 he wrote an eighth canto; but, opening as it did
with a lament for the passing of the Homeric epic of adven-
turous deeds, it continued to reflect his uncertainty. In 1923,
however, Pound rejected most of old Cantos I–III, especially
those parts which were based on Browning. He moved the
Odyssey translation from the end of old Canto III to make a new

[1] The above quotations are from old Canto I (*Poetry*, June 1917),
discarded in 1923.

125

Canto I. Old Canto VIII, with a new introduction that rejects
Browning, was moved forward to become Canto II. A new
Canto III was made up from fragments of the rejected cantos.
Cantos IV–VII were retained substantially the same as the
present versions.[1] By these revisions Homer became Pound's
guide, Aphrodite his muse, and Odysseus his central figure;
instead of being merely evocations of past literature, past
persons, and past places, reflected in the mind, the poem was now
motivated by the fictional pattern of a voyage, by encounters
with the living and the dead, and by a traditional epic idea, the
nostos (the return home).

From the time he arrived in London in 1908, intent on writing
an epic poem, Pound's own life had seemed to him an Odyssean
adventure and his studies of the past his 'background'. In a
1909 letter to his mother about the feasibility of a modern epic
(at Yale), he thought of Homer's Odyssey as a primary model,
though at the time Whitman's and Dante's overt use of themselves as epic figures seemed more adaptable. From the beginning, in his essays and reviews, he compares the modern experimental writer to an Odyssean adventurer into the unknown.
In his poems the voyage with Homeric echoes of exile and
discovery crops up incessantly. His first 'major persona' was
'The Seafarer'; he republished 'The Seafarer' in *Cathay*, (1915),
juxtaposing it to his second major persona, 'The Exile's Letter'.
In 1906 he had bought Andreas Divus's translation of Homer; in
1909 or 1920 he had conceived the Nekuia as a symbol of his
own voyage to Europe; between 1911 and 1914 had translated
the Odyssey passage of Canto I into 'Seafarer' metres; in 1915
he incorporated it into the original third canto. It is only natural,
then, that the Odyssey is one of the formative patterns of *Hugh
Selwyn Mauberley*, his summary of his London years.

---

[1] Publication of the 'old' Cantos I–III, *Poetry*, June–August 1917 (con-
densed somewhat for *Lustra*, American edition, 1917); IV, Ovid Press,
1919; IV–VII, *Poems 1918–21* (1921); VIII, *Dial*, May 1922. Myles
Slatin describes the history of composition leading up to *A Draft of XVI
Cantos* (1925) in 'A History of Pound's *Cantos* I–XVI, 1915–1925',
American Literature, May 1963. Pound made minor changes in several of

But if the Odyssey was so pervasive as a pattern for his own life and as a pattern of literary form, why did Pound wait so long before making Odysseus the major figure of *The Cantos*? One reason was that his conception changed after 1919: *The Cantos* was to be not a poem written from within modern civilization, but a poem about a break with modern civilization and a search for a new basis. This 'break' is reflected in his personal life, in *Mauberley*, and in Canto VII; it became for him a theory of history, of which the *nostos* is a symbol. Another reason lies in Pound's conception of epic as 'a poem containing history'. A modern epic had to build on tradition. It had to be based upon the present 'state of consciousness' as that state had been represented in literary form up to the time when the modern poet began *in medias res*. In 1915 the epic had seemed to stretch from Homer to Browning. Between 1915 and 1922, however, it became increasingly evident that the modern consciousness had been discovered and expressed in prose. Therefore Pound had to come to terms with the prose tradition.

Ford Madox Ford had impressed on Pound as early as 1911 the importance of 19th century prose, especially the style of Flaubert (Mauberley's 'Penelope', if not Pound's own). But although Pound at once sought in the theory and practice of imagism to incorporate this 'prose' dimension, which meant for him 'realism' and which enlarged the scope of poetry, his awareness of the range and uses of prose techniques and subjects underwent continuing development during his London years. Thus his first interest was Flaubert's style, *le mot juste*, more than other aspects of Flaubert's art or his overall literary achievement. A symptom of change appears as early as 1914: Flaubert's 'varnish' seemed to lack the 'solidity' of Stendhal's preoccupation with 'matter'. Pound's 1918 essays on Henry James and Remy de Gourmont were less studies of style than efforts to define in those writers a 'General summary of state of human consciousness in decades immediately before my own';[1]

these cantos for *A Draft of XXX Cantos* (1930), especially alteration and condensation of Canto VI.

[1] 'Date Line', 1934, *The Literary Essays of Ezra Pound* (1954).

that is, to bring literary treatments of the western mind up to date. He also discovered, however, that James and de Gourmont provided no answer to his own most pressing problem, the *form* in which the modern consciousness might be treated. This frustration is expressed in Canto VII, where he runs through a narrative tradition stretching from Homer, Ovid, the medieval epics, Dante, Flaubert, and James to himself. As a guide 'drinking the tone' of period atmospheres, James offers little help, nor, by itself, does the Gourmontian apperceptivity of 'the live man'. Canto VII and the original Canto VIII express nostalgia for the old epic subjects and forms, but suggest no integration of the epic and prose traditions.

In 1922, however, Pound gained a new awareness of the prose tradition as a development from the epic tradition. Pound had moved to Paris. Having given a new direction to his life he was seeking to give one to his poem. It was Flaubert's centennial year; Pound read René Descharmes's recently published *Autour de Bouvard et Pécuchet*. *Ulysses* appeared in book form. Pound, who had followed it chapter by chapter since 1918, saw it as a whole for the first time. Pound wrote several 'Paris Letters' for *The Dial* on Flaubert and Joyce. Of Flaubert he wrote : 'More and more we come to consider Flaubert as the great tragic writer, not the vaunted and perfect stylist. I mean that he is the tragedian of democracy, of modernity.'[1] Both Flaubert and Joyce were 'classic' in that they represent 'everyman' even while writing *l'histoire morale contemporaine*. Flaubert had adumbrated a new modern form in *Bouvard*; Joyce had perfected that form in *Ulysses* and at the same time conflated the novel and the epic. In his 'Paris Letter' of May 1922 and in 'James Joyce et Pécuchet' Pound announced that every writer had to make a critique of *Ulysses* for his own use, 'afin d'avoir une idée nette du point d'arrivée de notre art, dans notre métier d'écrivain.'[2] These essays were his critique.

[1] *Dial*, September 1922, p. 333.

[2] 'James Joyce et Pécuchet' (written in French), *Mercure de France*, June 1, 1915; reprinted, *Polite Essays* (1937); an English translation, *Shenandoah*, Lexington, Va., Autumn, 1952. 'Paris Letter', *Dial*, June 1922; reprinted, *Literary Essays*, as 'Ulysses'.

They reflect a focusing of his thoughts about ways to handle the modern consciousness in contemporary yet classic form.

The results of this new view of Flaubert and Joyce can be seen in 'On Criticism In General' (*Criterion*, January 1923), a summary of 'The better tradition' Pound had been seeking to define throughout his London years. This history of literature—from Homer to Joyce, adapted to his own use—takes full account of an idea he had adumbrated in 1913 but only now stated categorically : that with Stendhal vital literary expression—at least work of epic scope—had 'gone over to prose'. Since Stendhal the main line had developed out of Flaubert, passed through the Goncourts, Dostoievsky, and James, and come to a final fruition in Joyce (Pound's table includes associates and followers of the previous writers, but Joyce stands alone). After Joyce, what? Pound appends enigmatically 'Fenollosa on the Chinese Ideograph'. By so doing he suggests that the next work is still to come. That he called this essay his *De Vulgari Eloquio* makes clear that it is his authoritative basis for *The Cantos*. His decision to begin his own poem as a modern *Odyssey*, in the wake of the prose *Ulysses* — 'an epoch-making report on the state of the human mind in the twentieth century (first of the new era),' i.e., testimony of 'the break' — was more than accidental.

Pound uses at the beginning of the *Pisan Cantos*, reflecting the beginning and progress of his entire poem, the phrase 'Odysseus the name of my family'. Joyce is also of that family, for Odysseus (Joyce called him 'Ulysses') evolved in Joyce's imagination and in his work just as it did in Pound's. Joyce wrote a schoolboy essay on Ulysses as his favourite hero. He considered calling *Dubliners* 'Ulysses in Dublin' and based a story on him, but, sensing that such a figure was too encyclopedic for a short story, put it aside. Having completed 'the moral history of my country' he went on to write his portrait of the artist who is seeking to free himself from the bonds of home, nation, and church so that he can 'forge in the smithy of my soul the uncreated conscience of my race'. Joyce's presentation of the typical modern city as a formative principle for the first time in English fiction, showing how its customs, institutions, and spiritual atmospheres paralyse its life, and his rendering of the conflict between this deadening milieu and the creative spirit, prepared the sequel. In *Ulysses* Joyce retained Stephen, the figure of his own alienation, intellectuality, creative impulse, and sense of history, but complemented him with the more comprehensive Bloom, *l'homme moyen sensuel* of 1904. He set them in a full presentation of the historical city, a material entity almost as alive as its denizens (conversely, the Dubliners appeared to be reduced to the city's materiality). He left them in the shadow of the historical city's biological counterpart, the non-intellectual force of physical nature, Molly Bloom. *Ulysses* is a personal epic in which the modern city-dwellers live their daily lives and enact their fates against a social, political, and metaphysical background that includes the history of western civilization at least since Homer.

Joyce develops a single idea toward an ever larger, more inclusive, synthetic form, until *Ulysses* becomes the culmination of the western epic tradition. Pound was in a perfect position to follow Joyce's progress, which is a precise parallel of his own. From 1914 on Pound corresponded with Joyce steadily, received his works chapter by chapter on their way to the magazines, and promoted his work in various reviews. Pound admired Joyce above all other contemporary writers; if he were a prose writer, he said, he would wish to write like Joyce. It was in one sense 'the Joyce decade'. In 1938 Pound recalled:

In 1912 or eleven I invoked whatever gods may exist in the quatrain

> Sweet Christ from hell spew up some Rabelais,
> To belch and . . . and to define today
> In fitting fashion, and her monument
> Heap up to her in fadeless excrement.

'Ulysses' I take as my answer.[1]

Ulysses was the 'monumental' presentation of the modern

---

[1] *Guide to Kulchur* (1938), p. 96.

consciousness; it registered comically the uncritical 'unification' of 19th-century thought which made modern man a thesaurus of inert ideas. 'Modernity', for Pound, was the as yet undiscovered relations among personality, the proliferating mechanism of the modern city, and history. By expressing these relations *Ulysses* appeared to end an era and clear the way for the new.

Pound used Joyce's books as whetstones while he himself was seeking new artistic methods. In 1914 Joyce appeared as a prose imagist who had invented a new form for short prose fiction; based on the form of an emotion rather than the form of the short story, it was perfectly adapted to register modern life both objectively and as it struck the sensitive individual.[1] Joyce was able in *Dubliners* and *A Portrait* not merely to 'present' the urban surface, but to make evident 'behind' his work his own 'sense of abundant beauty', or personal vision. In his 1916 essay, ostensibly on *Exiles*, Pound raises the whole problem of genres and modern realism and decides that the novel, not the drama, is the form which the shaping intellect can use to encompass modern multiplicity. Yet Pound, then in the midst of writing the early cantos and afflicted by the problem of realism in poetry (he asks in old Canto I if he should 'sulk and leave the word to novelists?'), strains in his remarks on the cinema, with *A Portrait* and his own work in mind, toward the idea of a more concentrated, flexible form which might be built up out of dramatic speech, melody, and the image. In 1918, having reread *A Portrait* and read the first chapters of *Ulysses*, he perceived even more fully how Joyce's 'Swift alternation of subjective beauty and external shabbiness, squalor, and sordidness' enabled him to bring within his scope the most disparate matter of modern life, from lyric and symbolic to naturalistic, and to achieve a maximum concentration and historical depth. *Ulysses* appeared to be an even further advance, for in Bloom Joyce had

[1] The essays referred to in this paragraph are 'Dubliners and Mr. James Joyce,' *Egoist*, 15 June 1914; 'The Non-Existence of Ireland', *New Age*, 25 February 1915; 'Mr. James Joyce and the Modern Stage', *Drama*, February 1916; and 'Joyce', *Future*, May 1918, augmented by 'Ulysses' for *Instigations*, 1920. The first and fourth appear in *Literary Essays*.

'moved from autobiography to the creation of the comple-
mentary figure'. *Ulysses* was 'an impassioned meditation on life',
but the meditation was fictionalized: Bloom 'brings all life into
the book. All Bloom is vital'. In 1922 Pound's enthusiasm
increased. Bloom appeared to encompass everything: he was a
man immersed in modern life yet seen in the perspective of
history; at the same time he expressed in his *monologue intérieur*
the integrity of the personal life and the vitality of a mind
unconquered by the material world of things and forces. Bloom
was a focus for what Pound was seeking in himself as man, as
artist, and as the figure who spoke in his poems: he must
reflect the novelist as receiver and recorder of *l'histoire morale
contemporaine*, the historian who saw contemporaneity in the
perspective of the past, and the lyrist who could express freely
his desire and his ideal vision of the future.

In 'James Joyce et Pécuchet' Pound develops a synthetic view
of Flaubert's career as the 19th century novelist-historian who
had adumbrated a vision of the 20th. Flaubert had written works
of contemporary realism in *Madame Bovary* and *L'Éducation
Sentimentale*, and of historical exploration in *Salammbô* and
La Tentation de Saint Antoine; he had sought to summarize
these modes by historical juxtaposition in *Trois Contes*. But
Pound's most absorbing new interest was the structure of
Bouvard et Pécuchet. While *Madame Bovary* and *L'Éducation*
record 19th-century provincial and city life in 'une forme
antérieure', *Bouvard* foreshadows the future by inaugurating
a new form, the 'encyclopédie mise en farce'. *Bouvard* sub-
stitutes for the traditional form of the novel, with its naturalistic
plot, an external form that reflects the structure of the mind,
namely, *idées reçues* and the alphabet. The internal causality,
Bouvard et Pécuchet's 'Défaut de methode dans les sciences'—
motivating ideas but lack of a method to evaluate or use them
effectively—appeared to be a crucial insight into modern
mental reality. *Bouvard* gives the comic effect of men running
in place while their surroundings stream past; there is an illusion
of action, but it is really the stasis of a monument; despite the
friends' purposefulness, their multiple interests, and their force,

the mind is, as Pound put it, stuck in the mud, victimized by ideas which it receives passively rather than uses creatively. The book is an image of the mind as a single, paralyzed unification.

There was, however, another dimension to *Bouvard*. Flaubert was not merely presenting a *sottisier* and satirizing his characters; he was conducting what Pound called in his essay on *Exiles* 'a combat with the phantoms of the mind'. Flaubert used his own researches, in which he had discovered the encyclopedia to be the form of the mind of his time. He turned his researches into literature within that form, which both renders the mind and motivates it. Thus he fictionalizes his own struggle in his characters. The encyclopedia is his 'setting' or world, and his characters, like himself, are its victims. But Flaubert also stands outside of the fiction as the stylist, the heroic artist who exercises his act of art and whose energy gives the book life. The character is a mask, but the style is the man. In this sense Flaubert is opposing the creative personality to its environment: within it he is a victim; as the narrator he is the lyrist, or perhaps even would-be epist, a potential Odysseus whose motive is to renew the world.

Joyce's brilliant innovation in *Ulysses* synthesized Flaubert's work and his own; it also added to 'the international store of literary technique'. Pound lauded Joyce's form unreservedly. Instead of writing historical novels and realistic novels or using the static structure of the encyclopedia, Joyce had integrated within his Homeric 'scaffold' the chaotic multiplicity of modern life, an archetypal hero, a compelling plot, and a vertical depth which evokes history and myth: 'Joyce combine le moyen âge, les ères classiques, même l'antiquité juive, dans une action actuelle.' By comparison, Flaubert 'échelonne les époques', and *Bouvard* is inferior in architecture and narrative drive. Within the objective form of the scaffold Joyce could make autobiography, in the persons of Stephen and Bloom, his subject matter. Stephen, who has an historian's mind, is a victim of history, and Bloom, 'a receiver of all things' who has a novelist's, is a victim of his surroundings. Yet in their *monologues intérieurs* they express

the freedom of the mind and the emotions. Their 'tones of mind'
are personal on one side, yet on the other 'realist', for they
correspond to modern realities. These 'tones of mind' provide
the basis for the narrator's overview of his action. For Pound
the vitality of *Ulysses* rose from Joyce's presenting his 'tones of
mind' in a 'many-tongued and multiple language'. As the
controlling mind and synthesizing stylist who imposes on
Ulysses its varied forms and methods, Joyce includes the entire
fiction in his encompassing voice, a version of the epic voice.
Thus his vision of the modern world, and of the modern consciousness in the perspective of history, emerges as a personal
construction which yet derives full validation from its modern
surface, its naturalistic characterization and plot, and its
historical scaffold. Joyce's intellectual vitality and intensity
unite novelist, historian, and lyrist; in so far as the proportion of
balance are perfect, and imply or are suspended in a comprehensive philosophy of life, these three make Joyce a (modern) epic
writer. Joyce succeeds Flaubert as the ultimate Odyssean,
having at last made the figure of himself both the centre and
the encompasser of his fiction.

But although Joyce had freed the idealizing sensibility from
total subjection to the present, Bloom remained a receiver of
all things, Stephen remained detached from the outer world,
and *Ulysses* looked toward the past. For Pound the difference
between the passive hero and an active one was the difference
between prose analysis and poetic synthesis. In the face of the
prose tradition Pound had been trying sporadically since 1912
to define the possibilities and limits of poetry. In 1918, faced
with Henry James's representation of *moeurs contemporaines*,
which remained embedded in period costume and feeling, he
attempted a theoretical definition:

'Most good prose arises, perhaps, from an instinct of negation;
is the detailed, convincing analysis of something detestable;
of something which one wants to eliminate. Poetry is the assertion of a positive, i.e. of desire, and endures for a longer period.
Poetic satire is only an assertion of this positive, inversely, i.e.
as of an opposite hatred. . . . Poetry = Emotional synthesis,

quite as real, quite as realist as any prose (or intellectual) analysis. . . . This is a highly untechnical, unimpressionist, in fact almost theological manner of statement, but is perhaps the root difference between the two arts of literature.'[1]

For Pound the prose tradition had discovered the conditions of modern consciousness; poetry had to accept those conditions but go beyond them. 'Emotional synthesis' required the apperceptivity of an urbane, historically aware sensibility like that of de Gourmont, an 'artist of the nude' or 'permanent human elements' (like Pound's Propertius, or his Acoetes of Canto II). Only out of emotional awareness could a new consciousness (a new ethic and a new city) be built ('We base our "science" on perceptions, but our ethics have not yet attained this palpable basis'). Such a new ethic or 'city' began and ended with the personal: 'Civilization is individual. The truth is the individual.'[2] But any 'assertion of a positive' required volition as well as apperceptivity; poetry demands 'some sort of vigour, some sort of assertion, some sort of courage, or at least of ebullience that throws a certain amount of remembered beauty into an unconquered consciousness'.[3] Joyce's city was a bankrupt paralytic unification of which Joyce remained a 'receiver'; to revitalize urbanity or community the mind would have first to break down inert orders, then rediscover living fragments of thought and feeling from the matter of past and present, and finally reshape these by the creative effort of the poetic mind. By such notions Pound had been working toward a method of giving form to his concept of the heroic artist as a troubadour in the root sense: a 'maker and finder of songs' (the phrase comes from Whitman), whose 'making' would receive objective validation from his 'finding' of his matter and his forms in history and nature.

Pound defined epic from the personal standpoint as 'the speech of a nation through the mouth of one man' (1909), and from the objective standpoint as 'a poem including history'

[1] 'Henry James', *Literary Essays*, p. 324.
[2] 'Remy de Gourmont', *Literary Essays*, pp. 340, 345, 355.
[3] Pound is thinking of d'Annunzio versus Proust, *Dial*, November 1922, p. 554.

(1933). These definitions imply that the 'one man', the lyrist and in Pound's sense the hero himself, must be objectified, that is, identified with the nation or speech or 'world' which he took as his subject. Pound had assumed from the start the classic 'vocational' conception of the epic poet : that he was a synthetic or 'donative' artist who built upon his predecessors and whose work was a continuation of theirs, and that his own career was not merely a personal one, but itself a part of history. One of the things he was doing with Flaubert's and Joyce's careers was to give them a shape, especially Joyce's. Thus he saw Joyce as a figure who had worked through the lyric mode of *Chamber Music* to the novelistic mode of *Dubliners*; had then integrated the novelistic and lyric modes in *A Portrait*; had experimented with the objectivity of drama in *Exiles*; and had concluded this development in the epic synthesis of *Ulysses*. He also found parallels between *Dubliners* and *Trois Contes*, *A Portrait* and *L'Éducation*, *Ulysses* and *Bouvard*. In short, not only did Joyce epitomize in his work the modern artist's formation of an objective literary tradition, but his personal career was itself a pattern validated both by tradition and by a struggle which had turned that career into a classic monument.

Pound had been schematizing his own career during the fallow years 1920–1921 while he was reassessing his American and London past to seek a new direction (such reassessment is a personal version of the *nostos*).[1] In 'Main outline of E. P.'s work to date' (*Umbra*, 1920) he reflected the historical, novelistic, and personal strains. The 'Personae' of 1908–1911, his early dramatic lyrics, were objective expressions of past emotions in forms adapted from Browning, Yeats, and the 1890s. The 'Sketches' of *Ripostes* and *Lustra* had thrown the emphasis toward *moeurs contemporaines*, using the avant garde techniques Pound had denominated as imagism. The three

[1] It should also be noted that Pound had written in 1917–18 'Studies in Contemporary Mentality' (*New Age*), a survey of British magazines which he called in 'Date Line' his Flaubertian *sottisier*. All of Pound's prose collections are intended to 'have a design', and in that sense are efforts to give form to his public career as his poetry gives form to his poetic career.

'Major Personae'— 'The Seafarer', 'The Exile's Letter (and *Cathay* in general)', and *Homage to Sextus Propertius*—were efforts to define figures who would objectify, and place in a better or larger tradition than either the British or American traditions then available to a poet writing in English, his personal motives. *Propertius* (1918) was Pound's first successful large form to integrate the motives of lyrist, novelist, and historian. Previously he had written many 'series', all of which he subsequently broke down into single poems because they failed to achieve any unity except the unity of the single personality behind them (e.g., a collection of early personae intended as 'a more or less proportional presentation of life'; 'Und Drang' (*Canzoni*, 1911); and 'groups' of poems in *Lustra*). He had tried historical juxtaposition of the amatory customs of two cultures in *Homage à la Langue d'Oc*, a sequence of of Provençal adaptations Gourmontian in their expression of emotion, and *Moeurs Contemporaines*, Jamesian sketches of London (1917).

In *Propertius* Pound used the 'major persona' to give full expression to the state of civilization in London. *Propertius* is, however, the poem of a poet who, although opposing the prevailing civilization, speaks from within it. Even as he concluded *Propertius* his motive was expanding, leading him away from London toward a search for the new, as *Mauberley* and Canto VII make evident. In *Mauberley*, which he called (misleadingly) a version of *Propertius* with a modernist surface, he tried to summarize his life in London by placing it against the background of both the prose tradition (it 'condenses a James novel') and the epic tradition (including, one should not forget, Whitman). Mauberley, a figure like Frederick Moreau or Stephen Dedalus, reflects the modern artist in historical and Odyssean perspectives. Just as Joyce had multiplied himself in Stephen, Bloom, and the voice of his narrator to enlarge his form and thereby encompass a more complex reality, Pound divided the objectified passive figure Mauberley, artist-hero manqé, from the active narrator whose voice dominates the poem. But although *Mauberley* seeks to use an objectified

137

figure, at least nominally, it is still a 'study in form'; Pound is exploring the relation between the traditions of poetry and prose rather than having successfully fused them. Actually *Mauberley*, like Canto VII, records 'the break'—in all aspects of culture and in his own life—of which Pound became aware following World War I.

In *Poems 1918–21* Pound tried to suggest an even larger summary of his work, in Flaubertian fashion, by juxtaposing *Propertius*, *Langue d'Oc / Moeurs Contemporaines*, and *Mauberley* as *Three Portraits* of, respectively, Rome, Provence-London, and London. As in *Trois Contes* these historical tableaux all revolved around a theme line—for Pound's triptych, Propertius's 'My genius is no more than a girl'; in the sense that the portraits also constitute representations of London, he also seems to have been seeking on a larger scale than in *Propertius* alone the kind of vertical historical depth which Joyce was achieving in *Ulysses*. All of these reassessments and reorderings, however, reflect the misgivings about epic form Pound had expressed when he asked if he should 'sulk and leave the word to novelists?' His exasperation about the state of western civilization and his efforts to extend his conception of history to social, economic, and political dimensions were having effects on his poetry: partly growing pains, but partly also personal discouragement. He frequently (most often to Joyce) deplored the *passéism* of his subjects and forms; he repeated this misgiving in 1922 in congratulating Eliot on *The Waste Land*. As already noted, from 1919 to 1922 he was at an impasse about the increasing formlessness and obscurity of his poem. It is against this background that we should see his reactions to Flaubert and Joyce in 1922 and his reorganizing of his poem sometime in 1923.

In his 1909 letter to his mother Pound wrote that an epic writer needed 'a beautiful tradition', 'a unity in the outline of that tradition', 'a hero, mythical or historical', and the equivalent of divine machinery. He had begun his poem without either the outline or the hero, seeking to follow the method Dante had used to escape from such epic requirements ('he dips into a multitude of traditions and unifies them by their connec-

tion with himself'). Joyce's crucial innovation, his Homeric
scaffold, gave the prose and epic traditions the unity of outline
Pound is seeking in Canto VII and finds in his 1922 essays.
Pound's first canto represents, as well as the tragedy of 'Europe
exhausted by the conquest of Alsace-Lorraine', which can be
called the theme of Cantos I–XVI, a tiered historical depth in its
conflation of Homer, the Anglo-Saxon 'The Seafarer', and
Divus's Renaissance Latin version of the Odyssey, in the language and voice of the 20th century American. But more important it throws his poem forward with a compelling fiction : a
story of action, an archetypal hero, and the idea of the *nostos*.
By starting with the voyage to the land of the dead Pound made
the *nostos* symbolize a theory of history. It is the archetype for
'the break' and for his motive of exploring the past in order
to find the basis for a return journey which will itself be the
process of building a new civilization; according to the Homeric
parallel the *nostos* would be completed when the poet, in the
wake of Odysseus, became united again with Penelope (the
archetypal woman, for Pound a symbol of beauty) : their
union would symbolize a reconstituted Ithaca (the city of the
imagination, Pound's 'city of Dioce'). The *nostos* is also a figure
for a journey of the mind; as Pound wrote to Williams in 1908,
'the soul, from god, returns to him. But anyone who can trace
that course or symbolize it by anything not wandering. . . .' In
this visionary or Neoplatonic sense the *nostos* is the search for
what Pound called a 'philosophy', a metaphysic which would
validate an ethic, a morality, and a politics. Both the fiction
and the philosophy are based, however, on personal experience.
In the 'periplum', or voyage on which experience is encountered
directly, the hero sees many cities and manners of men and
knows their minds. He also enters the world of myth and
encounters divinities. Both kinds of encounter also become the
occasion for personal insights, the aesthetic perceptions ('gods,'
or states of mind) which form the basis of Pound's visions of a
permanent world of truth.

Pound modifies Joyce's use of the Odyssey by making his
scaffold merely imply form rather than impose a fixed progres-

sion. For, Pound's form had to be open: he was seeking to build up the new from the very bottom out of modern experience (Pound's method should be carefully differentiated from the 'mythical method' as Eliot defined it from Joyce and used it: 'manipulating a continuous parallel between contemporaneity and antiquity').[1] Thus whereas Joyce's scaffold adheres closely to Homer, Pound's is a universal archetype of epic form, an overarching ideal structure which the modern poet must in one sense fill and in another sense make new. Pound was careful even in designating the scaffold of *Ulysses* 'un moyen de régler la forme' to emphasize the stylist's conception and the work he built up within it:

'These correspondences are part of Joyce's mediaevalism and are chiefly his own affair, a scaffold, a means of construction, justified by the result, and justifiable by it only. The result is a triumph in form, in balance, a main schema, with continuous inweaving and arabesque.'[2]

In the most limited sense Pound's personae had been scaffolds, but they represented only isolated moments; the shaky division between mask and poet in *Mauberley* is symptomatic of Pound's need to separate the poet from the mask so that he can enlarge his scope. In the broadest sense the scaffold is the entire literary tradition, and in that sense a pattern of the human mind itself (one can see in the rejected early versions of Pound's poem the failure of an effort to use 'the tradition' or 'the mind of Europe' —and America—merely as an ideal concept hazily defined by the external, arbitrary scaffold of the Dantean or Whitmanian canto). The scaffold as Pound finally conceived and used it can be thought of as a potential 'overplot', while the direct experience can be thought of as welling up from a kind of 'underplot'. These two meet on the surface of *The Cantos* in the activity of the poet; the motive of *The Cantos* is toward their perfect integration.

Formally speaking, the point of Canto I is its momentary synthesis of epic form and the poet's own modern experience.

[1] ' "Ulysses," Order, and Myth', *Dial*, November 1923.
[2] 'Paris Letter', *Literary Essays*, p. 406.

Canto II, denying the Browning method of using history directly, without myth, introduces Pound's basic mode of sensibility, the 'magic moment' of insight into a permanent world constituted of the human figure, the elements, and the state of mind as a 'god'; his humanistic version of Christianity's revelation, conception, and incarnation. After these *trouvailles* (which imply the whole poem as do the exordium and invocation of the classical epic, though as 'prophecies'), Canto III returns to the present to express, as still part of the fiction, the failure of old Cantos I–III because of a lack of a scaffold: in doing so Canto III presents Pound's own meditations on a failed voyage, a failed 'magic moment', and a failed *nostos;* it ends in mere desolation. Cantos IV–VII, still rehearse as intermittent vision Pound's struggle of 1915–19 to accommodate the muse of epic, Calliope, who is providing the forms which arise in the modern poet's mind, and Truth, the muse of fact, who supplies unformed historical data, whether they be fragments from the past previously unformed or the modern poet's own life. The conflict, which emerges explicitly in the exordium to the Malatesta Cantos (VIII–XI), is resolved in those cantos as the modern poet speaks in many voices—narrator, chronicler of the times, retrospective historian, and Sigismundo's compatriot, among others—to bring Sigismundo's ethos to life in an epic frame. Thus, whereas the 'ply over ply' of 'tiered' history in Canto I was a poetic *trouvaille*, here the poet builds it up methodically out of unformed matter.[1] With the assurance gained the poet 'sees' modern 'facts' within the Homeric frame (Canto XII).[2]

[1] Myles Slatin (op. cit.) hypothesizes that Pound discovered his form and motive from his work on the Malatesta Cantos, spontaneously, as in an action painting. This is the side of the 'underplot', or 'fact'. But Pound had to have a coherent theory of history and literary history, defined as a potential 'overplot', as well as confidence in the spontaneous creative act.

[2] Canto XIII, Confucius, is a new 'potential' element, 'seen' because the poet can sustain vision; it does not become actuated until later in the poem. Canto XIII is Pound's version of Whitman's 'Passage to India'; it extends the scope of *The Cantos* toward its true epic subject, the idea and vision of 'one world' that had begun to emerge as a fact in 1914. Pound has tried to 'forge in the smithy of his soul the uncreated conscience of one world'.

Able now both to *enter* past forms and to *use* them, he sustains in Cantos XIV–XVI a neo-Dantean dream narrative during which he encounters the modern 'dead' as infernal states of mind, as anecdotes about the war, and as radio voices, all of which signify the fading away of western civilization as a viable culture. It is with Canto XVII, which picks up the interrupted 'So that' from the end of Canto I (he is now *with* the dead, all history now being one), that the Odyssean scaffold is fully actuated. Canto XVII introduces a coherent fictional venture, by the modern poet in his own person, into original myth, a mystical-artistic state of mind; though fleeting, it is a testimony that the effort to give form to experience is on the right track.

Within the Odyssean frame, then, Pound's overriding narrative voice, which often comes to the surface as the modern poet speaks in his own person, expresses the process of the mind as it moves through all eras seeking materials and capturing them in the myriad forms the mind uses to reify and communicate its discoveries. These forms are appropriated by a narrator who, as Pound had been in London, is city-saturated, historically and contemporaneously. The potential form of the archetypal scaffold and an encyclopædic principle which might be called 'the unlimitedness of forms' (Pound's polytheistic states of mind), make it theoretically possible to include any kind of experience. Like Flaubert and Joyce, Pound draws on all the arts (e.g., literature, history, journalism, philology, economics, theology, physics, music, politics) and all the techniques (e.g., narrative, monologue, anecdote, litany), thus solving Bouvard and Pécuchet's and even Bloom's 'Défaut de methode dans les sciences'. He assumes that the permanent forms of nature and the permanent forms of the human mind, which are reflected in whatever men have made (or will make), undergo perpetual metamorphosis (changes of phase, emergence and recession, perfection and decay, etc.); to renew these forms, to create new syntheses out of permanent materials, and even to invent, expresses not simple recurrences of cycles, but continuous creative renovation. The energizing principle of Pound's poem is not Flaubert's objective narrative voice nor the voice of

Joyce's unseen stylist. Rather the spoken voice of urbane conversation tries to reflect at once the creative process of aesthetic perception, free will, and intellectual shaping; the objective nature of its materials; and the moment in which conversation creates an audience whose view of reality is subject to change like the speaker's. The past, the past as it is brought to life in the present, and the present itself, as mental and emotional experience, are being discovered, absorbed, interpreted, and applied to create the future.

To what extent Pound's *Cantos* is wholly successful is still unclear It may not be possible for one man, however intelligent, perceptive, and purposeful (and many of Pound's ideas are certainly questionable), to induce from the fragments of civilization a new literary and cultural synthesis. There is no question, however, that he composed and reshaped *A Draft of XVI Cantos* with great care, not only introducing the Odyssey scaffold but interpolating elsewhere direct and indirect indications of its primacy. When we learn to read the *Cantos* more thoroughly in the light of traditional epic conventions; to assess exactly the carefully modulated relation of the contemporary speaker to his facts and forms; to interpret indicated connections between cantos; and to see modern poetic techniques in their proper perspective: then, I think, we shall see that Pound has achieved within his scaffold a more distinct progression—line by line, passage by passage, canto by canto—than has been so far discovered. But whatever the final judgment, it is precisely the effort 'to build the city of Dioce, whose terraces are the colour of stars', which makes Pound, like Joyce, one of the great witnesses to the artist's effort to encompass the 20th century. Though Pound's Europe, his structure of ideas, and perhaps his poem seemed to collapse, the dream remained 'in the heart indestructible', for, in the Pisan stockade, the voice continued. There is no mistaking that at Pisa a meeting takes place between the Odyssean poet and some goddess, confirming our feeling that a dispersed personality has reconstituted itself out of bits of its past, out of the wreckage of Europe, out of his Pisan surroundings, and out of earned permanent truths. If

Bouvard et Pécuchet is a monument to the Second Empire and *Ulysses* a monument to Europe on the verge of World War I, *The Cantos* may be a monument to the tragic failure of many visions held between the two wars. Joyce and Pound are both Flaubert's successors in an Odyssean tradition. Even more directly than Flaubert, attempting to resolve the post-romantic division between history and the self, they used their own lives as their subject matter and tried to make personality and history the two bases from which the present might pass into the future, giving new life to the achievements which make civilization a great expression of man.

Persephone's Ezra

———————————⬧———————————

I

The Flowered Tree as Koré

Of the twenty-three poems in Ezra Pound's first book of verse, the unpublished *Hilda's Book* now in Houghton Library at Harvard, written between 1905 and 1907 for Hilda Doolittle in whose possession it was during most of her lifetime, only 'Donzella Beata', 'Li Bel Chasteus', and 'The Tree' were salvaged for *A Lume Spento* in 1908. 'Donzella Beata' prefers a live girl to a Blessèd Damozel waiting in heaven, and 'Li Bel Chasteus' depicts Tristram and Iseult high above the common world in their rock haven. 'The Tree', however, begins a theme that has remained in Pound's poetry for sixty years. It is the first poem of the *Personae* canon, and is echoed as late as Canto CX ('Laurel bark sheathing the fugitive'). It is a poem under the spell of Yeats, kin to 'The Song of Wandering Aengus' and other evocations of an enchanted wood. The Pre-Raphaelite Yeats is everywhere in *Hilda's Book*.

> Autumn is over the long leaves that love us,
> And over the mice in the barley sheaves;
> Yellow the leaves of the rowan above us,
> And yellow the wet wild-strawberry leaves

begins Yeats's 'The Falling of the Leaves' (*Crossways*, 1889). The first poem of *Hilda's Book* opens with a hint of Whitman but proceeds as if by Yeats:

Child of the grass
The years pass Above us
Shadows of air All these shall love us
Winds for our fellows
The browns and the yellows
Of autumn our colors

But Celtic twilight and Yeatsian diction are but part of the
strange beauty of 'The Tree'. That a tree can be a persona at all
is startling. Joyce, years later, will have a tree speak in his poem
'Tilly' (*Pomes Penyeach*, 1927). Pound's poem trembles
between the imitative and a strong originality. It is as precious
as the early Yeats while having the masculine boldness of
William Morris. It is both Ovidian and Thoreauvian. It is
seed-rich in matters that will occupy Pound for years: the
theme of metamorphosis and the mimetic act of assuming a
mask and insisting on the most strenuous empathy. Daphne
and the figures of Baucis and Philemon will appear throughout
The Cantos. The most fructive theme, however, is that of
chthonic nature as a mystery, the Eleusinian theme. To understand 'many a new thing. . . . That was rank folly to my head
before' is to find a mode of perception other than one's own.
Omniformis omnis intellectus est, Psellus says in *The Cantos*,
quoting Porphyry. But why begin with the nymph's supernatural,
intranatural sense of things? The question is a large one, for
trees are everywhere in Pound's poetry, and become symbols of
extraordinary power and beauty in *Rock-Drill*, *Thrones*, and
the cantos now in draft form for the poem's conclusion.

Hilda's Book is green with trees, poem after poem. '*Dulce
myrtii floribus*', we read; 'sweeter than all orchards breath';
'She swayeth as a poplar tree'; 'the moss-grown kindly trees';
'some treeborn spirit of the wood / About her'. *A Lume Spento*
was originally titled *La Fraisne*, the ash tree; and the poem of
that name is a variant of 'The Tree', as is 'A Girl' in *Ripostes*.

In 1960 Pound chose for the translator Alfredo Rizzardi a
selection of his poems to be published in Arnoldo Mondadori's
Poeti dello Specchio series. From the twenty-three poems of

Ripostes as that book is preserved in the *Personae* canon, he chose 'N.Y.,' that charmingly ironic-romantic poem in which he persists in having the New York of 'a million people surly with traffic' appear as a girl praised by Solomon, 'a maid with no breasts, / . . . slender as a silver reed'; 'A Girl' ('The tree has entered my hands'); 'The Cloak', a poem about the claims of love and death and a paraphrase of Sappho's poem reminding a girl who refused her gift of roses that death is long and loveless (Fragment 55, Lobel and Page); *Δώρια*, another poem of love and death ('The shadowy flowers of Orcus / Remember thee.'); and 'Apparuit', a ghostly and splendid evocation of Persephone, in sapphics and with the touch of Sappho more finely upon it than any translation yet of Sappho into English. A glance at *Ripostes*—a book dedicated to William Carlos Williams, with the Propertian tag *Quos ego Persephonae maxima dona feram*, to which Williams replied in his *Kora in Hell* (1920)—will show that Pound selected for his Italian translator only those poems that contained the theme of Persephone as the sign of youth radiant before its doom or as the indwelling spirit of springtime. Conversely, Pound chose from the early *Personae* volumes (1908–1910) only those poems that are about Aidonian Persephone whose beauty is destructive, Helen and Iseult, the figure that will become Circe in *The Cantos*.

Pound was not without clues as to how to move from the neurasthenic dark of the nineteenth century Circe-world and its Hell-like *cul de sac*; he has acknowledged his debt to Whitman and Whistler. He had the end of the thread when he wrote 'The Tree'. But he preferred to go back to the very beginning of literature, to see its growth from sensibility to sensibility, and to arrive, if possible, with its masters who knew the art best. We find him instinctively turning toward robustness and clarity. There are many ways of studying Pound's evolution; his own criticism will probably remain the surest record. But everywhere we turn in his poetry there is the clear emergence of Persephone and her springtime as a persistent image and symbol. The first great search concentrated on the springtime of styles and cultures; with what sureness does he introduce the archaic Minoan undulations and Cretan basketwork braids into the Edwardian fog of *Mauberley*! (and he was working, except for the *Illustrated London News* and Sir Arthur Evans' *Mycenaean Tree and Pillar Cult* of 1901, well ahead of the world's knowledge of Knossan art; *Mauberley* was published a year before Evans' *The Palace of Minos*).

As if Persephone were his guide toward the light he sought, as if she, the power of renewal, had chosen him and not he her (as in the conceit in Canto LXXVI where we have 'Dafne's Sandro', the fleet laurel nymph choosing Botticelli as her painter rather than the other way round), his eye went to the master poets whose manner is limpid, sharp, clear and simple: Homer, Ovid, Dante, and Chaucer. So carefully did he study each that one can plausibly trace Pound's style wholly to Homer, or wholly to Dante, as it would seem; what we would be looking at is the unbroken tradition of the Homeric phrase in western literature, clear equally of metric, sound, image, and thought. We would also be looking at a special propensity to find conjunctions of trees and radiant girls, reminiscent of the Cretan and Mycenaean assimilation of pillar and tree as the goddess' sign. It is an atmosphere that can best be described as Botticellian or Ovidian. In Arnaut Daniel,

> Ges rams floritz
> De floretas envoutas
> Cui fan tremblar auzelhon ab lurs becs
> Non es plus frescs,

in Cavalcanti,

> Avete in voi li fiori, e la verdura,

in Dante,

> Tu mi fai rimembrar dove a qual era
> > Proserpina nel tempo che perdette
> > la madre lei, ed ella primavera,

in Li Po

> While my hair was still cut straight across my forehead
> I played about the front gate, pulling flowers,

he found a mode of poetry that moved him with a force that is easier to illustrate than to attempt a theory versatile enough to encompass all its dimensions. In 'The Alchemist' he brings such illustrious women as Odysseus saw at Persephone's request in Hades in conjunction with American trees, 'under the larches of Paradise / . . . the red gold of the maple, / . . . the light of the birch tree in autumn . . .'. The heart of the poem is a prayer to Persephone ('Queen of Cypress') in her other kingdom, the world under earth or ocean :

> From the power of grass,
> From the white, alive in the seed,
> From the heat of the bud,
> From the copper of the leaf in autumn,
> From the bronze of the maple, from the sap in the bough;
> Lianor, Ioanna, Loica,
> By the stir of the fin,
> By the trout asleep in the gray-green of water;
> Vanna, Mandetta, Viera, Alodetta, Picarda, Manuela
> From the red gleam of copper,
> Ysaut, Ydone, slight rustling of leaves,
> Vierna, Jocelynn, daring of spirits,
> By the mirror of burnished copper,
>   O Queen of Cypress,
> Out of Erebus, the flat-lying breath,
> Breath that is stretched out beneath the world :
> Out of Erebus, out of the flat waste of air,
>   lying beneath the world;
> Out of the brown leaf-brown colourless
>   Bring the imperceptible cool.

Apart from the satires and the studies of the forces counter to Persephone, such as the Hell cantos, which are about the abuses of nature, and the great 'Sestina : Altaforte', in which Bertran de Born welcomes Easter as good weather for a military campaign, there is little in Pound that is far away from Persephone and her trees.

It is curious that Michael Ventris was born when Pound was drafting the first canto. A man with *The Cantos* in his head sees this correlation of *periploi*—Odyssean voyages—as being within the *numen* that Pound, more than any man of our time unless it be Picasso and his Ovidian eyes, has recovered and charged with meaning. Canto I, set in Persephone's kingdom which is not the dead past but the communicable spirit of being, metamorphosed from the temporal to the eternal, is Homer's most archaic matter, his deepest plumbing of 'rite and foretime' (in David Jones' resonant phrase). It is the hero's necessary recognition of his life's roots in the powers that sustain him.

> Poured ointment, cried to the gods,
> To Pluto the strong, and praised Proserpine

These words contain strata, like a geological cross-section, or, to take an even more pertinent image, like the rings of growth in a tree, for they are Homer's words (first discernible date: the beginning of Mediterranean literature), Andreas Divus' words,

> Excoriantes comburere: supplicare autem Diis,
> Fortique Plutoni, et laudatae Proserpinae,

(second date: the Renaissance), cast in the Anglo-Saxon rhythms of *The Seafarer* (third date: the Renaissance of 1910, the linguistic renovations of which are still not understood, but which grow out of Morris' and Doughty's new sense of the genius of English), and they are words written with the intuition that their chthonic matter would continue to speak, as Ventris, Chadwick and Palmer found Persephone and Demeter in the Linear B tablets; Frobenius, 'the car of Persephone in a German barrow' (*Kulchur*, 244).

Persephone weathered the decline of antiquity, and survived the Middle Ages to emerge in the Renaissance. Ovid and Vergil had kept her in Italian tradition. Chaucer brought her to the north, 'Proserpyne, / That quene ys of the derke pyne.' Arthur Golding's Ovid of 1567 (when Ovid still, as for Chaucer,

150

meant the *Metamorphoses*) renders her myth with particular beauty; she is made accessible to the age as far more than a bit of classical iconography around which to shore up emblematic patterns (as in Francesco Colonna's *Hypnerotomachia* of 1499). Ovid's plastic terseness becomes an English narrative voice of lively extravagance:

By chaunce she let her lap slip downe, and out the flowres went.
And such a sillie simplenesse her childish age yet beares,
That even the very losse of them did move hir more to tears.

Milton's typological mind began the impressive baroque flourish that foreshadows Eve's temptation with an evocation of Persephone:

> Not that faire field
> Of *Enna,* where *Proserpin* gathring flours
> Her self a fairer Floure by gloomie *Dis*
> Was gatherd

And Shakespeare, enchanted by flowers, gave Perdita the speech that outdoes Poliziano in the imitation of Ovid's floral imagery:

> *O Proserpina,*
> For the Flowres now, that (frighted) thou let'st fall
> From *Dysses* Waggon: Daffadils,
> That come before the Swallow dares, and take
> The windes of March with beauty: Violets (dim,
> But sweeter then the lids of *Juno's* eyes

Thereafter she is everywhere, as firmly within English poetry as Latin or Greek. But as the Renaissance fades, she disappears from poetry. Neither the eighteenth century nor the early nineteenth thinks it sees anything in her myth, except to reflect the subterranean existence of her *Paradis artificiel* in such figures as La Motte Fouqué's *Undine* or Poe's *Ligeia.* Then all at once she is again in the open air, whether awakened by Sir James Frazer's *Golden Bough* or the new, charismatic interest in natural beauty that begins with scientific eyes (Humboldt, Agassiz, Darwin, Hugh Miller, Gosse) and is rapidly taken up by poetic ones (Thoreau, W. H. Hudson, Ruskin), or because of the new and pervasive interest in myth generated by archaeology, new texts and folklore.

Like Sappho and Chaucer, Ruskin wrote about girls as if they were flowers, about flowers as if they were girls (so that his botanical treatise called *Proserpina* has more of an archaic Greek flavour than any of the period's translations), and Lewis Carroll's Alice is a kind of Persephone. There is Tennyson's sombre, Vergilian 'Demeter and Persephone', Swinburne's 'The Garden of Proserpine' and 'Hymn to Proserpine'. The young Pound grew up in an ambience congenial to myth; the power it had over the minds of his generation can be seen in Frederic Manning's 'Koré', to which Pound wrote a reply that T. S. Eliot kept in the Faber *Selected Poems* but which Pound cancelled in the *Personae* canon.

Persephone enters Pound's poetry early and remains, and she is always there in an Ovidian sense, embodied in a girl or flower or tree, so that his most famous *haiku* is like a face Odysseus sees in Hades, reminding him of the springtime above in an image combining tree and girl : *petals on a wet, black bough.* In 'Heather'

> The milk-white girls
> Unbend from the holly-trees

'O Nathat-Ikanaie, "Tree-at-the-river," ' we read in 'Dance Figure', and in 'The Spring' (that subtle mistranslation of Ibykos), 'Cydonian Spring with her attendant train, / Maelids and water-girls . . .'. Her most poignant epiphany is as a ghost, Persephone bound in hell awaiting the spring.

> Les yeux d'une morte
> M'ont salué,

begins 'Dans un Omnibus de Londres', where the *frisson* depends on our recognizing Persephone by her Ovidian swans, which Pound has given Plutonian colours (Neare *Enna* walls

[as Golding puts it] there stands a lake *Pergusa* is the name. /
Cayster heareth not mo songs of Swannes than doth the same.) :

> Je vis les cygnes noirs,
> Japonais,
> Leurs ailes
> Teintées de couleur sang-de-dragon,
> Et toutes les fleurs
> D'Armenonville.
>
> Les yeux d'une morte
> M'ont salué.

These are the eyes of Jacopo's Venus in 'The Picture' and its
pendant, 'Of Jacopo del Sellaio,' that belonged to a model long
dead and are now pure vision,

> The eyes of this dead lady speak to me.

They are the eyes at the end of *Mauberley*, that do not know
they are dead. They are the ghostly eyes of the *Pisan Cantos*,
where they stand in relation to a continuum of images that
reaches back to the

> Souls out of Erebus, cadaverous dead, of brides
> Of youths and of the old who had borne much :
> Souls stained with recent tears, girls tender

of Canto I, the murdered bride Inez de Castro of Canto III,
the Ione and 'Eyes floating in dry, dark air' of Canto VII.
These eyes in Hades are one of the concomitants of Persephone's theme. Another is the alignment of girl and tree, as in

> And Sulpicia
> green shoot now, and the wood
> white under new cortex
> [Canto XXV]

or the appearance of Nausicaa, a type of Persephone, in a canto about women whose souls are chaotic, establishing a contrast between neurosis and health, confusion and clarity :

> Beauty on an ass-cart
> Sitting on five sacks of laundry
> That wd. have been the road by Perugia
> That leads out to San Piero. Eyes brown topaz,
> Brookwater over brown sand,
> The white hounds on the slope,
> Glide of water, lights and the prore,
> Silver beaks out of night,
> Stone, bough over bough,
>   lamps fluid in water,
> Pine by the black trunk of its shadow
> And on hill black trunks of the shadow
> The trees melted in air.
>
> > [Canto XXIX]

This theme prepares itself in the first thirty cantos, recurs less frequently but rhythmically through the American and Chinese cantos (XXXVI: woman radiant, a *ric pensamen* to the mind, *inluminatio coitu* to the heart; XXXIX: Circe, the richly dark, chthonic nature of woman—the two cantos form a diptych, and are brought together in XLVII, which is about the harmonizing of intelligence and the fixed order of nature : 'First must thou go the road / to hell / And to the bower of Ceres' daughter Proserpine'), and becomes in the *Rock-Drill* and *Thrones* sections a synergetic presence.

Beyond the poem's beginning in her underworld, Persephone is apt to be just off-stage, or invisibly contained. She is the spirit of natural metamorphosis; in the first thirty cantos her absence is as significant as her presence. In Canto XXI she, Pallas, and Pan, Titania and Phaetusa, Aetna's nymph at the entrance to the under-realm, are set in contrast to Midas, Plutus, and gold : the power to grow toward renewal, to think, to reproduce—against greed and ungrowing matter. At the end of XXI her rape is staged like Icarus' fall in Brueghel's painting, unnoticed, its implications unsuspected :

Dis caught her up.
And the old man went on there
beating his mule with an asphodel.

The loss of form through aimlessness, through moral slither,
through the continued use of form without content, or by
influences hostile to the organic nature of a form is a metamorphosis that is seedless, a stasis.

Life to make mock of motion :
For the husks, before me, move
[Canto VII]

One can follow throughout *The Cantos* the force that reclaims
lost form, lost spirit, Persephone's transformation back to
virginity. As Homer shows us a chastened and chaste Helen in
the Odyssey, so the first thirty cantos end with the moral
regeneration of Lucrezia Borgia, that archetype of the Circe-
world of the late nineteenth century from which every major
artist of the time had to extricate himself in order to discover
the moral nature of reality. She appears with the drunken
gaiety of Botticelli's Primavera, Dea Flora, and the Graces,
'foot like a flowery branch', 'Madame "ΥΛΗ"', a woman obedient
to all of nature's appetites, but with the balance and rhythm of
nature's seed-cycle regeneration.

Through the *Pisan Cantos* Persephone is the promise of
rebirth from the dark, an Ariadne in the labyrinth. 'When night
is spent,' ends the Pisan group, in which Persephone was prayed
to throughout. Pisa parallels the Homeric episode of Odysseus
captured by the Cyclops (of whom the brute violence of war is
an example), and the evocations of Persephone are under the
sign of Δημήτηρ δακρύων, nature impotent and dying.

with a smoky torch thru the unending
labyrinth of the souterrain
or remembering Carleton let him celebrate Christ in the grain
and if the corn cat be eaten
Demeter has lain in my furrow
[Canto LXXX]

But faith in all that Persephone has meant in the poem is unwavering.

> Elysium, though it were in the halls of hell,
> What thou lovest well is thy true heritage
> What thou lovest well shall not be reft from thee
>   [Canto LXXXI]

In watching a baby wasp, born in a nest in the corner of Pound's tent at Pisa, the poet brings the theme to one of its most resonant statements :

> When the mind swings by a grass-blade
>   an ant's forefoot shall save you
> the clover leaf smells and tastes as its flower
>
>
>   The infant has descended,
>   from mud on the tent roof to Tellus,
> like to like colour he goes amid grass-blades
>   greeting them that dwell under XTHONOS *ΧΘΟΝΟΣ*
> *ΟΙ ΧΘΟΝΙΟΙ*, to carry our news
>   *εἰς χθονίους* to them that dwell under the earth,
> begotten of air, that shall sing in the bower
>   of Kore,   *Περσεφόνεια*
> and have speech with Tiresias, Thebae
>   [Canto LXXXIII]

'Man, earth,' says Canto LXXXII, 'two halves of the tally.' Man is under Fortuna, the Pisan cantos say repeatedly, and the DTC at Pisa is 'a magna NOX animae' (Canto LXXIV), a very dark night of the soul, a hell out of which some spiritual recovery like the earth's from winter must happen.

The placing of events in time is a romantic act; the *tremendum* is in the distance. There are no dates in the myths; from when to when did Heracles stride the earth? In a century obsessed with time, with archaeological dating, with the psychological recovery of time (Proust, Freud), Pound has written as if time were unreal, has, in fact, treated it as if it were space. William Blake preceded him here, insisting on the irreality of clock time, sensing the dislocations caused by time (a God remote in time easily became remote in space, an absentee landlord) and proceeding, in his enthusiastic way, to dine with Isaiah—one way of suggesting that Isaiah's mind is not a phenomenon fixed between 742 and 687 B.C. Pound's mind has to be seen for the extraordinary shape it has given itself. To say that *The Cantos* is 'a voyage in time' is to be blind to the poem altogether. We miss immediately the achievement upon which the success of the poem depends, its rendering time transparent and negligible, its dismissing the supposed corridors and perspectives *down* which the historian invites us to look. Pound cancelled in his own mind the dissociations that had been isolating fact from fact for four centuries. To have closed the gap between mythology and botany is but one movement of the process; one way to read the cantos is to go through noting the restorations of relationships now thought to be discrete—the ideogrammatic method was invented for just this purpose. In Pound's spatial sense of time the past is here, now; its invisibility is our blindness, not its absence. The nineteenth century had put everything against the scale of time and discovered that all behaviour within time's monolinear progress was evolutionary. The past was a graveyard, a museum. It was Pound's determination to obliterate such a configuration of time and history, to treat what had become a world of ghosts as a world eternally present.

Whatever the passions and predilections that we detect in *The Cantos*, they are dispositions of mind that Pound is reflecting, not programmes he is advocating, not even matters on which he has passed judgment. The botanist may have a preference for conifers but he does not therefore omit mushrooms from his textbook. Pound's understanding of the world is always directed toward making us share the understanding he has found in other minds; we hear St Ambrose and John Adams condemn usury, not Pound; Confucius speaks for rectitude and probity; a good thousand voices speak. It was Pound's skill, the duty he assumed, to keep us from imagining that we are listening to ghosts, or that we are hearing dimly over vast time, or that the voices are meaningless.

Persephone, as a word, was, in the historical account of things, current among certain Greeks, Cretans, Sicilians, and Romans between such-and-such a year and such-and-such a year. Ethnology can also tell us that she is also known as Koré (The Girl), Flora, Persephatta, Persephoneia, and Proserpina. Any actual modern reference to her, in, say, the Greek hills, is a quaint bit of folklore, like the Cretans' still placing in the corpse's hand some token for Charon. The springtime, however, is eternal, though man's emotional response to it depends upon his sensibilities and education. And everything we call civilization depends upon that response. Man is aware of or blind to the order in which he lives by keeping or losing the tone of that response. From the beginning Pound was intuitively drawn to speaking of women and trees as if the one transparently showed something of the beauty of the other. From poem to poem this image grew; it is possible to point to where this or that detail was added in the enrichment, until coming across a late passage such as

> The purifications
> are snow, rain, artemisia,
> also dew, oak, and the juniper

> And in thy mind beauty, O Artemis,
> as of mountain lakes in the dawn.
> Foam and silk are thy fingers,
> Kuanon,
> and the long suavity of her moving,
> willow and olive reflected
> [Canto CX]

we find the ideogram to be a focus for meanings (the purpose of the ideogram in the first place) rather than a surface from which the eye uneducated by all that has come before it in the poem can discern anything beyond the beauty of the words.

For these words are not primarily lyric; nor are they a detail of memory, as they would be in Wordsworth, nor the epiphany of a visionary state, as they would be in Yeats. They are lines from an epic poem, their muse is Calliope, and their concern is with men in action. Calliope is The Muse with the Beautiful Eyes, and her business is to have looked and seen.

> Tell me of that man, Musa, who took the uneasy turn
> At all the crossroads, who came homeward in disaster
> From the plundering of the holy acropolis of Troia;
> Many towns has he seen, known the minds of many men,

begins the Odyssey, a poem about a man who thought trees were as beautiful as girls, girls as beautiful as trees; whose patrimony was an orchard and vineyard, whose peace, given him by Athena, is permanently before him and his children in the signature of the olive tree, who in the darkest trope of his wandering was sent by the witch-master of the lore of flowers and leaves, Circe, to the dwelling of Persephone, whose mystery is the power of eternal regeneration, in order that he find his way home.

In *Thrones* Persephone's tragedy is over: she has returned; her trees are in blossom. The voices that speak of her are easy, colloquial, at peace:

> And was her daughter like that;
> Black as Demeter's gown,
>
> > > > eyes, hair?
> Dis' bride, Queen over Phlegethon,
> > > girls faint as mist about her?
>
> The strength of men is in grain.
> > > > > [Canto CVI]

She is the power of moving from dark to light, from formlessness to form, from Circe, whose inhuman mind is instructive but tangential to the life of man, to Penelope, whose virtues are domestic, an unwavering continuum.

> > this is the grain rite
> > near Enna, at Nyssa:
> > > > Circe, Persephone
> > so different is sea from glen that
> > > > the juniper is her holy bush

159

GUY DAVENPORT

In 1958, after the thirteen Odyssean years in a fastness that had been an arboretum (and has kept its trees) before it became a prison, Ezra Pound, a free man, went first to the sea whose greatest poet he is in our time, and secondly to a particular apple tree in Wyncote, Pennsylvania, in whose boughs he read the lines of Yeats's that moved him to write 'The Tree' that stands foremost in his poems :

> I have been a hazel tree and they hung
> The Pilot Star and the Crooked Plough
> Among my leaves in times out of mind

The stars by which Odysseus navigated!

II

The Tree as Temple Pillar or Demeter

Jardins audacieux dans les airs soutenus,
Temples, marbres, métaux, qu'êtes-vous devenus ?
[André Chénier *Élégie XCVI*]

At the end of Canto XXX, before the laconic notation of Alessandro Borgia's death—for the opening three decades of the poem are essentially a vortex of turbulence and misdirection to which Alessandro's dark squalor makes a fitting signature—we are shown the colophon of a book printed in July of 1503 (Alessandro died the next month of that year). Girolamo Soncino, one of a family of Jewish printers who came to Italy from Nürnberg in the late fifteenth century, and Francesco Griffo da Bologna the type designer (who also cut type for Aldus Manutius, the Venetian printer whose editions of the classics spread the Renaissance beyond the scholars' walls) were brought to Fano by Cesare Borgia to found a press for books in Hebrew, Greek, Latin, and Italian. The text which is 'taken . . . from that of Messire Laurentius / and from a codex once of the Lords Malatesta' is Petrach's *Rime* which Soncino printed for Cesare Borgia in 1503—seventy-eight years before

160

the edition of the Petri at Basel which bibliographies are apt to list as Petrarch's earliest printing.

With characteristic obliquity in the angle of his gaze Pound stations the *Realpolitik* of the Borgias within the humanist tradition that has come down to us as a distinct activity. We can also observe that Pound is placing Cesare's patronage of the arts alongside Malatesta's and the Medicis'. And that Canto XXX is in spirit Machiavellian, from its opening *planh* against Pity to its alignment of Petrarch and the attempts of the Borgias to unify Italy; for *Il Principe*, like Canto XXX, ends with a melancholy hope that depends on both a dream of Petrach's and the firm hand of a Borgia or a Medici: '. . . acciò che, sotto la sua insegna, e questa patria ne sia nobilitata, e sotto li sua auspizii si verifichi quel detto del Petrarca :

> Virtù contro a furore
> Prenderà l'arme; e fia el combatter corto :
> Ché l'antico valore
> Nelli italici cor non è ancor morto.

The lines are from the 'Italia mia' canzone of Petrarch's and the word before the one that begins Machiavelli's quotation is 'pity.' But it is pity by which *virtù* takes up arms against Italy's enemies; it is solicitude for Italy. The theme of Italy as a high culture is more lyrically and directly stated throughout the poem (and Italia serves here as a type of the *patriae* and *urbes* that illustrate the theme of the city as the sacred reservoir of the continuity of civilization, and we should remember that Petrarch's allegorical Italia began her history as the city-goddess Roma).

Between a matrix of stars above and a matrix of stone and water beneath, the earth is given its form. 'Zeus lies in Ceres' bosom' (Canto LXXXI)—light shapes the dark seed into the wheat ear. The profoundest diagram of this process, no less for civilization's rhythm of inevitable decay and conscious renewal than for the green world, is the myth of Persephone. Yet her myth is of the kinesis of growth and germination, of loss and return. Her mother Demeter has been from the beginning the sign of the process's maturity, the harvest. Persephone is the living tree; Demeter is the tree carved, shaped, painted, capitalled with acanthus, translated into marble, even turned upside down (as at Knossos).

Ecbatana, Deioces' city as Herodotus describes it (Cantos IV, V, LXXIV, and LXXX) reflected in its seven concentric walls the circuits of the planets, and its acropolis was (as in the ziggurats of Sumeria and the Parthenon at Athens) a place for the meeting of man and god, and Pound remembers that mountains first served this purpose (Sinai, T'ai Shan, Olympos). The Prophet Ezra honours Cyrus' anxiety to restore the temple at Jerusalem ('for Yahweh is the god of that place'). Nineveh took its ground-plan from Ursa Major; Jerusalem began as a model in heaven, was translated into brick and stone for an historical existence and was by John of Patmos' time a heavenly paradigm again. Sigriya in Ceylon is an earthly model of the celestial city Alakamanda. (Leo Frobenius' *Erlebte Erdteile* is still the fullest and most perspicacious study for the sacred origins and designs of the walled, temple-centred city, though the subject has received brilliant attention in the fifty years that Pound has been building the subject into *The Cantos* : see especially Dumézil's *Jupiter, Mars, Quirinus* and *Tarpeia*, Giedion's *The Eternal Present*, and Eliade's *Cosmos and History*).

The figure of Italia (or Roma) persists on Italian money and postage stamps : a woman's head crowned by battlements. She is the city 'now in the mind indestructible' of Canto LXXIV. Toward this allegory Pound tends to move all the goddesses he evokes in *The Cantos*, until he has constructed one of the richest symbols in the whole poem. Persephone's wreath of meadow flowers will become interchangeable with Demeter's coronal of wheat. The goddess crowned with an image of her city is the Mediterranean's oldest emblem of sovereignty (the high priest of Babylon wore a replica of a ziggurat that is the model for the Pope's tiara today; the Pharaoh's double crown of the Two Kingdoms represented a pyramid). And the emblem was not only of the holy acropolis, with which Pound associates the tower of Danaë, human receptacle of divine seed and archetype for the poem of the women who bear children to gods, but of the outer limits as well—the man-made stone wall and the outer, magic, invisible wall which was put into place with music and incantation (like the Knossan maze and the wall that Achilles destroyed when he drove Hector counter-clockwise around Troy, undoing the spell that bound the city to Pallas' protection, or the walls of Alba Longa [*Aeneid* V. 583–602]).

It was Cybele, the Phrygian Demeter, who, as far as we know, first wore a crown of battlements, for she was not only the goddess of mountains, forests, and the wealth of nature, but was the giver of towers and city walls to mankind. In her is that marriage of flower and stone toward which Pound's early poetry moved, not quite knowing its way, seeing in stone something sinister (as had the major poets and painters of the nineteenth century) rather than the under-matrix of nature. Once we realize this double nature of Demeter's patronage, her protection of both field and city, we can see with what care Pound has chosen his pictures of her in all her transmutations. She first appears in the poem as Venus, with the towers and walls (*munimenta*) of mountain copper (*orichalchi*) at Cyprus as her allotted place. This initial conjunction of city and goddess is deliberately portentous and auspicious. From it will grow the definition of civilization everywhere implicit in *The Cantos*. In the Homeric Hymn to Aphrodite from which Pound takes 'Cypri munimenta sortita est', Venus appears disguised as a Phrygian princess, to beget with Anchises the city-builder Aeneas, transplanter of a culture to which, in time, an oracle will cause Cybele's turret-crowned image to be brought. Ovid in the *Fasti* (IV. 179–376) describes her arrival in Rome and explains her diadem of towers :

> at cur turrifera caput est onerata corona ?
> an primus turris urbibus illa dedit ?
>
> [219–20]

Yet the goddess was already in Rome. She was the Etruscan Vortumna, Goddess of the Turning Year, an indigenous Demeter whose name would get changed to Fortuna, and who

163

was to be fused with the allegorical Roma. In the *Aeneid* we can
feel the subtle confusion of Roma and Fortuna, for practically
every mention of Fortuna involves the destiny of Rome's walls.

> Qua visa est Fortuna pati Parcaeque sinebant
> Cedere res Latio, Turnus et tua moenia texi
> [Aeneid XII. 147–8]

Vergil of course was aware of the Phrygian origin of the wall-
crowned goddess :

> Et hujus, nate, auspiciis incluta Roma
> Imperium terris, animos aequabit Olympo
> Septemque una sibi muro circumdabit arces,
> Felix prole virum : qualis Berecyntia mater
> Invehitur curru Phrygias turrita per urbes
> Laeta Deum partu centum complexa nepotes,
> Omnes caelicolas, omnes supera tenentes.
> [*Aeneid* VI. 781–7]

Lucretius describes the goddess :

> Muralique caput summum cinxere corona,
> Eximiis munita locis quod sustinet urbes.
> [*De rerum naturae* II. 606–7]

The Greek Tyché also wears a crown of towers, whence Fortuna got hers. Doughty found somewhere in his erudition cause
to describe an allegorical figure of Claudius Caesar's triumph
over Britain as

> (Minerva seems!) *Colonia Nova*, Claudia;
> Like shielded goddess, with high turrets crowned.
> [*The Dawn in Britain* XVII]

The resonant *krédemnon* of Canto XCVI—the goddess Ino-
Leucothea's headdress—may be a doubled image, for *krédemna*
were the battlements of a city, and Leucothea is under the sign
of Fortuna. (*Krédemnon* : something that binds, a turban or
magic precinct around a city.)

Fortuna, evoked so lyrically in *Thrones* and *Rock-Drill*, is
another mask of the pervasive Mediterranean deity whom

anthropology has traced through a thousand guises by now and who—as Pound sees her—always emerges, whatever her name or attributes, as the chthonic, mysterious force whose harmony man must search out and adhere to or perish. As Castalia she comes crystal and clear from the dark earth (Canto XC, and as Arethusa and other spring nymphs throughout *Rock-Drill* and *Thrones*), inspiration of poets and Pound's further extension of the rivers of light in Dante's *Paradiso* and the opposite of the destructive floods in *Thrones* (rhyming with Petrarch's flood-imagery in the 'Italia mia' canzone, where the floods are the barbaric ravagers of Italy). Or she comes from the chaos of the sea (Aphrodite, Leucothea) as civilization itself grows from the dark of forest and wildness to the ordered perfection of a city.

An altar to Tyché stands at Eleusis, facing the sea. Fortuna eluded all the forces of time and Christianity that disguised or banished the other gods. She lived quite respectably in the mediaeval mind, where (as in Alan de Lille and Bernardus Silvestris) she becomes identified with Natura and moves suavely in and out of theology and philosophy. Goliardry and the *Carmina Burana* fashioned her into a striking figure, though her reputation, as now, vacillated between that of a strumpet and a powerful force worthy of placation and circumspect deference. In *Inferno* VII Vergil chides Dante for so misunderstanding Fortuna:

'He whose wisdom transcends all made the heavens and gave them guides, so that every part shines to every part, dispersing the light equally. In the same way He ordained for worldly splendours a general minister and guide who should in due time change vain wealth from race to race and from one to another blood, beyond the prevention of human wits, so that one race rules and another languishes according to her sentence which is hidden like the snake in the grass. Your wisdom cannot strive with her. She foresees, judges, and maintains her kingdom, as the other heavenly powers do theirs. Her changes have no respite. Necessity makes her swift, so fast men come to take their turn. This is she who is so reviled by the very men that should give her praise, laying on her wrongful blame and ill repute. But she is blest [*ma ella s' è beata*] and does not hear it.

Happy with the other primal creatures she turns her sphere and rejoices in her bliss [*e beata si gode*]'[1]

This is reflected in Canto XCVII as :

> Even Aquinas could not demote her, Fortuna,
> violet, pervenche, deep iris,
> beat' è, e gode.

and as :

> All neath the moon, under Fortuna,
> splendor' mondan',
> beata gode, hidden as eel in sedge,
> all neath the moon, under Fortuna

Fortuna is the goddess of *forsitan* : of perhaps. Her virtue is in 'ever-shifting change' (Canto XCVII), the constant motion that Thoreau thought was the very definition of life. Pound claims Fortuna as a positive force under the theme of metamorphosis (even if she wears the Gorgon mask of Nemesis); her unceasing turbulence is a natural mode, and all of man's actions are within it.

That Fortuna should come to the fore in the Pisan group and remain as a lyric presence grows from the Homeric ground-plan. All of Odysseus' adventures are either hairbreadth escapes or subtle enchantments. In the first half of the poem we find the adventures of enchantment, Sirens, Lotos Eaters, Circe. The Pisan DTC begins the adventures of entrapment and physical endurance, Scylla, Charybdis, Cyclops, and the shipwreck before Phaeacia. The mimesis of action, however, is Great Bass, as Pound calls it. We listen to it to calculate the aptness of the counterpoint, remembering that we are experiencing an *epos* of ideas released in interlocked phrases each of which is a musical phrase, an image, and as much of a grammatical coherence as the poet can allow. There is a larger grammar, where entire cantos count as ideograms; to see the meaning of the goddesses we must read the larger grammar. We have seen that Persephone and her green world move through the poem.

[1] John D. Sinclair's translation, London 1948.

PERSEPHONE'S EZRA

Cantos I–XXX are under the sign of Circe. XXXI–XLI are under the sign of three goddesses insofar as they have power over wild beasts; that is, are civilizing and taming forces: Aphrodite, Circe, and the Egyptian Aphrodite (roughly) Hathor. XLII–LI are under the sign of Demeter, as are LII–LXXI. The *Pisan Cantos* bring to a crescendo the theme of Demeter and Persephone, introduce Fortuna, and evoke Athena, Artemis, and Fortuna's planet the moon. *Rock-Drill* introduces Leucothea (an agent of Fortuna), and carries forward the amplified theme of all the natural goddesses, adding many from cultures other than the Mediterranean, Kwannon, the Buddhist goddess of Mercy, for instance. The visionary eyes of the goddess, flowing crystal, light 'almost solid', mermaids, nymphs, and many historical figures (Elizabeth I, Theodora, Jeanne d'Arc) embody the bright theme of the lady of spiritual power. *Thrones* approaches the imagery of the *Paradiso* in its translucent brilliance.

These images are not only radiant; they act as mirrors to each other in patterns of increasing clarity the more we understand the poem. Many distinct but congenial themes flow through the matters we have just been looking at (the half-visible parallel to Christianity, for instance, reaching from Eleusis, as Tadeusz Zieliński argues in *The Religion of Ancient Greece*, to the saintly ecstasies of the twelfth century), but what we are interested to watch emerge is the articulation of the offices of Demeter and Persephone into an image of extraordinary meaning and beauty.

A culture, in the sense that Leo Frobenius understood it (and hence Pound), has two dominant symbols, the male one of action, the female one of stillness and place (*Ruhe und Raum*). The male symbol is of direction, expansion, intensity, considering space as distance to traverse and measure, and is therefore volatile, unstable, destiny-ridden.

> Moth is called over mountain
> The bull runs blind on the sword, *naturans*
> > [Canto XLVII]

And in the same canto, and again of Odysseus:

First must thou go the road
                    to hell
And to the bower of Ceres' daughter Proserpine,
Through overhanging dark, to see Tiresias,
Eyeless that was, a shade, that is in hell
So full of knowing that the beefy men know less than he,
Ere thou come to thy road's end.
                    Knowledge the shade of a shade,
Yet must thou sail after knowledge
Knowing less than drugged beasts . . .

Canto XLVII aligns even the indomitable Odysseus with the fate of the yearly slain: Tammuz, Adonis, Osiris, for man the seed-scatterer is staccato, discontinuous. He runs on the sword; he perishes as the moth. The female is on the other hand a mountain, a cave, the fecund earth, considering space as a room. Woman for Pound is the stillness at the heart of a culture.

The Cantos, for all their ability to make the past transparent, are ultimately about their own century. Pound's despair over his own time, rarely stated personally in the poem, is nevertheless an astringent theme. The man who wrote the Hell Cantos (XIV–XVI) and who wrote in Canto XCVI

Good-bye to the sun, Autumn is dying
Χαῖρε ὁ ῞Ηλιος
whom the ooze cannot blacken
Χαῖρε clarore

said to the journalist Grazia Livi in 1963 (*Epoca* 50:652): 'The modern world doesn't exist because nothing exists which does not understand its past or its future. The world of today exists only as a fusion, a span in time.' We are, in Pound's image, inundated; we have 'heaped fads on Eleusis' (Canto XCVI). We have lost our clarity. The tragedy outlined in such hard detail in *The Cantos* begins deep in the nineteenth century when Europe was preparing a spiritual metamorphosis of extraordinary dimensions. The nature of this metamorphosis can still be seen only in symbolic configurations, although we can with some

certainty translate the symbols into what we imagine to be
historical facts. André Chénier (1762–94), writing a suite of
elegies that can be seen as the end of the meditative tradition of
sweetly melancholy verse that begins with Petrarch or as the
first Romantic inventions of an imaginary past of golden
splendour, begins to construct a vision that is both past and future
—we recover from the high cultures a spiritual reality that we
hope to claim. Like Watteau imagining a magical Cytherea he
could say:

> Partons, la voile est prête, et Byzance m'appelle.
>
> [*Élégie* XLVIII]

> 'Constantinople' said Wyndham 'our star,'
> Mr. Yeats called it Byzantium,
>
> [Canto XCVI]

Chénier hungered for the physical recovery of what there
might be left of the past:

> L'herbe couvre Corinthe, Argos, Sparte, Mycène;
> La faux coupe le chaume aux champs où fut Athènes.
>
> [*Elégie* XCVI]

Yeats' two great visions of Byzantium are derived from the
imagery of Shelley's *The Revolt of Islam*,

> this vast dome,
> When from the depths which thought can seldom pierce
> Genius beholds it rise, his native home,
>
> [I. L. 1–3]

The nineteenth century was obsessed with visions of paradises
and utopias: Blake's Jerusalem, Coleridge's Xanadu, Shelley's
Bosch-like lands of the spiritually cleansed, Rimbaud's and
Henri Rousseau's jungle gardens. Two poles of attraction, we
have seen, seemed to control these visions. One was Arcadian
and natural, with some of its roots in Christian thought, and
was a node for those Romantics who were seeking a world-order
consonant with nature (Wordsworth, Ruskin, the Transcen-
dentalists). The other was deliberately artificial, arcane,
symbolic. Novalis' *Heinrich von Ofterdingen* searching for his

blue flower, des Esseintes immured among his bibelots and curios, Yeats longing to be refined into a mechanical nightingale in a Byzantium under the spell of faery—Baudelaire (the spiritual heir of Novalis, Hoffman, and Poe) gives a name to the century's predilection for a counterfeit world, *les paradis artificiels*, a phrase that Pound saw as the ultimate etiolation of Villon's *Paradis paint, où sont harpes et lus*. Baudelaire was principally concerned to contrast the healthy mind with the drugged one, natural vision with that induced by opium. Helplessly he preferred the natural, but as the drunkard commends sobriety. He was committed to his '*nouveauté sublime et monstrueuse*' (as Guillaume Apollinaire called it). Practically all its practitioners saw the Décadence as a religious force, specifically an inverted, mirror-like parody of Christianity; Baudelaire, especially, saw *Les Fleurs du mal* as a kind of hymnal or missal. It contains litanies, prayers, meditations.

> Ô vierges, ô démons, ô monstres, ô martyres,
> De la réalité grand esprits contempteurs,
> Chercheuses d'infini, dévotes et satyres,
> Vous que dans votre enfer mon âme a poursuivies.
>
> *[Femmes damnées]*

What, to Pound's mind, the century was doing was imagining Persephone's reign in hell. And the artist is a prophet. He shows the first symptoms of what will become contagion. Persephone's hell is one of nature's modes—the dwarf world, as folklorists know it, a world with phosphorus for light, with strange parodies of growing nature (geode for fig, gems for flowers, crystal for water). Image after image betrays an unconscious longing to be released from the sterility of this gorgeously artificial Hades, though its evil consists solely in one's mistaking it for reality's wholeness. Poe symbolized its psychology by placing his demon raven atop a bust of Pallas: the irrational dominating the intellect. Rossetti's paintings became an endless series of portraits of Persephone in hell. The 'Veronica Veronese' of 1872 shows a young lady in plush (Miss Alice Wilding, the model) in a room hung with heavy cloth. She is reproducing on a violin the notes of her caged canary. Flowers made of jewels hang from her wrist; shells of ivory, gold, and pearl figure in her necklace. Once Pound had perceived that the major artists of the late nineteenth century had, for the most part uncosciously, taken Persephone grieving for another world as a dominant symbol, he was in a position to write both *Hugh Selwyn Mauberley* and the first thirty cantos. He had identified the chthonic Persephone with Circe, and the mirror-world in which nineteenth-century art had locked itself as a counterfeit paradise, a *paradis artificiel*. One of his responses was to write 'An Idyll for Glaucus', casting the problem of increasingly arcane subjectivity as that of a girl trying to communicate with the metamorphosed Glaucus (he has eaten a magic herb and become a sea-creature).

Three English writers began almost simultaneously to transmute this precious, ungrowing world of the imagination (reflecting what malady of the soul practically every artist of the twentieth century has tried to say) into visions of growth and organic fulfilment, to find again the ancient conjunction of flower and stone, underworld, world, and empyrean ('Topaz, God can sit on,' Canto CIV). All three, Joyce, Eliot, and Pound, were close students of Dante, and all three, however differently, were involved in the recovery of the Mediterranean past by archaeology and anthropology. In Dantesque terms, Eliot managed an *Inferno* (*The Waste Land*) and fragments of a *Purgatorio* (*Ash Wednesday, The Four Quartets*). Joyce constructed in *Ulysses* the century's *Inferno* and in *Finnegans Wake* a *Purgatorio*—a cyclic *Purgatorio* from which one cannot escape. Pound has attempted a *Paradiso*, a vision of the world's splendour encompassing, as he configures the design, both of Persephone's kingdoms, 'the germinal universe of wood alive, of stone alive' (*Spirit of Romance*, p. 72). It is in religion eclectic and is as interested in justice and piety as reflected in collective human behaviour as in the fulfilment of the soul's inwardness. Eliot's and Joyce's city is unquestionably hell. Pound chose to traverse the dark vision completely and posit the city as the one clear conquest of civilization.

Each of the first thirty cantos either ends with the image of a city wall or tower or contains such an image: even the comic Canto XII ends with the word 'Stambouli'. The darkest of these images are of ruin (III, IV, XVIII, XX) or treachery (V, VI, VII, XXVIII). The brightest are of Aphrodite's copper walls, Danaë's tower, Sigismundo's Rimini, Chinese dynastic temples, and Florence, Venice, and Ferrara at their height. Yet everything in *The Cantos* is seen in tragic deterioration up until Pound discloses in the Pisan group the enveloping idea of the past as a symbol alive in the present and holding within it the seeds of the future. It is here that he brings in the city 'now in the mind indestructible' and the oldest myth in the entire poem, that of Wagadu in Africa, a Soninke legend of a city, Wagadu, that was lost as a reality but remained in men's hearts.

'Four times Wagadu stood there in her splendour. Four times Wagadu disappeared and was lost to human sight: once through vanity, once through falsehood, once through greed, and once through dissension. Four times Wagadu changed her name. First she was called Dierra, then Agada, then Ganna, then Silla. . . . Wagadu, whenever men have seen her, has always had four gates, one to the north, one to the west, one to the east, and one to the south. These are the directions from whence the strength of Wagadu comes, the strength in which she endures no matter whether she be built of stone, wood, or earth, or lives but as a shadow in the mind and longing of her children. For, really, Wagadu is the strength which lives in the hearts of men and is sometimes visible because eyes see her and ears hear the clash of swords and ring of shields, and is sometimes invisible because the indomitability of men has overtired her, so that she sleeps. . . . Should Wagadu ever be found for the fifth time, then she will live so forcefully in the minds of men that she will never be lost again, so forcefully that vanity, falsehood, greed, and dissension will never be able to harm her.'[1]

In Canto XVI, emerging from the hell of the decivilizers, we have as a counter-vision:

[1] Leo Frobenius and Douglas C. Fox, *African Genesis*, London 1938, p. 109–110.

172

entered the quiet air
>> the new sky,
the light as after a sun-set,
>> and by their fountains, the heroes,
Sigismundo, and Malatesta Novello,
>> and founders, gazing at the mounts of their cities.

In Canto XVII: 'and the cities set in their hills.' In Canto
XXVI there is a Jerusalem painted by Carpaccio, which was also
a city foursquare, many times lost and now a vision in the mind,
as it (or she) was in the time of Isaiah and Jeremiah, in whose
pages the myth of Wagadu would be perfectly at home. In the
figure of the city that has become a throne—a spiritual power of
greatest force—Pound sees the one inclusive symbol of civilization. Here the odysseys of men come to rest and cohere with the
Penelope-work at the still centre. By Canto CVII Demeter has
become Queen of Akragas, and the cities through whose histories
The Cantos have moved become temples containing light, and
the processes of architecture the music by which Amphion lifted
the enchanted stones into place to ring Thebes with a wall.

>> Amphion not for museums
>> but for her mind
>>> like the underwave
>> [Canto CVII]

The museum, twentieth-century parody of a temple, is all that
we have, physically, of the past; and Joyce begins *Finnegans
Wake* in a museum. The early interpreters of *The Cantos* tended
to see the poem as a study of the man of willed and directed
action, as a persona of Odysseus. It is now clear that the poem
rests most firmly in a deeper, stiller sense of humanity, the city
and its continuity, symbolized by the goddess of field and
citadel wearing the sanctuary of her people as a crown.

BORIS DE RACHEWILTZ

Pagan and Magic Elements in
Ezra Pound's Works

T ime and again in the prose works of Ezra Pound we
come across remarks which appear to add up to a total
rejection of the use of symbols in poetry in favour of,
first, the image, then the image-in-action, and finally the ideogram. Yet it might be shown that Pound's original objection
applies only to the use of 'a symbol with an ascribed or intended
meaning', whereas he defines symbolism 'in its profoundest
sense' as 'a belief in a sort of permanent metaphor'[1] and goes on
significantly to explain that this does not necessarily imply 'a
belief in a permanent world' but 'a belief in that direction'.[2]

What he has in mind at this point is thus a symbol-in-the-
making rather than a fixed symbol which can be used outside of
its original context. Yeats's differentiation between intellectual
and emotional symbolism (*Ideas of Good and Evil*, 1903) is
useful as an aid to understanding this position. The 'intellectual
symbol' relies upon a set of established mythological or religious beliefs and has, at least to the initiate, an objective and
relatively clear meaning. The 'emotional symbol', on the other
hand, is a personal invention of the poet that derives from his
inborn tropisms. Wholly subjective in origin, its meaning only
reveals itself to the reader from its context within the poem as a
whole. It is evident that the intellectual or objective symbol,
however, must also have had a predominantly emotional or
subjective origin.

In his overruling passion to 'make it new', Pound has always

[1] Pound, *Gaudier-Brzeska*, London 1916, p. 99.   [2] *Ibid.*, pp. 97, 120.

exhibited a tendency to restore to intellectual, objective symbols some of their original subjective content, and this is the real reason why he holds the concrete quality of the image and the ideogram to be superior to the abstract cut-and-dried symbol. However, if the *Cantos* are to be regarded as 'a permanent metaphor' in the direction of 'a belief in a permanent world', certain recurrent expressions and images which gradually grow increasingly 'objective' necessarily assume the status of symbols. This process becomes particularly striking in the cantos of *Section: Rock-Drill* and *Thrones*, and it is with these quasi-objective symbols that we shall here be concerned.

Anyone familiar with the *grimoires* and other mediaeval texts in which formularies are found along with the complex diagrams of pentacles, the cyphers of angels and demons, the *nomina barbara et arcana*, will be less disconcerted than the general reader at the sight of these cantos, where the layout of the text and the insistent rhythms of the poetry so frequently bear the mark of ritual magic. The Neoplatonic belief, as expressed by the Jesuit Athanasius Kircher (1601–80) in his later years,[1] that Egyptian hieroglyphs are endowed with magic power, may be taken to explain Pound's frequent use of Chinese pictograms and eventually also of Sumerian and Egyptian hieroglyphs or even music in archaic black notation.

The belief that the written word is charged with thaumaturgic power is of very ancient origin; in fact it may be traced all the way back to the *graffiti* of the Neolithic civilization and even to the cave-art of Paleolithic times. This phenomenon stems from the untold power of the image: imo-ago, 'to rouse from the depths'.

In the cabbalistic teachings of the Sepher Jezirah, the acoustic element of the word has an equivalent in light, and the signatures of things, the *nomina arcana*, appear in this sphere as luminous letters.[2] In ancient Egypt, the priests, after chanting a hieroglyphic text 'in the right tone', used to obliterate whatever

---

[1] *Oedipus Aegyptiacus*, 1652–54, especially his translation of the obelisk of Minerva in *Obel. Isaei Interpretat*, 53, 78.

[2] A. Jounet, *La Chiave dello Zohar*, Bari 1936.

hieroglyphs represented maleficient beings so as to prevent their taking on life in the other world, where they might have harmed the dead.[1] In more recent times, the acoustic figures of Jules Lissajous and Ernst Chladni have shown that the spoken word has not only sound but shape.

So when we listen to Pound reading cantos in his quasi-liturgical cadence, with chanted passages in Greek or Chinese, we at once recognize the typical intonation of sacred texts and magical incantations. Julius Evola, in his essay *Poesia e realizzazione iniziatica*,[2] goes so far as to regard magic as the very origin of poetry, believing its imagery and rhythms to reflect the first stirrings of a higher conciousness. Certain metaphysical experiences, he suggests, can be expressed more effectively in poetry than by abstract thought. In India the oral teachings of the gurus follow a rhythmic pattern. The Sanskrit language is itself inherently rhythmical. This rhythmic element of language Evola believes to have been still present in ancient Greek and to have been gradually lost in more modern languages. Poetic rhythm, when not intended as mere sonority but attuned to certain rhythmical emotions, can restore it. Pound seems to have approached a subconscious realization of this when he wrote : 'I believe that every emotion and every phase of emotion has some toneless phrase, some rhythm-phrase to express it.'[3]

In this sense at least it would seem an acceptable proposition that certain traditional forms of poetry, by their inherent nature, contain definite elements of magic. As a poet ages, these elements tend to become more pronounced. When his visions no longer come freely of their own accord, the subjective symbols and formulas originally evoked by transcendental experience are then employed to invoke past visions. This development may be traced in the works of many poets, the case of Yeats being a classic example. It is also very much in

---

[1] P. Lacau, *Suppression et modification de signes dans les textes funéraires*, Zeit. f. Aegypt. Spr. t. LI, 1914.

[2] *Introduzione alla Magia quale Scienza dell'Io*, Rome 1955, Vol. III, p. 27.

[3] *Gaudier–Brzeska*, p. 97

evidence in Pound, but in his case differs from the norm in that a leaning towards magic was already noticeable in his earliest poems and, while largely absent from the poetry of his middle years, reasserts itself more strongly than ever before in his old age.

Thus in the poem 'La Fraisne' (*A Lume Spento*, 1909) we find the first appearance of the mythical ash-tree Yggdrasill, which is afterwards to recur in the late cantos LXXXV and XC (1955). The first printed version of this poem was preceded by a gloss in which the poet significantly calls to mind the ancient pagan cycle in the words :

'When the soul is exhausted in fire, then doth the spirit return unto its primal nature and there is upon it a peace great and of the woodland "*magna pax et silvestris.*" Then becometh it kin to the faun and the dryad, a woodland-dweller amid the rocks and streams "*consociis faunis dryadisque inter saxa sylvarum*" (Janus of Basel). Also has Mr. Yeats in his *Celtic Twilight* treated of such, and I because in such a mood; feeling myself divided between myself corporal and a self aetherial, "a dweller by streams and in wood-land," eternal because simple in elements "*Aeternus quia simplex naturae.*" Being freed of the weight of the soul "capable of salvation or damnation", a grievous striving thing that after much straining was mercifully taken from me; as had one passed saying as one in the Book of the Dead, "I, lo I, am the assembler of souls," and had taken it with him, leaving me thus *simplex naturae*, even so at peace and trans-sentient as a wood pool I made it.'[1]

This pagan reduction to *simplex natura* is none other than the alchemists' hermetic key to palingenesis. It is also here that we encounter Pound's first reference to ancient Egypt, one of the subjects to which he has responded with a certain ambivalence throughout his life, for although drawn to it repeatedly he has never felt for Egypt the same immediate affinity that he has for the China of Confucius and Mencius.

Ancient Egypt remains outside the range of Pound's sen-

---

[1] *A Lume Spento*, 1908, p. 14.

sibility on account of the transcendental nature of its beliefs. This accounts for his sudden elation on discovering, albeit late in life that, in King Khaty and the aristocrat Antef, Egypt had once had rulers whose recorded secular wisdom is sometimes comparable in quality to that of the sages of China, and which antedated and anticipated those of the Christian evangelists by almost two thousand years. Known from his stele in the British Museum to have lived in the reign of Sesostris I (12th dynasty, ca. 1970–1936), Antef is recorded as having voiced the injunction 'Give bread to the hungry, beer to the thirsty', which was to cause Pound to place him at the beginning of Canto XCIII in association with the 'panis angelicus'.

While this and Khaty's maxim 'A man's paradise is his good nature', first quoted in Canto XCIII and repeated in Canto XCIX, are entirely secular, the 'assembler of souls' to whom Pound referred in his note to 'La Fraisne' is brought up directly from the Egyptian Realm of the Dead, of whose chthonic inhabitants Pound has shown himself familiar :

> The gods of the underworld attend me, O Anubis,
> These are they of thy company . . .
> > ['Before Sleep', 1914]

Much later, in Canto XCII, we find the same deity invoked once more in the lines :

> O Anubis, guard this portal
> > as the cellula, Mont Ségur
> Sanctus

Anubis, who stood guard over the tent of the ritual resurrection known as Osirification, is here referred to as guardian of the cellula, i.e. the crypt, which corresponds to the *sanctum sanctorum* of temples. In macrocosmic terms this is the Cosmic Mountain, the abode of the god, while in the human microcosm it finds its counterpart in the *ignis centrum terrae* of the individual, i.e. the heart. In the esoteric language of ancient Egypt, the heart is referred to as *nether imy remet*, or 'god in man'.

It is interesting to note that in 'De Aegypto', a poem Pound wrote in 1907 (aetat 22) on reading something of the work of E. A. Wallis Budge, he pretends to personal mystical experience :

> I, even I, am he who knoweth the roads
> Through the sky, and the wind thereof is my body.

These lines are reminiscent of a passage in the *Texts of the Pyramids* describing the journey across the sky of the king who 'knows the routes'. In esoteric terminology the 'wind' invariably refers to man's first experience of cosmic power after he has divested himself of his body, a belief also reflected in the initiation ritual of Mithraism. This early anticipation of a lifelong theme only assumes its full depth of meaning in the late Canto XC, where Isis, the lunar goddess of ancient Egypt, is placed in association with the Kwannon, the compassionate bisexual Bodhisattva :

> Isis Kuanon
> from the cusp of the moon

The Egyptian goddess, in fact, appears repeatedly in the *Cantos*, as do also her attributes such as the 'horns' of the moon and the serpent head-dress of the Ureus, by which we are reminded of the Egyptian origin of the caduceus. It is also she whom we may discern in that intriguing syncretic entity 'Ra-Set', who is borne by the sun-boat through the underworld. In the Egyptian *Book of the Underworld*,[1] from which Pound drew his inspiration at this point, the 'Lady of the Boat' is the goddess in person.

In order to understand the full implications of Pound's references to Khaty and Antef on the one hand and to the 'Princess Ra-set' on the other, it is necessary to go back to the poet's source materials and also to consult some hitherto unpublished letters to the present writer that were written by Pound between 1954 and 1955, when he was composing the cantos in question. The maxims of both Khaty and Antef were derived from an Italian translation of hieroglyphic texts, the

[1] de Rachewiltz, *Il Libro Egizio degli Inferi*, Rome 1959.

Massime degli antichi Egiziani.[1] Letters from St Elizabeth's reveal his lively interest in his new discoveries : 'Congratulations / you have / humanized the egyptians / and Budge didn't, at least not to the point of getting into my head in 1907 mezzo sekolo fa . . . Kati and Antef as Kung and Mang ? . . . King KATI is the bright light of that collection. . . . A Man's paradise is his good nature. I should like that in hieroglyphs . . . Cantobile.' (August 15, 1954.) And a remark suggesting a belief in telepathic communication : 'Incidentally, I had repeated "Le Paradis n'est pas artificiel" in Canto Draft on 12 Ag[osto] / KATI's line arriv. on the 14th.' (August 16, 1954).

Further letters requested information on magic : 'Initiation details are most immediate . . . need.' And : 'Have you any more formulae (strong ones) for exorcism—Egyptian—of demon possession. Apollonius in Phil[ostratus] merely threatens the devils but Ph/ don't give formulae.' (September 25, 1954.) And again : 'I will meditate re / esoteric utilities / The Isis inscription [Iset weret] is, I think, the best immediate medicine.' (December 12, 1954.)

The association of Ra and Set that we have already noted in the 'Princess Ra-Set' may have its source in the commentary to the *Papiro Magico Vaticano*,[2] which induced Pound to ponder the problem of good and evil as it existed for the ancient Egyptians. In this papyrus, Set, the god of evil, is redeemed and allowed to enter the boat of the sun-god, Ra. Ra is the male god par excellence, while Set was always considered a 'typhonic' power, associated with moisture and passivity, which may be taken as feminine qualities. The concept of a maleficent yet necessary being is already present in the Osiris myth, where Set, bound in chains by Horus, is liberated by compassionate Isis, whom Pound immediately associates in his mind with the similarly compassionate Kwannon. 'Ra-Set' is therefore seen to emerge as a syncretic deity of the poet's invention, representing the essential cosmic equilibrium of good and evil. A parallel conception is inherent in the teachings of Plotinus, who, in a broad sense, does not recognize the existence of evil but only of

[1] de Rachewiltz, Milan 1954. [2] de Rachewiltz, Rome 1954.

a sort of compensation between the various levels of existence, while the universe as a whole is one beatific godhead. The same commentary also refers to the cabbalistic teaching of the Zohar, which claims that, when all the cosmic cycles are fulfilled, evil will be reabsorbed to become nothing more than a vestige of a former duality : 'At the end of time, Sama (poison) will be subtracted from the name Samael (the name of the devil) and only "El", the formula of god, will remain.'[1]

It should be remembered that in ancient Egypt, as also later in ancient Greece, goodness was regarded as an ontological rather than a moral value. Nofre, which means 'good' in the language of ancient Egypt, therefore also assumes the sense of 'perfection' or 'wholeness', while Wnnofre, one of the epithets of Osiris which Egyptologists earlier translated as 'The Good Being', is found in the light of later research to have been used more in the sense of 'The Complete Being'.

We might think that Pound had this conception of 'wholeness' in the back of his mind when, in Canto XCI, he combined the two ancient Egyptian male divinities, Ra and Set, and transformed them into a single female entity :

> The Princess Ra-Set has climbed
> to the great knees of stone,
> She enters protection,
> the great cloud is about her,
> She has entered the protection of crystal

This change of sex suggests that the poet's esotericism may in this respect have a microcosmic as well as a macrocosmic significance. In a microcosmic sense, i.e. *sub specie interioritatis*, the male and female components of Ra-Set would represent the full solar and lunar cycles, corresponding to the solar Ammonite and lunar Isis mysteries otherwise known as the Major and Minor Mysteries. The duality here encountered was already prefigured in *The Spirit of Romance* (pp. 93–4), where Pound wrote :

'When we do get into contemplation of the flowing we find

[1] A. Jounet, *La Chiave dello Zohar*, Bari 1936.

181

sex, or some correspondance to it, "positive and negative," "North and South," "sun and moon," or whatever terms of whatever cult or science you prefer to substitute . . . Substituting in these equations a more complex mechanism and a possibly subtler form of energy is, or should be, simple enough. I have no dogma, but the figures may serve as an assistance to thought. It is an ancient hypothesis that the little cosmos "corresponds" to the greater, that man has in him both "sun" and "moon." From this I should say that there are at least two paths —I do not say that they lead to the same place—the one ascetic, the other for want of a better term "chivalric." In the first the monk or whoever he may be, develops at infinite trouble and expense, the secondary pole within himself, produces his charged surface which registers the beauties, celestial or otherwise, by "contemplation." In the second, which I must say seems more in accord with "mens sana in corpore sano" the charged surface is produced between the predominant natural poles of the two human mechanisms.'

The same dualism is to be noted in the cantos in places where perceptions deriving from sensual experience are defined as 'fire' ('in coitu inluminatio', Canto LXXIV) and personified by deities such as Aphrodite-Kypris, Helen, Circe and Hathor, while perceptions deriving from the intellect are defined as 'light' and personified by, say, Artemis, Selena and Diana. The two forms of perception are elsewhere reified by 'the ball of fire' (Cantos XXXIX and XCI) and 'the great ball of crystal' (Canto XCVI), their order of succession—fire : light : crystal— being given in Canto XCI in the lines 'that the body of light come forth / from the body of fire', and 'from fire to crystal / via the body of light'.

While Pound on the one hand hypostatizes certain psychic forces within himself into a private pantheon, on the other he humanizes his gods. Where other poets may invoke the gods or, like Yeats, embrace theosophy as a means of escape from the world of humanity, Pound's efforts usually follow the opposite direction. Hence his preference for Ovid over Apuleius. The reason for this is made clear in *The Spirit of Romance* (p. 15) where, referring to Ovid's *Metamorphoses*, he concludes: 'The marvellous thing is made plausible, the gods are humanized, their annals are written as if copied from a parish register; their heroes might have been acquaintances of the poet's father.' This process by which the gods are brought down to a level where they can be empirically experienced also accounts for the repeated identification in his poetry of real persons with mythological characters. The humanization of the gods and, conversely, the mythologization of personal acquaintances, enables him to perceive human archetypes in gods and divine archetypes in humans. A process of osmosis is in this way established between the divine and the human world. This demonic participation results in an extension of the poet's identity in the manner he describes in his early poem 'Plotinus' (*A Lume Spento*, 1908):

> As one that would draw through the node of things,
> Back-sweeping to the vortex of the cone,
> . . .
> And then for utter loneliness, made I
> New thoughts as crescent images of *me* . . .

The 'crescent' or, as it were, growing images of the self, are later to assume the form of personae, or masks. A mask, by virtue of its function, may be said to have a certain wavelength over which its wearer is attuned to and in communication with the character of the person or deity it represents and so acts as both transmitter and receiver. This applies no less to the immaterial masks of poetry than to real masks, the function of which has been the subject of ethnological study.

The mode of conveyance used by the anima 'Princess Ra-Set' is described in Canto XCI in the lines:

> The golden sun boat
> > by oar, not by sail

accompanied by a drawing of an Egyptian craft that the poet has excerpted, along with the central concept, from the *Libro Egizio degli Inferi*,[1] an Italian version of the ancient Egyptian

---

[1] de Rachewiltz, Rome 1959.

Book of the Underworld dating back to the New Kingdom. There we find a description of the nightly progress of the sun through the underworld, along with various magic formulae by which humans may attain immortality. Although not visible in the drawing, the crew of the sun-boat is made up of the persons enumerated in the 'First Hour' of the Egyptian text: The Lady of the Boat (i.e. Isis),[1] Horus the Supplicant, The Bull of Truth, The Prudent One, Will, and The Oarsman, all being personifications of the qualities required for undertaking the voyage to the underworld. The symbolic oar signifies that the voyage is a carefully charted one that will not rely upon the fortuity of the winds.

The motif of the sun-boat achieves full significance only when it is seen as forming a thematic rhyme with a much earlier voyage to the underworld recorded in Canto XXIII:

> With the sun in a golden cup
> and going toward the low fords of ocean

A further point of interest in the present context is the way in which the nightly voyage of the sun is linked with Mithras and the destruction of the main Albigensian sites of Chaise Dieu, Mt Ségur and Excideuil. The sun, in fact, appears repeatedly in the *Cantos* in connection with a voyage to the darker regions. Thus in Canto XV, the poet, after his journey through Hell, emerges into the sunlight to sing the praise of 'Helios', and in Canto XVII, where he describes his vision of a subterranean sun in the lines 'Saw the sun for three days, the sun fulvid, / As a lion lift over sand-plain; / and that day, / And for three days, and none after / Splendour, as the splendour of Hermes', where the image of the lion would seem to stand for the chthonic lions which in the mythology of Asia Minor so often guard the threshold of the underworld. In Canto XCVII the motif is taken up yet again in the line 'and at Rhodos, the sun's car is thrown into the sea'. In the *Pisan Cantos* the sun, this time emerging from darkness, is identified with the creative

[1] According to some Accadian texts, the boat which carries the soul through the underworld is itself a deity.

word, the Paraclete and Logos, rising from consciousness, a vision reinforced by the Chinese pictograph *k'ou³* depicting a mouth, which Pound interpets after his own fashion as 'mouth, is the sun that is god's mouth' (Canto LXXVII). This is later thematically rhymed with a reference to Wondjina, an Australian aboriginal deity who created the world by 'naming' things, a very ancient magical rite found in most early cultures. Also in Pisa we find the poet cherishing the eucalyptus pod as a sun symbol in miniature : 'cat-faced, croce di Malta, figura del sol' (Canto LXXX). It may here be noted that according to magic doctrine : 'Eucalyptus will be used in all theurgic rites and in those that establish an accord between intelligences . . . the fruit is marked with the seal of the sun.'[1]

While the Greek conception of the nocturnal voyage of the sun rhymes thematically with the nightly progress of the Egyptian sun-boat, there is still another echo present : the voyage of the 'moon barge'. First launched in Canto LXXX, it appears in view again in Canto XC of *Section: Rock-Drill.* The lunar motif, previously introduced with the 'moon nymph immacolata', i.e. the nymph in the Japanese Nō play 'Hagoromo' (Canto LXXIV), with Diana of Ephesus 'in the cusp of the moon' (Canto LXXX), and with the personal vision of 'la scalza' (the bare-footed girl) in Cantos LXXIV and LXXVI, eventually assumes in Cantos XC and XCIII the atttributes 'Regina' and 'Isis-Luna'.

In *Thrones* a new component is added to this already complex symbol by the line 'all under the Moon is Fortuna' (Cantos XCVI and XCVII). Pound would here seem to be referring to the esoteric doctrine of the moon as the mediatrix of changes of fortune that are related to its various phases, and since not only Fortuna but also the Moirae, the Fates spinning the thread of life, are associated with the moon, the allusion may possibly also extend to the poet's personal fate. The Fates are further associated with the moon in an Orphic text, while Porphyry even observes that they are of lunar origin. The lines 'above

[1] Luce, *Opus Magicum, I Profumi,* in *Introduzione alla Magia,* Vol. I, p. 284.

the Moon there is order / beneath the Moon, forsitan' (Canto XCVII) recalls Plutarch's *De facie in orbe lunae*, a little-known text according to which man experiences two deaths, the first when his body is returned to the earth as a corpse and separated from the soul and the mind (νοῦς), the second when the soul is separated from the mind, an event which occurs on the moon when man's individual existence is reabsorbed into the cosmic cycle. Only initiates ascend beyond the lunar sphere to become what Plutarch calls 'conquerors'. This would seem to indicate an active 'conquest' of the lunar sphere, beneath which all remains unstable, in order to attain to a higher cosmic order. As Pound, in his aversion to abstract thought, apparently realized, the poet, inexorably tied to concrete sensory perception, must forever remain under the spell of the moon. 'Castalia like the moonlight' (Canto XC) takes on added significance when we recall that Castalia was thought of in the ancient world as the fount of poetic inspiration.

The habit of thinking or of expressing thought in terms of myths ('mythopoeia') is more readily understood when we call to mind that 'to live a myth' means to participate in an experience outside of historical time by means of a symbolic process in which imponderable forces become effective in the human sphere. Etymologically, the word symbol implies an act of throwing together, a dynamic process which is, by definition, almost opposite to that of analysis, which implies the act of resolving a complex whole into its component elements. In *Thrones* Pound avers: 'ne divisibilis intellectu / not to be split by syllogization' (Canto XCV). For him, the act of living a myth is thus a dynamic process quite unrelated to his reading, and involving complex multiple identifications such as we find throughout his works. A god, by his definition, is 'an eternal state of mind'. As a corollary it might be added that, in hermetic philosophy, 'to know' or 'be aware of' a god means to break through to and reunite with the creative state.

Pound already attempted to define this peculiar awareness in *The Spirit of Romance*:

'We have about us the universe of fluid force, and below us

the germinal universe of wood alive, of stone alive . . . As to his [man's] consciousness, the consciousness of some seems to rest, or to have its center more properly, in what Greek psychologists called the *phantastikon*. Their minds are, that is, circumvolved about them like soap-bubbles reflecting sundry patches of the macrocosmos. And with certain others their consciousness is "germinal." Their thoughts are in them as the thought of the tree is in the seed, or in the grass, or the grain, or the blossom. And these minds are the more poetic, and they affect mind about them, and transmute it as the seed the earth. And this latter sort of mind is close on the vital universe; and the strength of Greek beauty rests in this, that it is ever at the interpretation of this vital universe . . .' (p. 92).

This conception of the function of myth naturally allows the poet a certain amount of leeway in the subjective interpretation or modification of accepted versions. This becomes evident in some of the pseudo-historical sections of the *Cantos*, especially those concerned with early history, where the poet draws upon sources which will not stand up to critical scrutiny.

We have a typical instance of this in Pound's quotations from the works of the Scots amateur orientalist, Lt.-Col. L. A. Waddell (1854–1938), some of whose fanciful identifications of historical personages, particularly Sumerian and Egyptian, made in support of his strange theories, have in this way crept into the late Cantos. In Canto XCIV of *Section: Rock-Drill* we read, for instance:

> From the hawk-king
> > Goth, Agdu
> Prabbu of Kopt, Queen Ash
> > may Isis preserve thee
> Manis paid for the land
> > 1 bur : 60 measures, lo staio, 1 mana of silver
> as is said on the black obelisk
> > > somewhere about 27 o 4
> in the long boats east of Abydos.

Quite apart from the fact that Waddell's identifications of Goth,

Agdu, Prabbu of Kopt, Queen Ash are all purely arbitrary,[1] it is entirely erroneous to regard Sargon the Great as a pre-dynastic Egyptian ruler. The hieroglyph that Pound assigns to Sargon in Cantos XCIV and XCVII is borrowed from Waddell's *Egyptian Civilization—Its Sumerian Origin and Real Chronology* (1930). Waddell, in turn, borrowed it from the classic *History of Egypt* (1923) by Sir Flinders Petrie, who discovered in the course of his excavations in Abydos a predynastic tomb, already plundered in antiquity, which he attributed, on the strength of the inscription on a jar, to a little-known ruler 'Ka-ap'. Waddell later took the Egyptian cartouche surmounted by a falcon to be the seal of Sargon, and the fringe forming the upper part of the cartouche to be a three-column façade of a temple. This mis-interpretation was then adopted by Pound and so came to be introduced into the iconography of the *Cantos*. In Canto XCVII it turns up along with the insistent line 'The temple is holy / Because it is not for sale', which is further repeated several times in the same canto along with the cartouche and culminates in the illumination: 'From Sargon of Agade / a thousand years before T'ang.'

In Canto C the three-columned façade appears yet again as the pictogram of a temple, this time with the addition of the

[1] The foregoing names are all drawn from L. A. Waddell's *Egyptian Civilization, Its Sumerian Origin*, London 1930, where 'Goth' is claimed to be the dynastic line of Sargon the Great, whom Waddell considered to be the father of Menes, founder of the Egyptian dynasties. 'Agadu' or 'Agade' is supposed to be shown by the Indian seals to be the capital city of Sargon and Menes (!). 'Prabhu' (Pound's 'Prabbu' is a typographical error) was, according to Waddell, a form of the Sumerian title 'Par', corresponding to 'Pharaoh': 'the form Prabhu adopted by the Indian scribes was presumably to make this "Pharaoh" title intelligible to Indian readers,' pp. 4–5. 'Queen Ash' is supposed to be the wife of Sargon, whose name, again according to Waddell, is found on the Abydos vases. The reference to 'Manis' in Canto XCIV is from the same source, p. 53: 'one *bur* of land being reckoned as worth sixty *gur* measures of grain, and one *mana* of silver.' The famous black obelisk discovered by de Morgan at Susa in 1897 is likewise arbitrarily attributed to 'Menes'. As an example of Waddell's theories it is sufficient to note that he identifies Menes with Min or Minos of Crete and interprets the text on the ivory tablets found in Abydos to say that King Menes died in Ireland of a wasp's sting.

word 'hieron' (holy), having by now assumed the status of a symbol in the poet's mind. As will shortly be shown, the temple, like the sacred city and the altar, was traditionally regarded as the centre of the world, the point of intersection of the three zones, heaven, earth, and underworld, which Pound's associative mind has little difficulty in seeing represented by the three columns. Yet despite its inacceptability from the standpoint of egyptology, the hieroglyph and the interpretation that Pound gives to it under Waddell's false guidance might be said to retain some value as a personal vision, for to him the immanence of the 'temple' and its associations have come to take on a separate existence regardless of the unreliability of the source. His error is also compensated in part by the heightened significance that his symbol receives through a multiple thematic rhyme that endows it with a whole cluster of meanings which bring us back to the vision of ideal cities that reappear throughout the epic. The most important of these is the city of Deïoces (Ecbatana), mentioned by Herodotus, which Pound introduced in the first of the *Pisan Cantos* with the line: 'To build the city of Dioce whose terraces are the colour of stars' (Canto LXXIV), and the city of Wagadu of the Soninke legend, destroyed four times finally to arise again 'now in the mind indestructible'. Ecbatana, the temple city, conceived on the principle of the Sumerian ziggurat, represents the macrocosmic aspect of the sacred archetypal edifice, while Wagadu, the city 'in the mind', represents its microcosmic human aspect.

The cities of antiquity, like the temples and altars, were laid out according to a time-honoured canon which separated sacred space and time from secular space and time. Accordingly, any chosen space was qualified to become the *umbilicus mundi*, the centre of the world. The underlying idea was to create a cosmic centre—hence the symbols of the planets on the concentric walls of Ecbatana which mark off the sacred space. This archetypal conception may be traced back to the very earliest imagery found in art, whether proto-Indian or Aegean. Its archetypal nature is further reflected in the capital of the legendary 'perfect sovereign' of Chinese antiquity, which tradition situates at the 'centre of the universe', near the towering tree trunk, chien-mu, a mythological double of the ash-tree Yggdrasill in Canto LXXXV:

> That you lean 'gainst the tree of heaven
> and know Ygdrasail

The three cosmic zones of heaven, earth and underworld meet where the chien-mu enters the sky, again recalling Pound's emblematic temple. But perhaps the most interesting feature of this Chinese conception is that, in the capital, the gnomon standing on the exact meridian does not cast any shadow on the day of the summer solstice. This notion sheds light on the otherwise cryptic line in Canto LXXXV:

> a gnomon
> Our science is from the watching of shadows

which is, moreover, reminiscent of Plato's famous simile of the cave. The 'watching of shadows' is a constant search for the centre, the point where, on the day of the summer solstice, the imaginary line stretching from the gnomon to the sun forms the cosmic axis. The azimuth of the sun is then aligned on the gnomon, and no shadow is cast. In other words, the gnomon is in *medio mundi constructum*. These ideas, which are also reflected in the canons of esoteric architecture, reappear in Cantos LXXXV and LXXXVII in references to the 'Centrum circuli' and 'hic est medium [mundi]'. In Canto XC the theme is further elaborated:

> Templum aedificans, not yet marble,
> 'Amphion!'

And from the San Ku

> to the room in Poitiers where one can stand
> casting no shadow,
> That is Sagetrieb,
> that is tradition.
> Builders had kept the proportion,
> did Jacques de Molay
> know these proportions?
> and was Erigena ours?

The reference to the last Grand Master of the Order of Templars who was burnt at the stake as a heretic in Paris suggests that the proportion of the 'golden section' was known to the Templars as perpetuators of the tradition.[1] The question of Scotus Erigena, accused of the Manichean heresy, is here also brought up once more. It had been touched upon earlier in Canto LXXIV, where an affinity was suggested between Erigena, the Manicheans, and the Albigensians in the line ' "sunt lumina" said Erigena Scotus'. There, and in Canto LXXXIII, it was recalled that Erigena's grave had been desecrated under the pretext of searching for Manicheans: 'so they dug up his bones in the time of de Montfort (Simon)'. One of the possible motives for this desecration was, as Pound indicates, the desire to discover in Erigena's remains the bone luz and, by its removal, to prevent his resurrection on judgment day: 'the bone *luz*, I think was his take off', and later, 'or the bone *luz* / as the grain seed' (Canto LXXX).

In Agrippa's *De occulta philosophia*, I, 20, mention is made of 'a certain very small bone called luz . . ., which is incorruptible, which is not destroyed by fire but is preserved unimpaired, and from which, as a plant produces a seed, our body will come to life again as in the resurrection of the dead'. This provides a clue to the meaning of the 'partial resurrection in Cairo' in Canto LXXX and the connection between the bone luz and the grain seed. The gnomon that casts no shadow because it

[1] On the symbolism of the 'center' and esoteric architecture, see M. Eliade, *Cosmologie si alchimie babiloniana*, 1937, pp. 31 ff; E. Burrows, *The Labyrinth*, 1935, pp. 45–70; P. Sartori, *Über das Bauopfer*, in Zeit. für Ethn., XXX, 1898.

stands at the dead centre of the universe is thematically rhymed with the room in the tower in which one can stand without casting a shadow. In turn, the tower reintroduces the motif of Excideuil, the main site of the Albigensians that was first mentioned in connection with Arnaut in Canto XXIX: 'the wave pattern cut in the stone / Spire-top alevel the well-curb,' a theme which is picked up again much later in Canto CVII with the lines 'wave pattern at Excideuil / A spire level the well-curb'.

Used in a context in which it represents the centre of the universe, the gnomon finds a symbolic equivalent in the omphalos of ancient Greece, of which Pausanias (X, 16, 2) writes: 'That which the inhabitants of Delphi call omphalos is of white stone, and it is thought of as the center of the earth.' The symbolism of the gnomon and the tower is further associated with that of the mountain, here represented by Mt Ségur. The Mesopotamian temple was, in fact, called the 'mountain dwelling'. According to Islamic belief, the highest place on earth is the Ka'aba, which the position of the polar star shows to lie perpendicular to the earth's centre. It was this conception that gave rise to the custom of choosing elevated sites for the erection of temples and, later, monasteries. Canto LXXX presents an interesting synoptic view in the lines:

> Mt Ségur and the city of Dioce
> Que tous les mois avons nouvelle lune[1]

This would imply the existence of some relationship between the ideal city of Deïoces (Ecbatana) and Mt Ségur which, with its Abbey of Chaise Dieu, was the stronghold of the Albigensian heretics whom the Church persecuted with such venom, perpetrating, as Pound puts it in *The Spirit of Romance* (p. 101),

---

[1] This is a line from a poem by Charles d'Orléans (1391–1465) which Pound also quotes elsewhere: 'Tout dit que pas ne dure la fortune. / Un temps se part, et puis l'autre revient: // Je me comforte en ce qu'il me souvient / Que tous les mois avons nouvelle lune': The link between the moon and Fortuna ('All under the Moon is Fortuna'', Cantos XCVI and XCVII) which has already been pointed out should not cause us to overlook the lunar phases of memory and poetic inspiration ('The Muses are daughters of memory', Canto LXXIV). E. H.

'a sordid robbery cloaking itself in religious pretence'. The destruction of Mt Ségur by Simon de Montfort is described as early as in Canto XXIII along with a parallel: 'And that was when Troy was down.' In mourning the devastation of Provence and of its culture in the campaigns of extirpation against the Albigensians just as other poet-seers have lamented the fall of Troy, Pound brings out the poignancy of these events by associating the city of Deïoces with Mt Ségur as another stronghold of a higher knowledge passed down through dark ages. The continuity of this tradition links the rites of the Cathars, as the Albigensians called themselves, with those of the Bogomils of Thrace and, even further back, with Mithraism, to which Pound refers in Canto LXXVI:

> and in Mt Ségur there is wind space and rain space
> no more an altar to Mithras

Mithras is linked in turn with Mani, founder of the Persian Manichean sect, who attempted a synthesis between Mithraism and other oriental religions, Greek philosophy and Christian beliefs, very much in the way that the *Cantos* attempt a synthesis of human experience up to our time. In Canto LXXIV we find Mani referred to as an 'avatar'; hence the parallel in martyrdom drawn from the cage in Pisa in the line: 'Manes! Manes was tanned and stuffed.'

It would surely be no exaggeration to infer from all this that Pound's relationship to Christian beliefs is not quite orthodox. Indeed his own beliefs are modified throughout by that anthropological approach which he has described as being indispensable to modern thinking. In this connection we may read in his *Literary Essays* (p. 343):

'As Voltaire was a needed light in the eighteenth century, so in our time Fabre and Frazer have been the essentials in the mental furnishings of any contemporary mind qualified to write of ethics or philosophy or that mixed molasses religion. *The Golden Bough* has supplied the data which Voltaire's incisions had shown to be lacking.'

It is therefore hardly surprising that we find the *Cantos* so crowded with references to the fertility cults of Adonis, Tammuz, the chthonic trinity of Eleusis (Demeter, Persephone, Dionysus), and various agrarian as well as sexual rites. All this has been capably treated in other critical studies of Pound. What is of particular interest in the present context is that Pound approves of church ritual in so far as it retains traces of the older pagan meaning. 'The Church in sanity,' he wrote in a letter of June 18, 1954, 'RETAINED symbols, look at Easter show in Siena Cathedral (Egypt etc.) Ceres, Bacchus, and damn the blood washings . . .'. For this reason one of the rare priests with 'understanding' is brought to the fore in Canto LXXVII :

> Padre José had understood something or other
> . . .
> Learned what the Mass meant
>   how one shd/ perform it
> the dancing at Corpus   the toys in the
>   service at Auxerre
> top, whip, and the rest of them.

In his essay *Quand on dansait dans les églises*, Guy Breton writes: 'Up to the Middle Ages, the canons used to dance in church and monastery. In summer they performed sacred dances to the accompaniment of sung psalms on the large lawn in front of the church. Each city followed its own customs. In Auxerre the priests used to perform a ball dance in the nave of St Etienne. A new canon would hand the abbot a ball, which he then threw to the assembled canons, who would pass it around from hand to hand. During this procedure the new canon would execute a dance and sing a psalm—a ritual strangely reminiscent of those of the Inkas, where the motion of a ball was taken to represent that of the stars across the sky.'

From Breton's essay we see that the foregoing quotation from Canto LXXVII is intended to call to mind the pagan origin of the symbolic ritual of the mass as well as other elements, from the mitre to the crozier and the dance itself. We might compare objective symbols such as are found in church ritual with stock clichés which once also possessed the fresh appeal of new images. 'The etymologist', Emerson has said, 'finds the deadest word to have been once a brilliant picture. Language is fossil poetry.' Thus we see Pound, here as elsewhere, constantly at work breaking down outworn symbols into their original components, once more restoring them to some of their earlier power by making them new. This is, after all, quite an appropriate function for a poet in his role as a perpetuator of traditions temporarily lost from sight. Pound even carries this conception of the poet's subjective responsibility for the whole race a decisive step further. In a letter written in 1927 to his father he defines the themes of the *Cantos* as follows :

A.A. Live man goes down into world of Dead

C.B. The 'repeat in history'

B.C. The 'magic moment' or moment of metamorphosis, burst thru from quotidien into 'divine or permanent world.' Gods, etc.

The descent to the underworld can only be accomplished within one's own body, which represents the earth, and by purging the soul one may find the philosophers' stone. The objective is to realize a true transmutation and resurrection : *transmutemini de lapidibus mortuis in vivos lapidis philosophicos.*[1] This process is related by Zosimus, Olympiodorus and other early Greek alchemists with the creation of the world, the various phases of creation being repeated in the initiation ceremony and other rituals. Macrocosm and microcosm here coincide, and the individual initiation with its phases of 'descent' and 'rectification' finds its full counterpart on the supra-individual, collective plane of existence. The *Cantos* are the record of the descent into a neo-Dantean inferno, where the work of rectification is reflected in the labours which the poet thought it necessary to take upon himself for the sake of future society. In other words, the poet, in his function as *vates*, or as one of the 'antennae of the race', descends into the 'magna nox animae' (Canto LXXIV) by

Berthelot M., *La Chimie au moyen-âge*, Paris 1893, p. 124.

195

assuming a role in which he suffers vicariously the spiritual crisis of the age. Heedless of the dangers to which his mind is thereby exposed, he descends into the underworld, as Dante before him, albeit without the benefit of an Aquinas map, in his search for the philosophers' stone. He experiences all the terrors of this venture, which Plutarch has described: 'At first there are wrong starts and exhausting detours, journeyings through the dark, full of doubts and uncertainties, and nothing is achieved; then, before the end, come terrors of every kind, shivers and trembling, sweat and anxiety.'[1] The neophyte has to overcome dragons, demons and larvae as verbal reifications of the demonic forces that he encounters on his way. It is to these dangers that Pound refers in a broader and social rather than an initiatory context in a letter of 18 June, 1954 when he writes: 'Anteposition of: subjugation and perversion / against LIGHT. And the Paradiso, Dante model. The powers of hell, always ready to pervert IN ORDER to subjugate.'

Seen in this light, the crystal motif recurring throughout the *Cantos* might well be taken to represent the philosophers' stone. The lines in Canto IV: 'The liquid and rushing crystal / beneath the knees of the gods,' or the image of the goddess in Canto XXIII: 'and saw then, as of waves taking form / As the sea, hard, a glitter of crystal, / And the waves rising but formed, holding their form. / No light reaching through them,' or the vision of the 'crystal body' and of the 'sphere moving crystal, fluid' in Canto LXXVI, all bring to mind the hermetic inscription on the Porta Magica in Rome: *Aquam torrentum convertes in petram*.[2] The crystal combination of the fluid transparency of water and the solidity of stone predestines its use to symbolize the philosophers' stone.

Greek alchemical texts treating of the descent to the underworld describe the rock boulders encountered in the dark passages as the reanimated dead, redeemed through transformation so that the black earth may produce precious stones. While this, too, is to be taken *sub specie interioritatis*, it is

---

[1] Plutarch, in *Stobeo*, Flor. IV, 107; Porphyry, *Sententiae*.
[2] P. Bornia, *La Porta Magica*, 1915.

interesting to note how often precious stones such as jade, sapphire, topaz and amber appear in the *Cantos* and gradually come to acquire symbolic significance. Pound progressively refines his materials as if by calcination in hermetic fire until by the time we reach the *Pisan Cantos* the work itself has become as crystal: 'Serenely in the crystal jet / as the bright ball that the fountain tosses . . . as diamond clearness' (Canto LXXIV). And in one of his last canto fragments (CXVI) the poet asks: 'I have brought the great ball of crystal / who can lift it?'

In conclusion it might be considered whether the vast hyperbolic spiral of the unfinished *Cantos* has or has not led to an alchemical synthesis. Has the quintessence separated, as it were, the philosophers' stone from the amorphous rocks? The traditional criterion of the quality of an initiatory text in which 'with one day's reading a man may have the key in his hands' (Canto LXXIV) is the bite of the serpent, the *pathos* that leaves on the mind of the sensitive reader an indelible mark. In judging the *Cantos* from the particular aspect from which they have here been examined, we might perhaps accept a criterion that was originally established by Robert Frost: 'It is absurd to think that the only way to tell if a poem is lasting is to wait and see if it lasts. The right reader of a good poem can tell the moment it strikes him that he has taken an immortal wound—that he will never get over it.'

DONALD DAVIE

The Poet as Sculptor

I t is not often observed that the art of sculpture, as traditionally conceived, comprises two very different kinds of activity. Yet the carving of stone and the moulding of plaster (or of clay, so as later to make a bronze casting) are very different operations, and profoundly different because the artist's way with his material represents in miniature his way of dealing with the whole material world.

Some have thought that moulding and carving are not just different but antithetical. Adrian Stokes observed, in *The Stones of Rimini* (London 1934):

'Today, and not before, do we commence to emerge from the Stone Age: that is to say, for the first time on so vast a scale throughout Europe does hewn stone give way to plastic materials.... The use in building of quarried stone must ... increasingly diminish, and with it one nucleus of those dominant fantasies which have coloured the European perception of the visual world. In the work of men, manufacture, the process of fashioning or moulding, supersedes, wherever it is possible, the process of enhancing or carving material, the process that imitates those gradual natural forces that vivify or destroy nature before our eyes' (p. 24).

And elsewhere Stokes elaborates:

'In the two activities there lies a vast difference that symbolizes not only the main aspects of labour, but even the respective roles of male and female' (p. 110).

This last erotic analogy is several times pursued by Pound, nowhere more clearly and powerfully than in Canto XLVII:

So light is thy weight on Tellus
Thy notch no deeper indented
Thy weight less than the shadow
Yet hast thou gnawed through the mountain,
    Scilla's white teeth less sharp.
Hast thou found a nest softer than cunnus
Or hast thou found better rest
Hast'ou a deeper planting, doth thy death year
Bring swifter shoot?
Hast thou entered more deeply the mountain?

But, if the mountain is the female body ('By prong have I entered these hills'), it is also literally the mountain from which the sculptor quarries his marble block ('Yet hast thou gnawed through the mountain'), the quarrying being itself a sort of sculpture, a first stage in the carving. It is also ('Begin thy plowing . . . Think thus of thy plowing'—out of Hesiod in this same canto) the mountain that the farmer scores with his plough. And in *The Stones of Rimini* Adrian Stokes makes this analogy too: carving is not only like a man's way with a woman, it is also like a ploughman's way with the land. And let it not be thought that for Pound, any more than for Stokes, these analogies are fanciful; when Stokes speaks of 'fantasy' he means something as far as possible from free association— he means that in man's profoundest awareness of what he is doing these actions are not just alike but identical. It seems clear that we should range with them that way of dealing with words which regards them, as Pound says, as 'consequences of things' ('nomina sunt consequentia rerum', Thomas Aquinas); and with the other, the female role, the way of the modeller, that symbolist way with words which regards things, in the last analysis, as the consequences of the words that name them.

In Stokes's book on the Venetian use of colour, the analogous distinction in painting is between hue and tone; hue is the 'intrinsic' colour, tone that colour which is imparted to objects by the light as it strikes them this way or that, with this or that degree of intensity: and the distinctive achievement of Venetian painters, we are asked to think, lies in their attachment to hue as against tone. In Canto LII, which contains an extremely beautiful redaction of the sixth book of the *Lü Shih Ch'un Ch'iu*, or Spring and Autumn of Lü Pu-wei, Pound evokes in terms of ancient China a way of life that becomes ritual in its observance of the seasonable; and we learn, concerning the last summer month of the year:

> The lake warden to gather rushes
> > to take grain for the *manes*
> to take grain for the beasts you will sacrifice
> to the Lords of the Mountains
> > To the Lords of great rivers
> Inspector of dye-works, inspector of colour and broideries
> see that the white, black, green be in order
> let no false colour exist here
> black, yellow, green be of quality

There is nothing arbitrary about introducing the inspector of dye-works. In an ideally good society his office, the keeping of colours true, is a crucial one. In the canto preceding this we have read:

> Usury rusts the man and his chisel
> It destroys the craftsman; destroying craft
> Azure is caught with cancer. Emerald comes to no Memling
> Usury kills the child in the womb
> And breaks short the young man's courting.

And this in turn has repeated Canto XLV:

> Azure has a canker by usura; cramoisi is unbroidered
> Emerald findeth no Memling. . . .

For that matter Pound years before, in 'A Song of the Degrees' from *Lustra,* had already ranged himself with hue against tone:

I

> Rest me with Chinese colours,
> For I think the glass is evil.

II

The wind moves above the wheat—
With a silver crashing,
A thin war of metal.

I have known the golden disc,
I have seen it melting above me.
I have known the stone-bright place,
    The hall of clear colours.

III

O glass subtly evil, O confusion of colours!
O light bound and bent in, O soul of the captive,
Why am I warned? Why am I sent away?
Why is your glitter full of curious mistrust?
O glass subtle and cunning, O powdery gold!
O filaments of amber, two-faced iridescence!

For Pound, colour inheres in the coloured object, it is of its nature; just as the carved or hewn shape inheres in the stone block before it has been touched; just as words inhere, in the natures they name, not in the minds that do the naming. Not in painting any more than in poetry will Pound agree that 'it all depends how you look at it'. Nature exists as other, bodied against us, with real attributes and her own laws which it is our duty to observe.

Adrian Stokes, who met Pound many times in 1917, 1918, and 1919, both in Rapallo and in Venice, has written several books that make an illuminating, perhaps indispensable commentary on the *Cantos*. Stokes makes a great deal of the derivation of marble from limestone, which is of all stones the one that has most affinity with the element of water. He maintains that great carvers of marble, such as Agostino di Duccio, the sculptor of Sigismundo's Tempio,[1] express their material

[1] According to John Pope-Hennessy, *Italian Renaissance Sculpture* (London 1958), p. 328, much of this carving is now attributed to Matteo de Pasti.

through the medium of figures they carve from it; and that in doing so they try (unconsciously) to do justice to the stone's watery origin. This fantasy, he argues, would be particularly common and potent in Venice, built upon water, its power and prosperity based on naval supremacy and sea-going trade. Hence, he is particularly interested in the Istrian marble used by the Venetian builders and carvers:

'Istrian marble blackens in the shade, is snow or salt-white where exposed to the sun. . . .

'. . . For this Istrian stone seems compact of salt's bright yet shaggy crystals. Air eats into it, the brightness remains. Amid the sea Venice is built from the essence of the sea. . . .

'Again, if in fantasy the stones of Venice appear as the wave's petrification, then Venetian glass, compost of Venetian sand and water, expresses the taut curvature of the cold under-sea, the slow, oppressed yet brittle curves of dimly translucent water.

'If we would understand a visual art, we ourselves must cherish some fantasy of the material that stimulated the artist, and ourselves feel some emotional reason why his imagination chose . . . to employ one material rather than another. Poets alone are trustworthy interpreters. They alone possess the insight with which to re-create subjectively the unconscious fantasies that are general.'[1]

Those last sentences seem to be Stokes's oblique acknowledgment that he draws authority here from the early cantos, which, as we know, he had read with excitement some seven years before, and from one of these in particular, Canto XVII.

In Canto XVII there appears, to begin with, the very epithet for stone which Stokes was to use, 'salt-white'. Elsewhere in the canto Pound compresses into a single perception the whole process of the composition of marble from the incrustation of sunken timber by algae, through shell-encrusted cliff and cave, to the hewn stone of the palazzo with its feet in water. Thus 'Marble trunks out of stillness' are balks of timber encrusted

---

[1] *The Stones of Rimini* (London 1934), pp. 19–20.

by limestone deposits, but they are no less ('On past the palazzi') the hewn columns of some Venetian portico, which is 'the rock sea-worn' as well as the wood stone-encrusted. The light is said to be 'not of the sun', and this for all sorts of reasons : because it is light as reflected off water in the open air or inside a cave or inside a Venetian portico, because it is light refracted through water when we imagine ourselves submerged along with the just-forming limestone.

When, a few lines later, a man comes by boat talking of 'stone trees' and 'the forest of marble', he may be taken as one who brings to a Venice not yet revetted in stone the news of marble to be quarried, together with his excited sense of an affinity between city and quarry, a fittingness about bringing the stone of the one to dress the other; or he may be conceived as one who returns to another part of Italy with excited news of the city of stone on water that the Venetians are making. He speaks of the beaks of gondolas rising and falling, and of the glass-blowers from Murano in terms that look forward to Stoke's argument about the marine fantasies inspiring them. The transition from this, in two lines of verse, to 'Dye-pots in the torch-light', may be glossed from another book by Adrian Stokes :

'There is no doubt that the Venetian painters were directly inspired in their use of oil paint by the achievements of the glass makers at Murano.'[1]

This stone Venice is seen in the poem as a product of Mediterranean sensibility (related, for instance, to the Greek culture, similarly maritime, similarly marble-loving) and not, as Ruskin thought, related northward to Gothic. The place spoken of is identified as Venice only at the end of the canto, and then only obliquely (by way of two names, Borso and Carmagnola). And this is right, for the pleached arbour of stone, besides being Venice and besides being the quarries from which Venice was built, is the good place, a sort of heaven of cut and squared masonry, which the broken but indomitable hero earns by his resolution and courage.

[1] *Colour and Form* (London 1937), p. 111.

The *Cantos* force us to dismiss from our minds most of the familiar connotations of 'marmoreal' or 'stony'. Where 'marble' appears, or 'stone', it is a sign of resurgence and renewed hope. The most striking example is in Canto XVI where the first glimmer of convalescence after the passage through infernal regions, which occupied Cantos XIV and XV also, is a hand clutching marble. After the marble comes the new inflow, the embryonic, the new potential; and twelve lines later in Canto XVI a new amplitude and tranquillity: 'The grey stone posts, / and the stair of gray stone. . . .'

It is this casing in hewn and chiselled stone that, in the *Cantos*, justifies Sigismundo Malatesta. That is the achievement which Pound celebrates. And, if we understand why, we go near to the nerve of all the early cantos, for of all spiritual manifestations, the one that Pound at this stage showed himself surest about, and most excited by, was that which in the Renaissance went by the name of *virtù*:

> That hath the light of the doer, as it were
> a form cleaving to it.

The virtù which is the light of a personality cleaving to act or artifact, moulding and forming it, is all the more impressively *there*, all the more certainly a proof that the spiritual resources of the person can modify and indelibly mark the physical, when we perceive it as in the Rimini Tempio transmitted through intermediaries as well as through a medium—the *virtù* not of doer or artificer, but of the patron who caused things to be done, caused artifacts to be made. For the Tempio, according to Adrian Stokes, expresses not Alberti's personality nor Agostino di Duccio's, but Sigismundo's. This was the emphasis Pound was to give to Sigismundo in *Guide to Kulchur:* 'There is no other single man's effort equally registered.'

When Adrian Stokes wrote of the Tempio as Sigismundo's emblem, he was making another distinction besides that between the Renaissance patron and other kinds of patron. He insists that Sigismundo is 'projected directly into stone, not as a succession or a story', and that 'each characteristic passed easily into a form of art, non-musical, tense'. When he writes 'not as a succession . . . non-musical', he is deploring the confusion of non-successive arts like sculpture and architecture with the 'successive' art of music, a confusion that he lays at the door of Brunelleschi. Pound had made the same protest, but from the side of, and on behalf of, music:

'The early students of harmony were so accustomed to think of music as something with a strong lateral or horizontal motion that they never imagined any one, ANY ONE could be stupid enough to think of it as static; it never entered their heads that people would make music like steam ascending from a morass.'[1]

But what of literature, of poetry? Is not poetry necessarily a 'successive' art like music, carving its structures out of lapsing time? Certainly the Symbolists thought so, with their 'De la musique avant toute chose'. But Pound as early as *Gaudier-Brzeska* was opposed to symbolism on these grounds as on others, and was speculating about poetry by analogy with the spatial art of sculpture rather than the temporal art of music.

In 1927 he was still imagining his poetry in these sculptural and spatial terms. This appears from a letter written in that year to his father, a document which is invaluable in any case as it is the nearest we come to an exegesis by the poet of one of his own cantos, specifically, of Canto XX.

This canto opens with interlarded scraps of verse from the Provençal of Bernart de Ventadour and the Latin of Catullus and Propertius. It moves into a pleasantly relaxed and affectionate reminiscence of Pound's visit, on the advice of his teacher Hugo Rennert, to the scholar of Provençal, Emile Lévy, with a problem of vocabulary from Arnaut Daniel. Pound's exegesis for his father begins with the first line of a fourth section, 'He was playing there at the palla.' Pound writes that this section represents 'Nicolo d'Este in sort of

[1] Pound, *Patria Mia and The Treatise on Harmony* (London 1962), p. 80.

delirium after execution of Parisina and Ugo' (that is, of Nicolo's wife and his own natural son, who had been her lover). And Pound's note goes on:

'The whole reminiscence jumbled or "candied" in Nicolo's delirium. Take that as a sort of bounding surface from which one gives the main subject of the Canto, the lotophagoi; lotus eaters, or respectable dope smokers; and general paradiso. You have had a hell in Canti XIV, XV; purgatorio in XVI etc.'[1]

Nicolo's delirium plays with or plays over a great deal more than this. It includes, as Pound notes, memories of a passage of the *Iliad* when the old men of Troy talk of returning Helen to the Greeks and so ending the war; and this is confounded with another beautiful woman on another wall—Elvira, in Lope's play *Las Almenas de Toro*, which is described in *The Spirit of Romance*. Another episode that weaves in and out of Nicolo d'Este's disordered mind is the death of Roland. Against the tumultuous violence of love and war in Nicolo's delirium the serenity of what follows was to stand out seductively.

The same myth perceptions about the use of hewn stone or marble by sculptor and architect recur not only in Canto XVII but in many others besides.

> 'From the colour the nature
>   & by the nature the sign!'
> Beatific spirits welding together
>   as in one ash-tree in Ygdrasail.
>   Baucis, Philemon.
> Castalia is the name of that fount in the hill's fold,
>   the sea below,
>   narrow beach.
> Templum aedificans, not yet marble,
>   'Amphion!'

Amphion, thus invoked, stands inevitably for music and the power of music, especially as defined in *Guide to Kulchur* (p. 283):

---

[1] *The Letters of Ezra Pound* Ed. D. D. Paige (London 1951) p. 285.

'The magic of music is in its effect on volition. A sudden clearing
of the mind of rubbish and the re-establishment of a sense of
proportion.'
For the canto proceeds a few lines later to precisely a 'sense of
proportion':

> Builders had kept the proportion,
> > did Jacques de Molay
> > > know these proportions?

And the masonic associations of Jacques de Molay (accompanied by a reference we have met before, to a shadowless
room in Poitiers[1]) look forward to the achieved act, on the way
to which music's cleansing was only a necessary first stage. For
the achieved act is a stone or marble artifact:

> The architect from the painter,
> > the stone under elm
> Taking form now,
> > the rilievi,
> > > the curled stone at the marge

From 'not yet marble' to 'the curled stone at the marge'
graphs the movement toward perfection.

What the architect makes, however, is in the first place an
altar, as Clark Emery points out. For in between 'not yet
marble' and 'the curled stone' has come, along with material
familiar from earlier cantos (for instance the Adonis ritual
at the mouth of the river):

> Grove hath its altar.
> > under elms, in that temple, in silence
> a lone nymph by the pool.
> > Wei and Han rushing together
> two rivers together
> > bright fish and flotsam
> torn bough in the flood
> > and the waters clear with the flowing

---

[1] See *Guide to Kulchur*, p. 109.

Thus, the act is less an artistic achievement than a religious one; or rather it is a particularly solemn and worthy act of art in that it is a religious act also. For Pound's dislike of the Judaic element in Christianity stems specifically from the prohibition of graven images, since whenever religious apprehensions are not fixed in the images that an artist makes of them they are handed over instead to those who will codify them in prohibitions, and so betray them :

'To replace the marble goddess on her pedestal at Terracina is worth more than a metaphysical argument.'[1]

And it is for this reason that Pound always wishes the Hellenic element in Christianity to outweigh the Hebraic :

'Tradition inheres . . . in the images of the gods and gets lost in dogmatic definitions. History is recorded in monuments, and *that* is why they get destroyed.'[2]

Yvor Winters has challenged the basic assumptions of Pound's method perhaps more justly and searchingly than any other :

'There are a few loosely related themes running through the work, or at least there sometimes appear to be. The structure appears to be that of more or less free association, or progression through reverie. Sensory perception replaces idea. Pound, early in his career, adopted the inversion derived from Locke by the associationists : since all ideas arise from sensory impressions, all ideas can be expressed in terms of sensory impressions. But of course they cannot be : when we attempt this method, what we get is sensory impressions alone, and we have no way of knowing whether we have had any ideas or not.'[3]

This is admirably succinct. Moreover—what is more important —the state, in Winters's words, of not knowing 'whether we have had any ideas or not' is an accurate description of the state of mind we find ourselves in when we have been reading the *Cantos.*

One may still turn the force of Winters's objection. For this

---

[1] *Carta Da Visita* (Rome, 1942); translated by J. Drummond as *A Visiting Card* (London, 1952). Cf. *Guide to Kulchur*, Ch. 30.

[2] *A Visiting Card.*　　[3] *The Function of Criticism* (Denver 1957), p. 47.

state, of not knowing whether we have had ideas or not, may be precisely the state of mind that Pound aimed to produce—and for good reasons. Perhaps by his arrangements of sensory impressions (that is to say, of images) Pound aimed to express, not 'ideas', some of which admittedly cannot be expressed in this way, but rather a state of mind in which ideas as it were tremble on the edge of expression. Indeed, this is what we found him doing in Canto XVII, when he re-created the fantasy about the nature of Istrian marble which, arguably, inspired the builders of Venice. 'Fantasy', as used by Adrian Stokes in that connection, seemed to mean precisely the state of mind in which ideas tremble on the edge of expression. What we get in Canto XVII is not quite the idea of Venice held in the mind of the Venetian builder before he began to build; rather we have expressed the state of mind in the builder immediately before the idea crystallizes. In fact, the idea crystallizes only in the process of building, and the achieved building is the only crystallization possible.

Something very like this has been claimed for another poem of our time, 'Thirteen Ways of Looking at a Blackbird', by Wallace Stevens. This poem, according to Albert William Levi, re-creates 'that moment when the resemblances of sense and of feeling are themselves fused in such a way as to point to the resemblances between ideas'.[1] And Levi quotes from Stevens himself:

'The truth seems to be that we live in concepts of the imagination before the reason has established them. If this is true, then reason is simply the methodizer of the imagination. It may be that the imagination is a miracle of logic and that its exquisite divinations are calculations beyond analysis, as the conclusions of the reason are calculations wholly within analysis'. This is hardly acceptable as it stands: to call the imagination 'a miracle of logic' is to play fast and loose with the word 'logic', just as speaking of 'concepts of the imagination' is to loosen unmanageably the meaning of concept. Yet Stevens in

[1] 'A Note on Wallace Stevens and the Poem of Perspective,' *Perspective*, VII, 3 (Autumn 1954), 137–46.

a blurred and extravagant way is expressing what is reasonable enough: we live (at least some of the time) in arrangements of images which, as mental experiences, have a clear connection with those experiences that the reason is subsequently to establish as concepts. And thus it seems possible that Canto XVII and Canto XCI alike illustrate, as does Stevens's poem according to Levi, 'the moment at which the ideas of sensation merge (in most un-Lockian fashion) into the ideas of reflection.'

At least twice Pound has tried to re-create such moments in his prose. In his essay on mediaevalism, which was reprinted in *Make It New*, he wrote:

'We appear to have lost the radiant world where one thought cuts through another with clean edge, a world of moving energies *"mezzo oscuro rade,"* *"risplende in se perpetuale effecto"*, magnetisms that take form, that are seen, or that border the visible, the matter of Dante's *Paradiso*, the glass under water, the form that seems a form seen in a mirror. . . .' (p. 351)

And the reference to magnetism connects this with a passage from *Guide to Kulchur* (p. 152):

' "I made it out of a mouthful of air,' wrote Bill Yeats in his heyday. The *forma*, the immortal *concetto*, the concept, the dynamic form which is like the rose pattern driven into the dead iron-filings by the magnet, not by material contact with the magnet itself, but separate from the magnet. Cut off by the layer of glass, the dust and filings rise and spring into order. Thus the *forma*, the concept rises from death. . . .'

Here too 'concept' is used loosely. For it is plain that, speaking at all strictly, the *forma* and the concept are distinct. In the first passage, for instance, the *forma* evoked is something common to any number of mediaeval concepts; the one form can be, as it were, separated out into several distinct concepts, some belonging to physics, some to metaphysics, some to psychology, and so on. The one pattern informs all these different manifestations. And the point to be made is that Pound in the *Cantos* characteristically aims at re-creating not the concept, any or all or them, but rather the *forma*, the thing behind them and common to them all. By arranging sensory impressions he aims to state, not ideas, but the form behind and in ideas, the moment before that 'fine thing held in the mind' has precipitated out now this idea, now that.

The images of these passages from the prose—especially those of glass and water, and of glass under water—pervade the whole of Canto XCI. It begins with two lines of music in black notation set to words in Provençal; and continues :

> that the body of light come forth
>> from the body of fire
> And that your eyes come to the surface
>> from the deep wherein they were sunken,
> Reina—for 300 years.
>> and now sunken
> That your eyes come forth from their caves
> & light then
>> as the holly-leaf
>> qui laborat, orat
> Thus Undine came to the rock
>>> by Circeo
> and the stone eyes again looking seaward.

The lines of music make the important if obvious point that at the level of the *forma*, the artists of a period are at one with the conceptual thinkers; the *forma* is behind and in the music of the thirteenth century just as it is behind and in Grosseteste's work on the physics of light. And indeed, when Pound in *Guide to Kulchur* wants to illustrate how 'the *forma*, the concept rises from death', his example is from art, from the history of European song. The mediaeval *forma* that Pound particularly values is re-created whenever the tradition of song (originating, Pound thinks, in Provençe) is momentarily recovered, for instance by Henry Lawes in England in the seventeenth century. It is for this reason that Pound's version of the 'Donna mi prega' is dedicated 'to Thomas Campion his ghost, and to the ghost of Henry Lawes, as prayer for the revival of music'. The whole of Canto XCI is, from one point of view, just that prayer repeated. The 'queen', the *forma*, has been lost 'for 300 years'—three hundred years since the heyday of Henry Lawes, the cryptic reference thus taking up the square notes at the head of the page.

But it is important to realize that what is lost, according to Pound, is not just one technique of musical composition nor even one attitude toward such composition; what has gone is not a knack nor an expertise, but a *forma*. It is lost in one sense, but in another it never can be lost. The *forma* when it is manifest to thinkers and artists, informing their activities, is like 'glass under water'; when we say that it is 'lost', we mean that the glass has sunk back under the water so far that it can no longer be seen. The metaphor is more precise than any formulation in prose. The prayer, accordingly, is for the *forma* to rise through the waves again. At the same time the thinkers and artists must be looking for it; eyes must again look seaward. The waiting upon the *forma* must be a ritual ceremonious act, the invocation of a spirit or a god; and the waiting must also be expressed in art—the stone eyes are, for instance, those of the marble goddess replaced on her pedestal at Terracina; they express man's ceremonious waiting upon the elemental energies of air and water. It may be objected that we are given here not glass under water, but eyes under water; but eyes have most of the properties of glass together with an active *virtu* in themselves. The *forma* is an active and activating principle; and eyes under water is therefore a more precise ikon than the glass under water that Pound offered earlier in his prose.

The looseness of organization over long stretches of the *Cantos* is deliberate. For only if we are presented with references thus disorganized can we appreciate the drama of their gradual drawing together toward the high points of the poem, where what began as random associations are seen to organize themselves into constellations ever more taut and brilliant, and ultimately into the *forma*. This gradual clarifying and drawing together (which has an analogue in social organizations—see Canto XCIII, 'Swedenborg said "of societies" / by attraction') can be seen taking place not just inside a canto but over a sequence of many cantos.

The weight of Winters's objection falls elsewhere, however; and, surprisingly, Pound appears to have foreseen it and guarded against it. In one of his latest pieces of criticism, an introduction to reproductions of paintings by Sheri Martinelli, Pound has censured what he sees as a new orthodoxy derived from misunderstanding of a painter, Percy Wyndham Lewis, whom Pound had championed many years before:

'Lewis said something about art not having any insides, not meaning what several misinterpreters have assumed. I had a word in the early preface to some studies of Cavalcanti. Frate Egidio had already written against those who mistake the eye for the mind.'

Mistaking the eye for the mind is precisely what Winters accuses Pound of doing. The early preface to Cavalcanti is presumably the essay on mediaevalism, containing a passage that is indeed, as we have seen and as Pound implies, sufficient of itself to disprove Winters's contention. 'Frate Egidio' appears in the notes to Pound's version of 'Donna mi prega'; he is Egidio Colonna, an orthodox commentator suspicious of the heterodox Cavalcanti. And he appears also in Canto XCIV, which starts with several references to John Adams and what followed him in American thought about civics. It continues:

> Beyond civic order:
> > l'AMOR.
> Was it Frate Egidio—'per la mente'
> > looking down and reproving
> 'who shd/ mistake the eye for the mind'.
> Above prana, the light,
> > > past light, the crystal.
> Above crystal, the jade!

A hierarchy is established among kinds of creditable activity. The setting up and maintaing of civic order, exemplified by John Adams, is one sort of praiseworthy activity. Beyond this comes activity under the aegis of love. Beyond that comes 'the light,' beyond that 'the crystal,' beyond that 'the jade.' What is meant by 'the crystal' we have seen from Canto XCI; it is the

DONALD DAVIE

wooing into awareness, and the holding in awareness, of the *forma*. What lies beyond or even above this is 'the jade.' And a clue to what this may be is provided perhaps by an essay on Brancusi, which dates from as far back as 1921 :

'But the contemplation of form or of formal-beauty leading into the infinite must be dissociated from the dazzle of crystal; there is a sort of relation, but there is the more important divergence; with the crystal it is a hypnosis, or a contemplative fixation of thought, or an excitement of the "subconscious" or unconscious (whatever the devil they may be), and with the ideal form in marble it is an approach to the infinite *by form*, by precisely the highest possible degree of consciousness of formal perfection; as free of accident as any of the philosophical demands of a "Paradiso" can make it.'[1]

If this indeed is the right gloss on 'the jade,' it seems that last as first Pound is taking his bearings from the art of sculpture. But it is from sculpture seen in its aspect of carving, as making manifest what is extant. In the Brancusi essay Pound is insistent—what Brancusi gives is 'not "his" world of form, but as much as he has found of "the" world of form.' In the last analysis the art that comes of a marriage between the artist and nature is still, for Pound, superior to the art that comes by immaculate conception, self-generated—'I made it out of a mouthful of air.'

[1] *Literary Essays of Ezra Pound*, ed. T. S. Eliot (London, 1954), p. 444.

J. P. SULLIVAN

Ezra Pound and the Classics

Although it is arguable that Pound's finest criticism of ancient literature was through his translations and his remarks on translation, he offers enough *obiter dicta*, sometimes in defence of his principles and practice of translating, for us to recover something like a coherent attitude to particular areas of ancient literature and philosophy. It has to be stressed at the outset that Pound's criticism, like Eliot's, is at the direction of his poetic and critical interests—this in fact is part of its value—and that it is his positive insights rather than his negative judgments, the latter often reflecting not dislike but lack of interest or sympathy, which were particularly fruitful for those accustomed to a closed system of accepted evaluations of the main classical authors. Pound constantly attacked the growing academicism whereby 'the critical faculty is discouraged, the poets are made an exercise, a means of teaching the language'. He rightly objected that 'there is no discrimination in classical studies. The student is told that all the classics are excellent and that it is a crime to think about what he reads. There is no use pretending that these literatures are read as literature. An apostolic succession of school teachers has become the medium of distribution.'[1] This he saw as contributing to the fact that the modern world had lost a kind of contact with and love for the classics which not only the eighteenth century and the Renaissance shared, but even the Middle Ages, when so much of classical literature had been lost from sight.

Pound therefore in his translations, in his careful choice of

[1] *Literary Essays of Ezra Pound.* Ed. T. S. Eliot (London 1954), p. 239.

the opening of *Odyssey XI* to begin the *Cantos*, even his use for this purpose of Andreas Divus' translation, showed an early emphasis in his thinking on the continuity of, initially, the European poetic tradition and the importance of *making it new*— the classics only exist *in translation*, that is, if they *can* be translated at a particular time, and this has in turn implications for original poetry. Eliot's formulation in *Tradition and the Individual Talent* merely expands Pound's dictum in *The Spirit of Romance*[1] that 'all ages are contemporaneous':

'the whole of the literature of Europe from Homer and within it the whole of the literature of his own country has a simultaneous existence and composes a simultaneous order . . . what happens when a new work of art is created is something that happens simultaneously to all the works of art which preceded it.'

Perhaps Pound is more aware than Eliot was of the gradual closing down of vistas, the erratic removal from our literary consciousness of sometimes quite important areas of creation and thought—a melancholy fact which is obvious to some students of Shakespeare and ought to be to all students of classical literature. But this awareness, which shows itself in some of his negative appraisals, say of Pindar, is perhaps compensated by Pound's optimism about the modern poet's ability to revivify by critical insights areas apparently abandoned to oblivion and about the possibility of grafting on to our own tradition viable branches of oriental art and thought. Of course for Pound (and Eliot) the tradition, whatever its provenance, is a critically determined one and Pound would substitute for the bland spectator's indifferentism of the academic world a criterion of *experience*, which would not necessarily be the same for all ages —how else are we to account for the popularity of certain authors such as Ovid in the Middle Ages? Ovid doesn't touch the appropriate nerve in us—or at least not in the same way. Something is needed, a framework of reference, to deal with *our* experience and this will determine the choice: 'KRINO, *to pick out for oneself, to choose*. That's what the word means . . .' (*ABC of Reading*, p. 30).

[1] New York 1929, p. 8.

Pound's feeling of contemporaneity did not necessarily exclude the historical imagination, and more than many poets, Pound has a sense of the classical world and its legacy; this runs through the earlier Cantos in particular. And his willingness to look at an ancient poet not as dead material, but as living poetry, enabled him to discover, for instance, the irony in Propertius—he termed it *logopoeia*—that alone makes sense of certain parts of that poet's work.[1] In general, he valued certain areas of Latin poetry for the almost lost economy and exactness of language that is vital for cultural health: 'A people that grows accustomed to sloppy writing is a people in process of losing grip on its empire and on itself.'[2]

Pound's views on the classics changed as his own ideas on poetry developed; the case of Sophocles is the most notable example. But he never lost his admiration for Homer, particularly for the *Odyssey*. In his long essay, *Translators of Greek: Early Translators of Homer*,[3] he introduced the radical and important method, since taken up by academic critics, of looking at Homer through his translators, which is not the same as looking at Homer from a translator's point of view. The positive criticism and practice that emerges is patent and coherent enough.[4] He puts his finger on the fact that the Latin tradition is more accessible to English poetic sensibility than the Greek: 'Greek in English remains almost wholly unsuccessful, or rather, there are glorious passages but no long or whole satisfaction. Chapman remains the best English 'Homer', marred though he may be by excess of added ornament, and rather more

[1] See my *Ezra Pound and Sextus Propertius* (London 1965), pp. 58 ff.

[2] *ABC of Reading* (London and New Haven 1934), p. 34.

[3] *Essays*, pp. 249 ff.

[4] As for practice one may mention, besides the significant use of Andreas Divus' translation of the opening of *Odyssey* XI in Canto I, that Pound recognizes the time gap which has to be bridged between a translator and his original by using different layers of language rather than a straightforward 'modern' diction. The present and the past are displayed linguistically by the interaction of modern archaic elements, even old-fashioned translationese. (See my *Ezra Pound and Sextus Propertius*, London 1965, p. 80, for one particular use of this.)

marred by parentheses and inversions, to the point of being hard to read in many places.'[1] He is rather harder on Pope than strict justice warrants, but admits that he 'is easier reading, and, out of fashion though he is, he has at least the merit of translating Homer into *something*'.[2]

Matthew Arnold's famous characterization was: 'Homer is rapid in his movement, Homer is plain in his words and style, Homer is simple in his ideas, Homer is noble in his manner.'[3] A similar list of what Pound saw in Homer may be extracted from his scattered remarks. Apart from the *economy* which Chapman missed, Pound sees in Homer two further qualities that translators have been unable to capture: 'the magnificent onomatopoeia', and secondly 'the authentic cadence of speech'.[4] In so far as a translator approximates to onomatopoeia, to musicality, to sonorousness, or, on the other hand, to the authenticity of conversation, Pound approved of him: Andreas Divus managed at least to be 'singable', to keep hinting at 'the poetic motion', and to achieve simplicity of diction. Not unconnected with these qualities is the note Pound characterized elsewhere as 'freshness': 'The chief impression in reading Homer is freshness. Whether illusion or not, this is the classic quality. 3000 years old and still *fresh*. A trans. that misses that is bad.'[5] Of Book II of the *Odyssey*, he said further: 'Very definite sense: Telemachus growing up and asserting himself. It is the vividness and rapidity of narration, three little scenes, all alive.'[6] Seeing the *Iliad* and the *Odyssey* as immortalizing 'the shored relics of a very human and high state of culture', he more and more stressed the novelistic element in Homer, that is, the prose element, the narrative line, pointing to 'the quite H. Jamesian precisions of the *Odyssey*':[7]

'. . . In rough average I shd. say that its lessons for novelists may have received insufficient attention. The imaginary

[1] *Essays*, p. 249.　　　　　　　　[2] *Essays*, p. 250.
[3] *On Translating Homer*, ch. 3 *ad init*.　　[4] *Essays*, p. 250.
[5] *The Letters of Ezra Pound*. Ed. D. D. Paige (London 1951), p. 364.
[6] *Letters*, p. 360.
[7] *Guide to Kulchur* (London 1937), p. 31.

spectator, the study in moeurs, Castiglione's Il Cortegiano element, the knowledge of the whole life has been hammered by dozens of critics but perhaps not been sufficiently probed. The things that the *polumetis* knew were the things a man then *needed* for living. The bow, the strong stroke in swimming, the how-to-provide *and* the high hat, the carriage of man who knew how to rule, who had been everywhere, *Weltmensch*, with "ruling caste" stamped all over him, so that a red, cracked skin and towelled hair as he came out of the underbrush left him "never at a loss". He might as well have met Nausikaa in gibus and opera cloak.

'And as Zeus said: "A chap with a mind like THAT? the fellow is one of us. One of US."

'I hope that elsewhere I have underscored and driven in the greek honour of human intelligence

' "Who even dead yet hath his mind entire." '[1]

This stress on the prose virtues of Homer may be partially due to Pound's general dislike of epic (Vergil, Milton, etc.); allowing for such exceptions as *El Poema del Cid* and the *Iliad*, most epic displayed the qualities he most disliked in Pindar. A long poem or a long commissioned 'public' ode led to rhetoric or to the *longueurs* critics have claimed are necessarily part of epic: it could not be 'language charged with meaning to the utmost degree.' Even the *Iliad*, for instance, of which Pound claimed that 'the corking story' in it is not represented simply in the poem as it has come down to us, is not all gold: the *poetry* is intermittent. Pindar therefore comes in for such comments as: ' "Theban Eagle" be blowed. A dam'd rhetorician half the time' . . . 'the prize wind-bag of all ages' . . . 'big rhetorical drum'[2] and so on. His dislike of Pindar, the 'public' poet *par excellence* contrasts directly with his admiration for Sappho,[3] the supremely 'private' poet. The reasons may go deeper than his dislike for poetic inflation and his reaction to Pindar's bombastic, high-flown, and artificial language. A clue to the question perhaps is to be found in *Hugh Selwyn Mauberley*, where

---

[1] *Kulchur*, p. 146. [2] *Letters*, pp. 98, 138, 143.
[3] Cf. *Essays*, p. 27; *Letters*, p. 143.

Pound uses ironically a rephrased line from the second Olympian Ode :

> τίν' ἄνδρα, τίν' ἥρωα, τινα θεόν
> What god, man, or hero
> Shall I place a tin wreath upon!

Pindar, it would seem, stands for Pound as the paradigm of a public poet,[1] as opposed to Sappho, who cultivates her own Pierian roses and her private self-chosen concerns. Similarly in the *Homage* Propertius represents opposition to the Vergilian ethos that provides 'what the age demanded'. For Pound there is no-one worthy of the wreath; Pindar was conventional (*pompier*) and worse, and would lack no objects for his panegyrics. This sort of moral and social betrayal displays itself to Pound in Pindar's style as against Sappho's.

It is arguable that this set of moral and artistic criteria allowed Pound in the *Propertius* to go straight to the heart of the Augustan literary—and political—situation. He saw, not without justice, that these Augustan poets lived in a world which was not unlike our own at the time the *Homage* was being written (1917), and this made Propertius such an ideal *persona* for Pound's own preoccupations and ideals :

'The value being that the Roman poets are the only ones we know of who had approximately the same problems as we have. The metropolis, the imperial posts to all corners of the known world. The enlightenments. Even the Eighteenth Century is obsessed by the spectre of Catholicism, the Index, the Inquisition. The Renaissance is interesting, but the poets inferior. The Greeks had no world outside, no empire, metropolis, etc. etc.'[2] Pound rightly makes no attempt to separate out the purely literary and the socio-moral implications of the Augustan poets : hence his praise of Propertius is both for his language and tone, and his attitudes. On the one hand, he thought he discerned in Propertius the important quality of *logopoeia* (*Essays*, p. 33)

[1] *Contra* J. J. Espey, *Ezra Pound's Mauberley* (London 1955), p. 88.
[2] *Letters*, p. 141.

and saw him as 'tying blue ribbon in the tails of Virgil and Horace' (*Letters*, p. 246); and on the other, he says of the *Homage*:

'that it presents certain emotions as vital to me in 1917, faced with the infinite and ineffable imbecility of the British Empire, as they were to Propertius some centuries earlier, when faced with the infinite and ineffable imbecility of the Roman Empire. These emotions are defined largely, but not entirely, in Propertius' own terms. If the reader does not find relation to life defined in the poem, he may conclude that I have been unsuccessful in my endeavour.'[1]

Pound rightly divined that there was a strong critical difference between the so-called Alexandrian poets, the Neoterics and their successors, (represented for him by Catullus, Propertius, and Ovid) and the more conventionally central figures in our critical pantheon, Vergil and Horace. He saw the former as bringing something essentially new into literature, as far as the moderns were concerned. He was aware of their Greek roots, but pointed out that 'As we have lost Philetas, and most of Callimachus, we may suppose that the Romans added a certain sophistication; at any rate, Catullus, Ovid, Propertius, all give us something we cannot find now in Greek authors'.[2] What Pound instinctively saw with a poet's eye has been confirmed by recent criticism. Between Catullus and his long-winded epic contemporaries such as Volusius, who were writing in the established Roman tradition of 'public poetry' (the tradition of Ennius), and between Propertius, clinging to his Alexandrian masters, Callimachus and Philetas, and the Vergil of the *Aeneid*, there are distinct differences as to the proper methods and subjects of poetry. Pound is a little unfair to Vergil, who was himself in his earlier works, the *Eclogues* and the *Georgics*, as much of an Alexandrian as anyone,[3] but the *Aeneid* does bulk as the most conventionally esteemed work of Latin

[1] *Letters*, p. 310.
[2] *Essays*, p. 27.
[3] See, e.g., W. Clausen, 'Callimachus and Latin Poetry,' *Greek, Roman, and Byzantine Studies* 5 (1964) pp. 193 ff.

literature.[1] Pound, I think rightly, adds a note of irony to Propertius' praise of the *Aeneid* in Section XII of the *Homage*, for Propertius' point in the original is in fact that Vergil too was an Alexandrian before that work and wrote love poetry in the form of pastorals. Propertius' value to Pound was predominantly the note of irony which he brought to the task of protecting his chosen subject—love—against the Imperial claims for the sort of poetry 'the age demanded' and the chosen form, the low-pitched elegiac note, against the magniloquence of epic: *tenues* as against *duri versus*. Pound speaks therefore of Propertius' 'beautiful cadence', whereas for him 'Virgil is a second-rater, a Tennysonianized version of Homer'. (*Letters*, p. 138). This at least does justice to Vergil's greatest achievement, the perfection of the possibilities of the Latin hexameter, and Pound's description of him as *Tennysonianized* should not be taken *too* pejoratively, for Pound elsewhere gave Tennyson credit for some of his technical achievements: 'He refined the metric of England' (*Essays*, p. 277). But for Pound, Vergil, despite or because of his poetic—or political—conversion from Alexandrianism, added nothing new to the development of Latin poetic language. But when Pound is not building up Propertius at Vergil's expense, a more tempered view of the epic poet may be seen in *Notes on Elizabethan Classicists*, where Pound finds Gavin Douglas at least giving us 'a clue to Dante's respect for the Mantuan' (*Essays*, p. 245).

On Horace, Pound is more puzzling and ambivalent. He sides of course with Propertius as against Horace's 'public' Augustanism, but he includes him among the four Latin poets who matter, adding ambiguously 'Horace you will not want for a long time. I doubt if he is of any use save to the Latin scholar.' (*Letters*, p. 138). This is glossed elsewhere by the remark:

[1] In Section XII of the *Homage* Pound adds to Propertius' apparent praise of the *Aeneid* the words '*And to Imperial order!*,' a perhaps deliberately ambiguous phrase, which however makes it clear that he saw Vergil was here writing from an external rather than internal motivation. Compare his remarks elsewhere: 'But the man who tries to express his age, instead of expressing himself, is doomed to destruction.' *Gaudier-Brzeska*, p. 119.

'A specialist may read Horace if he is interested in learning the precise demarcation between what can be learned about writing, and what cannot. I mean that Horace is the perfect example of a man who acquired all that is acquirable, without having the root.' (*Essays*, pp. 27–8). Yet curiously some of Pound's most recent attempts at translating shorter Latin poems into English have been of Horace[1] and from these it may be seen that Pound values Horace for the strained compactness of his poetry, a quality he found for prose writers in Tacitus (*Letters*, p. 139). He saw in him the economy and intensity he himself so much admired without believing that he was a natural poet. It must be added, however, as a possible explanation of Pound's late interest in Horace, that Horace has long been regarded—for his attitudes rather than his verse—as the old man's poet *par excellence*. It may be that only in Pound's later years did the Horatian 'experience' strike a resonance in him.

In his earlier days Pound appears to have mistrusted Greek tragedy. He wrote of Murray's translations of Euripides :

'I am probably suspicious of Greek drama. People keep on assuring me that it is excellent despite the fact that too many people have praised it. STILL there has been a lot of rhetoric spent on it. And I admit the opening of *Prometheus* (Aeschylus') is impressive. (Then the play goes to pot.) Also I like the remarks about Xerxes making a mess of [illegible] in another Aeschylean play, forget the name [*Persae*]. Some choruses annoy me. Moralizing nonentities making remarks on the pleasures of a chaste hymeneal relation, etc., etc. Statements to the effect that Prudence is always more discreet than rashness, and other such brilliant propositions . . . I am too damnd ignorant to talk intelligently about the Greek drama. Still I mistrust it, dona ferentes, etc.'[2]

For Pound the rhetoric spent on Greek plays seemed paralleled by the rhetoric in them—again the fear of the poetically otiose.

---

[1] Notably, Odes I, 31; I, 11; III, 30 in *Confucius to Cummings, An Anthology of Poetry*. Ed. Ezra Pound and Marcella Spann (New Directions, New York 1964).

[2] *Letters*, p. 146.

In his impressionistic *How to Read*, we find this fear formally stated:

'The "great dramatists" decline from Homer, and depend immensely on him for their effects; their "charge," at its highest potential, depends so often, and so greatly on their being able to count on their audience's knowledge of the *Iliad*. Even Aeschylus is rhetorical.'[1]

This may be glossed by some further remarks in the *ABC of Reading* (pp. 69–70):

'The question of a word or phrase being "useless" is not merely a numerical problem. Anatole France in criticizing French dramatists pointed out that *on the stage* the words must give time for the action: they must give time for the audience to take count of what is going on. Even on the printed page there is an analogous ease. Tacitus in writing Latin uses certain forms of condensation that don't necessarily translate advantageously into English.'

But Greek tragedy has more static elements than modern drama, and while Pound was in search of 'language charged with meaning to the utmost degree' and working for the elimination of all non-functional words, then dramatic verse would be generally an object of suspicion to him. He would have to work towards a different conception of what a Greek drama at its best could be before doing more justice to at least a part of Attic tragedy. And in fact the earlier mild acceptance of Aeschylus as the best the Greek drama had to offer ('a great original'), despite the fact 'that he is not austere, but often even verbose after a fashion' (*Essays*, p. 273) begins to yield to an admiration for Sophocles. There is a recognition of 'Sophoklean economy' (*Essays*, p. 36 n.) and an addition to the paragraph in *How to Read* quoted above states that 'E.P.'s later and unpublished notes revise all this in so far as they demand much greater recognition of Sophokles' (*Essays*, p. 27 n.). Clearly this was working towards, or was the product of, Pound's fascinating translation of the *Trachiniae*. This

---

[1] *Essays*, p 27.

translation, *The Women of Trachis*, is the climax of his growing interest in Sophocles and Greek tragedy in general. In particular, his recognition of 'Sophoklean economy' is fully embodied in the translation, as one critic has well observed.[1] Pound's demand for poetic economy and intensity, derived partly from the early theories of Imagisme, led to the judgment that 'The Trachiniae presents the highest peak of Greek sensibility registered in any of the plays that have come down to us'. To bring out the economy and intensity, Pound took a number of short cuts, not all of which the critic or the scholar will find defensible, but his translation, despite the animadversions of the literalists, has behind it a critical insight, debateable but definite, without which no translation is ever worthy of the name. And *The Women of Trachis* has to be set beside the *Homage to Sextus Propertius* as a major attempt to restore to us an ancient original, which in an important sense had been lost. These Sophoclean qualities Pound had earlier seen only in the best Latin poets, such as Catullus and a few of the Augustans. He was led to this fresh insight, we are told, by rereading his treatment of the Fenollosa notes and versions of the Japanese Nō.[2] It is a tribute to his lack of dogmatism and willingness to change his mind—in literary matters at least—that he was eager to see for himself 'how Greek drama, and in particular how Sophokles, would measure up to similar or approximately similar treatment'. *The Women of Trachis* was the highly individual and interesting result, and his estimate of Greek tragedy and thus his whole literary estimate of the important world authors correspondingly changed. The change has been summarized by Pound himself as 'dress (in the military sense) on Sophokles'.[3] Of course, as with Horace, this conversion to Sophocles was not simply an application of theory or an experi-

[1] See H. A. Mason, *Arion* II. 2 (1963), p. 107.

[2] A further contributory event seems to have been Seferis' translation of *Cathay* into Modern Greek. Seferis had introduced China to Greece, as Pound would tell his visitors. See Michael Reck, 'L'époque élisa-béthaine' L'Herne, *Ezra Pound*. Ed. Michel Beaujour (Paris 1965), p. 165.

[3] *Confucius to Cummings*, (New York 1964) p. xi (Publisher's Note).

ment for its own sake. It might be suggested that at this period something in the play found an echo in Pound himself and produced the necessary inner solicitation that is vital for poetry or translation. It is possible to see in Heracles another mask, another *persona*, for the poet himself. The lines spoken by Heracles, particularly about his madness and the Shirt of Nessus, and the key phrase of Pound's interpretation of the play 'It all coheres,' may be related directly to his latter experiences and in particular to the words in the last fragment of the *Cantos* so far:

> A tangle of works unfinished.
>
> But the beauty is not the madness
> Though my errors and wrecks lie about me.
> And I am not a demigod,
>   I cannot make it cohere

and later:

>   i.e. it coheres all right
>   even if my notes do not cohere[1]

What was Pound out to discover in the classical authors he approved of? In one way he was using them as elements in his progress of poetry, and how he saw this progress was of course critically determined by his own work and preoccupations; in another way he found in them many different things. Melodic invention and narrative vividness, for instance, in Homer; economy in Sappho, Catullus, and (later) Sophocles; story-telling technique and mythological plausibility in Ovid; *logopoeia* and sophistication in Propertius; compression in Tacitus, and so on—things perhaps found elsewhere and in other authors, but representing in their classical formulation high points of poetic development and therefore suitable touchstones for good

---

[1] Canto CXVI (fragment) Ezra Pound: *Cantos 1916–1962—Eine Auswahl*, (Munich 1964), pp. 190, 192.

writing : 'The classics, "ancient and modern," are precisely the acids to gnaw through the thongs and bulls-hides with which we are tied by our schoolmasters'—'the one use of a man's knowing the classics is to prevent him from imitating the false classics.' (*Letters*, p. 168.)

Although the literary significance of the classics for Pound is initially the most striking, their cultural importance for him is not to be overlooked. The classics, whether Homer's epics or the 'Confucian Odes', are both the records and the germ of civilization. This view of the classics as *paedeuma* (in Frobenius' sense) involves not an *external* apprehension of what they have to say or convey, but rather seeing them as summarizing selectively and intuitively the whole experience of a given age or milieu. They represent, as it were, civilization in the sense in which it is meant in the half-humorous description of culture as 'what is left when one has forgotten everything one has ever learnt'. More seriously, the classics embody the *forma* of a given era, that half-conscious substratum of a civilization, which makes it possible for us to see in quite disparate art-forms in any given age a similar spirit or set of characteristics and allows the meaningful application of such terms as 'Attic', 'Hellenistic', 'Baroque', etc. Pound in the *Cantos* is attempting a similar ambitious task. But although the *Cantos* might be described as a *paedeuma* for the modern world as Homer's epics were for the Greek world, the work is not a 'public' poem in the way the *Aeneid*, say, strikes Pound as a 'public' poem and Pindar as a 'public' poet; the *Cantos* uses individual, lyrical and personal matter within a structure of tradition, not to expatiate on or describe some external *donnée* in which the poet is not personally involved, but to express through one man's experience and knowledge, empirical as well as historical, the underlying significance of a whole age and its relation to the past. The particularity of the poet becomes representative without his dealing in generalities or universals *per se*. This of course partially accounts for the historically determined nature of the work itself, its spilling over beyond its original conception. The content of the poem cannot be separated from the poet's experience.

There was another, equally significant dialogue with antiquity that exercised Pound—this time a more philosophical and critical debate about the very nature of poetry, with the discussion centring around Greek philosophy, particularly Plato and Aristotle. Plato's contribution is largely through Neoplatonism, as may be seen in the essay on Cavalcanti (cf. e.g., *Essays*, pp. 159, 161), and Aristotle, of course, might be mediated by later philosophers, Neoplatonic, Arabic, medieval and scholastic, Renaissance and so on, and Pound, as ever, is not particularly interested in the exact attribution of ideas to their authors. It might indeed be said, tendentiously, that the Neoplatonic elements in Pound are tempered throughout, consciously or unconsciously, by a sort of Aristotelian empiricism. At any rate, the dialogue concerned the nature of the poetic imagination and, by implication, the way to write poetry in the twentieth century. Pound's interest was as usual practical and eclectic, but it would be a mistake for that reason to underrate his very intelligent perceptions. Again, for Pound, philosophy, of all cultures, was contemporaneous and worth taking seriously. He approved of the Pythagoreans and some post-Aristotelian philosophers because 'Zeno, Epicurus, Pythagoras did teach a modus vivendi, did advocate modes of life, and did not merely argue about certain abstractions' (*Kulchur*, p. 25), just as he disapproved of the Greek philosophy that limited itself to arid and abstract discussion that had no connection with the world of men.

Pound's most extended discussion of Aristotle is of the *Ethics*.[1] And it is interesting to examine this first. Pound is unsurprisingly ambivalent. On the one hand the Stagyrite is 'a swine and a forger'; on the other, 'his lucidity as to the measuring function, and his implication of money of account are both admirable' (p. 325). He 'is not fit to clean the boots of Confucius' (p. 326), but 'With the start of the VIth book he ceases to be irritating. He has got onto his own subject and goes on quite nicely up to VI. vii. 4.' (*ibid.*). Pound is in fact

---

[1] *Kulchur*, pp. 304 ff.

very perceptive about the nature of Aristotle's philosophising, the quality that makes him such a sympathetic author to the modern school of Oxford analysis. Indeed considering the date of the book's publication, 1937, the following is an impressively intelligent statement:

'The "danger" of Aristotle arises partly from his not putting certain statements in the purely lexicographical form [cp. J. L. Austin's 'philosophical lexicography']. The "danger" for the reader, or class, being largely that of losing time in useless discussion. For example [III] ii. 3. Nobody deliberates about things eternal, such as the order of the universe.

'IF this is put as a statement about the use of the word (BOULUETAI), it does not lead to useless yatter.

'Lorenzo Valla wd. have written. Whatever mental process we indulge in re the eternal etc. we do not use the verb BOULEUOMAI in such cases. We do not . . . etc. spend time *deciding whether*, but *we observe that*.'   [*ibid*. p. 318]

'But even the most rabidly fanatical Aristotelian can scarcely claim that Arry had completely clarified his lexicographic intentions, i.e. sorted out what is or shd. be strictly lexicographic from what he supposed to express wisdom or observations on life and nature.'   [*ibid*. p. 319]

With the *Poetics*, the matter is more complicated. Although Pound several times quotes with approval Aristotle's dictum (Ch. 22. 16–7) that 'by far the greatest thing is the use of metaphor . . . it is the token of genius. For the right use of metaphor means an eye for resemblances', yet the whole of Pound's poetic theory is otherwise diametrically opposed to Aristotle's.

The *Poetics*, whatever its importance has been in European literary criticism, is a curious, almost un-Aristotelian work; someone once described it as the course of lectures delivered by Aristotle when the regular Professor of Poetry was on leave from the Lyceum. Apart from his observational analyses, the main purpose of the work seems to be vindication of epic and drama from the strictures of Plato. His defence is, roughly, that art does not represent particulars, but rather universal truths and it is therefore more serious and 'philosophical' than history, for 'a poet's task is not to tell what actually happened but what could and would happen either probably or inevitably' (Ch. 9. 1). Tragedy's social function, *pace* Plato, was that 'through pity and fear, it gives relief (*katharsis*) to these and similar emotions' (Ch. 6. 2).

Pound dismisses the metaphysic underlying the treatise by remarking :

'Aristotle being neither poet nor complete imbecile contented himself with trying to formulate some of the general interior and exterior relations of work already extant. He has presumably the largest bastard family of any philosopher. Ninkus, Pinkus and Swinky all try to say what the next writer must do.'[1]
But in fact the prescriptive *is* already there in Aristotle, and Aristotle's stress on form (cf. in particular *Poetics*, Ch. 6–7) is at least partially rejected or qualified by Pound :

'I am not going to say : "form" is a non-literary component shoved on to literature by Aristotle or by some non-litteratus who told Aristotle about it. Major form is not a non-literary component. But it can do us no harm to stop an hour or so and consider the very important chunks of world-literature in which form, major form, is remarkable mainly for absence.

'There is a corking plot to the *Iliad*, but it is not told us in the poem or at least not in the parts of the poem known to history as The Iliad. It would be hard to find a worse justification of the theories of dramatic construction than the *Prometheus* of Aeschylus . . . Lope has it, but it is not the "Aristotelian" beginning, middle and end, it is the quite reprehensible BEGINNING WHOOP and then any sort of a trail off . . . The component of these great works and *the* indispensable component is texture. . . .'[2]
It might be said in passing that this emphasis on texture at the expense of form goes some way towards destroying the older theory of literary genres that Aristotle and most ancient

---

[1] *Essays*, p. 74.
[2] *Essays*, pp. 394–5.

critics stood for. Thus the *Cantos* might be seen as a sort of lyrical dramatic epic.

To understand the basic disagreement Pound would have had with Aristotle we have to look a little closer at their literary theories. For Aristotle, in the drama plot is supreme with character secondary, and character, in so far as it was used, had to be developed in accordance with the laws of probability and consistency in general terms of a character's station, sex, etc. (cf. *Poetics*, Ch. 15), but this at once departs from the individuality and particularity that is essential to modern poetry as a whole and Pound's poetic theories in particular. Although Pound praised Aristotle for his stress on particulars in his philosophy ('he at least knew how generals are known from particulars'), Aristotle's stress on abstract syllogistic reasoning, from facts to generalities, or from observations to laws, has for Pound ominous implications for poetry and thought. He comments approvingly on Cavalcanti's simultaneously being 'for experiment', but 'against the tyranny of the syllogism, blinding and obscurantist' (*Essays*, p. 159). Thus when he follows up his translation of Cavalcanti's Canzone d'Amore in Canto XXXVI with the lines :

> Aquinas head down in a vacuum,
> Aristotle which way in a vacuum ?
> not quite in a vacuum.

he is clearly moving towards that line in mediaeval Aristotelianism that Ernst Bloch, in an essay in which Avicenna's ideas are contrasted with the thinking of the Aristotelian scholastic Establishment, has called the 'Aristotelian Left'.[1]

Pound invokes instead a more 'intuitive' theory which was influenced in its expression by, among others, the work of Ernest Fenollosa, who offered the statement 'Poetry . . . must appeal to the emotions with the charm of direct impression, flashing through regions where the intellect can only grope.'[2]

---

[1] Cf. *Avicenna und die Aristotelische Linke*, Suhrkamp Verlag (Frankfurt 1963).

[2] *The Chinese Written Character as a Medium for Poetry* (London 1936), p. 29.

In a way, Pound's theories on this subject are at the root of our modern poetic : which has been aptly described as 'the poetry of experience'. This stresses the unique particular, or the juxtaposition of particulars, rather than a logical progression or linkage of thoughts; it stresses character rather than coherent plot; the dramatic lyric rather than the drama with a beginning, middle and end. As Pound put it (as early as 1908) :

'To me the short so-called dramatic lyric—at any rate the sort of thing I do—is the poetic part of a drama the rest of which (to me the prose part) is left to the reader's imagination or implied or set in a short note. I catch the character I happen to be interested in at the moment he interests me, usually a moment of song, self-analysis, or sudden understanding or revelation.'[1] Pound is defining here his technique of *personae*, masks through which the poet himself may speak. In Pound's case, the character in such dramatic lyrics is not chosen out of a hat, but because of the particular reverberations 'at the moment' set up between the poet's preoccupations and the similar or kindred interests of the character.

Modern poetic, including, in their different ways, Browning's 'incidents in the development of a soul', Hopkins' 'inscape', Eliot's 'objective correlative' and even D. H. Lawrence's 'life', gives significance to *particulars* and character because the particulars generate their own meanings *in the poem* and thus their appropriate emotions in the reader. The particulars formulate their own values; empathy and understanding replace abstract judgment and the application of pre-existing values. Fundamentally, the instigation may be Romantic,[2] and it is true that this is not the only way of writing poetry, but it is hard to agree with such traditionalist critics as Yvor Winters that the whole notion is simply a post-empiricist fallacy, deriving from the Humean view that all our 'ideas' arise from the constant association of sense impressions.[3] But Pound's poetic by no

[1] *Letters*, p. 36.
[2] On this whole question, see R. Langbaum, *The Poetry of Experience*, (London 1957), in particular pp. 9–37, 210–35.
[3] See my *Ezra Pound and Sextus Propertius*, p. 89.

means implies that we are, as it were, stuck with particulars, naked facts, and nothing more. The poetic particular generates its own universe, but it is a universe which cannot be shared by another poetic particular. I cannot write :

> People in the New York subway—
> Petals on a long black bough.

We are in a different world. The 'mystical particularity' of a poem is that one cannot combine the well-known elements and produce equivalent effects. Of course for Aristotle the odd and the unique on the mundane plane are deviations or aberrations from a norm; in poetry the unique creates its own norm, which is not an arbitrary one, but may be relying on something other than itself, say, a myth, a belief, a way of seeing things. It is not however to be judged by that.

If poetry were like prose or philosophy, then such transferences as in my example—and translation—would be possible, but as Pound remarked 'certain things are SAID only in verse. You can't translate 'em' (*Kulchur*, p. 121). This is one of the reasons why Pound argued that the further poetry moved away from music, the supremely untranslatable art (for what would translation consist of?), the more it deteriorated.

The ramifications of this basic point are, of course, many. There is first of all the early emphasis Pound placed on the image as 'the primary pigment of poetry' (as Wyndham Lewis called it) : 'The image is the word beyond formulated language.' (*Gaudier-Brzeska*, p. 102). What is formulated is something that has grown out of more undifferentiated strata where the concept is still a rhythmical or pictorial entity which has yet to be put into musical (or other) speech. And similarly there is the belief that the juxtaposition of objects, images, persons and events, may render them intelligible without conceptual connection or grammatical links, as may be seen in the *Homage* and the *Cantos*. It issued also in an instruction to Imagists : 'Use no superfluous word, no adjective, which does not reveal something.'[1] Why? Because 'the natural object is *always* the

---

[1] *Make it New* (London 1934), p. 337.

adequate symbol' and 'a presented image . . . the perfectly adequate expression or exposition of *any* urge, whatsoever its nature.'[1] In poetry then the natural object is reinstated in all its dignity and particularity by a sort of poetic equivalent of Duns Scotus' *haecceitas*. The Platonic and Aristotelian stress on the impossibility of knowledge without universals, whatever its value in epistemology, belittles the individual object: for the poet the natural object IS its functions and this is its message.

Pound's brief remarks may be glossed by those of a poet closely associated with him, who says of his own ideas of what poetry should be:

'The true value is that peculiarity which gives an object a character by itself. The associational or sentimental value is the false. Its imposition is due to lack of imagination, to an easy lateral sliding . . . the thing that stands eternally in the way of really good writing is always one: the virtual impossibility of lifting to the imagination those things which lie under the direct scrutiny of the senses, close to the nose.'[2]

Or again, one might, in more modern terms, gloss Pound's theory with some of the reports of takers of hallucinogenic drugs such as LSD-25 about the compelling uniqueness of particular everyday objects on which their attention fastens, which would be analogous to Pound's 'scientific mystical empiricism'.

Aristotle's stress on metaphor as the mark of poetic genius may be misleading here by its very intellectuality: he defends metaphor as the perception of similarity in difference, as though the similarity were there waiting to be discovered by a superior

[1] *Make it New*, p. 337; *Polite Essays* (London 1937), p. 13.

[2] *Selected Essays of William Carlos Williams* (New York 1954), p. 11. Donald Davie, who quotes this passage *in extensiore*, adds: 'To all of this, with its emphasis on "the direct scrutiny of the senses," Pound would give a hearty assent, schooled as he had been (by Fenollosa and Gourmont alike) into admiring the controlled observations of empirical science as akin to poetic apprehensions.' *Ezra Pound: Poet as Sculptor* (New York 1964), p. 121. I cannot agree with his later strictures in Chapter VII that Pound might fail to see how natural science can also lead to and support an inert apprehension of particulars in an anti-poetic way. I should have thought Pound's critical remarks on Baudelaire made this clear: 'in many poems one "unpleasant" element is no more inevitable than another.'

intellect or method, after which everyone would agree that it had been there all the time. Now one might accept this in its minimal sense, but the theory rather underrates the creativity of such perception. Not everyone could create *that* metaphor, for the poet himself as a unique individual is involved here. He and he alone is stimulated into juxtaposing certain images or concepts in a fresh metaphor and if in so doing he reveals an aspect of reality, then it is not an aspect that *anyone* could have discovered. Poetry does not have to be 'what oft was thought, but ne'er so well expressed', but something that was perhaps never thought or even seen properly. Once such a metaphor is created, however, it may become accepted, revived, reused or 'made new'. And not all great poets are necessarily great inventors in this way.

Occasionally, such is Aristotle's prestige, he is invoked inappropriately as a supporter of Poundian theories. For example, Hugh Kenner associates 'the Aristotelian equation of a poem with an action' with the 'objective correlative'. But a detailed reading of Aristotle's text will not bear this association out : Aristotle was pleading a case for the universality of poetry against Plato's objection to its unreality. Aristotle's description of the ideal 'plot' is of one continually subject to limitations : of story, of morality, of emotions to be aroused by it (cf. *Poetics*, Chs. 13–14). This of course contrasts with Aristotle's more characteristic view in the rest of his philosophy that 'the concrete individual thing is substance in [the] primary sense', but here as in general he 'does not abandon the Platonic conviction that knowledge is of what is universal.'[1] Similarly, for Aristotle, an individual, a community, or a tragedy has a function and purpose, in relation to which it is to be judged a good or bad specimen of its species.

This, despite Aristotle's general insistence on particulars, leads to abstraction and is contrary to Pound's theories in general, even though he may claim that Aristotle is in various ways on his side. Pound owes more in practice to the sensuous-

[1] *The Philosophy of Aristotle*. Ed. J. R. Bambrough (New York 1963), p. 26.

ness and concreteness of the best European poetry and, for his theory, to Chinese and Japanese poetry and philosophy, as mediated through Confucius or the work of Fenollosa on the ideogram.[1] In fact, one of the best formulations of Pound's poetic is by a Japanese disciple of his, Katue Kitasono:

'The formation of poetry takes such a course as:

A. language   B. imagery   C. ideoplasty

'That which we vaguely call poetical effect means, generally, ideoplasty which grows out of the result of imagery.... What we must do first for imagery is (in this order) collection, arrangement, and combination. Thus we get the first line; "a shell, a typewriter and grapes" in which we have an aesthetic feeling. But there is not (in it) any further development. We add the next line and then another aesthetic feeling is born. Thus all the lines are combined and a stanza is finished. This means the completion of imagery of that stanza and then ideoplasty begins.

'This principle can be applied to poems consisting of several stanzas. In that case ideoplasty is formed when the last stanza is finished.

'Though it cannot be allowed as orthodox of poetry that imagery is performed by ideoplasty.... This violence is dared often by religionists, politicians, and satirists. Morality poems, political poems and satirical poems are written, almost without exception, with such an illogical principle.

'The phenomena in our life proceed, through our senses to our experiences, perceptions, and intuitions. It is intuition rationally that provides the essentials for imagery, and it is the method of poetry that materializes intuitions perceptively and combines. Consequently, exact imagery and ideoplasty are due to an exact method. Pure and orthodox poetry cannot exist without this theory.'[2]

[1] *Contra*, H. Kenner, *The Poetry of Ezra Pound* (London 1951), p. 72–3. It should also be said that Aristotle's doctrines of *mimesis*, inherited from Plato, have little to do, in my opinion, with the Imagisme described in *Gaudier-Brzeska: A Memoir* (London 1916), pp. 146–7.

[2] *Kulchur*, pp. 137–9.

Kitasono, of course, is seeing the creative process from the opposite end. This is the course the formation of poetry takes *in the reader's mind*, although the poet himself might also be the reader.

This indeed might be the point at which to quash the allegation that Pound is in some sense a 'nominalist,'[1] that is, he believes that universals are *universalia post rem* rather than *universalia in re* (Aristotle) or *universalia ante rem* (Plato). Pound does not profess to be an historian of philosophy and he has naturally not expressed himself on the metaphysical problem itself: his interest in such ideas is a poet's interest or, at most, the interest of a cultural historian and social thinker. Nevertheless if one tried to glean from his literary theories, his cultural criticism, and his practice in the *Cantos* any sort of statement of his position it would be roughly as follows: as the sort of poet he is, naturally sympathetic to the more Aristotelian position of *universalia in re* ('generals are known from particulars'). This would fit in well with his emphasis on the natural object, on the image, and on empirical science. He comments scathingly in his remarks on Browning's *Agamemnon*:

' "ideas" as the term is current, are poor two-dimensional stuff, a scant, scratch covering. "Damn ideas, anyhow." An idea is only an imperfect induction from fact.'[2]

Hence he stresses that:

'The image is not an idea. It is a radiant node or cluster; it is what I can, and must perforce, call a VORTEX, from which, and through which, and into which, ideas are constantly rushing. In decency one can only call it a VORTEX. And from this necessity came the name "vorticism". *Nomina sunt consequentia rerum*, and never was that statement of Aquinas more true than in the case of the vorticist movement.'[3]

But this poetic Aristotelianism, as it were, in Pound's earlier theory and practice is not the end of the matter. A rather different metaphysic may be found underlying the *Cantos* and this is a more complex business altogether. I think that Pound would set

[1] H. H. Watts, *Ezra Pound and the Cantos* (London 1952).
[2] *Make it New*, p. 147.   [3] *Gaudier-Brzeska*, p. 106.

his face firmly against a pure Platonist position, against, that is, the theory of universals existing in some timeless, unchanging and perfect state and standing quite apart from the particulars that instantiate them. For one thing, for him as for Aristotle, universals are firmly anchored *in time* and are perceived in history, future as well as past, and in the natural world of objects, at least by the man capable of understanding them: as Canto XC puts it—'UBI AMOR IBI OCULUS EST'. Hence springs his respect 'for the intelligence working in nature' and for empirical science, which is, theoretically at least, based upon a reverent observation of external reality. But there is also a Platonic tinge to Pound's thought. There are, as it were, 'ideas' struggling to express themselves dynamically, 'patterns' that underly the particular artistic, literary and social phenomena of a given age, but which are not to be identified with them. Such an 'idea' would be, for a given period, its *forma*:

'The *forma*, the immortal *concetto*, the concept, the dynamic form which is like the rose pattern driven into the dead iron-filings by the magnet, not by material contact with the magnet itself, but separate from the magnet. Cut off by the layer of glass, the dust and filings rise and spring into order.'[1]

It is in its germinal and developing state that the *forma* interests Pound: once it is dissected and ossified in intellectual history, it becomes a mere idea (in the bad sense), a *universale post rem*. The use of the metaphysical terms here is of course merely a useful analogy to understand the important (and less arid) thoughts that Pound is grappling with. And Avicenna's technical distinction between the three kinds of universals might well be invoked metaphorically to clarify what Pound is getting at. The *forma* of an age is logically prior to the different phenomena, literary, social, and artistic, in which it may be perceived, but it can only be seen *in* these phenomena by a creative and sympathetic intellect. Once concrete reality is left or disregarded we have Pound's 'poor two-dimensional' ideas, severed from their apprehensible ground.

To understand what Pound is after from a different point of

[1] *Kulchur*, p. 152.

view one has to look at a number of statements that he has uttered or has approved, and it has to be remembered that he is talking in terms of poetry, not philosophical prose. For there is an inherent tendency in critics to reduce (by analysis) poetry to prose in their explications. This is the process of abstraction: the pulverizing of images into their particles of 'meaning' for the whole poem. But a poem is not its 'message'—how banal most poetic 'messages' would be![1]

Pound points out:

'The syllogism, time and again, loses grip on reality. Richard St Victor had hold of something : sic:

"There are three modes of thought, cogitation, meditation and contemplation. In the first the mind flits aimlessly about the object, in the second it circles about it in a methodical manner, in the third it is unified with the object." '[2]

Here there seems a reminiscence of Aristotle's description in *De Anima* of the passive intellect (nous pathetikos) which actually becomes its objects in the act of knowing them. This is an image of the direct knowledge Pound demanded in the arts:

'I have a certain real knowledge which wd. enable me to tell a Goya from a Velasquez . . . this differs from the knowledge you or I wd. have if I . . . copied a list of names and maxims from good Fiorentino's *History of Philosophy* . . .

'It may or may not matter that the first knowledge is direct, it remains effortlessly as a residuum, as part of my total disposition, it affects every perception of form-colour phenomena subsequent to its acquisition.

'Coming even closer to things committed verbally to our memory. There are passages of the poets which approximate the form-colour acquisition.

'And herein is clue to Confucius' reiterated commendation of such of his students as studied the Odes.

'He demanded or commended a type of perception, a kind of

[1] See, e.g., Pound's letter to W. C. Williams in 1908 (*Letters*, pp. 36–40).
[2] *Kulchur*, p. 77.

transmission of knowledge obtainable only from such concrete manifestation. Not without reason.'[1]

In a sense this is taking the Aristotelian idea very literally. The image, say, or what is expressed in words by the poet is not abstracted for its 'meaning' but the mind directly apprehends the cluster of meanings that the poet wished to present without analyzing them discursively. Thus, like the Chinese ideogram, the poem or the part of the poem we are apprehending is, in Fenollosa's words, 'a bundle of functions'. This is an obvious characteristic of the *Cantos*. Granted that the poem is not trying to express a discursive meaning which could be grasped and expressed in abstract form, we might say with Donald Davie that

'this state, of not knowing whether we have had ideas or not, may be precisely the state of mind that Pound aimed to produce—and for good reasons. Perhaps by his arrangements of sensory impressions (that is to say, of images) Pound aimed to express, not "ideas", some of which admittedly cannot be expressed in this way, but rather a state of mind in which ideas as it were tremble on the edge of expression.'[2]

This illustrates then Pound's notion of the *forma*, something that underlies concepts and may later give rise to them, something that is apprehensible but not immediately expressible, so various and subtle may be its manifestations.

This may seem to take us a long way from Aristotle, whose world view was ultimately much more schematic, but something of the Aristotelian notion of 'form' is involved here. The form or mode of structure of a thing—e.g. of a tree—is precisely that by virtue of which it grows, and alters and comes to rest when it reaches the terminus of its growing. And conversely the power to grow and alter in a certain definite way is precisely the form or character of each thing.[3] In the essay on Cavalcanti, Pound applies this idea to a larger area, speaking of 'an interactive force : the *virtu* in short'[4] and comments that nowadays 'Even

[1] *Kulchur*, p. 28.
[2] *Ezra Pound: Poet as Sculptor* (London 1964), Ch. 12, p. 218.
[3] *Physics*, II. 1.   [4] *Essays*, p. 152.

Bose with his plant experiments seems intent on the plant's capacity to feel—not on the plant idea, for the plant brain is obviously filled with, or is one idea, an *idée fixe*, a persistent notion of pattern from which only cataclysm or a Burbank can shake it'.[1] This all-pervasive *forma* or *virtu* of an age has, for Pound, been lost and it is clear from this essay where he would put, in Eliot's phrase, 'the dissociation of sensibility'. There *forma* is at the service of cultural criticism; in the *Cantos* it offers an aesthetic, or rather a principle that unites the many disparate elements that have been the despair or the stumbling-block of critics.

It would be tempting to go into the Aristotelian origins, mediated by Aristotelian commentators and neo-Aristotelians, of Pound's motif of *light* and *intelligence*, the latter derived via the commentators' *intellectus agens* from Aristotle's *poietikos nous*, which actualizes the potentiality of knowledge in the *pathetikos nous*, by imposing the form of what is being known upon it. The middle ages saw the difficulty Aristotle had with this notion and gave it such interpretations as the Nous, the Logos, the Verbum, or the Divine and Creative Light (Dante's 'luce intelletual piena d'amore'). Despite the Christian accretions, 'I am the Light and the Life', Aristotle's own doctrines on light, an actuality or state of potentially transparent mediums such as air or water, have had some influence here. But how this influence operated takes us into fields far beyond the classics. All that has to be stressed is that Pound's dialogue with Aristotle and neo-Aristotelianism is far more pervasive in his critical theory and poetic practice than has yet been recognized.

[1] *Ibid.* p. 155.

Lay me by Aurelie:
An Examination of Pound's Use of Historical and Semi-Historical Sources

I

Ezra Pound is still often regarded as a crank, a great poet with a bee in his bonnet about usury, who has ruined his Cantos with Chinese ideograms and recondite references which one may skip for the sake of the 'good' bits, because, of course, he can 'rise' to occasional passages of magnificent poetry.

This view simply will not do. It might be worth recalling that Pound has said, in another context:

'I hope the reader has *not* "understood it all straight off". I should like to invent some kind of typographical dodge which would force every reader to stop and reflect for five minutes (or five hours), to go back to the facts mentioned and think over their significance for himself. . . .'[1]

Facts—'a sufficient phalanx of particulars' (Canto LXXIV)—are Pound's material, and the juxtaposing or ideogrammatic method of presenting them is the 'typographical dodge' he has invented to make us stop and reflect. Even in his prose he does not argue in an Aristotelian manner but ideogrammatically. If it makes most people slide over the very facts he wishes them to stop and reflect on, that is his risk, and their loss. For *The Cantos*, read properly, can give a sheer poetic enchantment not

[1] *Money Pamphlets by £* (No. 6, first published in Italian, Venice 1944), London 1950, p. 17.

242

to be found elsewhere, even to those who do not accept the
didactic value that Pound places on his facts.

'This is not a Short History of the Economy of the United
States', he wrote in the first of the *Money Pamphlets*:

'For forty years I have schooled myself, not to write the
Economic History of the U.S. or any other country, but to
write an epic poem which begins "In the Dark Forest", crosses
the Purgatory of human error, and ends in the light, "fra i
maestri di color che sanno". For this reason I have to understand
the NATURE of error. But I don't think it necessary to refer to
each particular case of error.'[1]

The interesting aspect of this statement is that in a way Pound
has written an economic history not only of the United States
but of many countries, though in a very unusual form, precisely
by producing his epic poem; and that he does find it necessary,
obsessively necessary, to refer to each particular case of error,
over and over again.

I say 'a very unusual form' and 'by producing his epic poem',
because of this very division so current even among sympathetic
critics, between the view of Pound as a first rate though erratic
craftsman, and the view of him as a cranky historian, economist
and general commentator on culture, who does not read the
correct, up-to-date, scholarly, orthodox books and is therefore a
bad historian, economist, and general commentator, though a
'great' poet. I do not think the two can be divided. We cannot
expect an epic poem to be a scholarly economic history in the
usual sense of the word, and Pound rightly denies that this is
what he has done. It is the work of a visionary, and that is its
value. The moment a visionary starts reading and accepting
all the orthodox scholarship of his day he ceases to be a visionary.
We only have to look up any old works of scholarship on any
subject whatsoever to see how quickly replaceable they became,
compared to the great works of art which are so frequently
unscholarly, anachronistic, fantastic even, but which, above all,
survive. 'Literature is news that STAYS news', Pound wrote

[1] *Money Pamphlets by £* (No. 1, first published in Italian, 1944),
London 1950, p. 5.

in his *ABC of Reading*,[1] and in the same book he announced
that 'no single language is CAPABLE of expressing all forms
and degrees of human comprehension' (admitting that this was
an unpalatable doctrine). Hence his disconcerting but essentially
poetic use of innumerable, sometimes 'unorthodox' but often
equally poetic sources in many languages and stages of languages.
Some of these sources, dismissed by experts as bad history or
bad economics, turn out to be much nearer to the basic truth
than the experts had supposed.

One of these, Laʒamon's *Brut* (Early Middle English, end
of twelfth century), crops up in *Rock-Drill* (Canto XCI),
apparently unnoticed by commentators. It is extremely ger-
mane to my argument, but before I come to this second and
main part of my essay, I should like to show, by an analysis of some
passages in the later Cantos from *Thrones*, what I mean by the
poet's treatment of sources, as opposed to that of the historian.

Thrones takes us to Canto CIX, and ends on a 'to be continued' note with an echo of *Rock-Drill* ('Oh you', as Dante
says / 'in the dinghy astern there', Canto XCIII—first quoted
in Italian in Canto VII):

> You in the dinghey (piccioletta) astern there!
> [Canto CIX]

Like *Rock-Drill*, however, it is flooded with light ('the light
there almost solid'—Cantos XCIII, XCV, *R-D*), the light of
Anselm ('incarnate awareness' Canto XCVIII), Ambrose,
Plotinus, Erigena, and others, but also the light of laughter
('But Gemisto: "Are Gods by hilaritas" '—Canto XCVIII).
Even the material consists more of what Pound regards as
examples of enlightenment than of errors, though there are
plenty of characteristically sharp asides: 'Ike driven to the
edge, almost, of a thought . . .' (Canto XCVII); 'and as for
those who deform thought with iambics . . .' (Canto XCVIII);
'and as for what happened after the king lost exclusivity /
even Del Mar gasps with astonishment' (Canto CIV).

[1] *The ABC of Reading*, London 1934 (Also Faber paperback, London
1961; New Directions Paperbook 89, New York 1960).

LAY ME BY AURELIE

Thrones is a Poundian (i.e. an a-chronological and echo-woven) history of money and good government, but money especially. 'Money is a kind of poetry', said Wallace Stevens,[1] and so Pound has made it. Canto XCVII opens with Abd-el-Melik (one of the Omayyad Caliphs, the first to have coinage), juxtaposed with Edward I. It is based on various sources, including Paulus the Deacon, Seneca, Landulphus Sagax, Matthew Paris, Mommsen, Gibbon, etc., all of whom he mentions, but chiefly on Del Mar, a nineteenth-century director of the U.S. Treasury Bureau of Statistics, and author of many books on the history of money.[2] Del Mar is always worth reading, as are most of Pound's sources. The *Monetary Systems* is in fact referred to by page in the second line:

> Melik & Edward struck coins-with-a-sword,
> 'Emir el Moumenin' (Systems p. 134)
>   six and ½ to one, or the sword of the Prophet

This refers to the fact that Mohammedan coins, unlike the Byzantine, had a silver content of $6\frac{1}{2}$ to one, and that Abd-el-Melik, the 'Emir-el-Moumenin', was represented on them with a drawn sword: Pound's wit, or perhaps Abd-el-Melik's, lies in suggesting that the fine metal content of the sword was at least as serviceable as was the sword in the Mohammedan expansion.

Pound insisted on Del Mar in a recorded conversation with D. G. Bridson broadcast in the B.B.C. Third Programme on 11 July 1960:

'And the Usura Cantos would be more comprehensible if people understood the meaning of the term 'Usury'. It is not to be confused with the legitimate interest which is due, Del Mar says, to the increase in domestic animals and plants. The difference between a fixed charge and a share from a proportion of an increase.'

[1] *Opus Posthumous*, ed. Samuel French Morse (London 1959) p. 165.
[2] Alexander Del Mar, *A History of Money in Ancient Countries* (London 1885), *Money and Civilization* (London, 1886), *A History of Monetary Systems*, (London, 1895, New York 1903, Pound using the latter). *Etc.*

As a mining engineer, Del Mar discovered that gold and silver were produced, on the average, at a loss, and were circulating through the world at a value in commodities and services far beneath the current cost of their production, though it had not always been so. This led him to formulate various tenets on the true nature and function of money, the facts of which, he held, had been obscured, chiefly by the Coinage Act of 1666. So Pound, in the above broadcast: 'Now as I see it, billions of money are being spent to hide about seventeen historic facts which the copyists in the Middle Ages or recently have been too stupid to cross out.'

There is, of course, an element of paranoia which disturbs even his most ardent admirers. There is an element of something unpleasant in most great artists, which ultimately comes to be regarded as the driving force of their greatness. Without it, they would not have had the curiosity, or the courage:

Mons of Jute should have his name in the record,
    thrones, courage, Mons should have his name in the record.
                                                [Canto XCVII]

This too is from Del Mar (*Systems*, p. 279), according to whom a sixteenth century magistrate of the Jutes in the Duchy of Schleswig had the courage to step up, alone and unarmed, and read a demand of deposition to Christian, the tyrant king of Denmark. His bravery led to Christian's abdication and flight, Del Mar says, and adds: 'This hero's name was Mons, and it deserves to be written over the gateway of every oppressor.'

'You can't have literature without curiosity,' Pound insisted to Bridson, and, later: 'Every man has a right to have his ideas examined one at a time.'

This is not the place to examine all of his ideas one at a time, but we can at least have the curiosity to see what Pound does with his sources. And he does not ask too much of us: he always gives his sources, if not at the first occurrence, then later, just as he sometimes translates his quotations and most of his ideograms.

Rock-Drill ended with yet another allusion to *kredemnon*, the

veil or mantle with which the sea-nymph Leucothea saved
Odysseus from drowning ('My bikini is worth your raft').
The first Canto of *Thrones* (the dots are those of Pound) opens :

Κρήδεμνον . . .
κρήδεμνον . . .
and the wave concealed her

Then, six lines below :

Thusca quae a thure,
from the name of the incense, in this province is
ROMA *quae olim* . . .
In the province of Tuscany is Rome, a city which formerly . . .
And Sabines with a crow on their flag.
Brennus came for the wine, liking its quality,
Bergamo, Brescia, Ticino,
& inviting his wife to drink from her father's skull
(Cunimundus) a cup which I, Paulus, saw . . .
that Tiberius Constantine was distributist,
Justinian, Chosroes, Augustae Sophiae,
lumina mundi, ἐπικόμβια . . . τὸν λαόν
or a hand-out. 586 chronologically
(more or less)
Authar, marvelous reign, no violence and no passports,
Vitalis beati
More water about San Zeno than had flowed since the days
of Noah
[Canto XCVI]

Paulus is Paul the Deacon, as is later made clear, otherwise
known as Warnefridus Diaconus, who wrote a history of the
Langobards (Migne 95). In Book I, ch. xvi, he describes the
provinces of Italy :

'Tuscia, which is so called from *tus* [frankincense], which its
people used to burn superstitiously in sacrifice to their gods.
. . . In the province of Tuscany is Rome, a city which formerly
was the capital of the whole world . . .'

Pound's ellipsis there is masterly, evoking not only the Langobard awareness of Rome's former grandeur but our own awareness and weariness of many other declines and falls. So with Brennus, king of the Senonian Gauls, who came because 'they had tasted the wine and were lured by greed', and who built Pergamus, Brixia, Ticinum; and Alboin, king of the Langobards, who also invaded Italy and ruled in Liguria, and who made his wife, Rosamund, drink wine out of a cup made from her father's skull, Cunimund, king of the Gepidae and his ex-enemy. Paulus adds: 'I saw king Ratchis holding this cup in his hand at a feast and show it to his guests.'

Pound never just translates. He takes what he wants, and with ellipses which can best be appreciated by knowledge of his source. His artistry in words is careful, lively and continuous. In Book III, ch. xii (i.e. two books later), we hear about Tiberius Constantine, fiftieth Roman emperor, who found gold under the flagstones of his palace and bestowed it on the needy (presumably in ἐπικόμβια, that is, money tied up in small linen bags and thrown to the people at festivals by the Byzantine emperors, 'or a hand-out', as Pound crisply glosses). The golden age of King Authar ('no violence, no ambushes, no one was unjustly detained, no one took loot or stole, everyone went where he pleased, safe and fearless') is not borne out by the facts, but Pound's one-line version is certainly pleasing. So in his telescoping of two different phrases in Paulus' description of a flood in Northern Italy: first 'such a deluge as has not occurred since the time of Noah' and later, 'the river Athesis [Adige] rose so high that round the church of the blessed martyr San Zeno, outside the walls of Verona, the water reached the upper windows, although, as St. Gregory, afterwards pope, also wrote, the water did not get into the church at all.'[1]

To the stories of Paul the Deacon are juxtaposed echoes, of course (e.g. of Antoninus who got down the percentage), but also the 'Eparch's book' or Edict of Leo the Wise (Leo VI, 886–912), from a fourteenth-century Codex discovered in

[1] The church of San Zeno Maggiore in Verona, with its individually signed columns and bronze doors, is important in Pound's ideas on sculpture and architecture. Mentioned in Cantos XLII, LXXIV, LXXVIII, XCI.

1892 by the Genevese Professor Jules Nicole, and edited by him in Greek and Latin under the title *Le Livre du Préfet*.[1] After exclaiming 'Here, surely, is a refinement of language', Pound breaks into sudden prose, almost, it would seem, as a brief gesture of defiant despair:

'If we never write anything save what is already understood, the field of understanding will never be extended. One demands the right, now and again, to write for a few people with special interests and whose curiosity reaches into greater detail.

Pound certainly has fun with the greater detail of this text. As with Chinese, he likes to comment on minor editorial matters: 'δέκα νομισμάτων (Nicole: purpureas vestes) τὰ βλαττία / but the ἀναιδῶς is rather nice, Dr. Nicole'; 'κατὰ τὴν ἐξώνεσιν νομίσματος ἑνὸς / that's how Nicole slanted it, grave on the omicron, / meaning one aureus, bankers / to profit one keration 2 miliarisia'; '& that Nicephorus / kolobozed the tetarteron / need not have applied to the aureus / or caused Nicole to understand token coinage'; 'have codified πολιτικῶν σωματείων / (To Professor Nicole's annoyance) Leo 886–911.'[2]

So with Baller's translation of *The Sacred Edict* in Canto XCVIII:

'Parents naturally hope their sons will be gentlemen.'

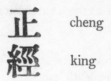

cheng

king

The text is somewhat exigeant, perhaps you will consider the meaning of

cheng

king

[1] *Le Livre du Préfet*, ed. Jules Nicole (Geneva, 1893).
[2] Actually 912.

Baller's footnote on the cheng king characters is ' "upright" in a Confucian sense. Here it applies rather to individual deportment than to rectitude between man and man.'

F. W. Baller edited *The Sacred Edict* of K'ang Hsi (Manchu dynasty) in 1892. From his introduction we learn that the original Edict, published in 1670, had sixteen maxims, each of seven characters, written in the highest literary style. His son and successor Iong-cheng (of Canto LXI) republished it in enlarged form, with expositions in simple literary style. Then a high official named Uang-iu-p'uh, who was Salt Commissioner in Shensi, felt that it was still too abstruse for simple people and translated it into colloquial. Baller adds that the student should learn these homely sayings, for the Chinese think in quotations, and one can thus add vivacity to one's style. He also thought the 'mere morality' of these maxims hollow, and that the people of China were still wrapped in darkness. He ends his introduction with a hymn, 'Thou bleeding Lamb . . . the best morality is love of Thee.' Pound's version, before he starts on the maxims, is as follows :

> And that Leucothoe rose as an incense bush
>   —Orchamus, Babylon—
>   resisting Apollo.
> Patience, I will come to the Commissioner of the Salt Works
>   in due course . . .
>   . . .
> But the lot of 'em, Yeats, Possum and Wyndham
>   had no ground beneath 'em.
>
>   Orage had.
>   Per ragione vale   [pu = not]
>
> Black shawls for Demeter.
>   . . .
> The cat talks—μάω—with a greek inflection.[1]
>   . . .

[1] mao : a cat (Baller, *Sacred Edict*, Vocabulary).

Uncle William two months on ten lines of Ronsard
But the salt works . . .

. . .

Patience, ich bin am Zuge . . .
ἀρχή
an awareness
Until in Shensi, Ouang, the Commissioner Iu-p'uh

volgar'eloquio 又樸 [1]

The King's job, vast as the swan-flight:
thought built on Sagetrieb.

[Canto XCVIII]

Then comes a loose and very funny translation of Ch. vii
(i.e. the 7th Maxim enlarged) of the Edict, on not trusting
Buddhist and Taoist monks; followed by bits of Ch. ix, on courtesy,
with selected ideograms from Baller's text, and a sudden:

And as Ford said : get a dictionary
and learn the meaning of words.[2]

. . .

A soul, said Plotinus, the body inside it.
'By Hilaritas,' said Gemisto, 'by hilaritas : gods;
and by speed in communication.
Anselm cut some of the cackle, and relapsed for sake of
tranquillity.

Thus the gods appointed john barleycorn Je tzu,
And Byzance lasted longer than Manchu
because of an (%) interest-rate.
Thought is built out of Sagetrieb,[3]
and our debt here is to Baller
and to *volgar'eloquio.*

[1] Chinese characters for Iu-p'uh.

[2] In interview with Ford Madox Ford published in *Pavannes and Divagations* (London 1960, New York, New Directions 1958).

[3] Leo Frobenius (*Erlebte Erdteile*, IV, Frankfurt 1929) advances the theory that man has an inborn *urge to use poetry as a means of giving expression to* and interpreting his past and almost forgotten culture and tradition.

Despite Mathews this Wang was a stylist.
Uen-li will not help you talk to them,
   Iong-ching republished the edict
But the salt-commissioner took it down to the people
   who, in Baller's view, speak in quotations;
   think in quotations :
'Don't send someone else to pay it.'[1]
Delcroix was for repetition.
   Baller thought one needed religion.
Without [2]muan [1]bpo . . . but I anticipate.[2]
   There is no substitute for a lifetime.

       [Canto XCVIII]

What Pound is doing is more than taking snippets of this and that and juxtaposing them together. He is telescoping time by his very choice of sources, so that we see the Manchu dynasty, not only in the light of, say, Plotinus and Gemisto, but through the eyes of the Victorian Baller superimposed with those of Pound, just as we saw the *Chou King* or Book of History in *Rock-Drill* through the eyes of the nineteenth-century Jesuit Father Couvreur plus those of Pound.[3] In the Chinese Cantos Pound had attempted something similar by summarising Chinese history via the eighteenth-century Enlightenment, the great age for discovering China and Confucian thought,[4] and juxtaposing these Cantos with those about eighteenth-century America. But Pound has come a long way since the Chinese Cantos, which few of his admirers have

[1] Baller, xiv, on prompt tax payment: 'Don't commission someone else to take them when he goes, or you will fall into the snares by which sharpers fleece people.'

[2] Cp. C. CIV: 'Without [2]muan [1]bpö / no reality . . .' which refers to Baller p. 43 (see also *The Muan Bpö Ceremony or the Sacrifice to Heaven as practised by the Na-khi*, article by J. F. Rock, Monumenta serica Vol. XIII, Pechino 1949, Journal of Oriental Studies of the Catholic University of Peking). Also in *Annali Lateranensi*, vol. xvi, 1952. Città del Vaticano.

[3] F. S. Couvreur, *Chou King*, first published Ho Kien Fou 1897, ed. Sien Hsien Fou 1939.

[4] Père Joseph-Anne-Marie de Moyriac de Mailla, *Histoire générale de la Chine, ou annales de cet empire*, 12 vols., Paris 1777–83.

been able to praise. His telescoping makes more demands, but is shot with poetry and humour. It demands that we look up his sources and have the curiosity which 'reaches into greater detail', that we get a dictionary and look up the meaning of words (and ideograms). 'Erigena with greek tags in his verses' he had exclaimed already in the opening canto of *Rock-Drill* (Canto LXXXV), and later: 'Awareness restful & fake is fatiguing' (*Chou King* XX. 18). But 'We flop if we cannot maintain the awareness' (XVI. 4), 'respect the awareness and / train the fit men.' 'Our dynasty came in because of a great sensibility' (accompanied by the splendid ling[2] ideogram which opens Canto LXXXV and is repeated in Canto XCVII). Or again:

> a gnomon,
> Our science is from the watching of shadows;
> That Queen Bess translated Ovid,
> Cleopatra wrote of the currency,
> Versus who scatter old records
> ignoring the hsien form.[1]
> [Canto LXXXV]

The experience, if one takes the trouble, is a very special poetic experience, part scholarly and part irrational, apocalyptic, timeless.

II

I hope that we are now more closely familiar with Pound's general methods, and so better equipped to look at the Laȝamon passage in Canto XCI. The whole canto is so closely woven that it must be read in full, if possible with the best commentary I have read on it, that by Professor Donald Davie.[2]

To summarize this briefly, he argues that the Reina whose eyes have been sunken for three hundred years (from the opening of the canto) is the *forma*, so important in Pound,

[1] Pound here gives the ideogram hsien[2], which stands for 'virtue'.
[2] *Ezra Pound: Poet as Sculptor* (London 1965) pp. 217–229.

which is lost and recaptured at various periods of human history, and which Pound was already talking about in *Guide to Kulchur*.[1] In *The Cantos* as a whole this ideal is of course sometimes moral, spiritual, governmental, economic, or, more usually, aesthetic, Aphrodite rising from the waves at any period when beauty is rediscovered ('So very difficult, Yeats, beauty so difficult', Canto LXXX). But Professor Davie is here chiefly interested in it as artistic *forma*, that is, not just a technique but a tradition, lost, in particular, since Petrarchism invaded Italy and Europe, but glimpsed now and again, and which Pound in this specific instance identifies with the Elizabethan tradition of music and poetry, and more specifically still with the Provençal origin of cantabile poetry, a snatch of which music in square notes opens the canto. The *forma* in this sense, Donald Davie argues here and throughout his book, is intimately connected with Pound's theories of light and colour, and of the artist drawing out of the material that which is inherent in it, rather than imposing upon it a wealth of significance by an act of will: in literature, the distinction between metaphor or the juxtaposed image, and symbolism; in sculpture, the distinction between carving and moulding, which is like creating money out of nothing in excess of natural wealth.

Donald Davie goes on to analyse the implications of these theories in Canto XCI, and brilliantly, linking the Reina with some of Pound's female archetypes that always accompany the *forma*, with Elizabeth of England as Virgin Queen, with the

---

[1] ' "I made it out of a mouthful of air", wrote Bill Yeats in his heyday. The *forma*, the immortal *concetto*, the concept, the dynamic form which is like the rose pattern driven into the dead iron-filings by the magnet, not by material contact with the magnet itself, but separate from the magnet. Cut off by the layer of glass, the dust and filings rise and spring into order. Thus the *forma*, the concept rises from death . . .' (*Guide to Kulchur*, London 1938, p. 152, quoted by Davie p. 219). He also quotes the famous passage from the essay on mediaevalism: 'We appear to have lost the radiant world where one thought cuts through another with clean edge, a world of moving energies . . . magnetisms that take form, that are seen, or that border the visible, the matter of Dante's *Paradiso*, the glass under water, the form that seems a form seen in a mirror . . .' (reprinted in *Make it New*, London 1934).

notion of immaculate conception so important in Pound ('I made it out of a mouthful of air'), with Diana, goddess of the moon and of the chase (who, incidentally, is said in Canto LXXX to have had compassion on the silversmiths at Ephesus, 'revealing the paraclete'), and, here particularly, with Ra-Set, an invented Egyptian goddess made up of Set, the evil male deity, and the sun-god Ra, whose hieroglyph the 'bark of dawn' (which accompanied the dead so that they could journey for ever with the god) is given, and who with Diana ties up with the sun and moon together as total light process, one of the earliest and most constant ideograms in *The Cantos*. Or Donald Davie again: 'This sets the key for what is the main business of these lines, the movement from sea water to sun . . . the idea of crystal clarity is being brought into harmony with the sun-derived ideas of vigor, fecundity, and ardor', but not as a crude opposition of pure spirit and impure flesh, on the contrary, Pound makes the presiding deities Zagreus (Bacchus) and Tamuz. 'The concluding passage of Canto XC . . . [was] only the latest of many passages in the *Cantos* making the point that any invocation of the spirits of air, of perceptions more than usually delicate and subtle, must also be an invocation of the chthonic powers, the spirits of earth and under-earth.'

When he comes to the Laȝamon passage, however, Professor Davie becomes inexplicably vague:

'The archaic language of the renewed invocation to the lost Queen—this time in her capacity as a goddess of earth, of woods, and of the chase—looks forward to the only slightly less archaic language of the lines about the birth of Merlin, which follow almost immediately. But it has the more important function of presenting, not as an idea but manifested concretely in words, that mediaeval sensibility in which the *forma* was present and operative as in the modern sensibility it is not.'

That's as may be. It is true that some of the lines in the passage in question (quoted below) are 'archaic' in the sense that they are direct quotations from Laȝamon, while others are 'slightly less archaic' in the sense that they are written by Pound, though the matter is from Laȝamon. But the significance of these variations is lost in the meaningless 'looks forward to' and the vagueness of 'that mediaeval sensibility'. The effect is to leave Pound high and dry in the sixteenth century, where he has certainly not remained. And the implications, to my mind very profound, of his using Laȝamon at all, or of mentioning Stonehenge, are totally ignored.

Here is the passage in full :

That the sun's silk

hsien³ tensile

be clear

ʽΕλέναυς That Drake saw the armada

       & sea caves

Ra-Set over crystal

[mnḏt]  moving

in the Queen's eye the reflection

& sea-wrack —

       green deep of the sea-cave

ne quaesieris.

       He asked not

nor wavered, seeing, nor had fear of the wood-queen, Artemis

       that is Diana

nor had killed save by the hunting rite,

       sanctus.

Thus sang it :

     Leafdi Diana, leove Diana

     Heye Diana, help me to neode

Witte me thurh crafte

     whuder ich maei lithan

     to wonsom londe.

       Rome th'ilke tyme was noght.

So that he spread a deer-hide near the altar,

Now Lear in Janus' temple is laid

[chên⁴] timing the thunder

Nor Constance hath his hood again,
  Merlin's fader may no man know
  Merlin's moder is made a nun.
Lord, thaet scop the dayes lihte,
  all that she knew was a spirit bright,
A movement that moved in cloth of gold
  into her chamber.
'By the white dragon, under a stone
  Merlin's fader is known to none.'
Lay me by Aurelie, at the east end of Stonehenge
  where lie my kindred
Over harm
Over hate
  overflooding, light over light
And yilden he gon rere
                    (Athelstan before a.D. 940)
the light flowing, whelming the stars.
    In the barge of Ra-Set
On river of crystal
So hath Sibile a boken isette.

'He asked not' refers grammatically back to Drake, who 'saw the armada' and, by implication, a vision 'of sea water as the signature of transcendent reality'.[1] But the actual context ('nor wavered, seeing, nor had fear of the wood-queen') at once brings up Actæon, one of Pound's favourite metamorphoses, to our minds.[2] By juxtaposition, or rather, here, by making two differ-

[1] Donald Davie, p. 224, on the earlier passage in the same canto, 'Light & the flowing crystal. . . . That Drake saw the splendour and wreckage / in that clarity / Gods moving in crystal.' Ἑλέναυς is of course Pound's usual short-cut allusion to the description of Helen in Aeschylus, when the chorus plays on her name: elenaus, elandros, eleptolis (*Agamemnon* 689–90), destroyer of ships, destroyer of men, destroyer of cities. The armada and vision are thus clearly linked with the thousand ships and the face of destructive beauty.

[2] The myth of Actæon among others serves to express the idea that beauty is very hard to possess. It is told in Canto IV (also in the early poem 'The Coming of War: Actæon'), and Pound weaves into it the story of the troubadour Vidal who dressed himself in wolf-skins for the love of Lady Loba and was hunted by dogs and shepherds. In both the hunter becomes the victim.

ent predicates depend on the one pronoun, Pound changes Drake
into Actæon. Moreover, Elenaus also reminds us that a third identity may be alluded to in the Drake/Actæon juxtaposition, namely
Agamemnon, who was linked in Canto LXXXIX with Judge
Marshall ('Judge Marshall, father of war. / Agamemnon killed
that stag, against hunting rites') in a reference to the sacrifice of
Iphigenia to the winds after the fleet had been windbound because
of Diana's anger at Agamemnon for having killed one of her
stags.[1]

By a further juxtaposition, moreover, Pound changes Drake/
Actæon/Agamemnon into Brutus, mythical founder of 'Brutaine'
or the British nation. For the next sentence 'Thus sang it',
which appears to refer back to the same 'he', introduces the
hymn to Diana sung by Brutus in Laʒamon's *Brut*. The story
(I summarize) runs as follows: Brutus was the great-grandson
of Aeneas who had escaped from Troy and become king of
Italy. Before the boy's birth, magicians had foretold a marvellous child who would slay his father and mother and be driven
from the land. Brutus was born, the mother died and later he
shot his father by mistake. He departed to Greece where he
found his Trojan kinsmen unhappy under Greek rule. He helped
to free them, eventually leaving Greece with the king's daughter
Imogen as part of the bargain. He and his men came to an
island called Logice, deserted and laid waste, except for wild
deer. His men found a destroyed castle and a marble temple
('the Worse'—i.e. the devil—'had it to wield') with the image
of a woman called Diana by the heathens ('the Devil loved
her'). So Brutus heard from his seamen who had been there
before. But Brutus, unafraid, entered the temple alone,
bearing a vessel of red gold, full of milk from a white hind
he had shot with his own hand, and wine separately. He
made a fire, walked nine times round it and called on her
whom he loved, kissed her altar, poured milk on the fire, and

---

[1] Cp. also Pound's early poem 'The Coming of War: Actæon', where
Actæon is connected with the 'hosts of an ancient people', the dead
warriors of Stonehenge. So Agamemnon, like Actæon sinning against
Diana, was a father of war.

spoke these gentle ('mild') words (Pound's quotes are in italics) :

> *Leafdi Diana: leoue Diana: heȝe Diana* . *help me to neode.*
> Wise me & *witer*e : þurh þine wihtful *craft.*
> *whuder ich mæi liðan:* & ledan mine leoden.
> *to ane wnsume londe* : þer ich mihte wunien . . .[1]

He promises to make a temple there in her name. He falls asleep and Diana tells him to go to Albion, where there is fowl, fish, deer, wood, water and desert, a winsome land, inhabited by giants, but empty of men. He is to build Troy there, and shall have royal progeny. After various adventures this is just what he does, coming up through Britanny and landing (like most British kings in the *Brut*) at Totnes, defeating twenty strong giants under their leader Geomagog, and building New Troy (Trinovant, though one of his kin called Lud renamed it Kaerlud which eventually became Lundin, according to the splendid eponymous etymologies that abound in the *Brut*).[2]

Pound's next line 'Rome th'ilke tyme was noght' is not a quotation from Laȝamon but what Professor Davie might already at this point have called 'slightly less archaic English' or what I shall later be calling 'synthetic Laȝamon' (i.e. by Pound). It is in fact only a foretaste of 'synthetic Laȝamon' for it comes from Robert of Brunne, a 14th century adapter of these British histories, and Pound has lifted it from a footnote by Madden. He has gone right back to the beginning of the *Brut*, when Aeneas lands in Italy :

[1] Lines 1198 ff, Madden, referred to in future with M before the line ref. I quote from Sir Frederic Madden's 1847 edition (Soc. of Antiquaries, 3 vols.), which counts half-lines as lines, because it is the one Pound used and because only one volume of the more modern edition by G. L. Brook and R. F. Leslie, E.E.T.S. 1963, has appeared. Rough translation: 'Lady Diana, dear Diana, high Diana, help me in my need. Teach me and counsel me through thy wise skill, where I may go, and lead my people to a winsome land where I might dwell.'

[2] The *Brut* was a free translation and expansion of Wace's *Brut*, itself based on Geoffrey of Monmouth's *Historia Regum Britanniae*, 1136, and the etymologies are those of Geoffrey. Sometimes Laȝamon uses Geoffrey direct. For discussion of Geoffrey's 'history' see below.

On Italiȝe heo comen to londe : þar Rome nou on stondeð.
fele ȝer under sunnan : nas ȝet Rome bi-wonnen.[1]

Pound is being 'slightly less archaic' here because he is
echoing Laȝamon as narrator, that is, much later than the event
narrated, and so chooses a narrator even later than Laȝamon,
though earlier than himself (our view of Rome being timeless),
an echo which is itself, perhaps, further echoed in the passage
from Paul the Deacon in Canto XCVI, analysed above. In other
words, he quotes directly from Laȝamon here only for the
prayer itself (*oratio directa*), to give it its oldest possible English
connotations, but uses a later narrator for the comment on
Rome, then slipping into his own modern English to indicate a
time-leap in the story itself.

For we then skip many generations in the next line, to the
story of Leir (Lear), which ends somewhat differently from
that of Shakespeare : Cordoille having married the king of the
Franks, she and her husband welcome her penitent father and
help him to regain his kingdom, where she then joins him after
her husband's death. Leir dies three years later, and she buries
him in Leicester (another eponymous etymology) 'in Janus'
temple, as the book tells' :

Inne Leirchestre : his dohter hine leide.
inne Janies temple : al swa þe bac tellet.[2]

[1] M. 106 ff. 'In Italy they came to land, where Rome now stands.
Many years under the sun, Rome was not inhabited.' Madden notes :
'In Wace the passage stands thus : "Ni ert de Rome uncore nule chose,/
Nene fut il puis de bien grant pose" which is rendered by Robert
of Brunne : "Of Rome th[t] ilke tyme was noght, / Ne long after was it
wroght".' Pound changes the MS. small t (=that) into an apostrophe.
Clearly the Brunne way of putting it was more to his purpose here. (*The
Story of England, by Robert Mannyng of Brunne, a.d. 1338*, ed. F. J.
Furnivall, 1887, I. 749). Brunne was a Gilbertine monk at Sempringham,
and Furnivall for some reason calls him a forerunner of Chaucer. No other
phrase in this Pound passage is taken from Brunne, who is much less
poetic than Laȝamon.

[2] M. 3722 ff. Geoffrey of Monmouth has a cave : Erat autem subter-
raneum illud conditum in honore bifrontis iani. The later Welsh and
(probable) translation of Geoffrey, known as the Tysilio, has a cave and
adds 'This house of earth was made in honour of the god called biffrons.'

LAY ME BY AURELIE

The ideogram chên⁴ that follows, with the gloss 'timing the thunder', is composed of the radical yü³ signifying rain (the pictograph shows the dripping roof of heaven) above the phonetic component ch'ên² which, used by itself means a period of time or, in certain contexts, temporal, vegetative changes, plants transformed by the elements.[1] Conventionally chên⁴ means 'tremble' or 'quake', as in an earthquake, but Pound is breaking it up etymologically with his gloss, which evokes (together with the sudden modern English) Shakespeare's Lear, himself a sort of Father Time figure, double-faced in his foolish past and the new year of his lesson learnt about Cordelia's love. But the whole meaning of the ideogram is also there (trembling, awe), recalling the other temple, Diana's,[2] and the vision of Brutus, Leir being after all part of his royal progeny foretold by the goddess.

After this leap forward from Brutus to Leir, itself firmly linked both back to Brutus and Rome, and forward to Elizabethan England by means of modern English, we are back in 'synthetic Laȝamon', that is, Pound/Laȝamon narrative, back

[1] Cp. C. CVI, where part of Brutus' prayer is repeated, together with the phrase 'the flowers are blessed against thunder bolt', which recalls the ideogram chên⁴ used here.

[2] Diana (or Artemis as the Greeks called her) is actually the female counterpart of double-headed Janus, the Roman deity of the door and the door-hinge (cf. A. B. Cook, Zeus, I, pp. 392–422). As such, Janus rules the double gates of birth and death, and his 'temple' would be the domain between death and birth, which is the earth itself. The concept of the gate, which is an important motif in the Cantos (cf. Canto XLVII, particularly the lines 'By this gate art thou measured / Thy day is between a door and a door,' or the repeated references to Gaius in the late Cantos XC, XCIV and C, 'and that all gates are holy'), is reflected in the trilithons of Stonehenge as well as in many other megalithic monuments. It is intimately related to the neolithic concept of the Cave-as-Tomb-and-Temple, where the cave represents the womb of the Great Goddess. The fact that Artemis was, among other things, a goddess of the underworld is clearly indicated by her Ephesian images, which show her as the goddess of many breasts who suckles the new-born dead. This aspect of Diana is reinforced in the story of Brutus' sacrifical offering of the milk of a dead hind as well as by her supposed liaison with the 'Worse'. 'Janus' temple' is thus seen to be identical with the 'house of earth' (cf. G. R. Levy, The Gate of Horn, London 1948). E.H.

from Shakespeare but forward from Leir. For the line about
Constance makes another leap in time to post-Roman Britain
(skipping Belin, Brennus, Julius Caesar, Augustus Caesar,
Luces, Severus, King Coel, Constantine and Helen) to Constantin the Fair, brother of Aldroein of Britanny (himself son of
Conan of Kent who had been given Britanny by Maximian as
peace-offering in a complicated story). The Britons are in
trouble as usual, under Febus of Rome, and send to Aldroein for
help. He sends Constantin who lands at Totnes and becomes
king. He has three sons : Constance, who becomes a monk through
his father's wish; Aurelius, surnamed Ambrosius; and Uther.

We have reached the beginning of Arthurian legend. After
Constantin's death the people choose Aurelius (Aurelie in
Laȝamon). But Vortiger, a crafty earl who is half-Welsh,
visits the monastery and persuades Constance the monk to
shed his hood and become king, with himself as steward.
Constance accepts, is smuggled out in a knight's cloak while a
swain is dressed in the monk's clothes ('the hood hanged down
as if it hid his crown'). The abbot, who thought the knights had
come to bid Constance 'hold his hood', is furious and threatens
to 'unhood' Constance. The people want Aurelie, for Uther is
too small and they won't have a monk as king. Vortiger produces Constance and explains that he is now unhooded. The
bishops are too afraid to protest. 'Constance deserted God's
hood and had sorrow'. For all this is part of Vortiger's crafty
plan. Constance knows nothing of government and lets Vortiger
rule 'except in the one single thing that he be still called king.'[1]
Vortiger laughs, makes an alliance with the Picts against the
Britons he loathes, and goes off to collect tribute from his lands.
The Picts seize the king, cut off his head and send for Vortiger,
who weeps and pretends the Picts have betrayed him by killing
the king while he was away. The Britons march against the
Picts and slay them to a man.

Wise men then take the children Aurelie and Uther over sea
into the less Britain to Biduz, the king, who brings them up.

[1] Cp. Shakespeare's *King Lear*, Act I, Sc.1 : 'Only we still retain / The
name, and all th' additions to a king ...'

Meanwhile Vortiger becomes a very cruel king, invites Hengest and Horsa from Alemaine (the Angles) and is reproached by his people for befriending the pagans. Vortiger's sons attack him, Hengest flees to Saxland, Vortimer the eldest son becomes a good king, while Vortiger wanders for five years all over Britain. But then the Britons become evil and take Vortiger back, who sends for Hengest again. Hengest promises peace, in a plain beside Ambresbury, 'now hight Stonehenge', where the Britons give up their weapons in token of good will and are massacred.

Pound has here telescoped a whole era of lost kingship and bad government into one sentence, which fuses all Laȝamon's 'hood' phrases (Robert of Brunne has none), where 'hood', in this full context, implies 'God's hood' or holy orders, or grace, as well as the crown, never really worn, and his head lost. Constance's foolishness is linked with Leir's (who was blind to love) just as Leir is linked, through the temple and the deer-hide, to Brutus and Diana.

Diana's prophecy about Brutus and his progeny is already rocked about. Hengest rules the kingdom, Vortiger flees to Wales. There follows the story of the castle he tries to build which keeps falling until a wise man (Merlin's rival) tells him that the cement needs the blood of a man born of no father. The boy Merlin is eventually found (Vortiger's men overhear other boys taunting him for having no father and a whore for a mother). The mother is sent for, who had become a nun (M. 15640: Nu wes Maerlinges moder: wundermere iwurðen / in ane haȝe munstre: munchene ihaded). She explains (I paraphrase): My father the king Conan loved me above all things, I was wondrous fair in stature, at fifteen years of age, and dwelt in a rich mansion with my fair maidens.

> þenne ich waes on bedde iswaued : mid soft mine slepen.
> þen com biuoren : þa fæirest þing þat wes iboren.
> swulc hit weore a muchel cniht : al of golde idiht.
> þis ich isæh on sweuene : alche niht on slepe.

CHRISTINE BROOKE-ROSE

þis þing glad me biuoren: and glitene [de] on golde.

ofte hit me custe : ofte hit me clupte.

ofte hit me to-bæh : & eode me swiðe neh.

þa ich an aende me bisæh : selcuð me þuhte þas.

mi mæte me was læð : mine limes uncuðe.

selcuð me puhte : what hit beon mihte.

þa anȝæt ich on ænde : þat ich was mid childe.

þa mi time com : þisne cnaue ich hæfuede.

Nat ic on folde : what his fader weoren.

ne wha hine biȝate : inne weorlde-riche.

ne whaðer hit weore unwiht : þe on godes halue idiht.[1]

I give most of the passage to show that Pound does not quote direct but takes what he wants. The three lines that come after the ideogram all refer to the same period, later than the previous but still remote enough in both time and historical veracity for a suggestion of archaism to feel right. The two lines after the Constance line, about Merlin's father and mother, are a faint echo of Laȝamon, in 'synthetic Laȝamon', which also manages to echo the boys' taunts to Merlin, as well as the comically crude sailor's story in Canto XII ('"I am not your fader but your moder," quod he'), but also, more faintly, the 'no-man' tag of Odysseus. And the moment we think of Odysseus in a context suggesting magic (Merlin), we can't help thinking of Circe, which takes us back to the beginning of this passage, when Brutus' men are frightened by the temple of the sorceress-like Diana (one of whose names was after all Hecate) on the island. Clearly Pound

---

[1] M. 15706 ff. Rough translation: 'Then I was wrapped in bed, softly in my sleep, when the fairest thing that was ever born came before me, like a great knight, all clothed in gold. This I saw in dream, each night in sleep. This thing glided before me, glittering in gold. Often it kissed me, often it embraced me, often it approached me, and came very close to me. When at length I looked at myself, it seemed very strange to me— my food was loathsome to me, my limbs unfamiliar, it seemed strange to me, what it might be. Then I perceived at last that I was with child. When my time came I had this boy. I do not know who on this earth his father was, nor who begot him, in this world's kingdom, nor whether it is an evil creature, or made on God's behalf.' Brunne has no golden creature, just an abstract 'being' (ywist).

himself made this connection too, for 'help me to neede' is repeated in Canto CVI in a Circean context.[1]

The 'archaic' or true Laȝamon line that follows ('Lord, thaet scop the dayes lihte') does not in fact belong to this story, but is taken from Aurelie's prayer before battle (see below). Here it serves to introduce the account of Merlin's immaculate conception, 'out of a mouthful of air', the magic, the *forma*, and because both Merlin and the *forma* are timeless, the account is given, neither in Laȝamon's words nor in 'synthetic Laȝamon' but in Pound's modern English, delicately cutting across the nun's own story.

Merlin duly explains that two dragons, North and South, red and white, are fighting at midnight under a stone below the castle, so that the earth sinks, and thus it turns out. Vortiger asks the meaning and is told that Aurelie and Uther are landing the next day at Totnes. Aurelie will have the kingdom first, but will be poisoned, then Uther, and he too will be poisoned. But there is to be much contest. Uther will have a son out of Cornwall, a wild boar, who will rule Rome (Arthur).[2] Pound telescopes all this into one phrase (in modern English), which mentions only 'the white dragon, under a stone' (Aurelie, who is to lie under Stonehenge), and then recalls (in 'synthetic Laȝamon', i.e. Pound/Laȝamon the narrator, but still in the same quotation marks as Merlin, thus fusing the two with the magician) that 'Merlin's fader is known to none'. A strange fusion of Odysseus/Pound/Laȝamon/Aurelie/Merlin thus takes place.

---

[1] but Circe was like that / coming from the house of smoothe stone / 'not know which god' / nor could enter her eyes by probing / the light blazed behind her / nor was this from sunset. / Athene Pronoia, / in hypostasis / Helios, Persæ: Circe / Zeus: Artemis out of Leto / Under wildwood / Help me to neede / By Circeo, the stone eyes looking seaward. . . . The temple shook with Apollo . . . And in thy mind beauty, O Artemis . . . Whuder ich maei lithan / helpe me to neede / the flowers are blessed against thunder bolt / helpe me to neede.

[2] The germ of this story is first found in Nennius (fl. 769) *Historia Britonum*, ed. Josephus Stevenson, London 1838, pp. 31 ff, where Merlin is called Ambrosius. The two dragons fight and the white one is defeated. Ambrosius explains this as an Omen that the Saxons will be driven out by the Britons. Pound's 'by the white dragon' thus touches on another lost theme.

Aurelie becomes king and fights Hengest. Before the battle he prays: 'ʒif ich mot ibiden: þat ich aʒæn ride. / & hit wulle *drihte*: þe scop þes daʒes lihte. / þat ich mote mid ifunde: biʒite mine ikunde. / chirchen ich wulle arære: & god ich wulle hæren. / ich wulle alche cnihte: ʒeuen his irihte.'[1]

With the exception of the later reference to Athelstan and the final reference in the passage to the Sibyl, this phrase from Aurelie's prayer and Brutus' prayer to Diana are the only direct quotations from Laʒamon. The phrase is linked with Merlin's mother, not just by attributing it to her arbitrarily but by Pound's telescoping method. The fact of the immaculate conception is given here in modern English, not only because it is timeless but to render the sobriety of her account in a way that the quaintness of direct quotation might not. But the mystery, and its possible divine origin, of which she herself has doubts,[2] is merely hinted at in this direct quotation, more like an oath on her part that her account will be true in the name of God, and left in 'archaic' English. The phrase is transferred, moreover, from a prayer before a battle of ethnic significance (Britons v. Saxons) to a context of mystery important in Pound's theories of light and imagination, and it thereby retains both connotations.

When Hengest is finally defeated and killed Aurelie goes to Ambresbury and sends for Merlin, asking him where he can find men who can hew stone to build a lasting work in memory of the many Britons massacred by Hengest.[3] Merlin tells him

[1] M. 16274 ff. The prayer is in rhyme. 'If I might abide, that I should ride back, and if the lord will it, who shaped the daylight, that I might in safety obtain my right, I will build churches, and worship God, I will give each man his right.'

[2] Pound amusingly casts doubt on the whole thing a page later: 'A spirit in cloth of gold, / so Merlin's moder said, / or did not say . . .' perhaps referring also to the duller versions like Brunne's where the phrase does not occur. Cp. Pound's comic version of mysterious birth in the sailor's story, C. XII, showing his ambivalent attitude of humour and high seriousness.

[3] He appears to have forgotten his promise to build churches. But see my discussion of the whole Stonehenge story below. To Geoffrey of Monmouth who 'invented' it, the memorial would be a church.

to go to Ireland and transfer the Giants' Ring Stones from Mount Kilara to Britain. After fighting the king of Ireland they find the stones but cannot move them. Merlin, however, uses some clever engines which make the stones light as feathers. On Whitsunday they hallow the new place called Stonehenge.

Aurelie duly dies, poisoned, and says: *& leggeð me an æst ænde: inne Stanhenge. | [ware liþ mochel of mine cun]*.[1]

When Uther eventually dies he does not say 'bury me by Aurelie' or indeed anything, but he is buried in Stonehenge: 'Then the people took the dead king . . . and carried him forth into Stonehenge, and buried him there, by his dear brother; side by side there they both lie'. (M. 19816 ff). Once again Pound telescopes two different parts of Laȝamon (Aurelie *asks* to be buried in Stonehenge, where lie his kin; Uther *is* buried there, near Aurelie). Clearly he cannot make such a telescoping by quoting direct, but then nor does he use 'synthetic Laȝamon' but modern English. The period is still remote and legendary, but this is a dying statement, as in a Will, and the shift to modern English gives on the one hand the right tone for such a statement (from the reader's viewpoint, a tone of do-not-misunderstand-me), and on the other it jerks us back to the present, not in the third person narrative we got in the Brutus/Leir and the Merlin's mother lines, but with 'me', as if it were the poet himself rather than Uther asking to be buried by Aurelie at Stonehenge. The whole passage began with a similar metamorphosis achieved by making a pronoun do more than double duty. Pound momentarily identifies with Uther, and since Uther's words were in fact spoken by Aurelie there is a treble identification.

Aurelie/Uther/Pound is thus to lie with his kindred beneath the monument at Stonehenge, 'Over harm / Over hate', the harm and the hate thereby acquiring a double meaning—Hengest's massacre of the Britons and racial wars in general, together with a more personal connotation, Pound's own harm and hate,

[1] M. 17842 ff. The interpolated line which Pound uses is from the other MS. printed parallel in the text. 'And lay me at the east end, in Stonehenge, where lie much of my kindred.'

both by and towards himself. The reference is all the more poignant if we remember that Diana's advice to Brutus to go to Albion and build a new Troy there, and her prophecy about his royal progeny, ultimately came to nothing. In Laȝamon, and therefore in Geoffrey, the history of the British people ends with the sad story of Cadwalader as an exile in Britanny, hearing of Athelstan's success. He gathers his ships but dreams of Christ telling him to go to Rome instead, where he must be shriven and die, for neither he nor any other Britons are ever more to possess England, which Alemainish men shall have, until the time comes that was declared by Merlin, when Britons shall come to Rome, and get Cadwalader's bones from the marble stone and carry them to Britain, and become bold, and prosper. His wise men consult the histories to see if Cadwalader's vision accords with the prophecies of Merlin and those of the Sibyl, and they find it does. So Cadwalader calls his sons and tells them about it, adding that Merlin said it in words 'and *Sibillie* þa wise : | *a bocken hit isette*.'[1] It is interesting that Pound, quoting this line at the end of the passage (after Athelstan), manages to link the prophetess (who is linked with Merlin as male prophet) back to 'Ra-Set' and the 'river of crystal', that is, total light (the sun and moon), part of which is Diana, and hence by implication back to Diana's prophecy to Brutus. He does not, of course, mention Christ (nor, for that matter, does Wace, who merely says 'a voice from heaven'). Cadwalader does what he is told, and his bones are still in Rome. Later, Laȝamon ends his history with these moving words : 'And the English kings ruled these lands, and the Britons lost it . . . so that nevermore were they kings here. And this same day came not, be it henceforth as it may; happen what happens, happen God's will. Amen.' (M. 32232–41). For Pound too, in a sense, lost England, and lost America, or they lost him. The important thing, however, is that this composite

---

[1] M. 32182–3. 'And Sibyl the wise set it in a book.' In Arthur's time the Sibyl is also said to have prophesied that three British kings were to win Rome : Belin, Constantine, and now Arthur. (M. 25141 ff.) Cp. Madden, Vol. 3, pp. 434 and 393 for notes on these Sibylline prophecies in the 13th and 14th centuries.

figure Pound/Uther/Aurelie lies under a great monument, 'over-flooding, light over light'.

The next sentence is the only other direct quotation from Laȝamon, and therefore in 'archaic English'. With it, we leap forward from Aurelie to the end of the history, much nearer to Laȝamon's own time, that is, two and a half centuries before it but some five centuries after the supposed events of the fifth century. 'And yilden he gon rere' refers, as Pound himself informs us, to Athelstan (924–940) who 'set up gilds':

hu Aðelstan her com liðen : ut of Sex-londen,
and hu he al Angle-lond : sette on his aȝere hond.
and hu he sette moting : & hu he sette husting.
and hu he sette sciren : & makede frið of deoren.
& hu he sette halimot : & hu he sette hundred.
& þa nomen of þan tunen : on Sexisce runen.
& ȝilden he gon rere : mucle & swiðe mære.
& þa chirchen he gon dihten : after Sexisce irihten . . .[1]

This reference to gilds and hundreds is not in either Wace or Geoffrey, both of whom end their history with Athelstan simply as king of all England (the first so to style himself on his coins —a fact from Del Mar). Nor does William of Malmesbury refer to gilds, despite a much fuller account of Athelstan. Laȝamon must here have had access to other information or oral tradition, although he is otherwise remarkably confused about chronology.[2]

The gilds in question are the frith-gilds or peace-gilds set up by the bishops and reeves of London (*Laws*, VI Athelstan).[3]

---

[1] M. 31989 ff. 'How Athelstan arrived here out of Saxland, and how he set all England in his own hand; and how he set up mooting, and how he set up husting, and how he set up shires, and made chaces of deer; and how he set up halimot, and how he set up the hundred; and the names of the towns in Saxish speech; and how he began to rear gilds, great and very large, and began to construct churches in the Saxish manner. . . .'

[2] Like Wace (who misunderstood Geoffrey) he brings Athelstan to England in the 7th century, some 65 years after the death of Ina (727–8).

[3] Code Textus Roffensis, Iudicia civitatis Londoniae, ed. F. Liebermann I/173–183, and with English translation by Attenborough, pp. 156–69, also in *English Historical Documents* (gen. ed. D. C. Douglas) Vol. I, ed. D. Whitelock, London 1955, pp. 387–391.

At first sight these are not commercial gilds in the later medi-aeval sense presumably intended by Pound, but purely judicial. There are twelve articles, detailing the arrangements by which the people of London and surrounding areas 'formed voluntary associations to undertake police duties, especially against cattle thieves . . . gildsmen were grouped in tens to make up a hundred with a chief called a hundred man. They were put under royal patronage by Athelstan, who allowed their members to share in the profits from any convicted thief. This scheme of self-help was so successful that Edgar's 'Law relating to the Hundred'[1] adopted it, extended it compulsorily and gave it an official and legal basis by allowing the gilds not only to arrest but also to try suspects with full use of the ordeal. . . . The hundred court met every four weeks under the presidency of the hundred reeve. . . . The hundred court had a jurisdiction as extensive and final as that of the shire and it was, in fact, the place where most judicial, police and commercial business was done.[2]

Pound does not make it clear at this point whether he knows the exact nature of these gilds, although in Canto LXXXVIII he had quoted from a law of Edward I, and in *Thrones* he quotes from the laws of Edgar (Canto CVII). The phrase from Laȝamon recurs in Canto XCVII in juxtaposition with Edgar's leather money (a fact from Del Mar), and is repeated in modern English at the end of that canto, after three ideograms pê[2] (a chief, leader, earl), ma[3] (horse), and tsu[3] (ancestor), which clearly refer back to '& Spartans in Mount Taygeto / sacrifice a horse to the winds' (itself a possible fusion with Agamemnon's sacrifice) but they may also be connected with Baller and the old

[1] The Hundred Ordinance, Code C.C.C.C., MS. 383, ed. Liebermann I/192–5, Whitelock op. cit., p. 393.

[2] G. O. Sayles, *The Mediaeval Foundations of England*, London 1952 (orig. 1948) p. 183. The gilds of Athelstan were the origin of the hundred, the but latter in some form is found among all Germanic peoples, evidently a tribal unit representing 100 persons or 100 hides of land, and revived by name in the 10th century to create some sort of order after the chaos of the Danish wars. Before then local government had centred on royal *tuns*, the royal reeves and bailiffs in charge of the king's private estates gradually encroaching on public life, financing levies, punishing criminals, collecting tolls from traders etc.

steppe custom of sacrificing the horses of dead chieftains;[1]
they would have a quadruple connotation if we suppose that
Pound has read VI Athelstan, with its cattle and its gild-chief
and its peaceful motives. In any case, the general idea of the
frith-gilds as a mutual help society covering the judicial, the
police, and the business aspects of cattle-trading, seems to accord
with Pound's principles of commerce and good government as
based on natural wealth, and above all against division—money
breeding without reference to the goods behind it, or, in culture
as in politics, specialisation and blinkers.[2]

Here, at any rate, this first Athelstan reference is given the
same numinous context that all glimpses of wisdom in human
history get from Pound :

> overflooding, light over light
> And yilden he gon rere
> > (Athelstan before a.D. 940)
> the light flowing, whelming the stars.

For Athelstan left this monument, just as Aurelie is said to
have left Stonehenge, and Pound is leaving *The Cantos*.

III

This brings me to the question of Stonehenge and the 'legendary' history of Britain as given by Laȝamon's ultimate source,
Geoffrey of Monmouth.

Stonehenge was not, of course, built in the 5th century A.D.,
and therefore not by Aurelius. Ambrosius Aurelius also appears
in Bede and Gildas, and was probably a real person, who
defended the Britons after the Roman withdrawal.[3] Geoffrey is

---

[1] Hugh Gordon Porteus in a letter.

[2] Cp. 'Nap III had the composition divided, / to each compositor in the
print shop / a very few lines, / none seeing the whole Proclamation'
(Canto LXXXV).

[3] Arthur E. Hutson, British Personal Names in *Historia Regum
Britanniae* (Univ. of California, Publications in English, Vol. V, 1944).
Lloyd, *History of Wales* (London 1939) p. 100. And Maynardier's discussion in Anniv. Papers by Colleagues and Students of G. L. Kittredge
(1913) pp. 119–126.

one of the 'romancers', who had an immense influence on the
vogue of 'matter of Britain' stories which had already begun
during the 12th century, but who—like Pound himself—has
been castigated by scholars as a bad historian (he is, however,
still read, rather than Bede, William of Malmesbury or Henry
of Huntingdon). Certainly his predecessors and contemporaries
do not present innumerable generations of pre-Roman British
kings from 'Brutus' on (though Brutus occurs in 'Nennius'),
indeed they do not deal with pre-Roman times at all.[1] Even in
the nineteenth century the editor of Gildas tells us in the typical
scornful terms which dog Geoffrey down the ages: 'Geoffrey of
Monmouth, upon whose veracity as an historian no reliance
can be placed, speaks confidently of a book by Gildas, *De
Victoria Aurelii Ambrosii*, a production which no one, it is
believed, except himself, has had the good fortune to see.'[2]
At the end of his history Geoffrey also adds a taunt to William
of Malmesbury and Henry of Huntingdon, leaving them his
Saxon kings but bidding them be silent as to the British kings,
since they did not possess a 'most ancient book, written in the
British tongue, which Walter archdeacon of Oxford brought out
of Britain.'

The quarrel about Geoffrey and the ancient book has gone on
for years. In 1929, Acton Griscom brought out his excellent
edition, together with a vast introduction in which he defends
Geoffrey as a historian for pre-Roman and Arthurian times, not
of course denying that he invented a great deal, but insisting
that he did have access to Welsh and Breton traditions at a time
when they were still familiar, before Saxon, Danish and Norman
invaders had destroyed the written records. His views have not
found favour, chiefly based as they were on the Welsh MSS
he claims could have been descended from this material, which
are all later than Geoffrey *as* MSS, and were all therefore

[1] Gildas and Bede start with a chapter on the geography of Britain
based on Pliny, Solicius and Orosius, then plunge straight in with Julius
Caesar up to the Saxons. Similarly William of Malmesbury in the 12th
century, bringing it up to his own times.

[2] *De Excidio Britanniae*, ed. Josephus Stevenson, 1838. The ref. is to
Hist. Reg. Brit. IV/xx.

dismissed as translations by scholars (who did not know Welsh). He prints one of them in translation, known as the Tysilio, together with Geoffrey's text, and insists that there are enough variations here and in others for some of the MSS at least not to be translations, although none is 'the most ancient book'.

More important to my mind is his argument from archæology, which often supports Geoffrey. He says examples could be multiplied but gives only two, unfortunately from post-Roman times.[1] But at least they show that where Geoffrey says something that is not in other histories he is not necessarily inventing.

Since Acton Griscom's edition, moreover, and indeed before it but inexplicably ignored by him, important discoveries have been made about Stonehenge, the chief of which corroborates in essence if not in Merlinerie Geoffrey's story about the transport of the stones. I quote from Professor R. J. C. Atkinson, who has himself worked on the most recent excavations:

'For a long time the story of the transport of the stones of Stonehenge from Ireland was regarded as a mere flight of fancy. But the growing belief that the bluestones came from some locality a long way off, finally identified as Pembroke-shire in 1923, and the high probability that they were carried from there most of the way by water, puts an entirely different complexion on the story. The correspondence between legend

---

[1] (a) the Venedoti or N. Wales men falling upon Roman legionaries on the bank of a small stream outside London and cutting off their heads (excavation along the bed of the Walbrook disclosed numerous skulls but almost no other bones); (b) the mention of Vortiger's son Pascentus being cordially received by the Irish king (stones with ogham characters discovered which mention Vortiger—until then always a 'mythical' British king, and there being no other record of this king being connected with Ireland; this is further strengthened by the fact that Vortiger lived in the ogham period, that there were Irish colonies in Britain in close touch with Ireland and that the name Vortiger is not duplicated elsewhere. (*The Historia Regum Britanniae of Geoffrey of Monmouth*, ed. Acton Griscom, London 1929, pp. 100–1). I may add that Vortiger's supposed wandering for five years all over Britain before he took over again might well have included Ireland.

and fact is so striking that it cannot be dismissed as mere coincidence; for to do so imposes at least as great a strain upon credulity as to suppose that behind this correspondence there lies a genuine memory of recorded events. Professor Stuart Piggot, who has discussed in detail the sources used by Geoffrey of Monmouth, concludes that we cannot rule out the possibility that he had access to a written or oral tradition, now lost but then still current in Wales, which embodied the story of the carrying of the bluestones from Prescelly to Stonehenge. Among the many extraordinary hypotheses concerning Stonehenge this is by no means the least credible. For the story of the carriage of so many stones over so great a distance would be one worthy of note and remembrance in the Middle Ages, and still more among the illiterate societies of prehistoric times, in which the oral transmission of tales of legendary and heroic feats was a commonplace.'[1]

Professor Atkinson gives a detailed account of Stonehenge, its present physical state, its origin, the sequence of construction and the probable techniques of transport and erection at various periods of addition, demolition and reconstruction. Prescelly

[1] *Stonehenge* (Pelican Book, London 1960, first publ. 1956) p. 185. The Piggot ref. is *Antiquity*, XV (1941), 269–86, 305–19. Despite the Piggot article, J. P. S. Tatlock (*The Legendary History of Britain—Geoffrey of Monmouth's Historia Regum Britanniae and its early vernacular versions*, Univ. of Calif. Press, 1950 pp. 40–2) continues to insist that Geoffrey invented his account of Stonehenge, on the grounds that (*a*) the parallel for a memorial to the dead would have been suggested to him by Battle Abbey, built by William the Conqueror in 1076 on the exact spot of his victory over Harold, *pro defunctis suis* (Henry of Huntingdon); (*b*) he gives a less vivid description of it than Henry and had probably not seen it (Tatlock even suggests the story was invented in answer to Henry who said no one knew what it was for); (*c*) Stonehenge, lost in the wilds of Salisbury plain where no one but shepherds went was a most unlikely place for legends to accumulate; (*d*) the story of the stones coming from Ireland and hither from the farthest ends of Africa was due to a natural desire to derive a mysterious thing from a mysterious origin, aided perhaps by rumours of such things existing there (as in other places). 'Modern semi-scientific conjecture [whatever he means by that] as to the actual origin of Stonehenge has no bearing on Geoffrey's account, simply because *there is no thinkable channel by which the prehistoric facts could have reached him*' (my italics), ftn. 160, p. 40.

was probably regarded as a holy mountain, which would explain the vast effort and the belief in the healing power of the stones. I would add that the techniques he describes would be amazing enough, in periods before the wheel, to have left a tradition of magical engineering that would easily give rise to Merlin's part in the story. From Professor Atkinson's Chapter V, I summarize his account of the various cultures probably concerned with the different stages of Stonehenge as given in his table (p. 101, end of Ch. 3)—the collation is mine, given in italics :

Pre-Stonehenge

Before 2300 B.C. Britain was populated by indigenous inhabitants, who were Mesolithic, who lived by hunting, fishing, gathering wild fruit. They are important for the old skills in gathering and preparing natural raw material, which would have been inherited by later cultures.

Around 2300 B.C. came the Windmill Hill Culture, that is, the first British wave of Western Neolithic peoples from somewhere in the Eastern Mediterranean, who had settled in Iberia, France, Switzerland, and the Channel coasts. They were agriculturers and stock-raisers. They built earthwork camps, cattle-corrals, long barrows, notably the Cursus, in Wiltshire, near Stonehenge.

Around 1900 B.C. came the Megalith Builders, also Neolithic. But they were the bearers of an attractive and potent religious doctrine expressed in the erection of vast and elaborate collective tombs such as Belas Knap in Gloucestershire and the West Kennet Long Barrow on Silbury Hill. Prof. Atkinson notes that tombs along S. W. France and the Bay of Biscay coast up to the Breton peninsula show the spread and persuasive force of the religious doctrine rather than the numerical strength of its bearers.

Stonehenge

Between 1900 and 1700 B.C. there was a wave of Secondary Neolithic, influenced by the previous cultures and therefore representing the first development of distinctively insular and British traditions. Unlike the indigenous and the Windmill Hill Culture they were nomadic, with small herds of ill-kept cattle, but they also fished, hunted, and had sporadic dealings in antlers, hides, vegetable ropes, fish, nuts, herbs. They exploited flint mines for the manufacture of axes which were traded over hundreds of miles, they had a tribal organisation and built embanked circular enclosures (probably sanctuaries), and wooden henge monuments (Woodhenge), also some upright stones (Stripple Stones, Bodmin & Penrith). To this period belongs what Prof. Atkinson calls *Stonehenge I*: *the construction of the bank, the ditch, & Aubrey Holes, the erection of the Heel Stone, Stones D & E, the timber structure (now gone), the cremation cemetery.* The religion at this time would probably have been earth-orientated, that is, towards the nether world and the chthonic powers.

Around 1700 B.C. came the Beaker Cultures, divided into the Bell Beaker from S. W. and Central Europe (the British immigrants probably from the Rhine) and the Necked Beaker, who mingled with warrior invaders from the Russian steppes (across theNorthern plain of Europe via the Rhine), and are characterized as a Corded-Ware-Battle-axe culture. The demand for metal objects opened up the trade routes to Ireland (a big European centre for metal work in copper and soon bronze), one of which routes lay along the S. coast of Wales, the same as the route for the transport of the bluestones. It is to this period, or perhaps nearer to the 16th century, that *Stonehenge II* belongs: *the transport of the bluestones from Pembrokeshire, the erection of the double circle, the filling up of the east end of the ditch at the causeway, the construction of the Avenue (to bring the stones up from the Avon), the dismantling of the timber structure, and other details.* There is evidence for supposing that the Beaker people, especially the Necked Beaker people, practised a sky-orientated religion.

About 1500 B.C. we have the Wessex Culture, in the Early Bronze Age. The primitive Neolithic cultures were by then in decline but the Secondary Neolithic and Beaker Cultures were still vigorous. The Wessex Culture is characterized by rich graves, warrior chieftains of Homeric and Saga type, and vast commerce. Objects were copied or imported from the principal centre of metallurgy in S. Germany & Bohemia, amber from entrepôts in South Central Europe on the North to Mediterranean route instead of direct from Scandinavia. There was probable trade with Minoan Crete and Mycenae, in relation to which the double-axe carved at Stonehenge is interesting, for it is similar to one in Britanny but also to the axe-cults in Mycenae, the *labrys*.[1] The same applies to a type of dagger. Atkinson even suggests the influence of a wandering or visiting Minoan architect on Stonehenge, its unique and sophisticated detail of design being unlikely in barbarians. In addition to this a rectangular escutcheon carving, similar to some in Britanny, which may perhaps represent a mother goddess cult figure, suggests a strong link between Wessex and the Breton peninsula : perhaps the Breton culture was itself an offshoot from Wessex. There is also evidence of concentration of power in the hands of a single strong man, whose memorial Stonehenge might perhaps be. It is from this time on that *Stonehenge III* was built : *1500 B.C., Stonehenge IIIa, the transport of the sarsen stones from near Marlborough, the dismantling (and storage in a safe place) of the double circle of bluestones, the erection of the sarsen trilithons, the Station Stones, the Slaughter Stone [not used for slaughter] and its companion. 1500–1400 B.C., Stonehenge IIIb, the tooling and erection of stones of the dressed bluestone setting, the digging and abandoning of the Y and Z holes (2 rings of holes intended for more stones but never filled, with traces of acute despair or apathy during the very digging, due perhaps to some calamity). 1400 B.C. Stonehenge IIIc, the dismantling of the dressed bluestone setting, the re-erection of these and of the remaining (stored) bluestones in the present circle and horseshoe.*

It is clear from this rough summary that Geoffrey had access to some genuine traditions concerning the Mediterranean

---

[1] Gave its name to the Royal Palace at Knossos. The axe Ⅎ pictograph is one that Pound is fond of, cp. Canto XCVII, 'what ax for clearing ?'

origins of what he calls the British people, their continuing va-et-vient and new landings (representing new waves perhaps), as well as their continuing links, friendly or hostile, with that area ('Rome'), with the Rhine, Southern Germany, Bohemia ('Alemaine') with Britanny and the Bay of Biscay ('Less Britain', 'Armorica') and Ireland. Certainly he (or the author of the 'most ancient book') formalized it with names of kings who no doubt never existed in the mediaeval sense Geoffrey had in mind. He imposed his own concepts on ancient times just as, for that matter, Shakespeare did.

The historical aspect of Geoffrey and of Stonehenge deserves consideration in such detail because it brings out a very similar aspect of Pound. Pound is not, of course, concerned with the historical truth of Laȝamon in this archaeological sense, for he is a visionary in much the same way that Geoffrey was, and like all visionaries he may (or at times may not) get hold of the essential truth by what can only be termed intuitive means. Put in the barest terms, Pound's interest in Stonehenge and the extraordinary telescoping of periods he achieves in this passage means this (I put legendary material in square brackets) : Britain, the home of the English language, was once a Mediterranean culture [guided to these shores by the goddess of the hunt and of the moon] and throughout retained its links with the Mediterranean area. A monument remains testifying to this, built [by the magic of Merlin (himself immaculately conceived), to commemorate the fallen in a Saxon massacre of the British, by Aurelius, a temporary victor over the Saxons], through early connections with both Ireland (the trade routes) and holiness (the holy mountain of Prescelly, the powerful religious doctrine of the Megalith builders from the Mediterranean via Britanny), as well as with Greece (Mycenae). In this link with Mycenae it represents the notion of perfect proportion so dear to Pound ('That is Sagetrieb, / that is tradition. / Builders had kept the proportion, / did Jacques de Molay / know these proportions?' Canto XC). The fact that the axis of Stonehenge is so important to the falling of the first light of sunrise on midsummer day may be linked with the importance of the axis in the unwobbling pivot on the one hand, and on the other with the perfect proportions of the tower in Poitiers, where no shadow falls in a certain room at a certain time, a reference which recurs often in these later cantos. But the Britons lost this land, and these traditions, this *forma*, only to glimpse it now and again, one of the immediate examples being Athelstan's 'monument', another the music of Henry Lawes, and its wiser kings lie buried under this monument (there is in fact one possibly pre-historic grave at Stonehenge), just as Lear lies buried in his temple. This monument is in fact a temple, where Brutus/ Actæon/Drake/Pound have their visions of the goddess, the temple where lie Aurelie/Uther/Merlin/Laȝamon/Geoffrey/ Pound. And the monument remains, a perfect example of what Donald Davie, quoting Adrian Stokes, calls the carver's as opposed to the moulder's art, the drawing out of wealth inherent in the material. The treatment of Laȝamon in Canto XCI is a superb example of the carver's art.

GEORGE DEKKER

Myth and Metamorphosis

Two Aspects of Myth in *The Cantos*

———————◦≫≫≫≫◦≪≪≪≪◦———————

I

Pound's pagan gods appear frequently in *The Cantos*. On most occasions they appear in the context of a myth or legend which Pound wishes to retell or recall. At other times, however, they seem to be making a personal appearance which does not occur for the sake of some story in which they figure. Bearing these distinctions in mind, it must nevertheless be confessed that the significance of these gods and of the myths in which they figure is sometimes rather obscure; indeed, the whole mythological apparatus in *The Cantos* recedes inevitably into the arcane regions of Acoetes' 'I have seen what I have seen' (Canto II). In the next section of this essay I shall do my best to explore these arcane regions. For the present, however, it will be more useful to consider two aspects of myth, which may be described briefly as 'myth as [im]moral fable' and 'myth as a record of a delightful psychic experience'. It is not always possible to make a hard and fast distinction between these, and the passages I select for discussion are not the clearest examples that I might give. A reader interested in this subject would therefore do well to study Cantos II and IV carefully before reading further.

In the later cantos Pound occasionally refers, rather enigmatically, to the powers of myth :

Remove the mythologies before they establish clean values
[Canto LXXXVII]

MYTH AND METAMORPHOSIS

> Bernice, late for a constellation, mythopoeia persisting,
> (now called folc-loristica)
>
> [Canto XCVII]

It is not until very late in *The Cantos* that Pound formally recognizes that myth has an independent status as an instrument of communication, roughly comparable to the categories he had established much earlier of 'logopoeia, melopoeia, and phanopoeia'.[1] There is no doubt, however, that his earlier use of myth was based on a recognition, if not of the special virtue of myths as a poetic instrument, at least of their potency as exemplary fables. The idea that they help to 'establish clean values' involves a good many things, such as religious awe in Canto II and sexual morality in Canto XXX.

One discussion of myth which may help to define Pound's use is to be found in Denis de Rougemont's *Passion and Society*, a book with whose central argument Pound would disagree emphatically:[2]

'. . . we are no longer at the stage of supposing that the mythical is tantamount to unreality or illusion. Too many myths now display their indisputable power over us. And yet abuse of the term has made a fresh definition needful. Speaking generally, a myth is a story—a symbolical fable as simple as it is striking—which sums up an infinite number of more or less analagous situations. A myth makes it possible to become aware at a glance of certain types of *constant relations* and to disengage these from the welter of everyday appearances.'

The immediate importance of this definition of myth is the way it seems to apply to the myths and troubadour biographies in Canto IV. The relations depicted in those fables certainly are, as de Rougemont says, *'constant'*; and Pound's treatment of them is certainly designed to focus attention on just that quality of 'constancy'.

The fables themselves are '[im]moral', which is to say that they deal memorably with archetypal human situations which

[1] 'How to Read', *Literary Essays*, p. 25.

[2] de Rougemont, *Passion and Society* (L'Amour et L'Occident), revised edition, London, 1956, p. 18.

give rise to moral problems. If they are taken as guides to conduct, their influence is of course 'immoral'; in the Cabestanh tale, for instance, we see one crime after another—adultery, murder, suicide: the stark and (as de Rougemont would say) *compelling* plot of romantic love. Dante recognized this problem in the Paolo and Francesca story, and Plato had recognized the general problem long before him. But in this violent little fable (which we remember, no doubt, because it is violent) there is an unforgettable sequence of clearly motivated yet blindly egotistical acts: at no point does one of these monoliths inquire whether he or she is damaging anybody else; each is a law unto himself, gesturing grandly in a world not unlike that of Jacobean tragedy. We shall see that in Canto XXX Pound develops these ideas in an unexpected and powerful way.

Before going on to Canto XXX, however, I should define the second aspect of myth which I mentioned—myth as 'the record of a delightful psychic experience'. This, it is obvious, is something quite different from myth as a moral fable; and it may be that 'myth' is a misnomer for what I have in mind. But my authority for this is Pound himself, and the idea has an interesting history:

'Poetry is a sort of inspired mathematics, which gives us equations, not for abstract figures, triangles, spheres, and the like, but for the human emotions. If one have a mind which inclines to magic rather than to science, one will prefer to speak of these equations as spells or incantations; it sounds more arcane, mysterious, recondite.'[1]

Mario Praz was, I believe, the first critic to suggest that this passage from the *Spirit of Romance* was the seed from which Eliot's 'objective correlative' sprang.[2] Another development is this:

'I believe in a sort of permanent basis in humanity, that is to say, I believe that Greek myth arose when someone having passed through delightful psychic experience tried to com-

---

[1] Pound, *Spirit of Romance*, (New York 1952), p. 14.
[2] Mario Praz, 'T. S. Eliot and Dante', *Southern Review*, Vol. II, no. 3, pp. 525–48.

municate it to others and found it necessary to screen himself from persecution. Speaking aesthetically, the myths are explications of mood; you may stop there, or you may probe deeper. Certain it is that these myths are only intelligible in a vivid and glittering sense to those people to whom they occur. I know, I mean, one man who understands Persephone and Demeter, and one who understands the Laurel, and another who has, I should say, met Artemis. These things are for them *real*.'[1]

'I have seen what I have seen', says Acoetes in Canto II; and it will be recalled that mad Piere Vidal seems to be experiencing such a vision in Canto IV. The essay from which this passage is extracted, though written as early as 1912, has in fact proved an invaluable confirmation of many of my readings. As a very early essay, however,—written before Pound began *The Cantos* —it has only a limited usefulness as a commentary on the poem as it now stands. It is clear, for instance, that the definition of myth which he gave there proved too limited. Yet the idea of a 'permanent basis in humanity' does obviously apply to myth as a moral fable as well as to myth as the record of a 'delightful psychic experience'.

I shall return later to this second aspect of myth in *The Cantos*, but it is time now to examine Canto XXX. The first part of that canto leads into the thickets of courtly doctrine, but this route will give a new perspective on Pound's use of myth as moral fable.

What Pound discovered in courtly poetry was something quite different from what Coleridge, Rossetti, and Morris discovered :

> Compleynt, compleynt I hearde upon a day,
> Artemis singing, Artemis, Artemis
> Agaynst Pity lifted her wail :
> Pity causeth the forests to fail,
> Pity slayeth my nymphs,
> Pity spareth so many an evil thing.

[1] Pound, 'Psychology and Troubadours', *The Quest*, Vol. IV, no.1, pp. 43–4.

Pity befouleth April,
Pity is the root and the spring.

This would appear to contradict Chaucer's *Complaint unto Pity*, in which he makes it quite clear all other courtly virtues are worthless unless 'Pity' is alive. In fact the convention of Chaucer's poem is that Pity is dead (lines 36–42):

> Aboute hir herse there stoden lustely,
> Withouten any woo, as thoughte me,
> Bounte parfyt, wel armed and richely,
> And fresshe Beaute, Lust, and Jolyte,
> Assured Maner, Youthe, and Honeste,
> Wisdom, Estaat, Drede, and Governaunce,
> Confedred both by bonde and alliaunce.

Nothing could be more conventional. The important point of this stanza, however, is that all of the courtly virtues are 'Confedred both by bonde and alliaunce', and that Pity, now dead, is an essential, indeed the chief, member of this confederacy. But by the same token, the death of 'Youth' would equally disrupt this allegorical confederacy. If 'Pity' were alive, in other words, and allied herself with 'Elde' or some equally uncourtly attribute, she would disrupt the entire courtly world. And this, very nearly, is what has happened in Canto XXX.

The Pity which Chaucer valued so highly is, then, quite a different creature from the Pity who 'spareth so many an evil thing'. But lest Pound's complaint against Pity be taken as a wholesale rejection of compassion and sympathy, I must point out at once that there is a crucial ambiguity in the line 'Pity is the root and the spring': in context, of course, the words 'of all that causes my complaint' are implied as an appendage to this line, but taken by itself, the line says something quite different— it says simply that 'Pity is the root and the spring'. The justification for detaching the line from its context is provided by the syntactical pattern, which consists essentially of a parallel series of transitive sentences (Pity causeth . . . Pity slayeth . . .

Pity befouleth . . .), followed by a sentence built around a copula (Pity is . . .). Pity, in essence, is 'the root and the spring' of any number of things, some good, some bad; and it is even, for that matter, the 'root and the spring' of *The Cantos*. But, like love itself (as we shall see shortly), what is essentially desirable can be perverted by indiscriminate use.[1]

> Now if no fayre creature followeth me
> It is on account of Pity,
> It is on account that Pity forbideth them slaye.
> All things are made foul in this season,
> This is the reason, none may seek purity
> Having for foulnesse pity
> And things growne awry;
> No more do my shaftes fly
> To slay. Nothing is now clean slayne
> But rotteth away.

These lines have apparently caused their author considerable worry, because we find him qualifying them in both the *Pisan* and *Rock-Drill Cantos*:

> J'ai eu pitié des autres
> Probablement pas assez, and at moments that suited my own
> convenience
> [Canto LXXVI]

> Pity, yes, for the infected,
> but maintain antisepsis,
> let the light pour.
> Apollonius made peace with the animals
> Was no blood on the Cyprian's altars
> [Canto XCIV]

Though I do not believe that these second thoughts in any way

---

[1] Pound may very well have had in mind *Inferno XX*, where Vergil reproaches Dante for having pity on the damned; however, Canto XXX is probably more directly indebted to the *Pervigilium Veneris*.

contradict the lines from Canto XXX, there is an apparent danger that a careless or ignorant reader might misconstrue them. Their first target is, no doubt, the Romantic Mediaevalists who sentimentalized and thus obscured the Middle Ages. The second target is the misuse of the word 'pity' and of the emotion it signifies. It is clear that this misuse involves a good deal more than erotic subjects: it includes especially those aspects of humanitarianism which had grown into an unassailable moral posture rather than an active force of social reform. But the handiest and least pretentious formulation of what Pound is driving at, I have found in Kingsley Amis's *Lucky Jim*, where Jim decides at last to abandon his neurotic girl friend in favour of a quite unpitiful beauty:

'For the first time he really felt that it was no use trying to save those who fundamentally would rather not be saved. To go on trying would not merely be to yield to pity and sentimentality, but wrong and, to pursue it to its conclusion, inhumane.'[1]

Pound then shifts to the classic triangle of Mars, Venus, and Vulcan. His 'Compleynt against Pity', which has rather general significance, is illuminated by a specifically erotic misuse of Pity:

> In Paphos, on a day
> > I also heard:
> . . . goeth not with young Mars to playe
> But she hath pity on a doddering fool,
> She tendeth his fyre,
> She keepeth his embers warm.

This, however, is classical myth as it was used by the Middle Ages, and one cannot do better than consult the Chaucerian translation of the *Roman de la Rose*: outside the garden of the Rose the lover sees portrayed the 'Deadly Sins' of courtly love; one of them is 'Elde', and I quote at some length, for reasons which will soon be apparent:

---

[1] Kingsley Amis, *Lucky Jim* (London 1954).

The tyme, that may not sojourne,
But goth, and may never retourne,
As watir that doun renneth ay,
But never drope retourne may,
Ther may nothing as tyme endure,
Metall, nor erthely creature,
For alle thing it fret and shall,
The tyme eke, that chaungith all,
And all doth waxe and fostred be,
And all thing destroieth he;
The tyme, that eldith our auncessours,
And eldith kynges and emperours.
And that us alle shal overcomen,
Er that deth us shal have nomen;
The tyme, that hath al in welde
To elden folk, had maad hir elde

But natheles, I trowe that she
Was fair symtyme, and fresh to se,
When she was in hir rightful age,
But she was past al that passage,
And was a doted thing bicomen.
A furred cope on had she nomen,
Wel had she clad hirsilf and warm,
For cold myght elles don hir harm.
These olde folk have alwey cold;
Her kynde is sich, whan they ben old.[1]

Possible though it may be, I do not claim that Pound had this passage in mind when he wrote:

She tendeth his fyre,
She keepeth his embers warm.

(It is more likely to be simply an allusion to Vulcan's occupation.) But it is certainly in keeping with the spirit of this passage when Pound goes on immediately afterwards to write:

[1] Geoffrey Chaucer, *Works*, ed. by F. N. Robinson (second edition, London, 1957), p. 569, lines 381–96 and 403–12.

Time is the evil. Evil.

                        A day, and a day
Walked the young Pedro baffled,

                        a day and a day
After Ignez was murdered.
Came the Lords in Lisboa

                        a day, and a day
In homage. Seated there

                        dead eyes,
Dead hair under the crown,
The King still young there beside her.

The shift to Camões's Portugal is violent and 'illogical', but emotionally it is right; for the terrible homage exacted by Pedro, insane flourish that it is, is as poignant as it is morbid. And though it is perhaps most ghastly because of its inadequacy as a revenge for the Lords' assassination of Ignez, it has an almost archetypal adequacy as an expression of human loss and of the irrecoverability of time :

> The tyme, that may not sojourne,
> But goth, and may never retourne,
> As watir that doun renneth ay,
> But never drope retourne may,

But Pedro's grief, terrible and affecting in itself, has by this ceremony become translated into a perverted, if 'poetic', gesture of the same order as Soremonda's 'No other taste shall change this', or her husband's savage revenge on her and Cabestanh. Memorable these acts are, and memorable their actors intend them to be—as monuments to their own outraged feelings and their own self-conscious capacity for outrage. In the sense that they act violently they are quite the opposite of the 'Pity' which Pound attacks in the first part of this canto; but they are quite alike in their assumption of a nearly unassailable moral posture. There is somewhat the same thing in Pound's Dido (Canto VII), where the suggestion of necrophilia anticipates Pedro's exhumation of his dead mistress or Pity's care for 'foulnesse' and 'things grown awry'.[1]

However, I might just as well acknowledge what is certainly true about the Middle Ages and its 'Pite': that the courtly society (so far as it existed) and its doctrine were a bizarre mixture of fantasy and ruthless 'realism'; and that mediaeval heroes like Richard Cœur-de-Lion committed mass atrocities and grand seigneurial gestures with equal ease. It would be foolish to suppose that Pound gives these things their due weight in his total evaluation of the Middle Ages. But he is not suggesting here or anywhere else in *The Cantos* that we should model ourselves on the Middle Ages or on China or on early-nineteenth-century America: but we *can* learn from them in certain areas, such as 'Pity', where the courtly doctrine exhibits a certain honesty of response or where the Confucian doctrine recommends that one save one's self before saving others.

Many myths, including some treated by Pound, enshrine sexual taboos. The taboos are still with us, necessary no doubt, for the old mythological violence is dangerous now as ever :

and Till was hung yesterday
for murder and rape with trimmings plus Cholkis
    plus mythology, thought he was Zeus ram or another one
        Hey Snag wots in the bibl'?
        wot are the books ov the bible?
        Name 'em, don't bullshit ME.

[mo⁴]　　莫　ΟΫ́ΤΙΣ

a man on whom the sun has gone down
the ewe, he said had such a pretty look in her eyes,
and the nymph of the Hagoromo came to me,

                        as a corona of angels
                        [Canto LXXIV]

[1] Pound's point of view here might usefully be compared with the point of view in *Lady Chatterley's Lover*, though the differences are perhaps more interesting than the similarities.

Pound's evident sympathy for Till is partly a matter of propinquity : as inmates in the Pisa D.T.C. they were both men 'on whom the sun has gone down'. But there is a recognition, too, that in a section of society where the search for knowledge is reduced to a quiz contest, one cannot expect moral scruples to hold the old mythological violence in check. A knowledge of the myths does not so much 'establish clean values' as remind us that a man like Till isn't necessarily an incomprehensible fiend, even when his 'trimmings' are carved with a switch-blade or a straight razor.

But if the myths still have a real force as embodied in Till, they have a very different reality as embodied in the 'nymph of the Hagoromo' who visits Pound in the D.T.C. This, apparently, is the sort of thing he had in mind when, thirty years earlier, he wrote : 'I know, I mean, one man who understands Persephone and Demeter, and one who understands the Laurel, and another who has, I should say, met Artemis. These things are for them *real*.' Until the *Pisan Cantos*, I am not convinced that these things are '*real*' for Pound. The impressionistic evocation of an Ovidian Eden in Canto IV is admirable in its own way, but it is chiefly an evocation of a scene; perhaps it should be regarded as an 'explication of mood'. The same thing can be said about Canto XVII. There are in fact many such passages scattered about the first thirty cantos, and they are rightly admired. But the goddesses do not come alive until the *Pisan Cantos*.

The 'Lynx' passage in Canto LXXIX is probably the best example of its kind in *The Cantos*; it is already famous, and it requires very little explication. I shall merely quote two passages from it which, in themselves examples of the best of Pound's work, will serve to advance my general discussion of Eros :

    Ἴακχε, Ἴακχε, Χαῖρε, AOI
        'Eat of it not in the under world'
        See that the sun or the moon bless thy eating
    Κόρη, Κόρη, for the six seeds of an error
    or that the stars bless thy eating

> O Lynx, guard this orchard,
> Keep from Demeter's furrow

> This fruit has a fire within it,
> > Pomona, Pomona
> No glass is clearer than are the globes of this flame
> what sea is clearer than the pomegranate body
> > holding the flame?
> > Pomona, Pomona,

This should certainly recall Canto XLVII very vividly to mind, for both are concerned with the Eleusinian Mysteries. Most remarkable about this passage, however, is Pound's oblique and very beautiful treatment of a young girl's fascination with sex. The symbolism is of course traditional, but it is Pound's particular approach to the Persephone story that makes it so radiant.

Aphrodite appears frequently in the *Pisan* and *Rock-Drill Cantos*, and she is the chief among many deities in the 'Lynx' passage:

> O lynx, guard my vineyard
> As the grape swells under vine leaf
> *Ἥλιος* is come to our mountain
> there is a red glow in the carpet of pine spikes

> O lynx, guard my vineyard
> As the grape swells under vine leaf
> > This Goddess was born of sea-foam
> > She is lighter than air under Hesperus
> > δεινὰ εἶ Κύθηρα
> terrible in resistance
> > Κόρη καὶ Δήλια καὶ Μαῖα
> trine as praeludio
> > Κύπρις᾿ Ἀφρόδιτη
> a petal lighter than sea-foam
> > Κύθηρα.

Maia, mother of Hermes, is chosen as the representative of

motherhood to set beside Delia the virgin and Kore the daughter,
and the implication of 'trine as praeludio' appears to be that
Aphrodite is 'three goddesses in one'—the Poundian Trinity.
In the next section we shall see that Aphrodite is (in some not
entirely penetrable sense) the controlling force in Pound's
world and thus in *The Cantos*.

II

Metamorphosis

Any exposition of *The Cantos* necessarily involves an attempt
to explain why Pound is so much concerned with metamorphosis.
One kind of metamorphosis is that which involves the transmission and translation of knowledge—an idea, an image, an
archetypal figure or deity—through various languages and
cultural situations. The legends of Tereus and Cabestanh seem
to be a case in point : though the circumstances of the stories
are in many respects dissimilar, the central episode, the revenge
for adultery, remains much the same; apparently there is
something in the cannibalistic feast-revenge which, however
times and customs change, remains fascinating to the folk
imagination. Perhaps the idea inevitably recurs, or perhaps it is
retained and reshaped in oral tradition, or perhaps it is taken
from a written source, i.e. Ovid, and translated by the mediaeval
mind into mediaeval terms; but in any case it is a constant
element in a world characterized by change, and its constancy
would seem to be a guarantee of its intrinsic validity as an
index to a 'permanent basis in humanity'.

Speaking broadly, this kind of metamorphosis is the basis of
Pound's poetic method in *The Cantos*. And yet to say so may be
misleading, since he is equally concerned with, say, the mediaevalism of the Middle Ages—as reflected in, for instance, the
unvarying sequence of details in the troubadour biographies.
The Middle Ages can be useful for our time only if we try to
understand them with some precision, as we have seen in the
case of the mediaeval use of the word 'Pity'. Likewise, when

Pound attempts to translate Homer by 'blood rite', he uses the nearest equivalent to Homer that he can find in English literature. It is at root a Confucian concern, or Confucian as Pound understands it. And there is nothing more central in *The Cantos* than this effort simultaneously to capture the constant element in the flux and yet to honour the thing *as it was* at the point where it was captured. In Canto XC, which I shall examine shortly, there is an effort to define the conception of reality which is behind this concern; it is a conception in which a second kind of metamorphosis plays an important part.

This second and more fundamental kind of metamorphosis is the kind that Ovid used as an organizing principle for his compendium of mythology, the *Metamorphoses*. The one constant, that is, which Ovid could use to bring his supernatural tales together was the constant change of form which his legendary characters underwent—from a man to a hawk, from a woman to a swallow. And, indeed, to a primitive mind the guarantee of the supernatural nature of a subject is its capacity to alter form dramatically. The result of Ovid's method in the *Metamorphoses* is a restless and fluctuating surface which is very much like Pound's picture of life. This kind of metamorphosis, it is clear, takes us again into those arcane regions concerning which Acoetes says, 'I have seen what I have seen'.

Canto XC begins with a mediaeval Latin epigraph which asserts that the human soul is not love but that love issues from it, and therefore the soul does not delight in itself, but in the love which flows from it:

> Animus humanus amor non est,
> sed ab ipso amor procedit, et
> ideo seipso non diligit, sed amore
> qui seipso procedit.

The point here seems to be that the dancer is admirable in so far as she dances. It is, in effect, a repudiation of the subject-attribute conception of reality, where the colour of an object is an attribute, somehow distinct from its essence. The introductory lines of the canto pick up this idea:

'From the colour the nature
      & by the nature the sign!'
Beatific spirits welding together
     as in one ash-tree in Ygdrasail.

On this showing colour is the active mode of being of an object, just as love is the active mode of being of the soul; and it is by the colour or the love that we know and value an object or the soul—that is, by its manifestations. Translated into mythological terms, as in the tree of Ygdrasail, this approach to reality instructs us that, though the roots of things are in heaven, we worship best by understanding their particular manifestations on earth.

The connection between pagan polytheism and this view of the world is quite clear. On the psychological level we observe, say, that sacred to Dionysus are the vine, the ivy, the rose, panthers, lions, lynxes, etc. They are, as in Canto II, manifestations of his power and affection; and they are, each of them, to be valued accordingly. This clearly suggests a form of Neoplatonism (derived chiefly, probably, from Erigena); but in its assignment of values it differs radically from Platonism proper and from many forms of Neoplatonism (Christian or pagan) which stress the inferiority of 'created things' and the desirability of turning away from them toward the Prime Mover. For Pound it is always *this* world that matters; and from his point of view the pagan gods are always, whether by patronage or metamorphosis, more concretely involved with this world than is the Christian god or the Neoplatonic One.

Committed as he is to a world of particulars inside time, where each decays, dies, or is subject to destruction, Pound is nevertheless deeply concerned with permanent values. On the one hand, permanence is achieved through the gods (in this case Hermes, patron of Amphion and inventor of the lyre), who express their supernatural will through perishable particulars:

       Templum aedificans, not yet marble,
         'Amphion!'

Or, less esoterically, through an oral tradition:

> to the room in Poitiers where one can stand
>> casting no shadow,
> That is Sagetrieb,
>> that is tradition.
> Builders had kept the proportion,

Admittedly, this is cryptic, but the legend of Amphion driving stones into order with the music from his harp has already appeared in *The Cantos*, as has a reference to the tower in Poitiers whose remarkable construction has left a room in which one may stand without casting a shadow. The power which, through Amphion's harp, compelled the stones into place in the wall of Thebes creates the temple, as yet a place of worship and not a monument of civic pride: the religious and creative force are united here, as they are in the 'Sagetrieb' which combines practical knowledge with a knowledge of religious symbolism. Stones or men may perish, but the wisdom of the race is handed down, or, lacking that even, the religious impulse reasserts itself.

Dropping down a few lines, we find in Latin (the closest thing to imperishability in language) a cryptic but central statement of Pound's conception of the world:

> Kuthera δεινά
> Kuthera sempiterna
>> Ubi amor, ibi oculus.
> Vae qui cogitatis inutile.
>> quam in nobis similitudine divinae
>>> reperetur imago.

Here are four separate phrases, grammatically unlinked, but not impenetrable. The goddess of Love has, as one of her epithets, 'eternal'; and this is not quite the same thing as saying that 'Love is eternal'. For the copula 'is' contains a suggestion of assertion which Pound does not want; 'sempiterna' and 'Kuthera' simply go together. This is the permanent element in Pound's universe, and it is typical that he prefers the goddess Kuthereia to the abstraction Amor. It is still more typical that he shifts quickly from the supernatural to the natural: 'Ubi amor, ibi oculus.' For, following the logic of the introductory lines of this canto, it is not the soul (or 'Kuthera') that delights, but the love that flows from it; and love, in flowing, manifests itself in actions, through concrete particulars. We respond to this love worshipfully by observing its manifestations, i.e. by directing our attention *outside* of ourselves. Hence the jeremiac 'Vae qui cogitatis inutile'—which is made meaningful by recalling 'Cogito ergo sum'. To the Poundian view of reality, Descartes's (or any Sceptic's) introspective method, of positing the universe on the basis of his own mental activity, is sacrilegious as well as perverse. And of course 'quam in nobis similitudine divinae / reperetur imago' is not merely the chief argument for human self respect; its corollary is the mediaeval 'Doctrine of Signatures', which holds that all created things contain the 'signatures' of divine forms and, as such, should be respected. Moreover, if the image of the divine is indeed found in us, we should act accordingly: i.e. reveal this kinship by an outflowing of love.

A brief summary may be useful at this point. Pound seems to envisage a natural world of more or less perishable particulars, which are not to be despised because they are perishable, but to be studied with affection because they are manifestations of divine love. Besides 'Kuthera sempiterna' there is a body of wisdom (practical and spiritual) which survives from generation to generation, and which is our guarantee that, whatever dark ages descend, civilization will rebuild. The capacity to renew is, of course, a capacity that each of us has, as a member of nature:

> 'Mother Earth in thy lap'
> said Randolph

(This is juxtaposed directly with 'quam in nobis similitudine divinae / reperetur imago'.) And, as we shall see, this view of the world is extremely hospitable to metamorphosis.

Pound then recalls Cunizza's liberation of her slaves and goes on to less congenial 'liberators':

liberavit masnatos.
Castalia like the moonlight
                              and the waves rise and fall,
Evita, beer-halls, semina motuum,
                              to parched grass, now is rain
not arrogant from habit,
        but furious from perception,
                                        Sibylla,

Castalia is the fountain on Mount Parnassus dedicated to Apollo
in which pilgrims to the Delphic shrine purify themselves.
'Evita' juxtaposed with 'beer-halls' suggests Eva Braun: this,
by way of imagery which may be taken to symbolize national
recovery, leads to one who is 'furious from perception'—
Adolf Hitler, it would seem. Pound's writing is so cryptic at
this point that the passage is subject to several possible interpretations, of which the one given might misrepresent his
intended meaning. A later reference to Hitler (in Canto XCIII)
is certainly less favourable than this one seems to be. It is
further useful to note that the conception behind this passage
and the actual imagery were in Pound's mind as early as 1912:

'And with certain others their consciousness is "germinal".
Their thoughts are in them as the thought of the tree is in the
seed, or in the grass, or the grain, or the blossom. And these
minds are the more poetic, and they affect mind about them,
and transmute it as the seed the earth. And this latter sort of
mind is close on the vital universe; and the strength of the
Greek beauty rests in this, that it is ever at the interpretation of
this vital universe, by its signs of gods, and godly attendants
and oreads.'[1]

The idea of resurrection is not present in this passage, but it
clearly indicates the basis of resurrection. In the lines from Canto
XC there is also the image '. . . the waves rise and fall', which
might be illuminated by this brief passage from Canto XLII:

[1] Pound, 'Psychology and Troubadours', *The Quest*, Vol. IV, no. 1,
p. 45.

> wave falls and the hand falls
> Thou shalt not always walk in the sun
> or see weed sprout over cornice
> Thy work in set space of years, not over an hundred.

It is in the nature of things, of men and civilizations, that they rise and fall. The serenity with which Pound contemplates this rise and fall of civilizations is one of the attractive features of the *Rock-Drill Cantos*—and yet how strangely it contrasts with the savage utopianism of Hitler, which was to have produced a world order that would last for a thousand years.

In the next block of verse Pound elaborates the theme of resurrection, though the active figure this time is (apparently) himself:

> from under the rubble heap
>   m'elevasti
> from the dulled edge beyond pain,
>   m'elevasti
> out of Erebus, the deep-lying
>   from the wind under the earth,
>   m'elevasti
> from the dulled air and the dust,
>   m'elevasti
> by the great flight,
>   m'elevasti,
>   Isis Kuanon
> from the cusp of the moon,
>   m'elevasti

It is not at all surprising that Pound turns from 'the rubble heap' to a natural world which he believes to be penetrated by a divine and vital force. (This occurs frequently in the *Pisan Cantos*.)
The common denominator of both Kwannon and Isis is compassion. Moreover, Isis, goddess of the moon and the underworld (among many attributes), represents a type of divinity common to almost all peoples of the ancient Mediterranean and Asiatic worlds. In this context she represents the natural cycle of death and rebirth, as does 'the great flight' (of migratory birds,

presumably, whose annual squadrons attest the persistence of the regenerative instinct).

Next Pound turns to one of the most ancient symbols of renewal and wisdom, then to fertility rites which echo Canto XLVII, and at last to a region of mythological serenity :

> the viper stirs in the dust,
>> the blue serpent
> glides from the rock pool
>> And they take lights now down to the water
> the lamps float from the rowers
>> the sea's claw drawing them outward.
> 'De fondo' said Juan Ramon,
>> like a mermaid, upward,
> but the light perpendicular, upward
> and to Castalia,
>> water jets from the rock
> and in the flat pool as Arethusa's
>> a hush in papyri.
> Grove hath its altar
>> under elms, in that temple, in silence
> a lone nymph by the pool.

It is again characteristic of Pound's world that serenity comes after (derives from) a period of intense creative activity. In fact many individual cantos, for instance Canto XLVII, follow this emotional curve. But, as Canto XC is the canto of rise and fall, the action begins again with even greater vigour :

> Wei and Han rushing together
> two rivers together
>> bright fish and flotsam
> torn bough in the flood
>> and the waters clear with the flowing
> Out of heaviness where no mind moves at all
>> 'birds for the mind' said Richardus,
> 'beasts as to body, for know-how'

One could preach a lengthy sermon on this text from Richard of St Victor (from whom most of the Latin quotations in this canto are taken); but as I must limit myself to the present context I note only that, though the bird moves more rapidly and freely through a different element, his flight depends on the same physical principles as does the movement of a beast. So it is with metamorphosis and natural growth in Pound's world: the sudden appearance of Dionysus' pards out of the aether may indeed be a revelation, but, for the mind accustomed to seeing individual lynxes, leopards, and roses as manifestations of divine forces, such metamorphoses belong to the same order of reality. And it is well to underscore what has already been said: that the soul is not love; that love is a flowing, the perception of which requires the eye; and that, of course, there is a visionary eye as well as a natural eye.

> The architect from the painter,
> > the stone under elm
> Taking form now,
> > the rilievi,
> > the curled stone at the marge
> Faunus, sirenes,
> > the stone taking form in the air
> > ac ferae,
> > > cervi,
> > > > the great cats approaching.
> Pardus, leopardi, Bagheera
> > drawn hither from woodland,
> woodland ἐπὶ χθονί
> > the trees rise
> > and there is a wide sward between them
> οι χθόνιοι myrrh and olibanum on the altar stone
> giving perfume,
> > > and where was nothing
> now is furry assemblage
> > > and in the boughs now are voices
> grey wing, black wing, black wing shot with crimson
> and the umbrella pines
> > > > as in Palatine,
> as in pineta, χελιδών, χελιδών

For the procession of Corpus
                come now banners
comes flute tone
            οἱ χθόνιοι
to new forest,
      thick smoke, purple, rising
bright flame now on the altar
              the crystal funnel of air
out of Erebus, the delivered,
              Tyro, Alcmene, free now, ascending
e i cavalieri,
              ascending,
no shades more,
              lights among them, enkindled,

It may be doubted whether, as a matter of historical fact, architectural form necessarily or even often follows the visual lead set by painting, though this may well be the case so far as Italian painting and architecture are concerned. In any event, it is an idea which helps one follow the development of this passage: the experience of metamorphosis (of the god's presence) leads to the institution of ceremony and places of worship, and these lead to the deliverance of vital spirits from the earth. The connection of this imagery with that of the fertility cults (especially the cult of Isis and the Eleusinian Mysteries) is sufficiently clear.

It is well to remember that 'Kuthera sempiterna' is behind all of this, for the shades are liberated through 'the crystal funnel of air', and crystal is the sphere of love where Cunizza was placed by Dante. One shade only, it seems, is not liberated by love:

      and the dark shade of courage,
            Ἠλέκτρα
      bowed still with the wrongs of Aegisthus.

Elektra remains behind, still trapped inside, incapable of forgiveness or regeneration. Then Pound closes Canto XC with a reassertion of the main principles on which it is based.

> Trees die & the dream remains
>> Not love but that love flows from it
>> ex animo
>> & cannot ergo delight in itself
>> but only in the love flowing from it.
>
> UBI AMOR IBI OCULUS EST.

There are other cantos, notably the second, in which meta-morphosis as such bulks larger; but there is no other canto, I think, in which metamorphosis is so clearly related to other, equally important components of Pound's world. For Pound metamorphosis is a revelation of the godhead, but it is not something that exists apart from the natural world; it is, rather, a more dramatic sign of the divinity which is immanent in the objects around him, whether they be works of art or works of nature. The creative force that reveals itself through meta-morphosis is the same force that drives the tree or the temple upwards. Or, in more human terms, we perceive that there is a permanent body of wisdom which survives in myth, in ritual, and in the craftsman's lore; and this wisdom survives to a large extent because it can assume new forms according to the demands of a new time and locality. But whatever form it takes, it embodies something of the divinity which may be discovered by a loving observation of the growing world.

WALTER BAUMANN

Secretary of Nature, J. Heydon

———————— ❧ ————————

S uppose the reader of the *Rock-Drill Cantos* has not become entirely impervious to the welter of proper names by the time he reaches page 33 and his curiosity can still be aroused as to the identity of one John Heydon, whom he finds there in juxtaposition with Mencius and a certain man called Jarge. If he wants to get to the end of the volume within a reasonable time he cannot afford too much of this kind of curiosity, but since the name recurs four times some forty pages later, in the course of Canto XCI, once with the rather striking and, one is inclined to think, ingenious designation, 'Secretary of Nature', he might not be able to resist the temptation any longer. In fact, it somehow seems that Pound is prodding the reader, especially if the line 'Formality. Heydon polluted. Apollonius unpolluted' (p. 76) happens to strike home. So he will turn to an encyclopaedia, but will find John Heydon in none of the big modern works, nor in the older ones, in any language, with the sole exception (just to prove the rule!) of *La Grande Encyclopédie* (Paris, 1886–1902), which would indicate that Heydon is ignored rather than 'polluted'. The scant fifteen lines in this French *Inventaire Raisonné des Sciences, des Lettres et des Arts* inform us that he was an English astrologer, born in London on 10 September 1629, so we turn to the *Dictionary of National Biography*, where, indeed, we find him and also possibly *the* cause of his latter-day pollution: A. E. Waite, who seems to have revived the campaign of vilification started by Heydon's contemporaries and promptly infected the contributor to the *D.N.B.*

Although most other writers on the occult sciences simply do not bother with him, there is at least one man apart from Pound who is willing to see more in Heydon, and this in spite of his close association with Waite : Lewis Spence. In his *Encyclopaedia of Occultism*[1] he attempts to defend him against Waite's accusation that he was 'no better than a charlatan', and comes to the conclusion that his plagiarism notwithstanding he 'must be credited with considerable assiduity' and that the mere titles of some of his pamphlets, now either lost or only advertised and never published, show 'how far Heydon waded into the sea of mysticism' and suggest 'that he was really more erudite therein than Mr. Waite imagines'. But the view of institutionalized learning, of the 'beaneries', as Pound would say, is certainly one of denigration. Thus the standard work dealing with the field at present, L. Thorndike's *History of Magic and Experimental Science*, groups Heydon with four other seventeenth-century astrologers who, 'although many of the intelligentsia scoffed at them as charlatans', above all enjoyed profitable business because their prognostications were listened to by both sides in the English Civil War, but singles out Heydon for a special word of disparagement, with the assistance of the German literary historian Daniel Georg Morhof (1639–1691), who called him a 'noted trifler'.[2] There is, however, one place where Heydon's literary labours are kindly spoken of; it is at the same time the only handbook that mentions him, and a work which Pound for one would consider the least likely. Harold V. Routh, in the chapter on 'The Advent of Modern Thought in Popular Literature . . .' in the *Cambridge History of English Literature* says :

'John Heydon sought to discover the secret of healing in the forces of nature, and has left a description of the Rosicrucian kingdom copied from the renascence Utopians and almost suggestive of *Erewhon*.' (vol. VII, p. 378).

[1] *A Compendium of Information on the Occult Sciences, Occult Personalities, Psychic Science, Magic, Demonology, Spiritism, Mysticism and Metaphysics,* New York 1960; originally published in London 1920.

[2] *A History of Magic and Experimental Science* (New York, 1958) VII, 331–2.

Although in consulting general works of reference and special studies concerned with the field in question we have progressed a good bit of the way towards an understanding of what Pound terms Heydon's pollution, it could nevertheless be argued that we have all but lost sight of the text of the *Cantos*. It is the great pioneer in the appreciation of Pound's poetry, Hugh Kenner, who states categorically that 'the words that can be looked up in a dictionary and the fields of reference that can be checked in the encyclopaedia are not the content of the poem. Verse that mentions cows, sheep, and grass need not be 'about' cows, sheep, and grass . . .'. If the rendering of 'a certain mode and degree of spiritual tranquility', as Kenner adds,[1] were indeed Pound's only aim, it would at least be partly possible to accept this, though the fact remains that an unknown foreign word is simply so much noise (perhaps a pleasant one) and that an unfamiliar name cannot convey much more. Of course, we could follow the policy suggested by Pound in connection with Gavin Douglas's Lallans: 'Don't be afraid to guess.'[2] Admittedly the context often invites this. Yet since Pound is more often than not fighting battles for his kind of 'Kulchur', and not just presenting moods, he clearly wants to be joined by the reader, who can certainly only fight, or refuse to fight, in Pound's army if he knows something about the weapons, the targets and the overall cause; and as Pound does not let him in on many of the details that could determine his allegiance, he has simply got to sneak into a library, and that distressingly often.

Clark Emery does not appear to have been very successful in his search for material on Heydon. At any rate, his comment that among other new images in Canto LXXXVII there is 'the rather ambiguous figure of John Heydon' is not in keeping with the aim of his book, i.e. to provide 'An ABC of Ezra Pound's Cantos'.[3] George Dekker, however, furnishes a very useful note on the 'Doctrine of Signatures', which apparently impressed

---

[1] *The Poetry of Ezra Pound* (Norfolk, Conn., 1951) p. 296.
[2] *ABC of Reading*, p. 117.
[3] *Ideas into Action: A Study of Pound's Cantos* (Coral Gables, Fla. 1958) pp. 154 and vii.

Pound above all in Heydon's handling of it, and links it with
the rest of Pound's arcanum,[1] and Donald Davie goes on from
where Dekker left off, offering further and so far the most
valuable illumination.[2] Kenner, whose essay 'Under the Larches
of Paradise' is a most inspired guide to the *Rock-Drill Cantos*,
gives this interpretation:

'The visible is a signature of the invisible, notarized by, for
instance, a seventeenth-century Neoplatonist, 'Secretary of
Nature, J. Heydon.'[3]

True, this is quite sufficient for the reader to get his general
bearings, but by immediately styling Heydon a 'Neoplatonist',
Kenner practically bullies the reader into believing that Heydon
was a genuine, recognized philosopher, whereas Heydon is not
mentioned as anything at all in any book on philosophy, and
this is of course why Pound is struggling to 'unpollute' him.
Moreover, as soon as we know that the coinage 'Secretary of
Nature' is listed in the *Oxford English Dictionary* as a term
quite current in the seveeteenth century, we may find that
Kenner's metaphorical language overreaches its aim in this one
instance.

Very commonly we encounter the people whom Pound
champions or abuses in the *Cantos* in his prose writings also.
And sure enough, Heydon appears there, too, very early in
fact, and in a work in which we would least expect to find, to
adopt the phrases of the vilifiers, a charlatan trifling with occult
lore. It is in the book on modernist sculpture, painting and
poetry, *Gaudier-Brzeska: A Memoir*. In section XVI, where
Pound talks enthusiastically about the new sense of form which
vorticist artists like Gaudier, Wyndham Lewis and Epstein
had awakened in him, we read this paragraph on the ultimate
effect of works of art:

'A clavicord or a statue or a poem, wrought out of ages of
knowledge, out of fine perception and skill, that some other man,

---

[1] *Sailing after Knowledge* London 1963, p. 83n.

[2] *Ezra Pound: Poet as Sculptor* New York 1964, pp. 213–32.

[3] Reprinted in Hugh Kenner, *Gnomon: Essays on Contemporary Literature*
(New York 1958) p. 285.

that a hundred other men, in moments of weariness can wake beautiful sound with little effort, that they can be carried out of the realm of annoyance into the calm realm of truth, into the world unchanging, the world of fine animal life, the world of pure form. And John Heydon, long before our present day theorists, had written of the joys of pure form . . . inorganic, geometrical form, in his "Holy Guide".'

And in the final note to the book :

'I refer the reader again to John Heydon's "Holy Guide" for numerous remarks on pure form and the delights thereof.'[1]

In 1915, when the Gaudier book first appeared, the reader, unless he dashed off to the British Museum, was hardly in a position to verify Pound's claim for Heydon, as the *Holy Guide*, which was 'Printed by T. M. for the Author. 1662.', was otherwise virtually unobtainable. Today even North American readers may consult it on microfilm.[2] When we look at the relevant passages in Book III, however, we are not particularly impressed, for we realize that when Heydon says, 'And it is observable, that if Nature shape any thing near this *Geometrical* accuracy, that we take notice of it with much content and pleasure' he is thinking in terms of well-known Greek aesthetics,

---

[1] 1939 reprint of first edition, pp. 157 and 167.

[2] 'English Books 1641–1700', Wing Reel 104, University Microfilms (Ann Arbor, Mich., 1961–64), H1670.

It appeared as six octavo volumes, most of them with lengthy dedications on unnumbered pages; the actual text amounts to just over 700 pages. The whole work is supplemented by 'An Index of the Particulars contained in the *Holy Guide*', which is really a table of contents mainly reproducing the argument printed at the head of most chapters and keyed to the numbered paragraphs. Many of the topics announced in these arguments are hardly touched on in the text; instead, Heydon is fond of referring the reader to his numerous other books. The grandeur of his design is particularly evident in the full titles, the first of which may serve as an example : 'The / Holy Guide, / Leading the way to / Vnite Art and Nature : / In which is maide plain / All things past, present, / and to come.'

A work of Heydon's on Wing Reel 103, H1666, entitled *The English Physitians Guide: or a Holy-Guide* . . . , 'Printed by T. M. for Samuel Ferris . . . 1662', has, in spite of an enormous amount of different preliminary matter, the same six books of text, but it also contains a portrait of John Heydon as frontispiece.

and that when he talks of the 'Pulchritude' of 'a rightly cut *Tetraedrum, Cube* or *Icosaedrum*' he is only saying that these 'gratifie the minds of men more, and pretend to more elegancy of shape, then those rude cuttings or chippings of Freestone that fall from the Masons hands'[1]–a statement which it is not difficult to agree with. Besides, was Pound really so hard pressed and unable to find any other more convincing and respected authority on the beauty of geometrical forms?

True, he did have recourse to a contemporary who had just begun to gain recognition as an authority on the subject: Wassily Kandinsky, whose *Über das Geistige in der Kunst* was already available in English translation at the time. That even the Vorticists respected this treatise may be inferred from the comments and selections which one of them, Edward Wadsworth, published in the first issue of *Blast*. But Pound preferred not to credit the reader of his *Gaudier-Brzeska* with a knowledge of Kandinsky's work, and instead told the history of 'In a Station of the Metro' (pp. 100–103), thus providing us with one of the most valuable insights into his creative mind, but forfeiting the propaganda value that Kandinsky might have had in a book that was intended to propagate the new painting and sculpture. Neither was Pound's excursion into mathematics, which was nothing new to the reader of *The Spirit of Romance*,[2] anything more than a striking analogy. Certainly, his turning Cartesian analytics into a kind of tracking system for 'the universal, existing in perfection, in freedom from space and time' (p. 106), performing what Pound had also claimed for the 'image', shows him as much interested in the 'pure and eternal qualities of the art of all men'[3] as Kandinsky. In fact, Pound might even have used Kandinsky to endorse his enthusiasm for Heydon, since the Russian-born painter also showed strong leanings towards occult sciences in those years. However, the real reason for mentioning Heydon was that Pound had at the time been fascinated by him in another connection, and this became

[1] Bk. III, Ch. VI, pp. 88–9.
[2] 1st ed., (London 1910) pp. 5 and 115–16.
[3] *Blast* I (20 June 1914), 119.

evident when, in August 1917, Canto III of 'Three Cantos' was
published in *Poetry*.

Whereas a good many elements of the abortive 'Three
Cantos' were used up in the definitive versions of the first few
Cantos, the beginning of Canto III was scrapped in its entirety,
which explains why the reader who has no access to the early
issues of *Poetry* considers Heydon a perfect stranger in the
Rock-Drill Cantos, unless he recalls the passage in *Gaudier-
Brzeska* and the parenthetical mention in *Guide to Kulchur*.[1]
It was Book VI of the *Holy Guide*, where Heydon relates how
he was given the 'Key and Signet' to the 'mysteries of the
Rosie Cross'[2] by the spirit Euterpe, that particularly inspired
Pound, but the cancelled passage is interesting for us mainly
because it indicates his attitude to Heydon in those years:

Another's a half-cracked fellow—John Heydon,
Worker of miracles, dealer in levitation,
In thoughts upon pure form, in alchemy,
Seer of pretty visions ('servant of God and secretary of nature');
Full of a plaintive charm, like Botticelli's,
With half-transparent forms, lacking the vigor of gods.
Thus Heydon, in a trance, at Bulverton,
Had such a sight:
Decked all in green, with sleeves of yellow silk
Slit to the elbow, slashed with various purples.
Her eyes were green as glass, her foot was leaf-like.
She was adorned with choicest emeralds,
And promised him the way of holy wisdom.
'Pretty green bank,' began the half-lost poem.
Take the old way, say I met John Heydon,
Sought out the place,
Lay on the bank, was 'plungèd deep in swevyn;'
And saw the company—Layamon, Chaucer—
Pass each in his appropriate robes;

[1] 'Whence I suppose what's-his-name and the English mystics with
reference to greek originals sometimes (John Heydon etc.).' (p. 225).
[2] Bk. VI, pp. 31–2.

Conversed with each, observed the varying fashion.
And then comes Heydon.

'I have seen John Heydon.'

Let us hear John Heydon.[1]

This is the kind of unblushingly naive writing that we find in a good many early poems, most of which Pound did not reprint in *Personae: Collected Shorter Poems*, presumably because they made him blush later on. As to the mingling with shades from all ages, this too is nothing unusual in the young Pound, as is most clearly seen in 'Histrion'.[2] At this stage, then, when Pound revelled in this sort of folly, he was not afraid of calling it just that. In fact we may gather from *Gaudier-Brzeska* that his whole fascination with things Platonic was initially akin to all this :

'. . . you had, ultimately, a "Platonic" academy messing up Christian and Pagan mysticism, allegory, occultism, demonology, Trismegistus, Psellus, Porphyry, into a most eloquent and exciting and exhilarating hotch-potch, which "did for" the mediaeval fear of the *dies irae* and for human abasement generally.' (p. 135)

---

[1] *Poetry*, X. 5 (Aug. 1917), 248. This sprawling 23-line passage is condensed to 10 lines in the reprint of 'Three Cantos' in *Quia Pauper Amavi* (London 1919) p. 28 :

> Another one, half-cracked : John Heydon,
> Worker of miracles, dealer in levitation,
> 'Servant of God and secretary of nature,'
> The half transparent forms, in trance at Bulverton :
> 'Decked all in green,' with sleeves of yellow silk
> Slit to the elbow, slashed with various purples,
> (Thus in his vision.) Her eyes were green as glass,
> Dangling a chain of emeralds, promised him—
> Her foot was leaf-like, and she promised him
> The way of holiest wisdom.

How actively Pound was engaged in recreating Heydon's vision can be seen in the imagery, which is not from Heydon (e.g. 'leaf-like') but is now familiar to the reader of the *Cantos*.

[2] See the discussion of 'Histrion' and its implications in M. B. Quinn, *The Metamorphic Tradition in Modern Poetry* (New Brunswick, N.J., 1955) pp. 22–25.

SECRETARY OF NATURE, J. HEYDON

As Heydon freely availed himself of this 'exhilarating hotch-potch' it was only natural for Pound to follow the passage on him with scraps from Neoplatonists. What is less natural is that these scraps were allowed to stay in the *Cantos*, while Heydon was dropped. Nevertheless, by the time Pound wrote *Guide to Kulchur* (1938), when he no longer referred to the 'Neo-Platonicks etc.' as 'hotch-potch' but, as may be seen from his Cavalcanti essay, had become more and more nostalgic for the lost 'radiant world'[1] they had been inhabiting, Heydon was still on the scene, and when he was working on the *Rock-Drill* section at St. Elizabeth's he asked Mrs Yeats to lend him the copy of the *Holy Guide* that her late husband had apparently had with him when the two poets had spent three war winters together at Coleman's Hatch in Sussex.[2] This time Heydon really came to stay in the *Cantos*, endowed with not only one function but five: 1. To endorse the Confucian-Mencian (scientific) concern and affection for the visible things in nature; 2. To join the constellation of the Neoplatonic 'Light' philosophers; 3. To provide further ingredients for Pound's own vision of Paradise; 4. To show him as one who has enjoyed the beatific vision; and 5. (most important, it seems) To rehabilitate him.

Evelyn Underhill speaks, in connection with the doctrine of Analogy, of 'the childish "doctrine of signatures" on which much of mediaeval science was built'.[3] Certainly, if by 'signature' is meant 'a destinctive mark ... on a plant or other natural object,' as an 'indication of its qualities, esp. for medical

[1] For a discussion of the nostalgia contained in this phrase from *Literary Essays* (p. 154) see Donald Davie, *Ezra Pound: Poet as Sculptor*, pp. 202, 219 and passim.

[2] 1913–14, 1914–15 and 1915–16. Pound's recollections of Stone Cottage in Canto LXXXIII are a good example of how he delighted in making fun of Yeats' fascination with the occult. In spite of this Pound himself obviously made much greater use of works like Heydon's than did Yeats.

[3] *Mysticism: A Study in the Nature and Development of Man's Spiritual Consciousness* New York 1912: 3rd ed., rev., p. 192. Cf. also her speaking of 'a previous and regrettable acquaintance with the "doctrine of signa-tures" ' in connection with George Fox and Boehme (p. 309).

purposes' (OED), for instance that a yellow flower is good for jaundice, it does seem rather childish, and when we read Heydon we are under the impression that for his Rosicrucian medicine he did use the word in this now ridiculous way. However—and this seems to have appealed to Pound most of all—Heydon says:

'Beasts have knowledge in the vertue of Plants as well as Men; for the Toad being overcharged with the poyson of the Spider, (as is well known) hath recourse to the Plantane-leaf. The Weasel, when she is to encounter the Serpent, arms her self with eating of Rue.

'. . . The Swallows make use of Celandine . . .' [Bk. III, Ch. viii, pp. 98–9] Only if we keep the swallows and the weasel[1] in mind does Pound's

> 'We have', said Mencius, 'but phenomena.'
> monumenta. In nature are signatures
> needing no verbal tradition
>
> [Canto LXXXVII]

make proper sense. The reference to Mencius[2] implies that we do not become familiar with these signatures unless we assiduously observe what we have around us and not only the 'monumenta' of history: first and last Pound urges us to 'Learn of the green world what can be thy place,'[3] because he believes that 'The plan is in nature / rooted.' Those whose main desire it is to escape from phenomena either dabble in 'mere epistemology' or do so, Pound hints at times, because of a 'bellyache' or because they are like 'Bhud: Man by negation'.[4] In a way, Pound's position resembles that of Goethe, who, likewise in the wake of Alchemists, held that it was the pheno-

---

[1] See *Rock-Drill*, Canto XCII, pp. 76 and 78:
  'so will the weasel eat rue,
  and the swallows nip celandine'.

[2] See James Legge, *The Life and Works of Mencius* (Philadelphia 1875) pp. 263–64 (Bk. IV, Pt. II, Ch. XXVI), with Legge's reference to science and Bacon.

[3] From the 'Pull down thy vanity' chant, Canto LXXXI, p. 99.

[4] All three from *Thrones*, Canto XCIX, pp. 61, 52, 54.

mena themselves that yielded the secret, if rightly approached, and it is a wonder that Pound never 'discovered' him.

That the right approach to tangible and visible nature depends on 'the quality of the affection'[1] Pound asserts and demonstrates most touchingly in the *Pisan Cantos*. In Pisa his familiarity with the reading of signatures as practised by men like Heydon provided him with metaphors for some of his strongest desires and hopes. The line ' "of sapphire, for this stone giveth sleep" ' and its echoes[2] are the clearest example, but his frequent naming of medicinal herbs, of 'menthe thyme and basilicum' and 'eucalyptus that is for memory'[3] is no less reminiscent of this tradition. From here we may pass on directly to Pound's observation of the pattern formed by the birds on the prison-camp wires and the clouds in the Pisan sky, two of the natural phenomena that inspired the most hopeful statement in the sequence, in Canto LXXXIV: 'out of all this beauty something must come' (p. 117).

When Heydon is placed on the roll of honour Pound gives him the epithet 'Secretary of Nature', which Heydon himself had printed on the title page of his *Holy Guide*. His detractors might of course say that this was rather presumptuous, as they would not regard him as 'one acquainted with the secrets of Nature' (*OED*), but this quaint old expression, at one time fondly applied to Aristotle, is one way of making Heydon unforgettable. That, in Pound's eyes, he deserves the company of Ocellus and thus implicitly of Pythagoras (Canto XCI) and Erigena (Canto LXXXVII) may be concluded from the fact that over half a dozen snippets from the *Holy Guide* easily fitted the crystal clarity[4] of Canto XCI:

> to ascend those high places
>   wrote Heydon
> stirring and changeable
>   'light fighting for speed' (p. 76)

[1] Canto LXXVI, p. 35 and Canto LXXVII, p. 44.
[2] Canto LXXIV, pp. 4 and 13 and Canto LXXVI, p. 37.
[3] Canto LXXIV, p. 13, etc.
[4] See Donald Davie's excellent discussion of 'crystal clear' in *Ezra Pound: Poet as Sculptor*, pp. 224–29.

The third of these especially must have met Pound's approval, hence probably the inverted commas, although they are all proper quotations from chapter II of Book I: '. . . but if God would give you leave and power', says Heydon, '*to ascend to those high places*, I meane to these heavenly thoughts and studies' (p. 26), and we may agree that Pound picked the contemplative gist of it, which, in isolation, may be said to evoke an elegiac note. The other two come from the passage where Heydon joyfully accepts the world as it is, with its mixture of good and bad:

'. . . were all alike, and one friend to another, all should be still and quiet, without succession, change and variety in the world, and so there should be no world; for God, when he cast his mind upon the building of the world, he went to make a beautiful and goodly work, meet for the Power, Wisdome and Pleasure of such a Builder, and therefore a *stirring and changeable* work, because there might be no cunning shown, no delight taken in one ever like or still thing; but *light fighting for speed*, is ever best in such a ground: let us away, and follow.' (p. 28)

One almost regrets that the naive charm of this account has all but evaporated in Pound's distillery, but we can be sure that Pound means the two phrases as a high compliment to a spiritual brother, for, although calm contemplation of the Divine Mind is one thing, his world, like Heydon's, does not rest there, but is one of dynamic processes, of growth and metamorphosis.

A little later in the chapter Heydon demands of the men engaged in studies like his that 'their riches ought to be imployed in their own service, that is, to win Wisdome and Vertue' and not just to attain honour and pleasure in society. Since the latter lie 'open (as all high things do) to the blast of Envy, so most commonly they will not be ruled' (pp. 31–2), i.e. if the desire for them gets out of hand, the sage may find himself in a vile controversy fired by jealousy. However the emphasis must not be on their exclusion, since, as Pound puts it in Canto LXXXVIII, 'Without honour men sink into servitude' (p. 40), but on keeping them under proper restraint. In adapting Heydon's reflection 'and if honour and pleasure will not be ruled',

Pound seems to have found a way to use Heydon even to back up Confucian lessons on civic virtues.

Pound's 'yet the mind come to that High City' is from the same chapter but, apparently to continue the contemplation begun with 'to ascend those high places', he changed the directional preposition, for Heydon says : '. . . let us know first, that the minde of man being come from that high City of Heaven, desireth of her self to live still that heavenly life . . .' (pp. 33–4). Pound's next three lines are quarried from Book II mainly in order, it would seem, to give examples of Heydon's erudition, and as Greek tags are always a recommendation to Pound the implicit praise is obvious.[1]

Heydon's 'that the whole Creation is concerned in this Number four . . .' (Book II, Chapter VI, p. 39), which is responsible for Pound's line 'and the whole creation concerned with "FOUR"', may remind the reader of Pound's own concern with visions like 'the baily of the four towers', the 'four coigns of the universe', etc.[2] The line 'And there be who say there is no road to felicity' (Canto XCI, p. 76), coming after the brief appearance of Leucothea out of the *Odyssey* ('my bikini is worth your raft') is from Heydon's chapter on beauty in Book III : 'And to say there is no such thing as *Pulchritude*, and some say, there is no *way to felicity*.' (p. 87) and suggests further personal agreement with Heydon.

If we think that Pound ever completely abandoned Heydon's vision of Euterpe on Bulverton Hill we are proved wrong by 'before my eyes into the aether of Nature', which comes from that point of the narrative in Book VI when 'her hour of Trans-

---

[1] Bk. II, Ch. I, p. 5; Ch. III, p. 11, 13. After quoting the Greek, Heydon gives Plato as the source and translates it as: 'Out of the Night, *both* day and skie *were born*.'

[2] Canto XL, p. 51 and Canto XCIX, p. 55 (*Thrones*). There are numerous other instances, e.g. '4 giants at the 4 corners' (Canto LXXIV, p. 7), i.e. the four 'guard roosts' (p. 6) of the D.T.C. in Pisa; 'Faasa! 4 times was the city remade, / now in the heart indestructible / 4 gates, the 4 towers' (Canto LXXVII, p. 43. Cf. also LXXIV, p. 20)—referring to the Wagadu legend—and 'But the four TUAN / are from nature / jên, i, li, chih' (Canto XCIX).

lation was come, and taking as I thought our last leave, she past before my eyes into the *Aether of Nature.*' (p. 34). In Canto LXXXVII, however, Heydon is to have, through Pound, another type of beatific vision :

> Oak leaf never plane leaf. John Heydon.
> Σελλοί sleep there on the ground.

The same sort of vision was also granted to another man :

> Hilary looked at an oak leaf
> or holly, or rowan.[1]

Scattered through *Rock-Drill*, and *Thrones* as well, we find similar moments at which the form of a leaf is perceived as a signature revealing the 'medicine' for that 'gt/ healing' of which Pound speaks near the beginning of Canto XCI, the awareness that the '*forma* the immortal *concetto*', time and again 'rises from death'[2] and that therefore 'the cosmos continues',[3] although man's vision of it is as short as a flash, jagged, and, one might even add, like the oak leaf.[4] The Selloi which attend Heydon's vision seem to suggest that while gazing at the pure form in the oak leaf he is, as it were, transported to Dodona, where they were the guardians of the oracles of Zeus, observed and listened to at one of the oldest and most famous oak-tree sanctuaries.[5] So Heydon, early spotted by Pound as a lover of pure form, of the rose that springs into order under the magnet's immaterial touch, has truly come into his own in Pound's Paradiso.

In placing men like Heydon, and Pound himself, in the Platonic tradition, we must once again point out that they belong to that branch of it which wants to 'save the phenomena' and is characterized by the 'search for the harmonious structure of the visible universe' and has nothing to do with the 'speculative

---

[1] Canto XCII, p. 82; cf. Canto XCV, p. 107 (*Rock-Drill*).
[2] *Guide to Kulchur*, p. 152. [3] Canto LXXXVII, p. 33.
[4] Cf. 'Le Paradis n'est pas artificiel / but is jagged' (Canto XCII, p. 80).
[5] See J. G. Frazer, *The Golden Bough* London 1925; abridged ed., p. 159.

symbolism of Plotinus,'[1] with that 'bellyache' and 'great perversion,' as Pound puts it in *Thrones* (p. 52). Thus it is important to stress that when Pound found the doctrine of signatures congenial to him he did not surrender to the symbolist tradition in literature, but merely acknowledged it as one aid to attaining 'the intellectual love of things', which is, as he says with Spinoza in *Guide to Kulchur*, 'the understanding of their perfections' (p. 73).

To back up the fine opening of Canto XCII :

> And from this Mount were blown
> > seed,

the first eleven lines contain one new snippet from Book III of the *Holy Guide* (Ch. VII, p. 92). Then comes the mention of two of the beasts that 'have knowledge in the vertue of Plants' from Chapter VIII, which has already been quoted :

> and that every plant hath its seed
> so will the weasel eat rue,
> and the swallows nip celandine

This is followed by what appears to be Pound's own handling of Heydonesque alchemy, leading up to his question about 'a sea-change'—which is presumably linked with 'That the tone change from elegy' in Canto XCI (p. 77)—and immediately afterwards to what may be taken to refer to Heydon :

> And honour?

Clearly the samples of Heydon's work which Pound supplies in the *Rock-Drill Cantos* are intended not least to prove that he was anything but a charlatan. Pound links him with Apollonius of Tyana because he too was to suffer denigration, but with the publication of F. C. Conybeare's translation of Philostratus' *Life* in the Loeb Classical Library, Pound maintains he has been thoroughly 'unpolluted'. In paralleling Heydon with Apollonius, Pound obviously wants someone to do for Heydon what Cony-

---

[1] See R. Klibansky, *The Continuity of the Platonic Tradition during the Middle Ages* (London, 1939) pp. 26 and 27.

beare did for Apollonius. Although there is little doubt that Heydon, like, say, the Latin translation of the *Odyssey* by Divus, is a chance pick, and although only men as deeply steeped in occult literature as Lewis Spence could tell us whether it was an unusually good one, a perusal of the *Holy Guide* cannot fail to show us that here was a man convinced that this life was the best life and, if only we would learn this, we should be healed and on the 'road to felicity'. This of course makes him a true Poundian hero. So why should someone not edit and thus 'unpollute' him? Even if his writing frequently deteriorates into mere recipe copying and his imagination is rather unbridled, his rhapsodic sweep, especially in the chapters on Numbers (Book II), is remarkable, and we might place him in the company of those who are thus spoken of in Canto LXXXVI:

> 'Sono tutti eretici, Santo Padre,
> ma non sono cattivi' (p. 23).

JOHN ESPEY

The Inheritance of
Τὸ Καλόν

A concern for Beauty occupies the centre of Pound's writing, and though many influences on his poetry and his aesthetic stem directly from the nineteenth century we should recall his enduring admiration of the Neoplatonists and note that his first definition of Beauty reached back to Plotinus by way of Coleridge when he wrote in 'In Durance' (1907):

> 'DAEMON,'
> 'Quasi KALOUN.' S.T. says Beauty is most that, a
> 'calling to the soul.'

His source in Coleridge reads:
'The Beautiful arises from the perceived harmony of an object, whether sight or sound, with the inborn and constitutional rules of the judgement and imagination: and it is always intuitive. As light to the eye, even such is beauty to the mind, which cannot but have complacency in whatever is perceived as pre-configured to its living faculties. Hence the Greeks called a beautiful object καλόν quasi καλοῦν, i.e. *calling on* the soul, which receives instantly, and welcomes it as something connatural.'[1]

The passage from Plotinus on which this is based follows and John Shawcross in his notes to the edition used by Pound (1907) remarks dryly (and not quite accurately) that 'Coleridge's etymology is ingenious, but without foundation.'

[1] S. T. Coleridge, *Biographia Literaria, with the Aesthetical Essays*, ed. J. Shawcross, (Oxford 1907).

319

Pound returned to the passage a few years later in his essay on Dante in *The Spirit of Romance* (1910), saying that 'Dante anticipates Coleridge's most magical definition of beauty— καλόν quasi καλοῦν. . . .' Thus Pound, early attracted by Plotinus, Porphyry, Iamblichus, and Ficino, worked from a concept of Beauty—or τὸ καλόν to use his own favourite term— as an actively evocative principle; and this first vision informs all his later responses and is the basis of his reaction to the Pre-Raphaelites (with specific reference to Rossetti) and to the Nineties (with specific reference to Dowson and Lionel Johnson), indicating the line that he followed and one that requires at least some clarification of how he came into contact with nineteenth-century aestheticism and of what it meant to him.

The immediate traces left by Rossetti on Pound's early work—the most interesting of which is the use of the line *Manus animam pinxit* from Rossetti's prose tale *Hand and Soul* in the poem 'De Ægypto'—are reasonably well known. Not so well known is the presence of what Pound has called Lionel Johnson's 'old-fashioned line of precision' in the action of verses such as

> Fair face gone from sight
> . . .
> Fair lips hushed in death
> Now their glad breath
> Breathes not upon our air
> Music, that saith
> Love only, and things fair

upon *Mauberley's*

> Young blood and high blood,
> fair cheeks, and fine bodies
> . . .
> Charm, smiling at the good mouth,
> Quick eyes gone under earth's lid.

Pound has noted that he first heard of Johnson from Cornelius

Weygandt in a course at the University of Pennsylvania, and has also mentioned his first guide to nineteenth-century aestheticism. This hint has, I believe, remained unexplored. 'One was guided by Mr Mosher of Bangor,' he writes, '. . . One was drunk with "Celticism," and with Dowson's "Cynara", and with one or two poems of Symons' "Wanderers" and "I am the torch, she saith" :

> I am the flame of beauty
> And I burn that all may see
> Beauty.

It is worth pausing at these references to Arthur Symons. The first illuminates Pound's early delight in vagabondage in its opening lines :

> Wandering, ever wandering,
> Their eyelids freshened with the wind of the sea
> Blown up the cliffs at sunset, their cheeks cooled
> With meditative shadows of hushed leaves
> That have been drowsing in the woods all day,
> And certain fires of sunrise in their eyes.

And the poem closes on a theme frequently echoed in Pound's early verse, the contrast between the safe and the free :

> Wanderers, you have the sunrise and the stars :
> And we, beneath our comfortable roofs,
> Lamplight, and daily fire upon the hearth,
> And four walls of a prison, and sure food.
> But God has given you freedom, wanderers!

Taken together with 'Wanderer's Song', its first stanza,

> I have had enough of women, and enough of love,
> But the land waits, and the sea waits, and day and night
> > is enough;
> Give me a long white road, and the grey wide path of
> > the sea,
> And the wind's will and the bird's will, and the heartache
> > still in me.

suggesting both the opening and the close of Pound's 'Cino':

> Bah! I have sung women in three cities,
> But it is all the same;
> And I will sing of the sun.
>
> .   .   .
>
> I will sing of the white birds
> In the blue waters of heaven,
> The clouds that are spray to its sea.

these lines give some indication of Symons' importance to the young Pound. And the poem from which he quotes may serve as a statement of the early, purely aesthetic concept of Beauty that was probably not much different from Pound's at that date.

MODERN BEAUTY

I am the torch, she saith, and what to me
If the moth die of me? I am the flame
Of Beauty, and I burn that all may see
Beauty, and I have neither joy nor shame,
But live with that clear life of perfect fire
Which is to men the death of their desire.

I am Yseult and Helen, I have seen
Troy burn, and the most loving knight lie dead.
The world has been my mirror, time has been
My breath upon the glass; and men have said,
Age after age, in rapture and despair,
Love's poor few words, before mine image there.

I live, and am immortal; in mine eyes
The sorrow of the world, and on my lips
The joy of life, mingle to make me wise;
Yet now the day is darkened with eclipse;
Who is there lives for beauty? Still am I
The torch, but where's the moth that still dares die?

But probably the most significant reference is to Thomas

Bird Mosher (of Portland, Maine, surely, rather than Bangor), for when one turns to the volumes of *The Bibelot*, which he edited and published between 1895 and 1915, one finds an already selected source book for Pound, though it is one that must be used with caution. In anticipation, it may be noted that the three poems by Symons mentioned above all appear in a selection from his verse in Volume IX (1903), with 'Modern Beauty' serving as an epigraph, printed in italics, followed by Verlaine's 'Fountain Court', dedicated to Symons, and the body of the selections headed by 'Wanderer's Song' and closed by 'The Wanderers.'

Mosher was the obvious publisher for the young Pound to approach with his first collection of poems, and though the Maine publishing pirate returned the manuscript Pound did not forget him. He sent Mosher a copy of *A Lume Spento* from Venice in 1908, and about six years later offered him the eight poems that make up *Cathay*, which were also returned. In a letter dated 3 December 1914 Pound wrote, 'You have had the honour of refusing some of my best work, also you kept me from printing my first book too soon. Your editions brought me various fine things which I should not otherwise have come upon so soon.'[1]

What is most useful here is a glance at the earlier volumes of *The Bibelot*, where one finds not only the emphasis on Celticism and the Pre-Raphaelites and the swish and slither of the Nineties, but a number of other things as well. One finds in the first volume, for instance, not only Rossetti's *Hand and Soul* but also Swinburne's translations of Villon's ballades, a group of medieval Latin songs in translation, selections from Sappho by various hands, and a group of Campion's lyrics, including 'When thou must home to shades of underground' with a note calling attention to Propertius; in the second volume, translations of Poliziano and Lorenzo de' Medici, as well as one of Pugliese

[1] This letter is contained in the collection of Mosher papers at the Houghton Library, Harvard University, and is used with the permission of the Librarian. The letter also contains some interesting comments by Pound on individual poems in *Cathay*. The Mosher copy of *A Lume Spento* is now in the Department of Special Collections at the UCLA Library. Unfortunately the accompanying letter has disappeared.

by Rossetti; in the third, translations of Bion and Theocritus, and Mackail's *Odysseus in Phaeacia*, a verse rendering of the *Odyssey*, Book VI; in the fourth, not only Rossetti's *Saint Agnes of Intercession*, but also Swinburne's memorial verses on Gautier and Baudelaire, a group of twenty-odd lyrics from Verlaine, and Edward Cracroft Lefroy's adaptations of Theocritus; in the fifth, not only Pater's *Aesthetic Poetry* and *Rossetti* but also a group of lyrics from Beddoes, and further translations of Villon; in the sixth, not only *A Little Garland of Celtic Verse* (including seven poems by Yeats and three by Lionel Johnson) and Arthur Symons' study of Dowson, but also Poliziano's *Orfeo* in John Addington Symonds' translation; in the seventh, not only a group of Swinburne's own poems but also Arthur Symons on Gerard de Nerval; in the eighth, not only F. W. H. Myers' *Rossetti and the Religion of Beauty* but also the full Latin text and four translations of the *Pervigilium Veneris*; in the ninth, not only the second *Little Garland of Celtic Verse* but also Symonds' *Popular Songs of Tuscany*, selections from the Greek Anthology, and Symons on Mallarmé; in the tenth, a substantial collection of Lionel Johnson's poems; in the eleventh, Wilfrid Scawen Blunt's *Esther* and Dowson's *Poems in Verse and Prose*; in the twelfth, not only more Swinburne but also Symonds' *Mediæval Norman Songs*; and in the thirteenth, twenty pages of Landor's poetry, opening with the first poem of *To Ianthe*, 'Past ruin'd Ilion Helen lives.'

This brings one to 1907 and includes only the most apparent of Pound's foci, but for anyone familiar with his enduring enthusiasms it is a suggestive list. This is not to claim that Pound read *The Bibelot* regularly or that a student of markedly independent mind who studies under William Shepard at Hamilton College and Cornelius Weygandt, Felix Schelling, and Hugo Rennert at the University of Pennsylvania would let himself be led by Mosher alone. (At the same time one should recall that Mosher was the American editor of the Pre-Raphaelite Brotherhood's short-lived periodical *The Germ*, of Rossetti and Swinburne, and publisher of *The Rubaiyat*.) But it is to suggest that, together with what one thinks of as the frequently rarefied and precious enthusiams of the Pre-Raphaelites and the Nineties and 'Celticism', Pound was absorbing additional material that helped form the standards by which he was to judge the period. 'The nineties have chiefly given out', he was to write in 1915, 'because of their muzziness, because of a softness derived, I think, not from books but from impressionist painting. They riot with half decayed fruit.'

At the same time, I suspect we tend to overlook that though the Pre-Raphaelites often seemed to forget that they were their own contemporaries, they did emphasize concrete imagery and a certain kind of pictorial exactness, and Rossetti translated a substantial body of work from the early Italians, including Cino da Pistoia and Cavalcanti, and Englished the *Vita Nuova*, for all of which Pound has saluted him. Thus Rossetti became guide not simply to Pre-Raphaelitism itself but to the sources of the movement, sources that Pound was to use in his own way. And although Lionel Johnson's precision might in 1915 be called 'old fashioned' by Pound and 'very different from the sort of precision now sought,' his poems could lead Pound to make certain distinctions, simultaneously reinforced by his reading of the nineteenth-century French poets. 'Johnson's poems were almost the last to catch one's attention. Their appeal is not so much to the fluffy, unsorted imagination of adolescence as to more hardened passion and intellect of early middle-age. . . . They hold their own now, not perhaps as a whole, but because of certain passages, because of that effect of neatness and hardness.' Pound summed up much of his feeling and where it led him when he wrote that 'no one has written purer Imagisme than he has, in the line

> Clear lie the fields, and fade into blue air.

It has a beauty like the Chinese.'

This conjunction of influences indicates the additional meanings τὸ καλόν began to gather to itself for Pound, just as the Greek had eventually ranged from the physically beautiful sense in Sappho to the sense of 'moral virtue'.

Already in its early use by Pound, as in the couplet (1916)

Tò Kalón

> Even in my dreams you have denied yourself to me
> And sent me only your handmaids

it carries, presumably, a creatively active implication. But Pound had begun enlarging its implications even before this. 'Love of precision' is his first additional association, occurring in *Patria Mia*, a discussion of American values and life, which he wrote in 1912. And as he felt more and more strongly the limitations of purely aesthetic studies he began to examine the products of art he admired—admired for their individuality, their precision, their exactness of definition, their cleanness of line, their freshness of vision, their 'hardness', with all these meanings now entering into *tò kalón*—as the results of specific forces. And though these products were in one sense contemporary, as Lionel Johnson had written—'And in beauty, in power of music and of phrase, the great poets are all contemporaries: an eternal beauty is upon the greatest works of art, as though they were from everlasting.' ('Note on Poetry', *Bibelot*, vol. x, 1904, p. 382.)—they were also products of history, which itself became in this sense contemporary precisely through these enduring monuments.

As so often in his development, Pound prefigured in miniature his larger themes; so it may be useful to look briefly at a poem in which art and aspects of society are discussed, a poem provoked by a specifically American occasion. In 1916 the city of Newark, New Jersey, celebrated the 250th anniversary of its founding and offered a group of prizes for poems honouring the occasion. Pound's entry is not included in *Personae*, though it can be read now in Charles Norman's biography as well as in the original collection published by the committee.

In 'To a City Sending Him Advertisements' Pound offers his first poem of any length in the rhetoric developing from his concentration on Propertius—the use of the phrasal rhythm as metrical unit, the balance of phrase against phrase, and repeated echoes of the 'imperial' Roman vocabulary that he was assimilating for his ironic handling of the Propertian text to produce a denunciation of empire. After questioning the city's intentions, Pound touches on the position of the artist in America, and then throws down his challenge :

> If each Italian city is herself,
>   Each with a form, light, character,
> To love and hate one, and be loved and hated,
>   never a blank, a wall, a nullity;
> Can you, Newark, be thus,
>   setting a fashion
> But little known in our land ?

This is followed by two stanzas on the dedicated life of the artist and then Pound, in a stanza that anticipates much of his *Homage to Sextus Propertius*, concludes with an expression of his doubts :

> If your professors, mayors, judges . . . ?
>   Readers, we think not . . .
> Some more loud-mouthed fellow,
>   slamming a bigger drum,
> Some fellow rhyming and roaring,
>   Some more obsequious back,
>   Will receive their purple,
>   be the town's bard,
> Be ten days hailed as immortal,
>   But you will die or live
>   By the silvery heel of Apollo.

In an essay entitled 'The Sunny Side of the Newark Poetry Competition' the editor of the published collection made some remarks (now also available in Donald Gallup's *Bibliography*) that provide a certain entertainment :

'That philosophic iconoclast, Ezra Pound, earlier exponent of the Imagist School of Poetic Palpitation, writing from London, assaulted our civic sensibilities in a poem of violence directed at the head, heart, and hands of Newark. Of his poem, one of the judges remarked that it is 'Captious, arrogant, hyper-critical, but of some merit.' Another judge cast it into the discard. But it won a prize and fits snugly into the rationale of the present volume. Also there is food for thought in our London poet's catechistic cadences. Let us not begrudge him the high appraisal of our poetry judges.'

As more than one person has pointed out by now, Pound was not a bad prophet, even though he won a limited honour in his own land; for though his poem received one of the lesser prizes, the first prize went to a set of verses by Clement Wood that opens

> I am Newark, forger of men,
> Forger of men, forger of men—

This is not important. What is important for our present purposes is that though Pound was bringing into relation *tò kalón*, precision, and a vision of society, the poet's role remains for him a somewhat detached and largely aesthetic one. Yet a partial condemnation of this view is implied by the subject itself and his handling of it, so it is not surprising that the two pivotal works of the period immediately following bring him closer and closer to a position of engagement. In *Homage to Sextus Propertius* the poet refuses to celebrate the conquests of empire, turning his back on public events to claim immortality for his memorializing of individual intensity and precision and private passion.

But in the succeeding modulation of the principal theme of *Propertius* that Pound makes in *Hugh Selwyn Mauberley* (1920) he deals with a consciousness distant from passion, and begins to consider the limits of a purely aesthetic definition of *tò kalón*; for in this society beauty is at the mercy of war and commercialism:

> We see *tò kalón*
> Decreed in the market place.

Searching, then, for an additional gloss to *tò kalón*, for a synthesis of the qualities he had come to associate with Beauty and the forces that made Beauty possible, he finally hit upon the single word 'order.' One must keep Pound's gloss in mind—

and indeed he insists upon it within the text—as one reads *The Cantos*, for it is '*tò kalón*/order' that is their impulse and their end. '*Tò kalón*/order' is the force that makes action possible and it is the end of that action. Odysseus is impelled by it and to it; it is the force that drives him, that in Leucothea's scarf preserves him, that he ultimately seeks. Its visible monuments include the church of St. Hilaire at Poitiers, Sigismundo's Tempio, the frescoes of the Schifanoia, the London Adelphi; its music is the music of the troubadours, of Janequin, of the notation to the Confucian *Book of Odes*; its passion is the light-filled love of Richard of St. Victor; its law is the justice of Coke; its mind is the balanced judgment of Mencius and Apollonius of Tyana and Khaty and John Adams and Thomas Jefferson.

By the time *The Cantos* were well under way, Pound used his equation directly in relation to the state when he wrote in *Jefferson and/or Mussolini* (written in 1933 and first published in 1935):

'Towards which I assert again my own firm belief that the Duce will stand not with despots and the lovers of power but with the lovers of

ORDER
tò kalón'

If the aesthetic of the latter part of the nineteenth century sometimes seems to us to suffer from an over-emphasis on art for art's sake, it is here that Pound's formula seems most vulnerable and to suffer from order for order's sake. For though '*tò kalón*/order' can be an evocation, a calling-forth of the individual, a recognition of the order of the created world, it can also, and in the state particularly, be something imposed from without and thus become a distortion of itself.

In the *Pisan Cantos*—first in Canto LXXIV and again in Canto LXXX—Pound repeats a remark made by Aubrey Beardsley to William Butler Yeats:

'beauty is difficult' sd/ Mr. Beardsley
    and sd/ Mr Kettlewell looking up from a
pseudo-Beardsley of his freshman composition
    . . .

Les hommes ont je ne sais quelle peur étrange,
            said Monsieur Whoosis, de la beauté

La beauté, 'Beauty is difficult, Yeats' said Aubrey
                                        Beardsley
    when Yeats asked why he drew horrors
    or at least not Burne-Jones
    and Beardsley knew he was dying and had to
    make his hit quickly

hence no more B–J in his product.

    So very difficult, Yeats, beauty so difficult.

    'I am the torch' wrote Arthur 'she saith'
                        [Canto LXXX]

The direct statement, with all its Nineties association and its
return to Symons' 'Modern Beauty' comes late in *The Cantos*,
but the 'difficulty' of beauty—'*tò kalón*/order'—is their most
profound theme, and the search for a solution of that difficulty
underlies all of Pound's political, economic, and historical
reading. His vision of it has blurred at times and he has recognized it where others can see only an ugly parody; but '*tò
kalón*/order' has remained central in the mind of a poet who more
than once has caught the glitter and felt the silvery heel of
Apollo on his shoulder.

HUGH KENNER

Blood for the Ghosts

I

That personae are donned as masks we learn from the etymology of the word and from much of Pound's early practice : thus we find him pretending, in Browning's way, to be the itinerant Cino—

> Bah! I have sung women in three cities . . .

or the inflamed Bertrans—

> Damn it all! all this our South stinks peace. . . .

That personae may also possess the way spirits do is a truth somewhat obscured by Pound's characteristic stress on expertise. A work of art, he keeps telling us, is someone's act of attention, detailed intimate attention, attention flowing down into the cunning articulation of sound with sound. The wordsmith's procedures—and it is from Pound that we have learned to talk of 'procedures',—suggest a donning of roles at all times equally deliberate, and we hear with condescension the 22-year-old Pound's avowal that the roles at times donned him :

> No man hath dared to write this thing as yet,
> And yet I know, how that the souls of all men great
> At times pass through us,
> And we are melted into them, and are not
> Save reflexions of their souls.
> Thus am I Dante for a space and am
> One François Villon, ballad-lord and thief . . .

... And as the clear space is not if a form's
Imposed thereon,
So cease we from all being for the time,
And these, the Masters of the Soul, live on.

This is 'Histrion', which went into books published in 1908,
1909 and 1910. The next time he turned aside from new work
to make a retrospective collection (*Umbra*, 1920) he dropped
it, being sure by then that it was badly written. Yet in 1908,
when his metric and rhetoric could be as sure as in 'Na Audiart'
or 'Praise of Ysolt', he had meant what 'Histrion' says, meant
it sufficiently to think it worth writing, though badly, and
though he never wrote out again what it says, he continued to
mean it. If we are properly prepared, if we have performed the
propitiatory rituals, the great dead may possess us.

Thus in Canto I shades speak to Odysseus, strong with the
blood he has brought them; Elpenor speaks, and Anticlea is
kept from speaking, and Tiresias speaks; and then the voice
that has been chanting the canto addresses a speaking shade
we'd not suspected : 'Lie quiet Divus.'

... I mean, that is Andreas Divus
In officina Wecheli, 1538, out of Homer.

For blood has been brought to Divus, twentieth-century blood,
and Divus has all this time been speaking, though not in his
Latin but in an English prepared for him : speaking through the
preparer of that English as Homer in 1538 had spoken through
him :

And these, the Masters of the Soul, live on.

Had no such English been prepared to receive his impress,
Divus (shade of a shade) could not have found his new voice.
The English had been prepared some years before, under the
auspices of the anonymous Anglo-Saxon Seafarer-poet. For it
was

wuniað þa wacran   ond þas woruld healdaþ,
brucað þurh bisgo.   Blæd is gehnæged,
eorþan indryhto   ealdað ond searað

that taught Pound in 1912 how to write

> Waneth the watch, but the world holdeth.
> Tomb hideth trouble. The blade is layed low.
> Earthly glory ageth and seareth.

and so made possible, in 1915 or '17, the idiom of which Divus' ghost avails itself:

> Bore sheep aboard her, and our bodies also
> Heavy with weeping, and winds from sternward
> Bore us out onward with bellying canvas,
> Circe's this craft, the trim-coifed goddess.

A familiar enough point, and by 1966 a commentators' staple; but the transaction wants a closer look. For if we examine again the lines from the ninth-century Seafarer-poet, we find that scarcely a word has passed through his 1912 disciple's mind without sea-change.

> —wuniað þa wacran   ond þas woruld healdað
> —Waneth the watch, but the world holdeth.

Close enough to the sound; but 'healdath' is plural and 'woruld' accusative; 'wacran' isn't 'watch' but 'weaker' [sc. folk]; 'wuniath' isn't 'wane' but (cf. German *wohnen*) 'dwell':

> 'A weaker sort survive and possess the earth.'

Similarly Pound's splendid phrase, 'The blade is layed low,' derives from a phrase ('Blæd is gehnæged') which sounds as if it ought to treat of blades, but according to the lexicon means 'glory is humbled'. For whatever trouble he did or did not take with the lexicon, the 1912 author of 'The Seafarer' was chiefly interested in the ninth-century sounds.

He was interested, that is, beyond philology, in how a bard breathed: in the gestures of tongue and expulsions of breath that mimed, about A.D. 850, the emotions of exile. 'I believe in an ultimate and absolute rhythm', Pound had written in 1910.[1] 'Rhythm is perhaps the most primal of all things known to us. . . . the rhythm of any poetic line corresponds to emotion. It is the poet's business that this correspondence be exact.' As to lexicography, 'The perception of the intellect is given in the word, that of the emotions in the cadence' from which it follows that the sense of the words will be important when the perceptions of the intellect are, as in a sonnet of Cavalcanti's; but less important in a poem like 'The Seafarer'.

And if emotions are psychic, *psyche* means 'breath'; and metre is breath measured. By rhythm and gesture, by rhythmic gesture: so, says Aristotle at the beginning of his *Poetics*, do the flute-player and the dancer imitate emotion. Bring both the dance and the flute within the body, and we have the bard, in the grip of his emotion, extemporizing. It is clear from the reduplications of his sense that developing the sense is the least of the Seafarer-bard's concerns; the meanings of the words fit in somehow, vessels into which to discharge his longing, as the structure of sound is built up, prolonged, modulated. And 'The Seafarer' being the kind of poem it is, Pound has made a similar English poem, so far as possible breathing as it breathed, intoning as it intoned, letting plausible words fall throughout the incomparable performance.

> May I for my own self song's truth reckon,
> Journey's jargon, how I in harsh days
> Hardship endured oft. . . .

He is interested neither in Anglo-Saxon lexicography, nor in the rules for its versification (which he commences to flout in the second line); but in how the bard's throat shapes air: his cadence (cadenza), his breath, literally his *psyche*. (*Psyche te menos te*, says Homer, equating the two: his breath and strength, all that it is to be alive). And Pound likes to quote what Yeats said of a poem, 'I made it out of a mouthful of air', a physical reality for the Irish poet who paced the downstairs room at Stone Cottage, intoning—

[1] Introduction (dated 15 November 1910) to *Sonnets and Ballate of Guido Cavalcanti*, reprinted in *Translations*, pp. 23–24.

that had made a great Peeeeeacock
　　　in the proide of his oiye
　　　had made a great peeeeeeeacock in the . . .
made a great peacock
　　　in the proide of his oyyee

　　　proide ov his oy-ee

—and likewise for the American poet upstairs who 31 years later recreated the process in Pisa, but for folk who *look* at poems (and write in their margins) only a bewildering fancy. Yet Homer (it is the thrust of our chief present knowledge of him) composed aloud, only aloud, building the *Iliad* out of mouthfuls of air, the Muse singing as his chest contracted, his breath governing the line, his heart beating against the stresses.

Psyche te menos te: and it was by learning to rehearse the Psyche's gestures of the Seafarer-bard that Pound prepared an English for Divus to speak through him when he was finally possessed by Divus, who had been possessed by Homer, who in his time had been possessed by Odysseus and prompted by a Muse. The *nekuia* that is now Canto I was perhaps 'easy to write' in a remarkable period when Pound wrote so much else; perhaps Divus/Homer took possession, once Pound had made ready the cadences and idioms, and filled his mind with the sharp-cut vowels and the shock of the alliterations; but 'to make oneself ready to do it . . .', as Brancusi said of a piece any maker of nine-pins might have thought himself capable of carving—'se mettre en état de le faire . . .'. The real labour preceded.

　　To break the pentameter, that was the first heave,

we are told in Canto LXXXI; for

　　. . . as Jo Bard says : they never speak to each other,
　　　if it is baker and concierge visibly
　　　　　it is La Rochefoucauld and de Maintenon audibly.

As courtly diction encysts French conversation, so the iambic pentameter imposed on speech an arbitrary measure, alien not only to the fall of stresses in speech but to the cadences in which Homer, at the beginning of all things, had enacted the bardic way of being alive in the presence of heroic imaginings. Pound's early cadences were Greek, as an early reviewer half-noticed :

'Sometimes there is a strange beating of anapaests when he quickens to his subject; again and again he unexpectedly ends a line with the second half of a resonant hexameter :

> Flesh shrouded, bearing the secret.

. . . and a few lines later comes an example of his favourite use of spondee, followed by dactyl and spondee, which comes in strangely, and as we first read it, with the appearance of discord, but afterwards seems to gain a curious and distinctive vigour :

> Eyes, dreams, lips and the night goes.'[1]

So 1909; and five decades later the terminal spondee is still Pound's personal signature :

> And was her daughter líke thát :
> Black as Demeter's gown,
> > eýes, háir ?
> Dis' bride, Queen over Phlegethon,
> > girls faint as mist abóut hér ?

The terminal spondee, he learned, governed a line receptive to many distinctive voices : Homer's :

> Thus with stretched sail, we went over sea till dáy's énd.

Ovid's :

> Black snout of a pórpóise
> > where Lycabs hád béen;

Sappho's :

> Fades light from séa-crést;

Kung's :

> If a man have not order withín hím
> He can not spread order abóut hím . . .

And as for the voice of Dante, which an ear trained on Wordsworth will force into an iambic norm, we have Pound's 1934
warning that Dante's line is 'composed of various different
syllable-groups, totalling roughly eleven syllables', and not to
be confused with ' "English pentameter", meaning a swat at
syllables 2, 4, 6, 8, 10 in each line, mitigated by "irregularities"
and "inverted feet".' Twenty-two years earlier he had noted[1]
that whereas some minds assimilate

> Nel mezzo del cammin di nostra vita

to

> If you fall off the step you'll break your ankle,

others hear a sonoric system comparable to that of

> Eyes, dreams, lips, and the night goes.
>   —Nel
> mezzo del
>   cammin di
>   nostra
>   vita.

Such were the preoccupations that guided years of technical
labour, labour aimed at working cadences and rhythms into
the blood : mastering the cadences of the dead, their breathing
(*psyche*); miming the beat their pulses shaped, the lips and
throat moving as theirs moved, that the whole man might be
open to their possession. So the tennis-player labours at his
strokes, practicing against the day when he may be supremely
matched; or the pianist works so that when Bach's spirit is

---

[1] In a *New Age* article, one of the 'Limbs of Osiris' series, never reprinted.
The 1934 quotation is from the review of Binyon's *Dante* (*Literary Essays*,
p. 204). See also the remarks on Cavalcanti's hendecasyllabics (*Literary
Essays*, p. 169). Pound there assigns his own discovery of the basis of Dante's
measure to his semester in Indiana (i.e. 1907).

understood at last his fingers will not prove unworthy. And in 1945, in Pisa, deprived of books and thrown upon the luck of encounters and visitations, Pound undergoes and registers in the *Cantos* encounters of three sorts, of which two are rationally predictable. We should expect him to encounter things objective and demonstrable, birds on wires, Pistol-packing Jones, la pastorella dei suini who reminded him of Circe; we should expect memory and imagination to conjure up beings purely visionary—

Dirce et Ixotta e che fu chiamata Primavera

(who 'suddenly stand in my room here'); we could hardly have expected the invading voices. For there are moments when he suddenly becomes someone other.

II

For instance, Walt Whitman. Whitman in 1905 was still 'a man of no fortune, and with a name to come' at the University of Pennsylvania, 'four miles from Camden' where he had died thirteen years earlier. This fact is remembered in Canto LXXXII, along with the indignation of Professor Riethmueller ('Fvy! in Tdaenmarck efen dh'beasantz gnow him'); the act of remembering it is the propitiatory ritual; and suddenly the poem commences to speak as it were from Whitman's consciousness.

'O troubled reflection
    'O Throat, O throbbing heart'
How drawn, O GEA TERRA,
    what draws as thou drawest
        till one sink into thee by an arm's width
    embracing thee. . . .

Where I lie let the thyme rise
                and basilicum
        let the herbs rise in April abundant . . .

Gea Terra is not part of Whitman's pantheon, but the opening words are his, abridged (with his consent, as it were) from two lines he had put into 'Out of the Cradle Endlessly Rocking'

BLOOD FOR THE GHOSTS

(O troubled reflection in the sea!
O throat! O throbbing heart!)

This poem of Whitman's recalls a bird singing night after
night 'in the moonlight on Paumanok's gray beach', calling for
his lost mate; and the young Whitman (who 'treasur'd every
note') stealing down to the shore to listen, and discovering in
the process his poet's vocation; and the ultimate word given
young Whitman by the whispering sea, which word is 'death'.
And now singing through Pound as the bird had sung through
him, the gray shade undertakes a reprise, the thyme and basilicum standing for Leaves of Grass, Whitman supplying motifs
and Pound the language. The longed-for mate in Whitman's
elegy becomes the earth-bride, *connubium terrae*. The sea-wind
blowing along Paumanok's shore ('I wait and I wait till you
blow my mate to me') gives the Canto

> wind : *'emòn tòn ăndra,*

the words of Theocritus' woman with the charm-wheel calling
her man back to her house. For dead poets can be of mutual
service, the voice of one bereaved singer supplying in courtesy
words for another ('Taking all hints to use them, but swiftly
leaping beyond them', says Whitman himself, giving the
sanction). Then Whitman's sea, with its 'low and delicious'
message,

> . . . death, death, death, death,

—this sea ('rustling at my feet, / Creeping thence steadily
up to my ears and laving me softly all over') finds austere
articulation as

> fluid *Chthonos*, strong as the undertow
> of the wave receding,

touched by which, Pound says,

> the loneliness of death came upon me
> (at 3 P.M., for an instant);

and as the voices fade Whitman's bird, tripled, presides over
the terminal cadence:

>   three solemn half notes
>   their white downy chests black-rimmed
>   on the middle wire
>   periplum

This extraordinary homage, a structural X-ray of Whitman's
intricate poem, in articulating itself has stirred into life many
voices: we can identify Theocritus, Nicolas Este, Aeschylus,
Kipling, and the Chinese sage who said that two emperors'
wills were as the two halves of the tally. Whitman himself,
in the very passage here resung as by his more learnèd ghost,
states the principle, recalling how he had cried to the bird,

> Now in a moment I know what I am for, I awake,
> And already a thousand singers, a thousand songs,
>   clearer, louder and more sorrowful than yours,
> A thousand warbling echoes have started to life
>   within me, never to die.

This is the doctrine of 'Histrion,' enunciated (Pound would say)
by a poet who had never the technical resources to articulate
distinctly, one from the other, those thousand singers, and is
now amplified, brought in touch with Theocritus and Aeschylus.

The resources, in the canto before us, are Pound's; so are
those of Canto I. Yet behind Canto I are the voices of Divus
and Homer; so behind the last page of Canto LXXXII is the
voice, the spirit, of Whitman: spirit: anima: psyche.

> We have one sap and one root,

Pound had written 32 years before, making compact with
Whitman.

> Let there be commerce between us.

In Pisa the offer of commerce was fulfilled.

III

In the canto before this one something still more eerie
is transacted: a drama of courtship with the eponymous

English decasyllabic itself, since Chaucer the language's most pervasive measure. This time 'the masters of the soul' are innumerable; like

> Miss Tomczyk, the medium
> baffling the society for metaphysical research

Pound rises to some of his most eloquent lines possessed by a host of voices. These ghosts commence to throng toward the end of Canto LXXX, passing 'by the dozen / who would not have shown weight on a scale'. Already, by that time, we have heard the voice of Browning ('Oh to be in England . . .') and the anonymous throat that shaped the drinker's refrain, 'Let backe and side go bare', and immediately afterward emotions directed by thoughts of Mary Stuart and the Wars of the Roses ventriloquize for eight Provençal words through the throat of Bertran de Born ('Si tuit li dolh elh plor elh marrimen') before being shaped for twelve lines more by the shade of Edward FitzGerald :

> Tudor indeed is gone and every rose,
> Blood-red, blanch-white that in the sunset glows
> Cries : 'Blood, Blood, Blood!' against the gothic stone
> Of England, as the Howard or Boleyn knows . . .

('Iram indeed is gone with all his rose', FitzGerald had written eight decades before, 'And Jamshyd's Sev'n-ring'd Cup, where no one knows'; as he did with the Seafarer-bard, Pound follows his model's intonation and breathing).

These stirrings, as toward the climax of a séance, suggest some major possession to come; and we shall soon have reason to observe that Bertran and FitzGerald have introduced into the poem two related measures not customary to it, the decasyllabic and the pentametric respectively. Within a page comes the reminder that 'the first heave' was 'to break the pentameter', which Pound saw as an unintelligent thickening (based on five stresses) of the Italian hendecasyllable (based on eleven syllables). He had worked hard to break it when he made, about 1910, his first versions of Cavalcanti :

. . . I síng how I lost a tréasure by desíre
And léft all vírtue and am lów descénded.

[Ballata I][1]

—not pentameters, but lines of 11 syllables, the first with
three stresses, the second with four. This had been a highly
imperfect renovation; eighteen years later he pronounced that
it had been 'obfuscated by the Victorian language', and offered
a more free-running sample :

Who is she that comes, makying turn every man's eye
And makying the air to tremble with a bright clearnesse
That leadeth with her Love, in such nearness
No man may proffer of speech more than a sigh ?

[Sonnet VII]

—lines of 12, 13, 10 and 11 syllables, respectively, cadenced
not metered.

Of verse that will pass as 'iambic pentameter' there is much
in Pound's published volumes, though very little in the *Cantos*.
One notes that he has always treated it as an archaic form,
through which Italian or Provençal voices may speak, and that
he has always demanded that it be heard not as iambic pentameter but as cadenced decasyllabic. One last specimen, 'Canzon :
The Yearly Slain', a poem of 1910 from *Provença:*

Ah! red-leafed time hath driven out the rose
And crimson dew is fallen on the leaf
Ere ever yet the cold white wheat be sown
That hideth all earth's green and sere and red;
The Moon-flower's fallen and the branch is bare,
Holding no honey for the starry bees;
The Maiden turns to her dark lord's demesne.

Austere end-stopped lines, each broken after the fourth (or in two
cases the fifth) syllable, so that we feel a uniformity of cadence—

Ah! red-leafed time /
And crimson dew /
Ere ever yet /

[1] *The Translations of Ezra Pound* (London 1953), p. 99.

—rather than of stress-count; a grid to exhibit the clear vowel sounds and the largely monosyllabic vocabulary, as remote as may be from the Tennysonian *rubato*.

Though one doesn't associate this measure with Pound, he expended much work on it, work the benefits of which stayed in suspension until 1945. His dealings with the decasyllable had been virtually terminated about 1911, when he left the *Canzoni* behind him; it was always, for him, an Italian rather than an English form; in 1929 the essay 'Guido's Relations' summarized his view of its anomalous English life. And there the matter rested until Pisa.

But in Pisa Bertran and FitzGerald nudged into the *Cantos* the old metrical motif, FitzGerald's example serving to remind us of a long, specifically English tradition. And three pages later the English tradition suddenly reasserts itself by way of the Cavalier song-writers, as a cadence ends with

> at my grates no Althea.

For Lovelace, writing 'To Althea, from Prison' has entered the flow of another prison-poet's reminiscence; Pound is recalling

> When Love with unconfined wings
> Hovers within my Gates;
> And my divine *Althea* brings
> To whisper at the Grates . . .

It is the seventeenth century, and time has flowed out like a great wave, to leave him possessed by the eponymous spirit (spiritus : psyche : air) that articulated itself to clear-cut lute-sound and viol-sound :

> Has he tempered the viol's wood
> To enforce both the grave and the acute ?
> Has he curved us the bowl of the lute ?

These are plucked strings; the clear consonants zone the sharply junctured vowels. It is writing to set against the Envoi to *Mauberley*, when he had imitated the boom of a grand piano :

Go, dumb-born book . . .

'Dumb-born': sounds to be prolonged *ad libitum*: not at all like

> To enforce   both the grave   and the acute.

Throughout these lyric strophes he is undergoing, it seems, in the 'aureate sky', some interrogation as to his worthiness, his craft; following which (is it some inaugural rite once more?), supported by Lawes and Jenkins, Waller and Dowland, he suddenly finds himself speaking words of Chaucer's:

> Your eyen two wol sleye me sodenly
> I may the beauté of hem nat susteyne

lines addressed by Chaucer to 'Merciles Beauté', and by Pound through him to the eternal Aphrodite, known always in the *Cantos* by the emblem of her eyes. And these pure English (Middle English) decasyllabics are followed by the contemporary speaking voice:

> And for 180 years almost nothing.

Then decasyllabic reasserts itself, in the tongue of Dante whom Chaucer read and paraphrased:

> Ed ascoltando al leggier mormorio[1]

'And listening to the light murmur'—of many voices, none yet dominant—

> there came new subtlety of eyes into my tent
> whether of spirit or hypostasis

—one line spoken, one line measured, and the measured line the decasyllabic once more, its third occurrence, modern English this time, though dealing in Tuscan precisions of terminology, as though finding its way into Pound's cosmos from trecento Italy. Then three more irregular lines; then, surprisingly, the anonymous genius of English metric asserts itself:

[1] Not Dante's words, but his tongue; it is, Pound has said, "Not a quotation, merely the author using handy language."

Sáw but the eýes and stánce betwéen the eýes

—a full-blooded iambic pentameter, not simply ten syllables but five unmistakeable stresses. It is the more remarkable because Pound is apparently musing *in propria persona*; such rare decasyllables as the *Cantos* have previously accommodated occurred in set-pieces like the version of Sigismundo's 'Lyra' ('Ye spirits who of olde were in this land'—Canto VIII).

He continues to muse, in short irregular lines; another iambic pentameter arises as from the deeps—

casting but shade beyond the other lights

—to be countered by three lines of Imagisme, school of 1912:

> sky's clear
> night's sea
> green of the mountain pool

And these three lines total ten syllables. The English mainstream measure is slipping past the well-tried defences of the years when the pentameter was 'broken'. But not slipping past unaltered; for the decasyllabic line to which these Imagiste lines add up is by no stretch of mensuration pentametric, nor even iambic:

skÿ's cléar, / níght's séa, / gréen of the móuntàin póol

This is a line composed, as the third Imagiste canon had it, 'in the sequence of the musical phrase, not in the sequence of a metronome.' And it is followed, this ghost line, by a line clearly printed as decasyllabic, not iambic pentameter at all but a ten-syllable line with stresses heavily grouped, closing in the paired (indeed here tripled) stress that is Ezra Pound's key-signature:

shone from the unmasked eyes in hálf-másk's spáce.

A process has traversed in half a page the history of English versification from Chaucer to 1945, decasyllabic becoming pentameter, pentameter encountering Imagiste resistance and metamorphosing into a more idiosyncratically stressed line, this time with Pound's hallmark on it.

And now the attainment of this honourable truce opens the poem to many anonymous masters. We have been watching enacted in this passage the work of preparing a language, as by working with 'The Seafarer' a language was once prepared for Homer and Divus. That work had been done before the poem was begun; this work is recapitulated in the course of the poem itself. So far the preparations; now for the ghosts; no assignable ghost this time, Whitman or Guido Cavalcanti or Divus, but simply the English tradition of weighty moral utterance, a grave didacticism that finally returns to paraphrased Chaucer as to its tonic. It announces its presence with the sonorous lines on Love, a Poundian decasyllable moving unresisted, line after line after line :

> What thou lov'st well shall not be reft from thee
> What thou lov'st well is thy true heritage
> Whose world, or mine or theirs
>   or is it of none ?

Then Vanity and the Ant enter out of Ecclesiastes, lending to this mounting utterance the implied authority of the translators commissioned by King James :

> The ant's a centaur in his dragon world.
> Pull down thy vanity, it is not man
> Made courage, or made order, or made grace,

—though Greece with its centaur and China with its dragon are joined to the Biblical ant in triple authority. Again and again the Poundian double stress terminates a line

> . . . nót mán
> . . . máde gráce
> . . . púll dówn
> . . . thý pláce

Yet undeflected by mannerism the decasyllabics march on, generally end-stopped, varied by resources—anaphora, internal rhyme, witty diction ('scaled invention', said of a beetle) that so delight the mind as virtually to conceal the didactic reiteration.

Chaucer paraphrased ('Master thyself, then others shall thee beare') terminates the passage as Chaucer quoted had opened it; decasyllabics break into halves

> A swollen magpie in a fitful sun
> Half black half white
> Nor knowst'ou wing from tail

and four trisyllabled rhymes—

> Fostered in falsity,
>   Pull down thy vanity,
> Rathe to destroy, niggard in charity,
> Pull down thy vanity,
>   I say pull down.

—terminate the cadence.

So considerable, however, is the decasyllabic momentum that it asserts itself twice more in the nine-line coda to this remarkable canto, and recurs to open the canto that follows :

> When with his hunting dog I see a cloud

Does another canto, of the 114 that we have, open with a line in that measure? It seems to be exerting on Pound the hypnotic pull it has so often exerted on the English tradition. But the real world intervenes :

> 'Guten Morgen, Mein Herr' yells the black boy
>   from the jo-cart

—a voice from the camp, innocent of iambs; and the camp roll-call recommences :

> (Jeffers, Lovell and Harley
>   also Mr Walls who has lent me a razor
>   Persha, Nadasky and Harbell)

The ghosts are scattered. For speech, unless the speakers are reciting Shakespeare, will not sustain the measure into which

English craft has recast so much speech; and Pound's mind, his metrical adventure behind him, returns to thoughts of Swinburne, who had laboured to introduce Greek meters into Tennyson's England.

It has been a strange adventure. Is there another passage in literature that can number among the protagonists in its drama the metre itself? Swinburne hauled out of the sea by French fishermen, reciting them Greek ('might have been Aeschylus') provides a faint parallel; the Greek language itself, falling on astonished unlearned ears, was a component in *that* drama, though not the Greek metres. Pound dwells for a few lines on the vivid incident. What did they drag from the sea? They dragged as it were Arion; or varying the figure, as it were Odysseus: a queer fish, from a world where the sphere of adventure is the imagination, and where mastery achieved by labour may open the mind to possession by minds past. So Odysseus took sheep with him in the black ship, that he might provide blood for the ghosts. The soldiers who interfered with Pound's liberty made an equally strange catch to wall up in their compound under the arc lights, and the ditch they dug around his cage 'lest the damp gnaw through my bones' recalls the fosse in which sheep's blood flowed in Hades. Their barbed wire did not wholly a prison make: not enough to exclude the Masters of the Soul.

Rhythm and Person in *The Cantos*

I

A metre, and even a predominant rhythm, emerges in a poem as the expectation of the reader gets conditioned line by line. After a second line of iambic pentameter, we expect the third line to be iambic pentameter also; when it is, we expect the following lines to be. If extra syllables are permitted early in the poem, we are less surprised when they crop up in the last lines.

Usually the metrical base of the rhythm is fairly simple: we have recognized iambic pentameter, and can rest. In *The Cantos*, however, multiple expectations are turned loose, sometimes simultaneously, in sections that themselves diversify into prose, free verse, and metre. Free-verse sections predominate and, in their simple linear movements through the varied 'instances'[1] of the sound, are deployed eclectic reminiscenses of metred 'designs': blank verse lines, French syllabic lines, hendecasyllables, Greek dipodic units, common English measures like iamb and trochee, and less common ones that perhaps also recall the Greek. The reminiscences multiply, design submerges design, each turning the other into instance: as one *persona* submerges another in the adaptive singularity of the speaking poet's own voice. This, to begin with, overcomes the English heroic line, as John Berryman points out (*Partisan Review*, April, 1949), quoting these lines from Canto LXXXII:

[1] This is Ramon Jakobson's term for the speech-segment of natural language in a poem, as opposed to the artificial design of a metre.

1 Swínbùrne my ónly mìss

2 and I dídn't knòw he'd beên to sèe Lándòr

3   *ánd* thèy tóld me thís thàt an' tôther

4 and whèn óld Máthèws wént hè sáw the thrêe téacùps

5   twó for Wàtts-Dúnton who líked to lét his téa coòl.

6 So òld Élkin hàd ónly óne glòry

7   He díd cârry Álgernòn's súit càse *once*

8 when hè, Élkin, fírst càme to Lóndon.

9   But gíven whàt I knòw nów Ì'd hàve

10   gót thròugh it sómehòw . . . Dírce's shàde

11   or a bláckjàck.

'Consider the two opening dactyls here', Berryman says, 'and then the spondee-two-dactyls-and-trochee of the beautiful sixth line.' And the metres he hears are some of the many designs present in the submerging instances of this deliberative voice. Yet the metric foot, like all features of design, must be recognized by a norm the lines gradually establish, and what can the norm be here? The second, third, and fourth lines can be heard also as variations on an iambic (not a dactyllic) norm. The second line can also be taken as a hendecasyllabic (especially in a poem that imitates Dante and quotes Italian), or else as a blank verse line with a feminine ending. The third line, with its ten syllables, can be heard as syllabic verse; or, again, as accentual iambic pentameter. The fourth line can be taken, among other possibilities, for exhibiting the design of alexandrine, complete with an exact count of twelve syllables and a medial caesura. Against these norms one would hear the first line as instance-variations on a design of iambic trimeter, not as dactylic. And one could hear the sixth line not only in Berryman's dactylic design, but also as an instance of semi-dactylic variation on the design of blank verse, with a kind of choliambic ('limping iamb') substitution of trochee for iamb at the end in '*glory*' (with an echo of satirizing *glory*, the classical function of choliambics).

Or, again, one can hear lines two, three, and four getting sucked into the dactyllic-spondaic orbit. And not only that;

accordingly, Hugh Kenner states one possibility in the form of a denial: 'this isn't one of the Greek meters salted with an abnormal proportion of long syllables'—but yes, it is that too.

Or, again, one can take the measure dipodically, as recalling Greek lyric strophes. The first line is a regular cyclic dactyl, the sixth a pair of cyclic dactyls, the logaœdic metre of Pindar. The phrase after the dots in lines ten and eleven is a perfect resolving glyconic, used, as in classical poetry, for its normal function of resolving a series of cyclic dactyls or pherecratics. If any one metre predominates, in fact, it is that varied staple of classical strophe, the cyclic dactyl ($/-/--/$). And the pivotal line five may be taken for a varied series of three of them. Classical metres allow, with the strength of a dipodic or larger base, for far greater variation of instance against design. Taking such allowances, one could scan the whole passage here by using only classical dipodies: glyconics and pherecratics, cyclic dactyls and reizianums, etc.

These three mutual possibilities of design-scansion—Greek dipodies, or else iambs, or else trochees and dactyls ('falling rhythm,' with the stress first)—are not superimposed on each other as sprung rhythm may be said to superimpose one metre upon another. They are not superimposed because they are only possibilities: no one emerges as a main design. Design is only suggested, precisely as it is only suggested in the overall coherent-diffuse organization of the poem. Instance here resolves into an interchangeable series of three (or more) designs—and there are more regular metrical passages elsewhere in the *Cantos* for further interchange, as well as occasionally the less regular passages of quoted letter or prose document. Along with, say, three possibilities over a whole passage, momentary possibilities also crop up (alexandrine in line 4; choliambic in the terminal trochee-after-a-downbeat of lines two, three, four, and six). The effect is of great modulation (multiple design) and of great freedom (masterly instance), an effect comparable to that of prose poetry, where the instances are so diverse we attend to each one: instance becomes design. Or the poem slows down, as Kenner goes on to say: 'its nature is to isolate *each* of the words so that we have not primarily "lines" diversified with a pattern of stresses but a succession of unshake-able terms.' Lines, however, are exactly what we do have: the movement of the line is the one unambiguous feature of design in this poem, as in most free verse: this stable feature permits all the other permutations of design and instance to take place. The 'terms' seem to be suspended in an equilibrium of two or three gravities, two or three possible designs, all at once, and the rhythmic movement of the poem can be 'slow' without losing any of its improvisatory freedom, at no point resembling the even slowness of a ritual procession. Syntax itself, to borrow Donald Davie's phrase, becomes music, because an underlying polyphony of dual and triple key sig-natures returns us to the syntax, to the cadences—as prose poetry does, but without the starkness of prose poetry.

Many musics still mingle in the unstopped ear of this Odys-seus, and the words ride in their equilibrium along the doubled melodic lines, 'unshakeable terms', in Kenner's phrase. Instance is not counterpointed against design, but design against design, so that instances multiply their effect through reciprocally-slowing designs. Because the voice is fluid, we move on: because it is retarded, we dwell on word and phrase, as Pound himself does in Canto XXIX :

> That leads out to San Piero. Eyes brown topaz,
> Brookwater over brown sand,
> The white hounds on the slope,
> Glide of water, lights and the prore,
> Silver beaks out of night,
> Stone, bough over bough,
>   lamps fluid in water,
> Pine by the black trunk of its shadow
> And on hill black trunks of the shadow
> The trees melted in air.

Since the design-reminiscences move adaptively, the presence of an extra slack syllable may tip the design-possibilities not in one but in two or three directions. The definite article, then, functions not only as a delicate semantic alternative, but as a magnified rhythmic alternative. Bare nouns and monosyllabic adjectives produce stress syncopations: *Eyes brown topaz,* *Brookwater over brown sand.* The third line sharpens the focus by adding the slack of 'the' before each of its two nouns, and producing, among other possibilities, the momentary illusion of strong dipodic single design (-//- -/). The slight variation between the predominant bare stress nouns and the nouns with the definite article, between singular nouns (*sand, slope*) and plural (*eyes, hounds*), comes to a head in the pair of nine-syllable lines that recapitulate 'with or without article' and 'singular-or-plural' in a single instance: *the black trunk/black trunks.* One of these—necessarily—has three syllables, the other two: but the shorter one is the plural. Moreover, this difference is offset by a positional identity: adjective and noun come both times at the fourth and fifth syllables, and each line has nine syllables. So the first *trunk* rises out of the wood—three syllables against nine—slightly more, in its cadence, than the second *trunks* does. Audible alternation becomes, and serves, a visual alternation, the precise image of the first line, and the precise shift to the second. Another step and the sight is gone from the eyes:

The trees melted in air.

If the two previous lines have an identical number of syllables, this line in turn is identical with the line before them not only syllabically but accentually too—except for one item, the definite article on which so many changes have been rung:

lamps fluid in water
The trees melted in air

The article picks up, so to speak, the overhanging slack in *water* and puts it at the beginning of the line. Syntax resolves as music resolves, and this sequence turns out, as we enter the next canto, to have been preparing for a music momentarily more formal in its design:

Compleynt, compleynt I hearde upon a day,

which moves through its own variations to changes rung on a prose quotation from a chronicle :

> And in August that year died Pope Alessandro Borgia
> Il Papa morí

A natural voice turns out to be echoing—or momentarily not, as it chooses—a multitude of formal musics; so in the *Cantos* a conversational self-portrait conceals its instances of latent content in manifestations of selves and attitudes. Pound's rhythm, like his organization, is not eclectic but syncretic, and the growing together of its constituents is made to seem to be heard in its very process of transformation.

II

The rhythmic virtuosity is not displayed for its own sake. It could only have been invented, in fact, to perform the poetic task of providing a musical ground for the shifts and convergencies in the *personae*-persons, the masks and faces, of the poem. The person of the *Cantos* is both multiple and moving; the motion of the face and its masks, instead of governing the shifts from short poem to short poem, has become the organizing principle of a very long one.

Within the *Cantos*, the fact that Pound declares the sections to be sections of the same poem allows him to enlist for that poem the flux of the self. *A Draft of XXX Cantos* is permitted to retain its title and remain a draft, while at the same time being incorporated into the larger work that transmutes it. If Pound reads Chinese history, impelled to do so by the intention of writing cantos, then a long stretch of the *Cantos* is filled with bits from the particular Chinese history he reads, out of which certain image-event nubs are concatenated, selected but scarcely 'digested'. The exiled American returns to the letters of John Adams and Jefferson : the next cantos comprise mosaics of quotations from their letters. Pound is imprisoned at Pisa : and the person of the poet strips off his masks for reminiscences triggered by actual visual associations, the mountains and peasants he can see from his tent mingling with bits he hears or remembers; the shape of the *Pisan Cantos*, ruminative, sorrowing and recapitulative, has become adaptively what the shape of time has dictated.

To see the *Cantos* as conversational improvisations (Blackmur, Tate) on the one hand, or on the other hand as some newer 'rose-in-the-steel-dust' version of a classical repetition with variation (Kenner), is to ignore the interaction of the speaking self with what the self has thought over. The poet of the *Cantos* represents a person too moving in his multiplicities to allow either for random fragmentation or for any sort of structured organization. When Kenner asserts that the *Rock-Drill Cantos* repeat, canto for canto, the themes of the first 'Draft' cantos, he has only taken a particular facet of the generality in the *Cantos* so as to slant toward some special order the more complex seeming-order that the poem creates. Kenner's particular correspondences happen to hold. So do others, and still others, among other parts of the *Cantos*—correspondences with those same parts, and with others. The ideograms are only there, in space, the space of a page that sets them in some kind of relation; and in time, the time of the sequentially read, rhythmed poem that is constantly adaptive so as to salvage itself (*From the wreckage of Europe, ego scriptor*) from the all-destroying time of history (*Time is the evil. Evil . . .*).

Already in *Personae*, as the title indicates, Pound has sent his own voice (*per-sona*) through the lives of poets actual (Provençal, Chinese, Anglo-Saxon, Latin) or invented (Hugh Selwyn Mauberley). His own person lies behind the *persona*. The process of using another real life entails, of course, a selection from that life of matter appropriable for masking the living poet. Sensitive to the dialectic of this process in *Personae*, Pound calls attention to it by restricting some poems to mere 'translation'. Others he builds along the lines of asking the strategic question about the process he is employing : how can one understand the flux of another life by looking back at details of it from a stable if adjustable point of view. A search for the real Bertran de Born organizes 'Near Perigord', and the process of the search occasions the one coherent thread of comment through the poem. The search for the past breaks the confected persona into fragments, 'a broken mirror of memory', in Kenner's phrase: the means towards composing the persona becomes also the instrument of discomposing it. In constructing 'Near Perigord', Pound has deliberately put the fragments about Bertran together in such a way that they will never cohere. The woman with whom the poem ends abruptly has been introduced under Dante's epigraph about the schismatic Bertran, 'And they were two in one and one in two' (*Ed eran due in uno, ed uno in due, Inf. XXVIII, 125*):

> She who could never speak save to one person,
> And all the rest of her a shifting change,
> A broken bundle of mirrors. . . . !

Here, and in the 'translation' poems, the language of the poet is modified by adopting into itself fragments not from the language of life but from other books, fragments that are kept from being assimilated or disguised beyond recognition in order that their second-handedness may function in the poem. When he uses other books this way, Pound is only making over for his own use a relation traditional since the Renaissance between the book and a person's self-knowledge. We use books to know the self, and introspection for us characteristically entails the roundabout process of going to something not within the self but outside the self, a book—in contrast to the mediaeval practices of spiritual discipline, which, however, themselves got codified in their later stages into such books as Ignatius' *Spiritual Exercises*. Montaigne's announced purpose was to know, in his own spirit, the human *esprit ondoyant et divers*. To accomplish that purpose he went on no pilgrimage and entered no monastery, but instead shut himself up in a third-floor tower, a tower lined with books. Over the tower he set a quotation not from the Word of God but from a Stoic philosopher He gradually came to know himself by the indirect means of a mosaic of quotations, and the history of the three editions of the *Essais* is largely a history of fleshing out the meandering prose by a diversity of quotations. The trials of the self, the *essais*, are made through books, and more books—fragments of books, as in Pound.

In the 'translation' poems of *Personae*, such as *Homage to Sextus Propertius*, Pound keeps entirely to the book; the antithesis between book and life when the book is about life is made to reflect the antithesis between self and other when the other is an admired poet. The term *homage* implies the distance between the face of the speaker and the severe mask he has adopted. The distance is also preserved by the fact that the translated quotations from Propertius are arranged into a pattern of Pound's own and are also slanted in the direction of satire (Kenner's point) and of literary precept—of directions, as it were, for doing what Pound is doing when he follows the directions. The homage resides in taking Propertius as a *persona*, the *persona* resides in performing translation as an homage. Not all Pound's translations are included in *Personae*. Those that are included thereby gain this added dimension: they are called *personae*.

This dimension expands in the *Cantos*. The Odysseus of Canto I is not merely a Propertius-like *persona* for the poet whose personal voice breaks out with the new theme and juxtaposed double-*persona* of Canto II: *Hang it all Robert Browning / There can be but the one Sordello*. Canto I itself breaks away from translation before the end, which *Homage* does not do. The recurrent and emerging characters, Odysseus and Sordello, Malatesta and Adams, Confucius and the Chinese emperors, the god Dionysus and Dante himself, stand to the verbal acts of the multiplied Pound-self as the multiple quotations stand to the invented words of the poem. *Personae*-fragments appear in blocks, like the ideograms with which they sometimes merge. In *Cantos* Pound has managed to bring together two techniques to which he devoted prolonged study, the technique of the *persona*, and the 'imagistic' technique of the ideogram.

The ideogram has been correctly regarded as the structural principle basic to the *Cantos*, and to understand its function there as a mirror for the person of the speaker a close examination of its linguistic technique is required. What meets the eye of the poet need not be a book; it may be something seen (as a quotation can itself be levelled to the status of an image, something seen, or of an ideogram, a stylized presentation of something seen. The Chinese quotations—as quotations, images and ideograms—resume all three.).

In his imaginative beginnings Pound applies himself to endowing the visual image with a precision that is so elusive as to suggest some vagueness quite contrary to precision. In his famous image about the Metro, Pound acts almost as though he were a Rimbaud 'fixing vertigoes':

> The apparition of these faces in the crowd:
> Petals on a wet, black bough.

Or consider the function of the image in the following, far more elusive poem:

L'ART, 1910
> Green arsenic smeared on an egg-white cloth,
> Crushed strawberries! Come, let us feast our eyes.

The visual precision here seems to be imitating a still-life painting, and the title seems to refer to something that could include a kind of painting. The relation between poem and title appears to be that between signifier and signified: arsenic-cloth-strawberries points to 'L'Art, 1910'; pretends to be, indeed, a sort of ideogram for it. But when we inspect this seeming precision, it disappears into the vagueness of generality. We are left with a pure impression, as though Pound had reversed for a poem his dictum about the prose artist:

'It is the almost constant labor of the prose artist to say "Send me the kind of Rembrandt I like" in terms of "Send me four pounds of ten-penny nails".'

He goes on to call the Rembrandt statement an 'utter cryptogram'. 'L'Art, 1910' sets up its own cryptogram, pretending precision (the ten-penny nails kind of statement, at which 'Imagisme' aimed) in terms of generality (the Rembrandt statement).

In this little poem the visual side of the image is clear to the eyes that are invited to feast on it (*egg* and *strawberry* suggest food, as *arsenic* suggests an ingestible poison). The signification of the image, however, gets obscured in the generality of the title: 'L'Art, 1910' could stand for a moment in history, or else a surrealist medley of all the arts taken together at a given moment of time. No mediation is possible between the visual clearness and the semantic obscurity: the meaning for which the text of the poem is an ideogram is utterly important in the poem and utterly inaccessible.

A comparable obscurity of signification, residing in a clarity of visual perception, is generated by the single images in the *Cantos*, from Ecbatana to the gloom where the gold gathers the light against it. The single ideograms there, present to the eyes, seem to be mediated by the speaking person; it is *him*, in turn, they seem to be revealing by their mediation. But a circular process is really set up; we have the illusion that all the blocks in the *Cantos* can be read back and forth in the light of each other. Actually in their conjunctions they are as isolated from final signification of any classical sort as is the single image of 'L'Art, 1910'. Indeed, since no one of them singly has a clearer signification than 'L'Art, 1910', they cannot be taken together for a Gestalt of signification. This brings us back to the self of the speaker, but he in turn merges with other selves, very much the way one image merges with other images.

Each individual canto is made up of blocks of statement, and each block tends to centre in a visual perception (ideogram) or an event from someone's life (*persona*), or occasionally in something that possesses the dual character of ideogram and *persona*. Ideogram exists, then, 'paratactically', on an absolute level with *persona*, so that one cannot be signifier and the other signified. Beyond the smaller blocks within cantos, each canto itself constitutes a larger block, usually a *persona*, which is set off against other blocks: the Odysseus-block of Canto I sets off a Sordello-block in Canto II; the two set off a Cid-block; all set off a Dionysus-block, etc.

The movement from one small block to another is adaptive,

and 'improvisational'. The blocks can be long or short, as the numbered cantos themselves may be. They respond, as they are posed, to the freedom of the 'speaking poet'. One need not end Canto XXIX to begin Canto XXX, since its block is set against the block of the other canto. Cantos are not separated by a greater distance than that which separates the sections within a canto, because there is nothing but white space to measure the distance and the self is all (multiple) one:

> Glide of water, lights and the prore,   (1)
> Silver beaks out of night,
> Stone, bough over bough,
>   lamps fluid in water,
> Pine by the black trunk of its shadow
> And on hill black trunks of the shadow
> The trees melted in air
>   [Canto XXIX]

> Compleynt, compleynt I hearde upon a day   (2)
> Artemis singing, Artemis, Artemis
> Against Pity lifted her wail:
> Pity causeth the forests to fail,
> Pity slayeth my nymphs,
> Pity spareth so many an evil thing.
> ... [10 lines about Pity] ...

> In Paphos, on a day
>   I also heard: (3)
> ... goeth not with young Mars to playe
> But she hath pity on a doddering fool,
> She tendeth his fyre,
> She keepeth his embers warm.

> Time is the evil. Evil.   (4)
>   A day, and a day   (5)
> Walked the young Pedro baffled,
>   A day and a day
> After Ignez was murdered.

Came the Lords in Lisboa　　　　　　　　　　(6)
　　a day, and a day
In homage. Seated there
　　dead eyes,
Dead hair under the crown,
The king still young there beside her.

Came Madame ῾ΥΛΗ　　　　　　　　　　　　(7)
Clothed with the light of the altar
And with the price of the candles
'Honour? Balls for yr. honour!　　　　　　　(8)
Take two million and swallow it.'
　　　　　　　　　　　　　　　[Canto XXX]

The link between the end unit of XXIX (1) and the long start of
XXX (2), trees and forests, is no less than that between Pity (2)
and the Venus-Mars (3) opposition; the second link lies
between Pity and the illustration of pity, but via a change
from Greece (Paphos) to Rome or a Renaissance view of Rome
(Mars).

So the link between (3) and (4) may be 'doddering' and
'time,' though the links are not that set: the link may lie
between 'Pity' and 'time' by way of self qualification: 'Pity is
the evil; or no, Time is'. The movement is temporal, a pure
succession, 'a day, and a day,' that links the love of Pedro I
of Portugal for Inez da Castro (Canto III also), perhaps via
Venus (3), with time (4), and with his bafflement of Odysseus-
like wandering after her murder (5). And temporal succession
continues, from the bafflement (5) to his order, on ascending
the throne, that his nobles do homage to her corpse (6). This
raises the question of form (lovable life) and matter (the
body) as related to love, a question already dominating the
block of Canto VII and now repeated by linking the dead Ignez
(5) with Madame Hyle (matter) personified after the fashion
of medieval allegory, 'Lady Philosophy', etc. (7) and here
representing Lucrezia Borgia, who travelled to Ferrara in great
pomp to wed the Duke Alfonso d'Este who, having regard for
his fiancée's past, had wangled a considerable dowry from the

Pope. Death in time may (6) involve religion (7) which costs money, something in usurious times more important than honour (8), and hence a link, via contrast, between buying votive candles and swallowing one's honour to make two million. Usury makes us leave beautiful ladies altogether, who coruscate through the successions here, the 'beauty on an ass cart' of XXIX (1), Artemis (2), Venus (3), Ignez (4–6), Madame Hyle (7). Abstractions also undergo metamorphosis—Beauty, Pity, Time, Matter [Hyle], Usury. Moreover, there is a movement traceable from visual perception (1) to invocation (2) to anecdote (3–5) back to visual perception (6–7). Each ideographic unit, by carrying so many connections, possesses the sheer indecipherability of 'L'Art, 1910,' even when ideas dominate it: because the ideas have their poetic function, *as distinct from their signification*, only by juxtaposition to other ideas. We know where Pound stands on pity and on usury, and what he thinks usury has done to civilization, but not how these strongly held notions relate to love or last things, to Odysseus or Pound (except by simple negation). Usury is understood as clearly as the 'Pine by the black trunk of its shadow' is seen here; but its relationships in the poem stand in obscure ideographic, aesthetic combination with other elements. So the visual scene of (1) can be broken down into several smaller ideograms (a) glide, (b) lights and prow, (c) silver beaks, (d) stone, (e) bough, (f) lamps, (g) pine, (h) hill, (i) trees. And the more sensory the poem becomes, the harder its relations are to grasp: the speaking poet moves to pure visual perception, which sets a limit for his eyes just as pure quotation sets a limit for his thought; he comes up against the barrier of 'otherness'; both limits are moved up to and away from. His thought, his self-definition, coruscates through the poem. The adaptations of the diction tell us as much, from the *persona*-archaism of 'Pity causeth the forests' and the very spelling of 'compleynt' to the harsh 'quoted' slang of 'Honour, balls for yr. honour,' and the abbreviated spelling of 'yr.'. The visual precept of 'imagisme' can be incidental here; or central, as often in the *Pisan Cantos*. The personal accent of the poet

362

improvising an archaized 'poetic' speech and the ideographic
set of a word 'older' than those surrounding it, interact through
the speaking person who is the history he projects.

He lives into that history he builds, living into history as the
poem, and the life outside the poem, grow : the Pound of 1922
could never have dreamt of Pisa, and he is caught in the tragedy
of the dream he did have, like the peasant who is taken because
he was doubtless actually seen by Pound to provide the beginning of the *Pisan Cantos* :

> The enormous tragedy of the dream in the peasant's
> > bent shoulders (1)
> Manes! Manes was tanned and stuffed (2)
> Thus Ben and la Clara *a Milano* (3)
> > by the heels at Milano
> That maggots shd/ eat the dead bullock (4)
> DIGONOS, δίγονος but the twice crucified
> > where in history will you find it? (5)
> yet say this to the Possum : a bang, not a whimper (6)
> > with a bang not with a whimper,
> To build the city of Dioce whose terraces are the
> > colour of stars. (7)
> The suave eyes, quiet, not scornful (8)
> > rain also is of the process. (9)
> What you depart from is not the way (10)
> and olive tree blown white in the wind (11)
> what whiteness will you add to this whiteness, (12)
> > what candor?

Here the units move with the speed of emotions that the actual
sights stir on the prison-barred eyes, 'out in the open'. They
move, too, with the great calm (*suave eyes, quiet*) of recapitu-
lation; the question of form and substance, in life and embalm-
ment, has been posed so repeatedly by now that Ignez does not
have to be mentioned again for parallel with Manes. Malatesta
can come out in the open and appear as Mussolini (3) : Pound
has come out in the open to correct his slangily-named taciturn
friend T. S. Eliot (5).

The ideograms build up, condense, and also expand in emotional effect. Because the person expands, his identity is to be found in the anonymity of an expanding series of ideographic units; they themselves are as cryptic as he; they are as imagistic, as spatially *there*, as he is temporally moving. There can be no end but the death of the writer to the person of this hero. No end, because his obscurity moves into the future of a life not yet come to term; it moves, too, into the very clarity of the blocks he offers as signatures for a self who can set out the full play of his ideas. That full play succeeds just because it must abide by changing rules, rules of relation between self and other, self and self, self and the seen, self and the word. Anonymity and identity are not fused: they keep changing off. We are enabled to come at them just for that reason. The book stays open.

Traitor or Laureate: The Two Trials
of the Poet

In the United States, poetry has been for so long not so much bought and read as honoured and studied that the poet has grown accustomed to his marginal status. Unlike the novelist, he takes his exclusion from the market place as *given*, not a subject for anguish and protest but a standing joke, partly on him, partly on those who exclude him. Edmund Wilson was able to ask, as early as the 'thirties, 'Is Verse a Dying Technique?' and the mournful answer is implicit in the mournful cadence of the question. But Mr Wilson did not, of course, pose the question for the first time; behind his concern there is a tradition of discovering the end of verse which goes back as far as Thomas Love Peacock's 'Four Ages of Poetry' and the earliest impact of advanced technology on the imagination of the West.

Long before the poets of the United States had found an authentic voice, the survival of poetry itself had come to seem problematical; and certainly today there is no American poet who does not suspect that his own verse is likely to live (once his small circle of admiring friends has died) in the classroom and library, rather than in the hearts of men. Meanwhile, he is inclined to feel, he must somehow sustain himself on the long, difficult way toward academic immortality, and to do so he must choose between being subsidized by foundation grants and university sinecures, or earning his keep at some job completely unconnected with the making or reading of verse. Wallace Stevens was an actuary in, and then vice-president of, an insurance company; Robert Frost tried for a while to farm; William Carlos Williams was, all of his adult life, a family doctor; T. S. Eliot began his career as a bank clerk. Each choice is perhaps a metaphor for each poet's view of himself and his work: Stevens aspiring to the precision and objectivity of statistical analysis; Frost longing to root words in the soil; Williams thinking of himself as a healer and adviser to ordinary men in their daily suffering; Eliot viewing himself as the guardian of the treasury of culture. But all together, these choices surely reflect a common awareness of a common plight, the poet's inability to subsist on his poetry alone.

That plight, however, has sent more poets into the classroom than (with whatever metaphorical intent) into the great world of production for profit; even Robert Frost, for instance, ended up teaching, once he had discovered how little he could earn tilling the soil. It is not, I think, only the poet's aversion to a world of competition and economic risk which has led him more and more to seek refuge in the college, but a sense that there he is close to his own future, to the posterity for whom he writes. Certainly there he can, if he likes, tout himself and his friends, as well as abuse his rivals and detractors; and there he can set the captive youngsters before him the task of understanding and loving (or, at least, of seeming for a moment to understand and love) certain poems, including his own, more important to him than any of the goals—erotic, athletic, or technological—which those same youngsters pursue once out of sight. Sometimes he fears, in fact, that the *only* reading such poems will get in the world he inhabits is precisely this vicarious or symbolic one, between college walls and class bells.

All of the Southern agrarian poets from John Crowe Ransom to Randall Jarrell have ended up teaching at one university or another; and numerous other poets of quite different styles and persuasions from them and from each other (Delmore Schwartz and Robert Creeley, John Berryman and Richard Wilbur, for instance) teach regularly if they can, irregularly if they must, or, best of all, enjoy the status and pay of teachers with a minimum of classroom duties. Even among the maddest of our poets, there are not a few to whom the academy seems the only real place preferable to the Nowhere that otherwise attracts their total allegiance. Sometimes, indeed, it seems as if the path which leads back and forth between the classroom and the madhouse is the one which the modern American muse loves especially to tread.

Yet the poet is finally aware that in the university he is expected not so much to write poetry, or even to teach it, as to be a poet: to act out a role which is somehow necessary to the psychic well-being of society as poems are not. And, similarly, it is the assumption of his poetic *persona* for which he is paid by grants and subsidies, and applauded at symposia and writers' conferences. After a while, it may even seem to the poet that he is being paid not to write; but this is not really so, and it is only a kind of desperate self-flattery which leads him to indulge in the conceit. In point of fact, our society does not really care whether he writes or not, so long as he does not do it on the time they ask him to spend in embodying publicly what they have rejected in themselves: a contempt for belonging and order and decorum and profit and right reason and mere fact; a love for exile and irrelevance and outrage and loss and nonsense and lies.

It is not merely himself that the poet is asked to play; if it were, there would be no temptation involved worth resisting. It is rather a *myth* of himself, or, more properly, perhaps, a myth of the poet in general which he is called on to enact. And he has, as a matter of fact, a choice of roles, for the morality play in which he is urged to assume a part demands, like all literature on the level of mass culture, heroes as well as villains, good guys as well as bad guys. But how can a poet be a hero? How can the projection of what the great audience rejects function for that audience as 'good'? To be sure, we can imagine best-selling poets on the analogy of best-selling novelists, unequivocal spokesman for the mass audience and its values; but there is so steep a contrast between 'best-selling' and 'poet', between what the great audience demands and what verse, any verse, does, that the concept is soon abandoned.

At any rate, since the time of Longfellow at least, the largest public in the United States has decided it does not need such hybrids in the realm of verse. The fictionist, the journalist, and, more recently, the script-writer for movies or television, performs much more satisfactorily any tasks which could be imagined for them. The servile sub-poet does not cease to exist entirely, but he is barred from the place where poetry is chiefly read, judged, and preserved, the academy, and relegated to the world of commerce, where he produces greeting card mottoes, or to ladies' clubs, where he flatters vanity, or to the mass magazines, where he provides filler for the spaces between editorials and short stories. In return for such meagre employment, he is asked to endure the indignity of being read, or listened to, without being noticed or remembered.

The 'hero' of the popular socio-drama we have been discussing is not so simple and obscure a mouthpiece; he is, in fact, both problematical and ambiguous : a hero-villain, a good rebel, an admirable non-conformist. And what makes him good or admirable is his presumed attitude toward the great audience which notices him without ever reading him; for that audience, by certain mysterious processes of cultural transmission, comes, after a while, to know—or believe it knows—who in the realm of art is really on its side, who regards it without something less than contempt. The one thing it will never forgive a writer is despising its reading ability, which, to be sure, it does not usually get around to practising. Such despite it regards as the ultimate treason, being willing, on the other hand, to forgive any challenge to its values or beliefs so long as that despite is not visibly present. As the critic at his best forgives a writer almost anything for writing well, the non-reader at his worst forgives him almost anything for writing ill—or simply for having the courtesy to *seem* to do so.

How can the great audience tell, after all, who is, in this sense a friend and who a foe? The point is, of course, that they cannot really tell at all, that they are likely to be fooled by the most elementary sorts of duplicity, since all their judgments are rendered on the basis of a handful of lines quoted for the benefit of their immediate mentors (schoolmarms and leaders of P.T.A. discussion groups) in the columns of, say, the *Saturday Review*, the *New Yorker*, the front page of the *New York Times Book Review*, or the back pages of *Time*. As a matter of fact, the reviewers for such journals exist precisely in order to serve as prosecuting attorneys for the great public in its continuing case against the artist; and what they must establish in order to prove guilt is *that a given writer has produced passages which cannot be misconstrued or half understood without the reader's being painfully aware of his own failure.*

It is not, then, mere difficulty which constitutes the *prima facie* evidence of a writer's contempt for the mass audience, but *unaccustomed* difficulty, a difficulty different from the kinds long so familiar in the classroom that no one any longer expects himself to do more than recognize and label them: Shakespeare, Dante, Whitman, etc. Certain writers are, in fact, more flagrantly difficult than others, and sometimes they are deliberately so; but the public's consciousness of the writer's role in this regard does not always coincide with his own. As far as American serious poets are concerned, though all of them have known for generations that the onerous advantages of best-sellerdom are denied them, they have responded in two quite different ways: some of them writing *as if* for a very few, and some of them, nonetheless, writing *as if* for a popular audience.

What is, or at least, from any historical point of view, ought to be involved is rather a matter of stance than of genuine expectation; because in fact there is little correspondence between the poets' theoretical and actual audiences. Walt Whitman, for instance, theoretically popular poet that he was, had, at the time of publication and, I should guess, will have forever after, a much smaller readership than the theoretically anti-popular poet Edgar Allan Poe. Certainly school children, that largest audience of all, have never been urged to read Whitman as they have been urged to read Poe. Yet this has not kept certain later poets (irony breeding irony in the tangle of misunderstanding), dedicated to widening the audience of verse, from invoking Whitman as their model; while others, content to address an élite, have made their ideal Edgar Poe, at least as reinterpreted by the French *symbolistes*.

In the mid-nineteenth century, the great public needed neither Poe nor Whitman, having still at their disposal the respectable academic bard, Henry Wadsworth Longfellow, and not yet having acquired that fear of Harvard professors which now plays so large a role in political as well as literary matters on the level of mass culture. Both Poe and Whitman were, therefore, found guilty in the treason trial for which only Poe had braced himself: Poe of drunkenness and drug-addiction and the celebration of death; Whitman of blasphemy and obscenity and the celebration of sex. Poe, at least, knew always that he was on trial, while Whitman, more naïvely and more typical of the American writer, thought of himself as wooing an audience, which in fact saw itself not as his beloved but as his judge.

Essential to an understanding of the difficulties of the American writer (especially, but not exclusively, the poet) is an awareness of this conflict of imagined roles, the clash of metaphors on the border between art and life. The relationship of the poet to the audience in the United States is—in *his* consciousness—erotic or sentimental; the relationship of the audience to the poet is—in *its* consciousness—juridical. While the writer may fancy himself pleading a tender suit, or carrying on a cynical seduction, the reader is likely to think of himself as hearing evidence, deciding whether to say, not 'no' or 'yes', but 'guilty' or 'innocent': guilty of treason, or innocent by reason of insanity—or even, as in the case of Ezra Pound, *both* at once.

It is, of course, Pound who comes into our minds when we reflect on the trial of the poet. A century ago it might have been still Poe or Whitman, but neither of these long-dead (and therefore for us inevitably sanctified and forgotten) figures is capable now of stirring passion in the minds of sub-literates, who have no memory. Each age must have its own, brand-new defendants, and the mass audience sitting in judgment in the middle of the twentieth century has tried and sentenced the poet once more, yet as if for the first time, in the person of Ezra Pound. Indeed, they have condemned him with what, from their standpoint, is perfect justice. I do not mean merely that Pound was, indeed, guilty of the charges of abetting anti-Semitism (and more recently anti-Negro feelings), praising Fascism, and condemning the best along with the worst in his own country; the popular mind in America has often regarded with favour enemies of democracy, Jews, and Negroes. I mean that all of the ambitious long poems of our time have been written under Pound's guidance or inspired by his example: Eliot's *The Waste Land*, for instance, and Hart Crane's *The Bridge*, and William Carlos Williams' *Paterson*: all of those fragmented, allusion-laden, imagistic portraits of an atomized world which have so offended the Philistine mind. And I mean, too, that in his *Pisan Cantos* Pound, driven by his tribulations beyond the circle of his bad literary habits and his compulsive political idiocies, has caught the pathos and the comedy involved in the relationship between artist and society in the twentieth century with absolute precision. Both the self-pity of the artist and the complacent brutality of the community that needs and resents him have been dissolved in irony only to be re-created as improbable lyric beauty. These are offences hard to forgive for those convinced that they should judge and not be judged— certainly not by a mad poet.

Precisely the qualities, however, which have made Pound the prototypical enemy of the people in our time have attracted to him not only certain impotent young cranks who might have been successful Hitlers had time and circumstances conspired, but also the sort of disaffected young poet who turns out in the end to have written the poetry by which an age is remembered. Both kinds of Poundians wrote on the walls of bars and taverns 'Ez for Pres', both dreamed him as their ideal anti-President in the time of Eisenhower, while Pound in fact still sat in an insane asylum in Washington—to which he had been remanded, just after World War II, by a jury of his peers even more eager to find him nuts than to declare him a traitor. And what worthy living poet would such a jury not have found crazy enough to confine, whether or not he had made treasonable broadcasts for Mussolini?

The answer is easy: Robert Frost, through whose intervention Pound was finally released from the madhouse and allowed to return to the place from which he had once raged against his country. For Frost only could our whole nation have consented to parole Pound, just as for Frost only could it mourn officially and without reservations. Certainly it could not have mourned so for, say, T. S. Eliot, who, however sanctimonious in his old age, had once swapped citizenship; or for E. E. Cummings, who despised punctuation and the slogans of advertising; or for Wallace Stevens, who had obviously not even cared to be understood. Indeed, long before his death, the great audience had found Frost guiltless of the ultimate treason, the betrayal of what it defines as 'sanity', and considers itself to possess in an eminent degree. Had certain poems of his not become so standard a feature of grade school and high school anthologies ('Mending Wall', for instance, or 'Stopping by Woods') that one finally could respond to them no more than to yet another reproduction of the Mona Lisa? Were not other verses of his distributed every year as Christmas cards by his publishers, and were not still others quoted from station platforms and the backs of trains by candidates for political office?

Had he not even been invited by President Kennedy to read a poem of his own composing at the inaugural ceremonies, and had he not actually written one for the occasion, ending with the complacent boast that his appearance there itself inaugurated 'A golden age of poetry and power / Of which this noonday's the beginning hour'? Fortunately, fate fought for him against the adulation of politicians and the crowd, that kindly comic fate which protects great men from their own delusions; he could not read the text, the sun too bright in his ageing eyes, and had to give up a television première in favour of more conventional modes of publication. But the damage had already been done; Frost had become in effect the first Poet Laureate of the United States, an honour and indignity no other

American had ever endured. And the nation, which is to say, the mass audience, smiled at his discomfiture and applauded his honours.

But why did they feel so at ease in his presence? Was it merely that he had lived so long? There was enough in his career to dismay them, had they known or cared. He had begun as alienated from them as any poet they had ever cast in the role of utter villain; had fled to England already middle-aged and convinced apparently that he could make his American reputation only second-hand; had withdrawn from the pressures of getting and spending, as well as the obligations of citizenship, to sit alone in a back-country which its own inhabitants were deserting as fast as they could; had boasted all his life long of preferring loneliness to gregariousness, night to day, cold to warmth, melancholy to joy; had mocked in more than one poem the penny-saved-penny-earned philosophy of the American Philistine's laureate, Benjamin Franklin; had celebrated himself as a genius 'too lofty and original to rage', and hinted that his message was not for everyone but hidden away 'under a spell so the wrong ones can't find it'.

In a long and, I suspect, not much read poem called 'New Hampshire', Frost has spoken, for once, without defensive pretence or disguise, as an artist—though he assumes the mask of a novelist rather than that of a maker of verses—and has identified without equivocation the bitterness that underlies his vocation as a poet.

> I make a virtue of my suffering
> From nearly everything that goes on round me.
> In other words, I know where I am,
> Being the creature of literature I am,
> I shall not lack for pain to keep me awake.
> Kit Marlowe taught me how to say my prayers:
> 'Why, this is Hell, nor am I out of it!'

He has spoken elsewhere quite as frankly of his audience, remarking, with the quiet and devastating irony that characterizes his best verse:

They cannot look out far.
They cannot look in deep.
But when was that ever a bar
To any watch they keep?

Yet reading this epitaph upon the grave of their fondest pretensions, the great public, which does not recognize irony, could see only what short words Frost used and how he respected both the syntax and the iambic measure which they had learned in school to honour, if not use. If he was 'lofty and original', he did indeed keep it a secret, as he slyly declared, from the 'wrong ones', from the very ones who made up his mass following, who hated all other living poets, but loved him because he seemed to them a reproach to those others who made them feel inferior with their allusions to Provençal and Chinese poetry, their subverted syntax and fractured logic, their unreasonable war against the iambic, their preference for strange, Mediterranean lands and big cities. Even if they themselves inhabited such cities, the Frostians knew that it was not fitting to write poetry about them; one wrote, like Frost, *not* Eliot or Pound, about hills and trees, streams and animals. Was this not what the Romantic poets, whom certain wiseacre moderns liked to mock, had written about; and did they not now venerate the memory of those poets whom they had despised, perhaps, in school, but who at a distance benefited by the illusion of attractiveness which attaches itself to terrors far enough removed: home, mother, the bad weather of our childhood?

Pound and Frost: these become the ideal antagonists of contemporary culture for the popular mind, which knows such myths better than any poems. The award of the Bollingen Prize for Poetry to Pound in 1949, while he was still a patient in St Elizabeth's Hospital, made it all a matter of public record. First the intellectual community itself was rent by disagreement about the wisdom of honouring the verse of one whose ideas they condemned (at the high point, an eminent poet challenged to a duel a well-known editor who, alas, never realized he was being challenged); and then the great audience, which has never noticed before or since any other winner of a poetry prize, found a voice in Robert Hillyer and through him joined the debate. In a series of articles for the *Saturday Review*, that second-rate poet vented his own frustration, as well as the public's rage, at the best poetry of the century, using Pound as his whipping-boy and Frost as his whip.

For this reason, then, we must come to terms with the legend of Pound and Frost, on our way toward a consideration of their verse. Indeed, not only the mass audience (to whom Pound is a curse-word in Hillyer's diatribe and a picture in *Life*, Frost an honorific in the same diatribe and a face on the television screen) but the poets themselves have been victimized by the myths mass culture has imposed on them. Under pressure, the poet tends to become his legend : Frost begins to believe he invented New England, and Pound to consider himself the discoverer of the Italian Riviera. And who is crude enough to remind the one that he was born in California, the other that he came from Hailey, Idaho? In the end, Frost almost succeeded in turning into the cracker-barrel philosopher from Vermont he played, spouting homely wisdom and affecting to despise the crackpot ideas of all intellectuals, while Pound came near to transforming himself into a caricature of the cosmopolitan aesthete, a polyglot unsure before the fact whether the word trembling on his lips would emerge as Greek or Catalan or pure Mandarin.

Worst of all, Frost finally permitted himself to be cast—in complete contempt of his deepest commitments, which are to alienation and terror—as the beaming prophet of the New Frontier, court-jester to the Kennedy administration, even as Pound was content to mug his way through the role of traitor-in-chief to a nation, though he seemed more a clown in the entourage of Mussolini. And for accepting such public roles at the cost of scanting the private tasks imposed on them by their talents, these two chief poets of our time must stand trial in quite another court, the court of criticism. Before the tribunal of critics, they will not be permitted to plead that they voted right (or wrong), or even that they were in their writings comprehensible (or obscure)—only that, keeping faith with their gifts, they wrote certain lines which no literate American, perhaps no educated man anywhere, will willingly forget.

Similarly, the charges against them will not be that they voted wrong (or right), or that they were obscure (or comprehensible)—only that, pursuing their own legendary images, they wrote dull or trivial, arch or pedantic, smug or self-pitying verse; that, moreover, by their poses, they have made even their best work unavailable to certain readers: passionate liberals and sensitive Jews in the case of Pound, the disaffected urban young and a vast number of Europeans of all persuasions in the case of Frost; and that, finally, by a strange sort of retrospective falsification, they have seemed to alter the meaning, the very music of the lines in which they have, in fact, transcended the limitations of their roles and of the weaknesses in themselves out of which the mass mind created those roles to begin with.

How much time will have to go by before we are able to read either one of them without these prejudices? If there were, indeed, a justice in the world higher than that of the critics, as the critics' is higher than that of the mass audience, both Pound and Frost would be condemned to spend that time in purgatory—a single chamber in a shared purgatory, where Frost would say over and over to Pound:

> And lonely as it is that loneliness
> Will be more lonely ere it will be less—
> A blanker whiteness of benighted snow
> With no expression, nothing to express.
>
> They cannot scare me with their empty spaces
> Between stars—on stars where no human race is.
> I have it in me so much nearer home
> To scare myself with my own desert places.

while Pound would shout back ceaselessly:

> Thou art a beaten dog beneath the hail,
> A swollen magpie in a fitful sun,

TRAITOR OR LAUREATE

Half black half white
Nor knowst'ou wing from tail
Pull down thy vanity
          How mean thy hates
Fostered in falsity,
          Pull down thy vanity,
Rathe to destroy, niggard in charity,
Pull down thy vanity,
          I say pull down.

Notes on the Contributors

Walter Baumann, Lecturer in German at the University of Toronto until October 1966, now at Magee University College, Londonderry, Northern Ireland. A graduate of Zurich University, his doctoral dissertation *The Rose in the Steel Dust: An Examination of the Cantos of Ezra Pound* appeared in Swiss Studies in English, a series published by Francke Verlag, Berne, in 1967. He has written on Max Frisch and Hermann Broch in *Colloquia Germania*, the *Modern Language Quarterly* and *Seminar*, and on Ezra Pound in *Seminar* and the *Journal of English and Germanic Philology*.

Christine Brooke-Rose, *Ph.D.* (London), has studied Middle English and Old French poetry. She is the author of *A Grammar of Metaphor* 1958, seven novels, short stories, and literary criticism in *Essays in Criticism*; the *Review of English Literature*; the *Times Literary Supplement*, etc.

Albert S. Cook, Chairman of the Department of English, State University of New York at Buffalo. Author of *The Dark Voyage and the Golden Mean, a Philosophy of Comedy* 1949, 1966; *The Meaning of Fiction* 1960; *Oedipus Rex: A Mirror for Greek Drama* (Textbook) 1963; *The Classic Line, a Study in Epic Poetry* 1966. Poetry: *Progressions* 1963. Translations: *Oedipus Rex* 1960; *The Odyssey of Homer* in English verse translation 1966.

Guy Davenport teaches English and Comparative Literature at the University of Kentucky, Lexington, Kentucky. He has also taught at Washington University, St Louis, Missouri; Harvard; Haverford, Philadelphia, Pa. Edited *The Intelligence of Louis Agassiz* 1963. Translations: *Carmina Archilochi* 1964; *Sappho: Poems and Fragments* 1965. Poetry: *Flowers and Leaves* 1966; *Cydonia Florentia* 1966.

Donald A. Davie, Professor of Literature at the University of Essex, England, has also been Visiting Professor at the University of California at Santa Barbara and at Grinnell College, Iowa. He is the author of *Purity of Diction in English Verse*; *Articulate Energy*, *The Heyday of Sir Walter Scott*; *Ezra Pound, Poet as Sculptor* 1965, and five books of verse. Edited *Russian Literature & Modern English Fiction* 1965.

George Dekker lectures in literature at the University of Essex. He is the author of *Sailing After Knowledge: The Cantos of Ezra Pound* 1963 and *James Fenimore Cooper, The Novelist* 1967.

Richard Ellmann, Professor of English at Northwestern University since 1951, is the author of *Yeats: The Man and the Masks* 1948; *The Identity of Yeats* 1954; *James Joyce* 1959, and has edited *Selected Writings of Henri Michaux* 1951, *My Brother's Keeper* by Stanislaus Joyce 1958, and Vols. II and III of *Letters of James Joyce* 1966; *Eminent Domain: Yeats Among Wilde, Joyce, Pound, Eliot and Auden* 1968.

John Espey, Professor of English at the University of California at Berkeley, is the author of *Ezra Pound's Mauberley: A Study in Composition* 1955, as well as three books of reminiscences of life in China and one novel.

Leslie Fiedler teaches at the State University of New York at Buffalo. He has also taught at the Universities of Montana, Columbia, Princeton and at the Universities of Rome, Bologna and Athens. He is the author of *Love and Death in the American Novel*; *An End to Innocence*; *No! In Thunder*; *Pull Down Vanity*; *Waiting for the End* 1964; *The Second Stone* 1966; *Love and Death in the American Novel* 1967.

Hugh Kenner, Professor of English at the University of California at Santa Barbara, is the author of *The Poetry of Ezra Pound* 1951; *Wyndham Lewis* 1954; *Dublin's Joyce* 1956; *Gnomon* 1958; *The Invisible Poet: T. S. Eliot* 1959; *Samuel Beckett* 1961; *Flaubert, Joyce and Beckett: The Stoic Comedians* 1964; *The Counterfeiters* 1968.

N. Christoph de Nagy, Professor of American Literature at the Universities of Basle and Berne, formerly Professor of

English and American Literature at universities in Canada and the U.S.A., is the author of *The Poetry of Ezra Pound: The Pre-Imagist Stage*, Berne 1960, 2nd edtn. 1968; *Ezra Pound's Poetics and Literary Tradition: The Critical Decade*, Berne 1966; *Michael Drayton's 'England's Heroical Epistles': A Study in Themes and Compositional Devices*, Berne 1968.

Boris de Rachewiltz, archaeologist and ethnologist, has specialized in Middle Eastern and African cultures. Was assistant to Prof. L. Keimer of Cairo University and has directed excavations in Egypt and Jordan, and ethnological missions among the Beja. Several translations of hieroglyphic texts, including the 'Book of the Dead' from the Turin papyrus and 'The Magic Papyrus' of the Vatican Museum. Author of some fifteen books on Egyptology, archaeology and ethnology, of which *Egyptian Art*, *African Art*, *Religion and Magic in Egypt* and *Black Eros* have appeared in English. His interests include the study of esoteric traditions and magic.

Forrest Read, Associate Professor at the University of North Carolina, where he teaches modern literature. He is the author of several essays on Ezra Pound and has edited *Pound/Joyce*, a volume of Pound's letters to James Joyce and essays on Joyce's work published in 1967.

J. P. Sullivan, a graduate of Cambridge University and formerly Fellow of Lincoln College, Oxford, England, is Professor of Classics at the University of Texas. He is also an editor of *Arion* and the author of *Critical Essays on Roman Literature, Elegy and Lyric*; *Critical Essays on Roman Literature, Satire*; *Ezra Pound and Sextus Propertius, A Study in Creative Translation* 1964; *The Satyricon of Petronius, A Literary Study* 1968.

A Chronology of the
Poetry and Prose by Ezra Pound
discussed in this book

The arabic numerals are page references

CHRONOLOGY

Personæ (1935)
Alf's Eighth Bit (first published in the 'New English Weekly' 1934), 78–9

The Translations of Ezra Pound (Collected 1953)
Canzon IV of Guido Cavalcanti's *Canzone d'Amore*, 14–15; Introduction to Cavalcanti's Poems, 21; Sonnet VII of Guido Cavalcanti, 342; 'Ballata' I of Guido Cavalcanti, 342

Sophokles—Women of Trachis (1956)
42, 224–6

Pavannes and Divagations (1958)
Neath Ben Bulben's Buttoks Lies, 81–2

CANTOS

A Draft of Thirty Cantos (*I–XXX*) 1930
Canto *I*, 18, 30, 35, 126, 139–41, 150, 153, 163, 216–17, 332, 335, 338, 340, 357, 359; Canto *II*, 29, 126, 135, 141, 280–1, 283, 294, 336, 357, 359; Canto *III*, 126, 141, 153, 172, 361; Canto *IV*, 30, 126, 141, 162, 172, 196, 257, 280–3, 288, 290, 292; Canto *V*, 42, 126, 141, 162, 172, 336; Canto *VI*, 126–7, 141, 172; Canto *VII*, 127–8, 137–9, 141, 153, 155, 172, 244, 288, 361; Cantos *VIII–XI* (Malatesta Cantos), 128, 141; Canto *VIII*, 141, 158–9, 345; Canto *XII*, 141, 172, 264, 266; Canto *XIII*, 141, 337; Canto *XIV*, 142, 149, 168, 204, 206; Canto *XV*, 142, 149, 168, 184, 204, 206; Canto *XVI*, 142, 168, 172–3, 204, 206; Canto *XVII*, 29, 31, 82, 142, 173, 184, 202–3, 206, 209–10, 290; Canto *XVIII*, 172; Canto *XX*, 30, 33, 172, 205–6; Canto *XXI*, 30, 154–5; Canto *XXIII*, 29, 31, 42, 146, 163, 184, 193, 196; Canto *XXV*, 24, 30–1, 153; Canto *XXVI* 173; Canto *XXVII* 30; Canto *XXVIII*, 172; Canto *XXIX*, 153–4, 192, 352–3, 360–2; Canto *XXX*, 38, 155, 160–1, 192, 281–6, 288–9, 292, 353–5, 360–1

A Draft of Eleven New Cantos (*XXXI–XLI*) 1934
(Nuevo Mondo Cantos)
Canto *XXXV*, 155; Canto *XXXVI*, 14, 154, 231; Canto *XXXIX*, 154, 182; Canto XL, 315

The Fifth Decad of Cantos (XLII–LI) 1937
(Siena Cantos—Leopoldine Reforms)
Canto *XLII*, 248, 297–8; Canto *XLV*, 19, 170, 200; Canto
XLVII, 27, 154, 167–8, 198–9, 261, 291, 299; Canto *XLIX*,
26; Canto *LI*, 200

Cantos LII–LXXI 1940
(China Cantos)
Canto *LII*, 200; Canto *LIX*, 39; Canto *LXI*, 250

Pisan Cantos (LXXIV–LXXXIV) 1948
Canto *LXXIV*, 14, 26, 38, 42, 80, 84–5, 129, 143, 156, 162–3,
170, 182, 185, 189, 191–3, 195, 197, 242, 248, 289–90, 313,
315, 329, 363; Canto *LXXVI*, 80, 84, 143, 148, 155, 170,
185, 193, 196, 285, 313, 338, 355; Canto *LXXVII*, 84, 155,
170, 185, 193–4, 313, 315; Canto *LXXVIII*, 248; Canto
LXXIX, 85, 185, 290–2; Canto *LXXX*, 26, 78, 155, 162,
185, 191–2, 254–5, 329–30, 341; Canto *LXXXI*, 20, 73, 156,
161, 312, 335, 340, 343–4, 376–7; Canto *LXXXII*, 43, 61,
155–6, 338, 340, 347–51; Canto *LXXXIII*, 68–9, 79–80,
155–6, 170, 191, 311, 335; Canto *LXXXIV*, 313

Section: Rock-Drill de los Cantares (LXXXV–XCV) 1955
Canto *LXXXV*, 46, 177, 190, 253, 271; Canto *LXXXVI*,
318; Canto *LXXXVII*, 44, 69, 190, 280, 305, 312–13, 316;
Canto *LXXXVIII*, 270, 305, 314; Canto *LXXXIX*, 26, 258;
Canto *XC*, 25–7, 46, 84, 165, 177, 179, 185–6, 190–1, 206–7,
238, 255, 261, 278–9, 293–302; Canto *XCI*, 30, 32, 35, 69,
180–3, 210–13, 244, 248, 253–79, 303, 313, 315–17; Canto
XCII, 178, 312, 316–17; Canto *XCIII*, 178, 185, 212, 244,
279; Canto *XCIV*, 27, 149, 187–8, 213, 261, 285; Canto *XCV*,
50, 186, 244, 247, 316

Thrones de los Cantares (XCVI–CIX) 1959
Canto *XCVI*, 164, 168, 182, 185, 187–8, 192, 247–9, 260, 281;
Canto *XCVII*, 165–6, 184–6, 188–9, 192, 244–6, 253, 270,
277, 281; Canto *XCVIII*, 82, 244, 249, 250–2; Canto *XCIX*,
30, 178, 312, 315; Canto *C*, 27, 32, 188, 261; Canto *CII*, 82;
Canto *CIV*, 171, 244, 252; Canto *CVI*, 159, 265, 336; Canto
CVII, 173, 192, 270; Canto *CIX*, 244

CHRONOLOGY

General Index

―――――――――――

The numerals on the right refer to pages in this book. Footnote references and concealed references are not shown separately.

389

GENERAL INDEX

GENERAL INDEX

GENERAL INDEX

GENERAL INDEX